Dew pt
Condensation
Sckro chart
Climate Zones
Air movement

Moisture Control Handbook

Principles and Practices for Residential and Small Commercial Buildings

Joseph Lstiburek

*Building Science Corporation
Chestnut Hill, Massachusetts*

John Carmody

*Underground Space Center
University of Minnesota*

*Designed and Illustrated
by John Carmody*

JOHN WILEY & SONS, INC.

New York   Chichester   Weinheim   Brisbane   Singapore   Toronto

Copyright © 1994 by John Wiley & Sons, Inc. All rights reserved
Published simultaneously in Canada

This publication is designed to provide accurate and authoritative information in
regard to the subject matter covered. It is sold with the understanding that the
publisher is not engaged in rendering professional services. If professional
advice or other expert assistance is required, the services of a competent
professional person should be sought.

Library of Congress Cataloging-in-Publication Data:

Lstiburek, Joseph W.
    Moisture control handbook : principles and practices for
  residential and small commercial buildings / Joseph Lstiburek and
  John Carmody ; designed and illustrated by John Carmody.
      p. cm.
    Includes bibliographical references and index.
    ISBN 0-471-31863-9
    1. Dampness in buildings. I. Carmody, John. II. Title.
TH9031.L78   1993
690'.893—dc20
                                                    93-11064

Printed in the United States of America

20 19 18 17 16 15

Contents

Preface

The original version of this handbook was a product of the U.S. Department of Energy (DOE) Building Envelope Systems and Materials (BTESM) Research Program centered at Oak Ridge National Laboratory (ORNL). The major objective of the research effort in building moisture control is to provide information to builders, contractors, and building owners that will lead to the construction of energy-efficient walls, roofs, and foundations. The first edition of this handbook, published in 1991, represented one in a series of design tools produced to provide the most current design information.

For the first edition, ORNL formed a review panel of moisture experts to provide technical guidance for this effort. This group reviewed the outline as well as several drafts of the handbook, and through this process strengthened the technical content.

The construction details shown for heating, mixed, and cooling climates are based on moisture transport principles. A growing number of designers realize it is too costly and too risky to completely keep moisture from penetrating building envelopes. Building envelope materials occasionally have high initial moisture levels, and degradation of siding, sheathing, membranes, sealants, caulking, and flashings can contribute significantly to the moisture load. Thus, the approach is to keep moisture levels low within building assemblies by providing a path for moisture to periodically escape. A design strategy that assumes building envelopes may get wet and permits them to dry, presents a more forgiving and perhaps less costly alternative.

This handbook, revised by the authors, represents yet another step in helping designers and builders to understand and utilize moisture control strategies. It is very satisfying to see products seeded with a few public dollars lead to successful commercial products. The contents of this book include a systematic method of evaluating moisture problems and moisture control strategies. The handbook provides a valuable set of principles to have on hand as your designs evolve into future buildings.

Jeffrey Christian
Manager, Building Envelope Systems
    and Materials Program
Oak Ridge National Laboratory
P.O. Box 2008
Building 3147, MS-6070
Oak Ridge, TN 37831-6070

Acknowledgments

This handbook represents a major revision, expansion, and refinement of the original *Moisture Control Handbook* prepared by the authors for the U.S. Department of Energy. Both this handbook and the earlier version on which it is based were made possible by the contributions and assistance of many people.

Sam Taylor of the U.S. Department of Energy was instrumental in the initiation of this project. He conceived of this handbook as a means of collecting and presenting existing information in a form useful to designers and builders. In addition, the handbook project was intended to identify areas where information was lacking, and thus, would serve as a needed element of the DOE Building Moisture Research effort. Sam's continuing contributions throughout the development of the project were appreciated.

The moisture handbook project was managed by Jeff Christian of Oak Ridge National Laboratory. The authors appreciate his contributions, criticism, and particularly his patience in coordinating this complex project over a long period of time.

Professor John Timusk, University of Toronto; and Gustav Handegord, formerly of the National Research Council of Canada, were the technical advisors to the project.

George Tsongas, Portland State University; Lester Shen, University of Minnesota; John Tooley and Neil Moyer, Florida Natural Retrofit; and Jim White, Canada Mortgage and Housing Corporation, provided guidance and advice. Finally, the manuscript was improved considerably by the editing of Pam Snopl.

Joseph Lstiburek
Building Science Corporation
Chestnut Hill, Massachusetts

John Carmody
Underground Space Center
University of Minnesota

Introduction

Moisture problems in buildings are prevalent throughout North America, almost independent of climate. They are viewed as the single largest factor limiting the useful service life of a structure. Elevated levels of moisture in buildings also can lead to serious health effects for occupants.

In residential buildings, homeowners (or their builders) may be faced with costly repairs in addition to suffering the health-related consequences of mold growth. In commercial structures, moisture problems can lead to lost revenues and litigation resulting from structural deterioration as well as worker health problems related to indoor air quality. In some cases, facilities must be closed while hundreds of thousands of dollars are spent on repairs, often incorrectly or ineffectively.

Until recently, very little consensus on moisture control existed in the building community. The information available was typically incomplete, contradictory, usually limited to specific regions, and in many cases misleading.

This handbook is intended to help homeowners, architects, mechanical engineers, and building contractors to understand mold and moisture problems in housing so that they can be prevented or corrected. While this book focuses on residential construction, many of the basic problems, principles, and solutions are similar for all building types.

In order to understand and prevent moisture problems, a building must be viewed as a complex system of interacting variables. Some of these interacting mechanisms include heat flow, air flow, moisture flow, and chemical and biological reactions within the building. People's behavior patterns, climate, building envelope design, construction practice, condi-tions during construction, and building operation are all factors influencing moisture problems and solutions.

The remainder of this introduction includes (1) a review of historical changes in housing construction that have led to increased moisture problems, (2) a set of goals for effective building design and construction, (3) a discussion of the variables involved in understanding a building as an overall system, and (4) a description of this handbook.

HISTORICAL CHANGES TO HOUSING CONSTRUCTION

In the last 50 years there have been some important changes to the way in which we build and operate buildings. These include: (1) the introduction of thermal insulation, (2) the development of tighter building enclosures, (3) the elimination of active chimneys, and (4) the introduction of forced air heating and cooling systems. These changes have influenced the occupants' health, safety, and comfort as well as the durability and affordability of the structure.

Thermal Insulation

When thermal insulation was widely introduced in the 1950's, its primary purpose was to reduce the heat flows into and out of buildings to make them more comfortable. Later, as energy conservation became important, insulation levels were increased to reduce operating costs. Clearly, thermal insulation is effective in achieving these goals.

A little understood by-product of the addition of thermal insulation, however, was the reduction of the drying potential of the building enclosure. Since heat and air flow through the building assemblies (roofs, walls, and foundations) are reduced, their ability to dry is diminished should they get wet from either interior or exterior sources. This impact of insulation is similar regardless of climate.

Tighter Building Enclosures

Building enclosures have become much tighter since the 1950's (Figure I-1). A typical building today is almost twice as tight as its counterpart built a few decades ago. The increase in tightness occurred as a result of the introduction of new materials and production techniques (sheet goods such as plywood, drywall, and precast panels), as well as a desire to increase comfort (eliminate drafts) and reduce energy usage (high heating and cooling costs). A tighter building results in a lower exchange of air between the interior conditioned space and the exterior. The lower the air change, the less the dilution of moisture and interior pollutants such as formaldehyde, other volatile organic compounds, radon, and carbon dioxide. This trend toward lower air change occurred simultaneously with the introduction of hundreds of thousands of new chemical compounds, materials, and products which were developed to satisfy the growing consumer demand for goods and furnishings.

This increase in interior pollutant sources combined with the decrease in the dilution of the air has resulted in higher indoor air pollutant concentrations. In commercial construction this has manifested itself in Sick Building Syndrome (SBS) complaints and cases of Building Related Illness (BRI). In residential construction the tighter enclosures also resulted in the reduction of a typical chimney's ability to exhaust combustion products which leads to spillage of these products, backdrafting of furnaces, water heaters, and fireplaces, and the associated health and safety problems. The most noticeable symptom of these changes is the increased levels of moisture in typical buildings. This manifests itself with mold and mildew on interior surfaces in cooling and heating climates as well as condensation on the interior of windows in heating climates.

Elimination of Active Chimneys

In residential and small facility construction, the trend towards using electric heating, heat pumps, and power vented, sealed combustion furnaces has resulted in the elimination of the traditional active chimney. Active

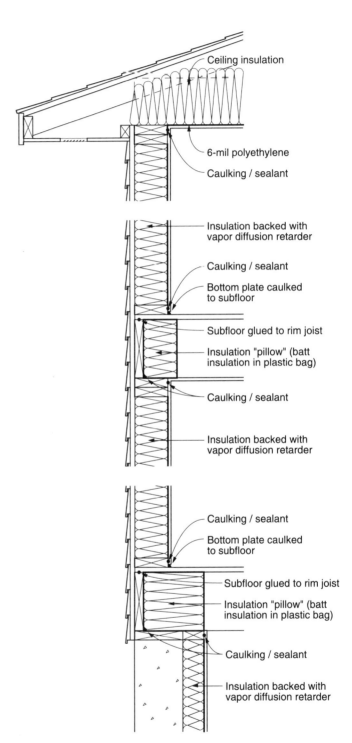

Figure I-1: This wall section illustrates tightly sealed, well-insulated construction. Increased insulation and tighter building enclosures improve energy use and thermal comfort, but can contribute to higher accumulations of moisture and various indoor air pollutants within the building envelope.

Ceiling insulation

6-mil polyethylene

Caulking / sealant

Insulation backed with vapor diffusion retarder

Caulking / sealant

Bottom plate caulked to subfloor

Subfloor glued to rim joist

Insulation "pillow" (batt insulation in plastic bag)

Caulking / sealant

Insulation backed with vapor diffusion retarder

Caulking / sealant

Bottom plate caulked to subfloor

Subfloor glued to rim joist

Insulation "pillow" (batt insulation in plastic bag)

Caulking / sealant

Insulation backed with vapor diffusion retarder

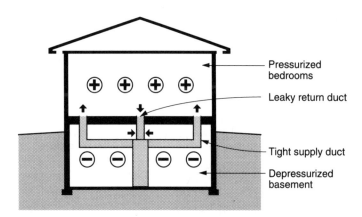

Figure I-2: *In heating climates, a forced air system with leaky return ducts leads to pressurized living areas and depressurized basements. Warm, moisture-laden air is driven into the above-grade building assemblies, while radon and moisture from the soil is drawn into the basement.*

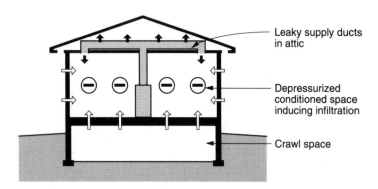

Figure I-3: *In cooling climates, a forced air system with leaky supply ducts that are placed outside of the conditioned space leads to depressurized living areas. Warm, moisture-laden air from the exterior is drawn into the above-grade building assemblies.*

chimneys were exhaust fans which extracted great quantities of air from the conditioned space and resulted in frequent air changes and the subsequent dilution of interior pollutants. Eliminating the "chimney fan" has led to an increase in levels of moisture and interior pollutants. Active chimneys also tended to depressurize conditioned spaces during heating periods, which reduced wetting of building assemblies from interior air transported moisture and led to a more forgiving building envelope.

Heating and Cooling Systems

In terms of building technology, forced air heating, ventilation, and air conditioning systems are rather recent innovations. Moving relatively large quantities of air around within building enclosures of increasing tightness has led to serious health, safety, durability, and operating cost issues.

In heating climates, supply duct systems are more extensive than return duct systems (Figure I-2). There are typically supply registers in each room, with common returns. Rooms are pressurized and common areas are depressurized by the combination of more extensive supply systems with leaky return ducts and interior door closure. The depressurization and pressurization of conditioned spaces is increased as the building envelope becomes tighter. This can lead to the infiltration of radon, moisture, pesticides, and soil gas in foundations. In addition, warm moisture-laden air can exfiltrate into wall and roof cavities, resulting in problems since higher levels of insulation have created lower drying potentials.

In cooling climates, supply ducts are often run exterior to the building envelope in attic, roof, and crawl spaces (Figure I-3). The supply ducts typically leak, leading to the depressurization of the building enclosure. Interior door closure with common return systems can also depressurize the main body of a building. The depressurization of the conditioned space results in the infiltration of hot, humid air from the exterior and subsequent problems with comfort, mold, mildew, and high cooling costs.

GOALS FOR EFFECTIVE DESIGN AND CONSTRUCTION

The major changes in housing construction over the past three decades have generally improved comfort and energy conservation, but they have also contributed to structural deterioration, major insurance and warranty problems, as well as health, safety, and comfort concerns.

It is not practical to return to constructing leaky building enclosures that lacked thermal insulation, and had less efficient heating and air conditioning systems. The marketplace demands sophisticated, high performance buildings operated and maintained intelligently. As improved building systems are evolving, it is important to state the basic goals of housing design and construction. These are health and safety, durability, comfort, and affordability. Achieving each of these goals depends in part on understanding and resolving moisture problems in buildings.

Health and Safety

Indoor air quality is the major factor that influences short-term and long-term health of occupants and is directly related to the concentration of pollutants within building enclosures. The source of pollutants in conditioned spaces, in order of impact, are:

- Combustion products
- Moisture and biological products
- Radon
- Formaldehyde and other volatile organic compounds (V.O.C.'s)
- Particulates
- Carbon dioxide

Each of these pollutants can be controlled by reducing the source. For example, properly installed gas or oil appliances and fireplaces can eliminate combustion by-products. Tight foundations coupled with air pressure control will prevent radon infiltration. Formaldehyde can be eliminated or reduced by using building products with zero or low formaldehyde emission ratings. The presence of other V.O.C.'s can be controlled by storing cleansers and cleaning agents outside of the conditioned space or by using safe, alternative products. Air filtration can control particulates and elimination of unvented space heaters controls excessive carbon dioxide and nitrogen by-products.

Mold and dust mite infestation produce the major health concerns related to excessive moisture in buildings. Strategies to prevent this problem are presented throughout this book. For example, control of excessive negative pressures and unconditioned make-up air in cooling climates will reduce the presence of moisture. Also, a correctly designed and constructed foundation will reduce the presence of moisture in heating and cooling climates.

Durability

It makes sense for the building industry to produce and operate facilities that will stand the test of time. A building should have a useful service life three to four times the mortgage period. If the mortgage period is 25 years, the useful service life should be between 75 and 100 years. While many facilities built at the turn of the century are still performing their function with grace and dignity, the same is not likely to be said a hundred years from now about many of today's buildings.

The development of a durable building starts with proper design and material selection. It also requires correct installation by the contractor as well as care and maintenance by the owner/occupant. It is unlikely that buildings will be maintained if they are not designed and built from the very start to be easily maintainable. Finally, the owner/occupant needs to be educated about the maintenance requirements of the building.

Historically, the single greatest factor affecting the durability of buildings has been excessive moisture. Moisture causes wood products to decay, metals to corrode, paint and coating systems to separate from substrate, and concrete and masonry to effloresce, spall, and flake. Changing moisture levels cause elements, assemblies, and entire buildings to move. Moisture problems often lead to maintenance nightmares. Control of moisture is proving to be a prerequisite for a durable building in all climate zones.

Comfort

Comfort involves satisfying the sensory perceptions of people. Comfort parameters include:

- Temperature/thermal comfort
- Moisture/relative humidity
- Odors/indoor air quality
- Vibration/noise
- Light/daylighting and illumination

There is an interrelationship between humidity and other comfort parameters such as temperature and odors. The ASHRAE psychrometric chart establishes the standard comfort zones for summer and winter (see Chapter 1). These comfort zones approximately cover the following ranges:

Winter Comfort Zone:
    Temperature: 20-24°C (68-75°F)
    Relative Humidity: 30-60%

Summer Comfort Zone:
    Temperature: 23-26°C (72-78°F)
    Relative Humidity: 25-60%

Affordability

The concept of affordability has different meanings for different people. Most will agree, however, that the market value of a house or commercial structure is one measure of its affordability. This figure is based on several components including the one-time cost of building construction, land, and financing. However, many are beginning to recognize that an affordable building must also minimize long-term operating costs for utilities and maintenance. Avoiding moisture problems plays a role in creating affordable housing by reducing costly repairs and maintenance.

FACTORS INFLUENCING DESIGN AND OPERATION OF BUILDINGS

Resolving moisture problems in buildings requires an approach that views the entire house, its external environment, and its occupants as an interrelated set of factors. Otherwise, if buildings are viewed as a set of isolated components or systems, solving one problem may simply create another one—or worse, the problem may never be diagnosed and solved correctly in the first place. By having an overall understanding of building systems, not only can moisture problems be addressed effectively, but other comfort, health, and energy use problems can be resolved simultaneously.

The factors influencing building design and operation can generally be divided into three groups: (1) climatic and environmental conditions, (2) building occupants, and (3) building systems and components. The manner in which buildings actually perform is governed by basic principles of building science including mechanisms of heat, air, and moisture flow, as well as chemical and biological reactions.

Climatic and Environmental Conditions

There are many ways to define climatic zones in North America. For the purpose of making recommendations regarding moisture control, a very simple division into three basic zones is acceptable (Figure I-4). These zones, defined more precisely in later chapters, are characterized by the type of environmental control they require for most of the year (heating, cooling, or mixed). Within these zones are areas of relative wetness or dryness as well as special microclimatic conditions. These variations in wetness within a particular climate zone generally do not dictate different strategies for moisture control. Instead, wetter conditions will simply indicate more potential for significant problems, and that building assemblies will be less forgiving than in dryer conditions.

Designing in response to the climate is an important concept, especially with respect to moisture problems. In heating climates one designs for heat and moisture that predictably move from the interior of the building to the exterior, while in cooling climates the reverse is true. In either case, it is relatively easy to design for a climate that is limited to all heating or all cooling conditions. When both heating and cooling are required over large portions of the year, design can be more complex since trade-offs must be made. This is particularly true when the climates are also wet, and therefore less forgiving.

In addition to being influenced by overall climatic and microclimatic conditions, a building's design and operation can be affected by the contaminants around and within the building. These include contaminants that may be built into or brought into the building.

An obvious example of the influence of the external environment can be found in a building placed on soil with high radon concentrations. External pollution sources also include outdoor air contaminants as well as excessive noise and vibration. Within the building, materials and furnishings contribute contaminants such as formaldehyde, while appliances may produce undesirable combustion products. The building occupants, as described below, also influence pollutant sources within a home.

Building Occupants

By controlling temperature and humidity, the occupants of a building significantly influence comfort, durability, health, and safety. Buildings in heating climates cannot be

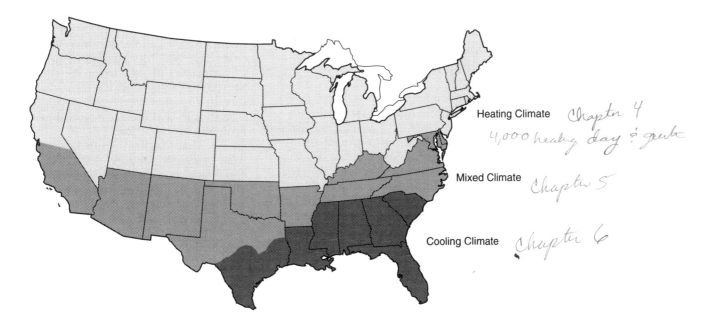

Heating Climate   *Chapter 4*
4,000 *heating day & greater*

Mixed Climate   *Chapter 5*

Cooling Climate   *Chapter 6*

Figure I-4: United States climatic zones used for moisture recommendations.

operated safely and maximize durability if maintained at high levels of interior humidity during heating periods. Likewise, in wet, cooling climates buildings cannot be operated safely or maximize durability if interior temperatures are too low during the hot, humid cooling periods.

People also influence the indoor environment in other ways as well. They produce carbon dioxide, odors, heat, and moisture. In addition, they make choices that introduce various contaminants into the interior environment (i.e. hazardous chemicals, paint cleaners, cleansers, and tobacco smoke).

Building Systems and Components

A building consists of the building envelope and the subsystems contained within it. Building envelopes, which enclose the conditioned space, separate the interior and the occupants from the exterior environment. The building envelope is composed of assemblies including the exterior walls, foundation, ceiling, roof, windows, and doors. Subsystems include the equipment that heats, cools, and ventilates the conditioned space, as well as the structural, plumbing, and electrical systems.

The building itself must be viewed as a complex set of interrelated systems and

components. A change in an element or subsystem can change the performance of an assembly, the building envelope, and ultimately change the characteristics of the entire building. In recent decades, there have been revolutionary developments in products, materials, and systems and the technology of construction has become quite complex. The building envelope and mechanical system interact with and influence interior environmental conditions as never before. For example, many buildings experience excessive depressurization of rooms, corridors, or interstitial spaces which can be a powerful mechanism in drawing moisture into building assemblies.

Mechanisms Underlying Building Performance

It has been stated that the building components, assemblies, and subsystems interact with each other. Moreover, the building interacts with the people who occupy it, as well as the environmental and climatic conditions in which it is placed. In order to diagnose, solve, and prevent moisture problems, as well as meet the broad goals for effective building design outlined earlier, these interactions must be understood. The underlying physical mechanisms that govern these interactions—heat flow, air flow, moisture flow, as well as chemical and biological reactions—are described in the first three chapters of the book.

ORGANIZATION OF THIS HANDBOOK

This handbook approaches moisture problems in buildings from several perspectives. The first three chapters present problems and fundamental principles related to moisture in buildings. Chapter 1—*Mold, Mildew, and Condensation*—examines surface moisture problems. The second chapter—*Moisture Movement*—examines how building assemblies get wet from both the exterior and interior; and Chapter 3—*Design Considerations for Building Assemblies*—introduces the concepts of acceptable performance, moisture balance, and the redistribution of moisture within building assemblies.

Chapters 4 through 6 apply the concepts outlined in the previous chapters and present specific moisture control practices for three basic U.S. climate zones (heating, mixed, and cooling). Each of these chapters begins with a set of strategies to be applied to the whole building, followed by a series of recommended wall, roof, and foundation assemblies. The commentary relating to each detail provides a brief summary of its key characteristics. More detailed explanations of the principles utilized in the development of the details can be found in the early chapters. Finally, Chapter 7 provides a series of brief case studies that illustrate typical moisture problems and solutions.

This handbook attempts to provide the basic principles for successfully designing and constructing building assembly details. Those readers desiring further information and depth are directed to the bibliography at the end of the book. References are provided where the specific issues raised may require further explanation, or where it was felt necessary to direct readers to particularly relevant research findings.

Whenever a specific construction practice in a particular climate presented in this handbook deviates from conventional practice or is unfamiliar, the reader is urged to consult with local code authorities to ensure its acceptability and compliance.

Moisture Control
Handbook

CHAPTER 1

Mold, Mildew, and Condensation

The most common surface moisture-related problems, regardless of climate, are mold, mildew, and condensation. The single most important factor influencing these problems is relative humidity near surfaces. Understanding the factors that govern relative humidity will enable builders and designers to control surface-related moisture problems.

RELATIVE HUMIDITY AND VAPOR PRESSURE

The terms *absolute humidity, humidity ratio,* and *vapor pressure* refer to the same concept: air contains varying amounts of moisture in the gas or vapor form. The actual amount of moisture contained in air is referred to as *absolute humidity*. More precisely, the absolute humidity is the ratio of the mass of water vapor to the mass of dry air. This is also referred to as the *humidity ratio*.

Air is a mixture of several gases including oxygen, nitrogen, carbon dioxide, and water vapor. The total air pressure exerted by a volume of air in a given container on that container is the sum of the individual or partial pressures of the constituent gases which make up the air. The *vapor pressure* is the partial pressure of the water vapor gas on the container.

The amount of moisture air can hold is dependent on its temperature. The warmer air is, the more moisture it can hold; the cooler air is, the less moisture it can hold. Air is said to be saturated (or at 100 percent relative humidity) when it contains the maximum amount of moisture possible at a specific temperature. Air holding half the maximum amount of moisture at a given temperature has a relative humidity of 50 percent. *Relative humidity* is defined as the ratio of the amount of moisture contained in the air to the maximum amount of moisture the air can hold at a given temperature.

Impact of Moisture Amount on Relative Humidity

Figure 1-1 illustrates the concepts of relative and absolute humidity. Three sealed containers each hold the same amount of air (1000 pounds) and are kept at the same temperature (57° F). The containers are assumed to be airtight, watertight, and vaportight. At a temperature of 57° Fahrenheit, 1000 pounds of air is capable of holding approximately 10 pounds of water at a maximum.

The air in container A is completely dry—the relative and absolute humidities are both zero. Three pounds of moisture in the form of water vapor has been added to container B while the temperature remains the same. The absolute humidity (or humidity ratio) of container B is .003 (3 pounds of moisture/1000 pounds of air), while the relative humidity is 30 percent (3 pounds of moisture/10 pounds of maximum moisture capacity at 57° F). Container C holds 10 pounds of moisture in the form of water vapor. The absolute humidity (or humidity ratio) of container C is .010 (10 pounds of moisture/1000 pounds of air), while the relative humidity is 100 percent (10 pounds of moisture/10 pounds of maximum moisture

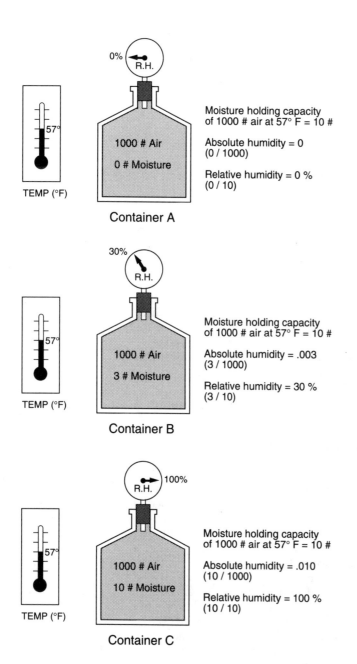

Moisture holding capacity
of 1000 # air at 57° F = 10 #

Absolute humidity = 0
(0 / 1000)

Relative humidity = 0 %
(0 / 10)

Container A

Moisture holding capacity
of 1000 # air at 57° F = 10 #

Absolute humidity = .003
(3 / 1000)

Relative humidity = 30 %
(3 / 10)

Container B

Moisture holding capacity
of 1000 # air at 57° F = 10 #

Absolute humidity = .010
(10 / 1000)

Relative humidity = 100 %
(10 / 10)

Container C

Figure 1-1: Impact of moisture content of air on relative humidity.

capacity at 57° F). The air in container C is at the saturation point—it cannot hold any more moisture in the form of water vapor. If additional moisture is introduced into container C, it will condense into liquid water.

Impact of Temperature on Relative Humidity

Figure 1-2 further illustrates the concepts of relative and absolute humidity and how they vary with temperature. As in Figure 1-1, three sealed containers each hold the same amount of air (1000 pounds). The containers are assumed to be airtight, watertight, and vaportight. Container D is at a temperature of 57° Fahrenheit and holds 5 pounds of moisture. At this temperature, 1000 pounds of air is capable of holding approximately 10 pounds of water at a maximum. Thus, the absolute humidity (or humidity ratio) of container D is .005 (5 pounds of moisture/1000 pounds of air), while the relative humidity is 50 percent (5 pounds of moisture/10 pounds of maximum moisture capacity at 57° F).

The amount of actual moisture in container E remains the same as in container D (5 pounds), however the temperature is increased to 77° Fahrenheit. At this warmer temperature, the air is capable of holding more moisture than it can at a colder temperature—1000 pounds of air can hold 20 pounds of moisture at maximum saturation. Because the actual amount of moisture remains the same in container E, the absolute humidity remains at .005 (5 pounds of moisture/1000 pounds of air). However, the relative humidity is reduced to 25 percent (5 pounds of moisture/20 pounds of maximum moisture capacity at 77° F).

In container F, the amount of actual moisture still remains at 5 pounds, but in this case the temperature is decreased to 37° Fahrenheit. The air is capable of holding less moisture at this colder temperature than it can at a warmer temperature—1000 pounds of air at 37° F can only hold 5 pounds of moisture when saturated. As with containers D and E, the absolute humidity remains at .005 (5 pounds of moisture/1000 pounds of air). Because of the diminished capacity of cold air to hold moisture, however, the relative humidity is increased to 100 percent (5 pounds of moisture/5 pounds of maximum moisture capacity at 37° F).

In Figure 1-1, the three containers are held at a constant temperature while the moisture content of the air increases. This raises both the absolute humidity and the relative humidity.

All three containers in Figure 1-2 hold precisely the same amount of moisture, yet the relative humidity increases as the temperature is reduced and decreases as the temperature rises. These simple illustrations demonstrate that relative humidity can be increased two ways— by increasing vapor pressure (moisture amount) and by decreasing temperature. The relationship between temperature, relative humidity, and absolute humidity is presented graphically on a simplified psychrometric chart in Figure 1-3.

The relationship between temperature, relative humidity, and vapor pressure can often be counterintuitive. For example, cold air is not capable of holding very much moisture, so cold air is dry in an absolute sense and has a low vapor pressure. However, the small amount of moisture present in the cold air is often very close to the maximum amount of moisture the air can hold at that temperature, so the air is at a very high relative humidity. Since the capacity of the air to hold moisture is reduced as temperature is decreased, only a very small addition of moisture is required to bring it to saturation.

In attempting to diagnose problems related to moisture in buildings, both relative humidity and temperature must be measured. In addition, since temperature and humidity can vary within spaces and buildings, taking measurements at several locations is desirable.

MOLD AND MILDEW IN BUILDINGS

Molds are simple plants of the group known as fungi that grow on the surfaces of objects. Mold discolors surfaces, leads to odor problems, and deteriorates building materials. In addition, mold growth can lead to allergic reactions in susceptible individuals as well as other potential health problems (hypersensitivity, other infectious diseases). Certain fungi found in indoor air produce mycotoxins which have been found to be carcinogenic (induces cancer), teratogenic (induces birth defects), immunosuppressive (reduces immune system performance), and oxigenic (poisons tissues) (Spengler et al. 1991).

Other agents of biological contamination can occur in many forms. Viruses, bacteria, protozoa, algae, and vapors derived from living organisms can become airborne (bioaerosols). Bacteria and fungi contribute to "organic dust" and have been linked to outbreaks of sick building syndrome (SBS). Furthermore, dust mites and cockroaches

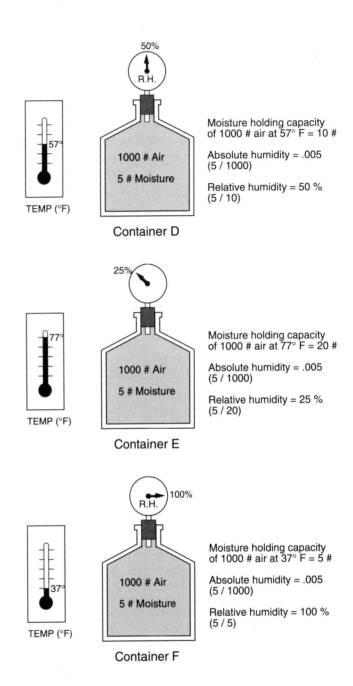

Figure 1-2: *Impact of temperature change on relative humidity.*

Note: Volumes of containers need to change slightly as temperature changes to follow the Ideal Gas Law.

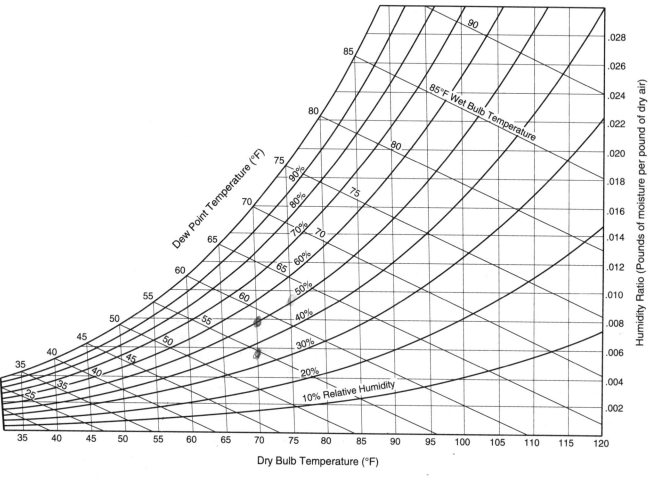

Figure 1-3: Simplified psychrometric chart.
Based on the chart in the 1989 *ASHRAE Handbook of Fundamentals.*

produce particulates which are allergenic or antigenic. Bioaerosols are also associated with tuberculosis, Legionnaire's disease, humidifier fever, hypersensitivity, pneumonitis, aspergillosis, allergic rhinitis, and viral respiratory infection. Fungal and bacterial growth can be curtailed if moisture levels are limited in organic materials. Dust mite growth can also be similarly inhibited. Relative humidities limited to 70 percent or lower at the surfaces of organic materials are typically necessary to limit these forms of biological growth (Samuelson and Samuelson 1990, AHMA 1991).

Most fungi have wind-borne spores, which are microscopic and buoyant. These suspended spores enter buildings as part of natural and controlled air change. Although exterior airborne concentrations vary seasonally, mold spores can be considered to be always present.

Molds cannot manufacture their own food, however they can utilize many commonly available compounds, such as starches, sugars, cellulose, lignins, fats, proteins, and complex hydrocarbons. Accordingly, many building materials provide nutrients for fungi. Examples are wood products, cotton fabrics, wool fabrics, hemp fabrics, organic dust and lint, soaps, oils, paints, adhesives, certain plastics, and vinyls.

Most fungi grow when the temperature is between 50 degrees and 100 degrees Fahrenheit, with optimum growth occurring between 75 degrees and 95 degrees. Some types of fungi can grow at temperatures as low as 35 degrees and as high as 120 degrees (AHMA 1991).

Molds also require moisture for growth. Moisture is necessary for the production of enzymes and other metabolic activities in order to digest carbohydrates, fats, and proteins. The optimum relative humidity for most fungal growth is 70 percent (Spengler et al. 1991).

The following conditions are necessary and sufficient for mold and other biological growth to occur on surfaces:

1. Mold spores must be present.

2. A nutrient base must be available (most surfaces contain nutrients).

3. Temperature range must be between 40 degrees and 100 degrees.

4. Relative humidity adjacent to surface must be above 70 percent.

Of these conditions, relative humidity near surfaces is the most practical to control. Spores are always present in outdoor and indoor air. Almost all of the commonly used construction materials can support mold growth, making control of available nutrients quite difficult. Finally, human comfort constraints limit the use of temperature control.

By maintaining relative humidities near surfaces below 70 percent, mold and other biological growth can be controlled. Since relative humidities are dependent on both temperature and vapor pressure, mold control is dependent on controlling both the temperature and vapor pressure near surfaces.

Mold Growth in Heating and Mixed Climates

In heating climates, mold grows on interior surfaces during the heating season. Typically, the interior surfaces of exterior walls are cool from heat loss while moisture levels within the conditioned space are too high. Mold growth control is facilitated by preventing the interior surfaces of exterior wall and other building assemblies from becoming too cold and by limiting interior moisture levels. The key is to prevent relative humidities of adjacent surfaces from rising above 70 percent. The thermal resistance of the building envelope and the local climate determine the interior surface temperatures of exterior walls and other building assemblies. Controlled ventilation and source control limit the interior moisture levels.

Where interior moisture levels during the heating season are limited to 25 to 35 percent relative humidity at 70 degrees Fahrenheit, relative humidities adjacent to the cooler interior surfaces of exterior walls (of typical thermal resistance) typically fall below 70 percent and mold growth is controlled. The colder the climate (for the thermal resistance of

any given building envelope) the lower the interior humidity necessary to prevent 70 percent relative humidities from occurring adjacent to cool interior surfaces of exterior walls. Building enclosures of similar thermal resistance (building code minimums) located in Minneapolis, MN and Cincinnati, OH should be limited to different interior moisture levels during the heating season. A 25 percent interior relative humidity at 70 degrees Fahrenheit would likely be appropriate for Minneapolis, whereas in Cincinnati, interior relative humidities up to 35 percent at 70 degrees Fahrenheit would likely be appropriate. Correspondingly, the higher the desired interior relative humidity, the higher the thermal resistance necessary to control relative humidities adjacent to interior surfaces.

During the heating season in mixed climates, interior moisture levels should be limited to the 35 to 45 percent relative humidity range at 70 degrees Fahrenheit. This limits the relative humidity adjacent to the interior surface of exterior walls to below 70 percent for the typical thermal resistance found in most building assemblies in this climate zone.

Where excessive ventilation or excessive air change by infiltration/exfiltration occurs during the heating season, uncomfortably low relative humidities can also occur. When relative humidities drop below 20 percent, membranes in the human respiratory system begin to dry, and defenses against infection may become compromised. At low relative humidities contact lens wearers become uncomfortable, and static electricity discharges can affect equipment and people. Relative humidities should be maintained above 25 percent during heating periods.

Mold Growth in Cooling Climates

In cooling climates, interior mold growth also occurs because interior surfaces are typically cold from air conditioning, while interior moisture levels are too high. When exterior hot air is cooled, its relative humidity increases. If the exterior hot air is also humid, cooling this air will typically raise its relative humidity above the point at which mold growth can occur (70 percent).

Cold spots can be created on the interior gypsum board surfaces where cold (air conditioned) air is blown against an interior surface due to poor diffuser design, diffuser location, or diffuser performance. Although this cold air is typically dehumidified before it is supplied to the conditioned space, it can create a mold problem on room surfaces as a result of high levels of airborne moisture within the room contacting the cooled surface. This typically leads to a rise in relative humidity near the surface and a corresponding mold problem.

If exterior humid air comes in contact with the interstitial cavity side of cooled interior gypsum board, mold and other biological growth can occur. Cooling this exterior hot, humid air by air conditioning or contact with cool surfaces will raise its relative humidity above 70 percent. When nutrients are present mold and other growth occurs. This is exacerbated with the use of impermeable wall coverings such as vinyl wallpaper which can trap moisture between the interior finish and the gypsum board. When these interior finishes are coupled with cold spots (from poor diffuser placement and/or overcooling) and exterior moisture, mold and other growth can occur.

Accordingly, one of the most practical solutions in controlling mold and other biological growth in cooling climates is the prevention of hot, humid exterior air, or other forms of moisture transport, from contacting the interior cold (air conditioned) gypsum board surfaces. This is most commonly facilitated by maintaining the conditioned space at a positive air pressure relative to the exterior and installing of an exterior vapor diffusion retarder. Airtight construction helps to effectively pressurize building assemblies.

Interior moisture levels within conditioned spaces in cooling climates should be limited to 60 percent relative humidity at 75 degrees Fahrenheit. This can be accomplished by dehumidification and source control to prevent mold growth on the interior surfaces within the conditioned space (AHMA 1991).

Experience has also shown that where conditions for mold growth are controlled, other biological growth such as dust mite infestations can also be controlled. For dust mites to grow, 70 percent relative humidities are also necessary. Carpets located on cold surfaces such as concrete slabs are particularly sensitive to dust mite growth. Carpets on cold surfaces should be avoided, or these surface temperatures should be elevated by the use of appropriate thermal insulation (EPA 1991).

CONDENSATION

When the relative humidity reaches 100 percent, moisture can condense. The temperature at which the air/vapor mix reaches 100 percent relative humidity is called the *dew point*

temperature. Moisture can condense on a surface if the temperature of that surface is below the dew point temperature of the air/vapor mix adjacent that surface. Condensation can provide an environment for the growth of mold, mildew, and other biological pathogens. In addition, it can lead to the deterioration of building materials if it is allowed to collect.

The colder the surface, the higher the relative humidity adjacent to that surface. The coldest surfaces in a room always have the highest relative humidities adjacent to them. The coldest surface in a room will likely be the location where condensation happens first, should the relative humidity rise to 100 percent. The coldest surface in a room is therefore referred to as the *first condensing surface*.

The same strategies that control mold and mildew growth also control condensation on surfaces—increasing surface temperatures and reducing vapor pressures (moisture levels) near surfaces.

GENERAL STRATEGIES TO CONTROL MOISTURE PROBLEMS

Increasing Surface Temperatures

A classic example of a moisture problem in a heating climate can occur in an exposed closet on an exterior wall (Figure 1-4). The closet has a higher ratio of surface area to volume compared to other conditioned spaces, resulting in a greater heat loss. In addition, it is also more exposed to the wind. If it is poorly insulated, the closet is likely to be significantly colder than the adjacent bedroom because of this higher heat loss rate and the fact that it is separated from the conditioned space with no independent source of heat.

It is reasonable to assume that the vapor pressure in the bedroom is the same as the vapor pressure in the closet, and since the closet is colder, the relative humidity in the closet will be much higher than that in the bedroom. For example, if a relative humidity of 35 percent at a temperature of 70 degrees Fahrenheit is measured in the bedroom, then there is a low amount of moisture in the conditioned space (see Figure 1-4). Assuming the vapor pressure (absolute humidity) is the same in both spaces, a closet temperature of 50 degrees Fahrenheit results in relative humidity of 70 percent—high enough to experience mold and mildew growth. With even lower temperatures or higher moisture levels in the closet, the relative humidity may rise to 100 percent, resulting in condensation and possibly the deterioration of materials and finishes.

The temperature of the closet can be raised by increasing the heat flow to the closet or decreasing the heat flow out of the closet. Increasing the heat flow to the closet can be as simple as leaving the closet door open. The open door will promote air circulation, and the air circulation will carry heat into the closet, warming the closet and reducing its relative humidity. Louvered closet doors can have the same effect. Heating the closet by leaving a light on inside (a 150-watt bulb generates 150 watts of heat) or by installing a heat register will also reduce closet relative humidity. Installing a heat register in a closet, however, is an inefficient use of heating energy and should be used only as a last resort.

Heat flow out of a closet can be reduced by insulating the exterior closet walls and by preventing the wind from *short-circuiting* the thermal insulation by blowing into the wall cavities (*wind-washing* of the insulation). Wind-washing can be controlled by installing a tight building paper or tight sheathing on the exterior of the wall.

Reducing Vapor Pressure

Similar to the previous example, a bedroom with a closet on the exterior wall is shown in Figure 1-5. In this case, however, there is a relative humidity of 60 percent and a temperature of 70 degrees Fahrenheit in the bedroom. This indicates a relatively high amount of moisture present in the conditioned space. Unlike the previous case where the closet was significantly colder than the bedroom, the temperature in the closet is only slightly reduced—65 degrees Fahrenheit. Assuming, as before, that the amount of moisture in the closet and in the bedroom are the same, the relative humidity in the closet rises to 70 percent. This relative humidity in the closet—high enough to experience mold and mildew growth—results from too much moisture in the house rather than from cold surface temperatures. Of course, with even higher moisture levels in the closet, the relative humidity may rise to 100 percent, resulting in condensation and related problems.

To control mold and mildew growth as well as possible condensation in the closet, the relative humidity must be reduced. In this case the vapor pressure in the closet and house can be reduced by using three methods: source control, dilution, and dehumidification.

Source control, the most energy efficient of the three approaches, involves limiting the amount of interior airborne moisture that enters the space. Common examples of source control are the direct venting of bathrooms, clothes dryers, and kitchen stoves to the exterior. Other strategies include the construction of dry basements and crawl spaces, the venting of space heaters directly to the exterior, the removal of unvented kerosene space heaters, and the storage of firewood outdoors rather than indoors.

Dilution involves the use of air change, or the exchange of interior moisture-laden air with exterior dry air. If the exterior air is dryer than the interior air, the greater the air change,

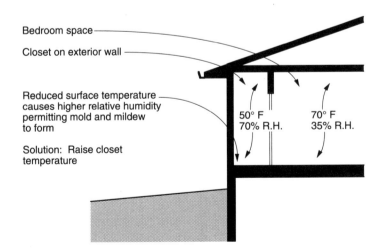

Bedroom space

Closet on exterior wall

Reduced surface temperature causes higher relative humidity permitting mold and mildew to form

Solution: Raise closet temperature

50° F
70% R.H.

70° F
35% R.H.

Figure 1-4: Bedroom with closet on exterior wall experiences surface moisture problem from low surface temperature.

the greater the dilution of interior airborne moisture levels. Dilution can occur through natural air change (uncontrolled infiltration and exfiltration) or through mechanical ventilation utilizing fans or blowers. Dilution by air change is only possible where the exterior air is dryer than the interior air. In cooling climates or during cooling periods this is often not the case. As such dilution of interior airborne moisture levels utilizing outside air is limited to heating climates and during heating seasons. A common example of dilution control is installation of an exhaust fan that operates by timer or dehumidistat control.

Dehumidification involves the removal of moisture from a space and usually involves the cooling of warm, moisture-laden air to reduce its ability to hold moisture, thereby forcing the moisture to condense. Dehumidification is coupled with air conditioning in cooling climates or during the cooling season. Dehumidifiers are commonly used in basements or bedrooms in many climates throughout the year.

COMMON EXAMPLES OF SURFACE MOISTURE PROBLEMS

As explained in the previous section, most mold, mildew, and condensation problems are either related to low surface temperatures, high interior humidity levels, or some combination of both. Moisture problems related to low surface temperatures may not be eliminated by increasing ventilation or air change strategies which are designed to reduce interior humidity levels. Likewise, moisture problems related to high vapor pressures may not be eliminated by increasing surface temperatures. Understanding which factor dominates—low surface temperature or high vapor pressure—will limit the choice of effective strategies.

An example of this would be an old, leaky, poorly insulated home in a heating climate which is suffering from mold and mildew. Since the house is leaky, it has a very high natural air change that dilutes interior airborne moisture levels and therefore maintains a very low interior vapor pressure. Providing mechanical ventilation in this house by installing a fan in an attempt to control interior mold and mildew will likely not be effective since the interior moisture levels are already low. Increasing surface temperatures by insulating the exterior walls, thereby reducing surface relative humidities, would be a better strategy to control mold and mildew in this instance. Other common examples of surface moisture problems follow.

Setback Thermostats

Setback thermostats have proven to be very effective in heating climates to reduce energy consumption during the heating season. House temperatures are dropped at night when occupants are sleeping and raised to normal comfort levels when occupants are awake. However, when temperatures are reduced at night, a corresponding increase in relative humidity also occurs, which can result

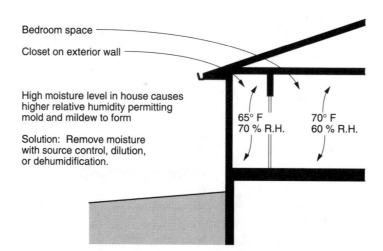

Bedroom space

Closet on exterior wall

High moisture level in house causes higher relative humidity permitting mold and mildew to form

Solution: Remove moisture with source control, dilution, or dehumidification.

65° F
70 % R.H.

70° F
60 % R.H.

Figure 1-5: Bedroom with closet on exterior wall experiences surface moisture problem from high interior relative humidity.

in mold and mildew growth at cool surfaces.

Heating climate mold and mildew can be controlled in many instances by increasing interior temperatures during heating periods. Unfortunately, increasing temperature also increases energy consumption. An appropriate balance needs to occur between the desired goal of reduced energy consumption and the avoidance of surface moisture problems.

Closed-Off Rooms

Many occupants close off unused bedrooms or other rooms during heating periods to reduce heating bills. Since air and room temperatures are reduced, this practice can result in high relative humidities in these rooms, leading to mold and mildew growth. Thus, the benefits of energy conservation should be weighed against the possibilities of damage from mold and mildew growth. Should rooms be closed off, control of interior vapor pressures (moisture levels) may be necessary.

Exterior Corners

In heating climates, exterior corners are common locations for mold and mildew growth as well as possible condensation. The higher relative humidities in exterior corners are due to the corners being colder than other surfaces. This condition results from:

1. Poor air circulation

2. Wind blowing through corner assemblies (wind-washing)

3. Low insulation levels due to framing practices

4. Greater surface area of heat loss

Lack of airflow at corners due to poor circulation and/or obstructions such as furniture results in less heat being carried to corner surfaces, making them colder (Figure 1-6A). Sometimes, rearranging furniture to remove air flow obstructions from a corner is all that is required to control mold and mildew growth. Homes with forced air heating systems and/or room ceiling fans have lower incidences of mold and mildew growth than homes with low levels of air movement.

Wind typically increases in velocity at corners, often increasing heat loss at corner surfaces (Figure 1-6A). When wind enters corner assemblies and blows through, or short-circuits the thermal insulation (wind-washing), the interior surfaces (gypsum board) can be

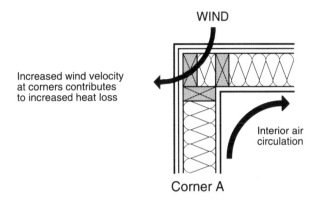

Corner A

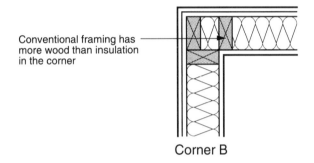

Corner B

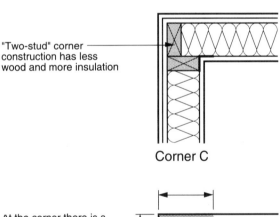

Corner C

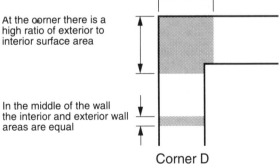

Corner D

Figure 1-6: Heat loss effects at building corners.

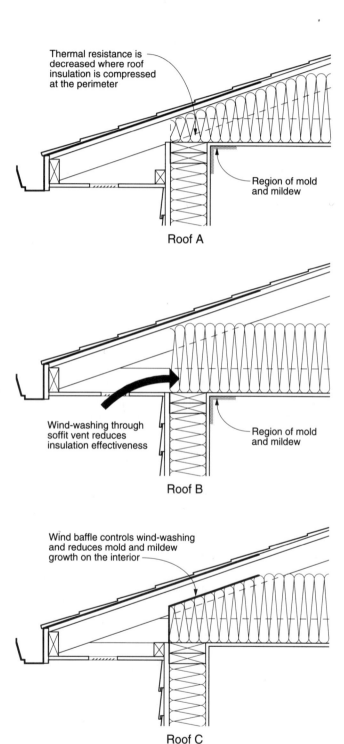

Thermal resistance is decreased where roof insulation is compressed at the perimeter

Region of mold and mildew

Roof A

Wind-washing through soffit vent reduces insulation effectiveness

Region of mold and mildew

Roof B

Wind baffle controls wind-washing and reduces mold and mildew growth on the interior

Roof C

Figure 1-7: Heat loss effects at ceiling edge.

cooled significantly. This air flow is distinct from infiltration. Infiltration is air movement through the wall, whereas wind-washing typically involves air flow entering a wall at one location at the exterior and exiting at some other exterior location.

Corner lumber framing practices often result in more wood than insulation in a corner. The resultant lack of thermal insulation leads to colder corner surfaces (Figure 1-6B). Recent framing innovations (i.e., two-stud corners) reduce heat loss at corners as well as reduce quantities of framing material required (Figure 1-6C). The advent of insulating sheathings has also significantly reduced the incidence of corner mold and mildew.

Corner geometry results in a greater exterior surface area of heat loss per unit of interior surface area than at other wall surfaces (Figure 1-6D). This also results in cooler surfaces near corners.

Exterior Wall/Roof Intersections

Cool interior surfaces in heating climates also can occur where exterior walls intersect roofs. Ceiling thermal insulation often is reduced in thickness at building perimeters due to roof geometries, resulting in greater heat loss at perimeters, and thus cool spots (Figure 1-7A). The cool spots lead to higher surface relative humidities and mold and mildew. The use of specialized roof framing details (i.e., *high-heel* trusses) has allowed greater thicknesses of ceiling insulation to be installed at building perimeters to reduce heat loss at these locations. However, the thicker roof assemblies can lead to greater heat loss than standard framing when these thicker roof assemblies are coupled with soffit ventilation. The higher roof framing makes it easier for air entering at soffit vents to short-circuit the thermal insulation (wind-washing) (Figure 1-7B). Therefore, wherever soffit ventilation is utilized, wind baffles are also necessary to control wind-washing to reduce mold and mildew growth at building perimeters (Figure 1-7C).

Air Conditioned Spaces

In cooling climates, the problems of mold and mildew can be as extensive as problems in heating climates. The same principles apply: either surfaces are too cold or the moisture levels are too high. Cold surfaces in cooling climates arise from the air conditioning of enclosures. When exterior hot air is cooled, its relative humidity increases. If the exterior hot air is also humid, cooling this air will typically raise its relative humidity to the point at which mold growth can occur (70 percent). In some cases, the relative humidity may rise to 100 percent, resulting in condensation.

A common example of mold growth can be found in hotel rooms in cooling climates where cold conditioned air is blown against an exterior wall surface. This creates a cold spot on the gypsum board inside the exterior wall. Although this cold air is typically dehumidified before it is supplied to the conditioned space, it can create a mold problem within an exterior wall cavity. This occurs if exterior humid air enters the wall cavity as a result of an air pressure difference and comes in contact with the cooled surface of the gypsum board within the cavity.

This is particularly a problem in hotel rooms due to the common use of impermeable wall coverings such as vinyl wallpaper, which can trap moisture between the interior finish and the gypsum board. When these interior finishes are coupled with cold spots and exterior moisture, mold growth can be significant. Several solutions are possible: (1) preventing the hot, humid exterior air from contacting the cold gypsum board by controlling air pressure differences and air leakage openings, (2) eliminating the cold spots and elevating the temperature of the surface by relocating ducts and diffusers, (3) increasing enclosure temperatures by preventing the overcooling of rooms, or (4) increasing the permeability (breathability) of interior finish materials.

Thermal Bridges

The cooling of any surface leads to an increase in surface relative humidity, which can lead to mold and mildew growth as well as possible condensation. Localized cooling of surfaces commonly occurs as a result of *thermal bridges*. Thermal bridges are regions of relatively high heat flow conductance in a building envelope. An example of a thermal bridge is an uninsulated window lintel, or the edge of a concrete floor slab in commercial construction (Figure 1-8). An even more common example is the wood stud of a typical exterior frame wall (Figure 1-9) where insulation is installed between studs in the wall cavity. The wood stud has a greater conductivity to heat flow than the insulation, and therefore provides an easy path for heat to bridge the wall. The result is a cold spot at the interior face of the gypsum board where it is in contact with the stud. This

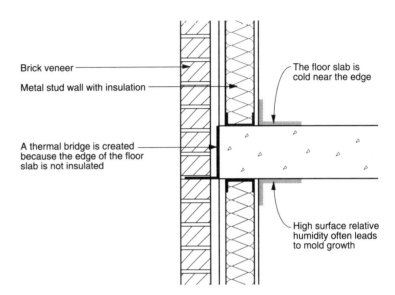

Figure 1-8: Thermal bridge at wall/floor intersection.

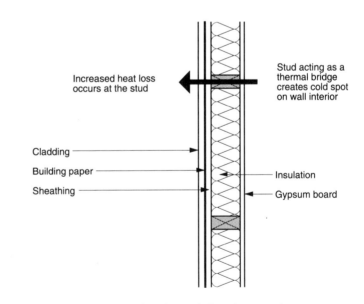

Figure 1-9: Thermal bridge through framing members.

can lead to a higher surface relative humidity at this location and potentially to mold and mildew growth. The use of insulating sheathings significantly reduces the impact of thermal bridges in building envelopes.

Concealed Condensation

The use of thermal insulation in wall cavities increases interior surface temperatures in heating climates and therefore reduces the likelihood of interior surface mold, mildew, and condensation. However, by reducing heat loss, the use of thermal insulation also reduces the temperature of the outer portions of the wall assembly which may increase the likelihood of concealed condensation within the wall cavities.

In a heating climate, the first condensing surface in a wall cavity is typically the interior surface (back side) of the exterior sheathing (Figure 1-10). The temperature of this surface is reduced by increasing the insulation in the wall cavities. Concealed condensation can be controlled by reducing the entry of moisture into the wall cavities or by elevating the temperature of the first condensing surface.

Elevating the temperature of the first condensing surface in a heating climate wall assembly can be accomplished by installing insulation on the exterior side of the first condensing surface. For example, an insulating sheathing installed on the exterior of wall framing increases the temperature of everything on the interior side of the sheathing (Figure 1-11). The rigid insulation can also be installed over plywood or OSB sheathing, thereby warming the cavity side of the sheathing and creating a temperature increase at the first condensing surface.

The first condensing surface in a cooling climate is typically the back side of the interior gypsum board or other finish material (Figure 1-12). Assuming the interior is air conditioned,

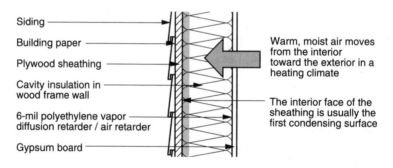

Siding

Building paper

Plywood sheathing

Cavity insulation in wood frame wall

6-mil polyethylene vapor diffusion retarder / air retarder

Gypsum board

Warm, moist air moves from the interior toward the exterior in a heating climate

The interior face of the sheathing is usually the first condensing surface

Figure 1-10: The inside face of the sheathing is usually the first condensing surface in a heating climate wall assembly.

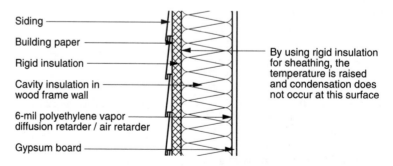

Siding

Building paper

Rigid insulation

Cavity insulation in wood frame wall

6-mil polyethylene vapor diffusion retarder / air retarder

Gypsum board

By using rigid insulation for sheathing, the temperature is raised and condensation does not occur at this surface

Figure 1-11: Rigid insulation sheathing reduces the likelihood that condensation will occur at the interior surface of the sheathing.

warm moist exterior air condenses as it comes in contact with the cool interior finish material. The temperature of the first condensing surface in a cooling climate can be elevated by installing impermeable insulating sheathing to the interior of the wall framing, between the wall framing and the interior gypsum board (Figure 1-13). In this manner, the first condensing surface is moved toward the exterior of the wall and becomes the cavity side of the insulating sheathing rather than the interior gypsum board.

Windows

Windows are typically the coldest visible surfaces in a room, and are therefore the location where moisture is most likely to condense. Condensation may occur because the interior airborne moisture level is rising, or the exterior air temperature (and the temperature of the interior surface of glass) is dropping.

The interior surface of a window is often the first condensing surface in a room. If the amount of condensation is substantial, water may run down the glass surface eventually leading to deterioration of wood sashes or sills.

Historically, to control condensation, window surface temperatures were raised by the use of storm windows, the replacement of single glazed windows with double glazed windows, and later with triple glazed windows as well as selective surface and gas-filled windows. The colder the climate, the greater the required thermal resistance of window surfaces and the greater the required sophistication of the glazing systems.

When condensation occurs on the interior surface of a window, airborne moisture in the vapor phase is removed from the air and deposited on the interior surface of the window. The colder the window surfaces, the greater the amount of moisture removed from the air. The window is acting as a dehumidifier

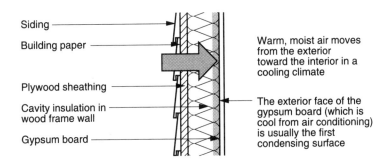

Siding

Building paper

Plywood sheathing

Cavity insulation in wood frame wall

Gypsum board

Warm, moist air moves from the exterior toward the interior in a cooling climate

The exterior face of the gypsum board (which is cool from air conditioning) is usually the first condensing surface

Figure 1-12: The exterior face of the gypsum board is usually the first condensing surface in a cooling climate wall assembly.

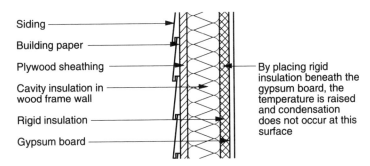

Siding

Building paper

Plywood sheathing

Cavity insulation in wood frame wall

Rigid insulation

Gypsum board

By placing rigid insulation beneath the gypsum board, the temperature is raised and condensation does not occur at this surface

Figure 1-13: Rigid insulation beneath the gypsum board reduces the likelihood that condensation will occur at the inside surface.

for the room (unless the condensed moisture re-evaporates).

The temperature of the first condensing surface usually sets or limits the maximum vapor pressure that can exist in a room. The greater the amount of moisture generation or entry in a space, the greater the amount of moisture deposited on the condensing surface. Vapor pressures will rise only when the rate of moisture generation or entry in a space exceeds the rate of moisture removal by the condensing surface. However, when moisture generation or entry stops or is reduced, equilibrium will occur at a vapor pressure limited by the temperature of the first condensing surface in the room. For all intents and purposes, the temperature of the first condensing surface controls moisture behavior in that room.

In order to operate the room at a higher vapor pressure, the temperature of the first condensing surface must be raised. As homeowners and occupants in heating climates began to humidify building enclosures during the heating season for comfort reasons, window surface temperatures had to be raised to control condensation, hence this became one of the reasons for developing higher performance glazing systems. In a sense, the advent of higher performance glazing systems has led to greater incidence of moisture problems in heating climate enclosures because they can now be operated at higher interior vapor pressures without visible surface condensation on the windows.

In older building enclosures, the thermally poor glazing systems limited interior moisture levels by condensing moisture. The visible condensation often alerted occupants to the need for ventilation to flush out interior moisture. In effect, the windows acted as an early warning system to identify excessive moisture and other indoor air pollutants.

CHAPTER 2

Moisture Movement

In order to control moisture levels and moisture movement in buildings, the mechanisms governing such movement must be understood. Appreciating the magnitude of each transport mechanism is crucial in developing an effective design and construction strategy. When working with limited resources, it is unwise to concentrate a disproportionate share of those resources and effort on relatively minor factors, while allowing major factors to be ignored.

The four moisture transport mechanisms predominant in building science are:

1. Liquid flow

2. Capillary suction

3. Air movement

4. Vapor diffusion

Moisture movement, and therefore any moisture-related problem, is typically a result of one or more of these mechanisms. Each mechanism can act independently and must be dealt with during design and construction. The first mechanism, liquid flow, is primarily responsible for moving moisture into the building envelope from the exterior. Capillary suction typically moves moisture into the building envelope from the exterior and also redistributes condensed moisture within building envelopes.

The latter two mechanisms, air movement and vapor diffusion, can move moisture both from the exterior as well as from within the conditioned space into the building envelope, depending on exterior and interior conditions. For example, when a building in a cold climate is being heated, air movement and vapor diffusion typically result in a net movement from within the conditioned space into the building envelope. When a building in a warm climate is being cooled, air movement and vapor diffusion may result in a net movement of moisture from the exterior into the conditioned space.

This duality of movement is dependent on both climatic and interior conditions and is often overlooked by designers and builders. It is not unusual to find cold climate building envelope designs employed in warm climate regions. Even more challenging to the builder and designer are conditions where both heating and cooling occur for extended periods of time.

Of the four transport mechanisms, the most significant are liquid flow and capillary suction, where groundwater and rain are the moisture sources. Controlling groundwater entry below grade and rain entry above grade have traditionally been the preoccupation of generations of builders and designers, and it is no different today. Liquid flow and capillarity are also recognized as the primary factors in the wetting of materials. Air transport and vapor diffusion make less obvious contributions to moisture problems.

Liquid Flow

The first and most significant moisture transport mechanism a designer and builder must deal with is liquid flow. This involves groundwater and rain moving under the

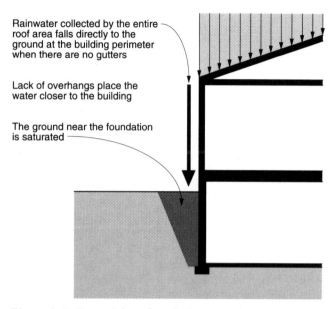

Rainwater collected by the entire roof area falls directly to the ground at the building perimeter when there are no gutters

Lack of overhangs place the water closer to the building

The ground near the foundation is saturated

Figure 2-1: Potential surface drainage problems.

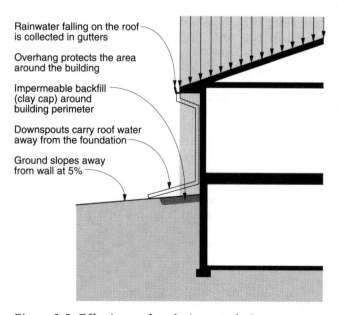

Rainwater falling on the roof is collected in gutters

Overhang protects the area around the building

Impermeable backfill (clay cap) around building perimeter

Downspouts carry roof water away from the foundation

Ground slopes away from wall at 5%

Figure 2-2: Effective surface drainage techniques.

influence of a driving force, typically gravity or air pressure. This mechanism is responsible for moving moisture from the exterior into the building envelope. Leakage will occur if three conditions prevail: (1) groundwater or rain is present, (2) an opening or hole in the building envelope exists, and (3) a driving force (gravity, momentum, surface tension, and/or an air pressure difference) is present. Understanding these conditions gives designers and builders flexibility in developing various strategies to control this moisture transport mechanism.

Designers or builders can seldom control whether groundwater or rain is present. However, they may be able to influence the magnitude (or source strength) of the groundwater and rain by proper site selection (minimizing wind exposure and building on elevated dry ground). To some degree, builders are able to control the number of openings or holes in a building enclosure. While driving forces such as wind or gravity cannot be controlled, they can be influenced by cladding geometry, flashings, and drainage.

Since it is difficult to build an enclosure without openings, controlling the effects of the driving forces, rather than eliminating openings, is the most effective approach for controlling liquid flow. In the portions of the building envelope below grade, gravity (hydrostatic pressure) can be controlled by the use of the *drain screen*. Above grade, momentum, surface tension, and air pressure differences across exterior cladding can be controlled by the use of the *rain screen* principle. Both of these techniques are described below.

It is also possible to provide a barrier below grade (*waterproofing,* or the elimination of below-grade openings) to resist hydrostatic pressure, and to provide a barrier above grade (face sealing or *weatherproofing,* i.e., the elimination of above-grade openings) to resist rain entry. However, waterproofing and weatherproofing (face sealing) are more dependent on workmanship and the appropriate choice of materials than both the drain screen and rain screen.

GROUNDWATER

The following strategies can be implemented to control groundwater effectively: (1) use surface drainage to reduce the rate at which surface water and rainwater enter the ground adjacent to a building, (2) use subsurface drainage to prevent groundwater from entering the building enclosure below grade, and (3) eliminate below-grade openings or provide a barrier/membrane to resist hydrostatic pressure (waterproofing). The first two strategies have historically proven to be more effective than waterproofing. Often, all three strategies must be used in conjunction to ensure an adequate system.

Roof and Surface Drainage

The following steps have historically proven effective to reduce the surface and rainwater entering the ground adjacent to a building:

1. Gutters and downspouts

Roof assemblies typically concentrate rainwater collected from an entire building's *footprint* at the building's perimeter (Figure 2-1). Use gutters and roof overhangs to control rainwater from roofs. Gutter and downspout systems should direct water away from the building above grade, and not tie into a below-grade drainage system (Figure 2-2).

2. Ground slope

Poor site location and/or site grading practices can lead to surface water flow toward building foundations. Slope the ground away from foundation walls, and use swales as necessary to redirect surface runoff (Figure 2-2). The ground near the building should be compacted or overfilled to compensate for backfill settlement.

3. Impermeable cap over backfill

Rainwater and surface water absorption by backfill material can cause groundwater to concentrate at building perimeters. Locating heavily irrigated flower beds and gardens immediately adjacent to building perimeters has similar effects. Backfill the upper portions of foundation excavations with an impermeable material (a clay cap as shown in Figure 2-2). Locating a sloping sidewalk adjacent to a foundation also works well in preventing water absorption by the ground; however, this strategy needs to consider the effects of *splash-back* on wall/cladding assemblies.

Free-Draining Backfill (Drain Screen)

A drain screen controls below-grade water by placing free-draining backfill material immediately adjacent to foundation walls (Figure 2-3). This free-draining material, typically sand or gravel, allows for the free flow

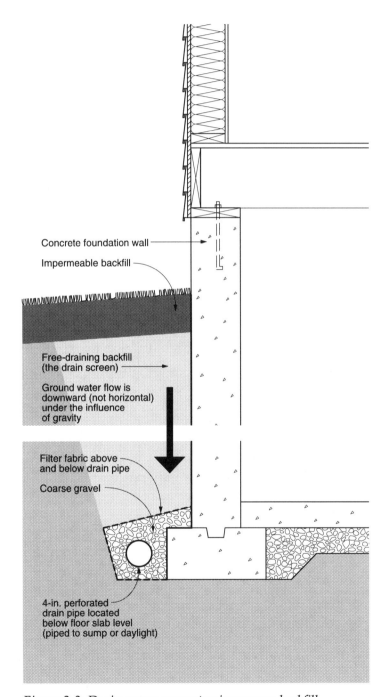

Concrete foundation wall

Impermeable backfill

Free-draining backfill (the drain screen)

Ground water flow is downward (not horizontal) under the influence of gravity

Filter fabric above and below drain pipe

Coarse gravel

4-in. perforated drain pipe located below floor slab level (piped to sump or daylight)

Figure 2-3: Drain screen concept using porous backfill.

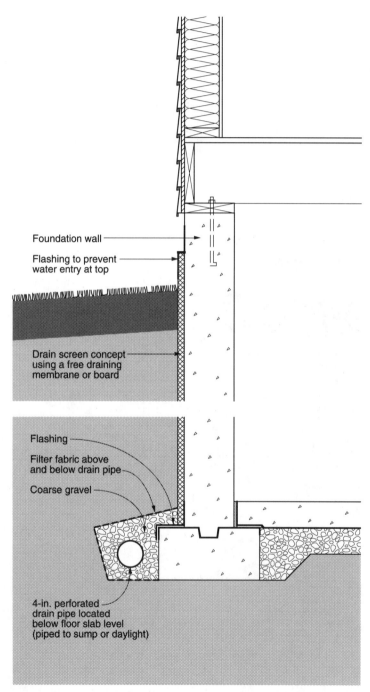

Foundation wall

Flashing to prevent
water entry at top

Drain screen concept
using a free draining
membrane or board

Flashing

Filter fabric above
and below drain pipe

Coarse gravel

4-in. perforated
drain pipe located
below floor slab level
(piped to sump or daylight)

*Figure 2-4: Drain screen concept using a free-draining
board or membrane.*

of water downwards toward a subgrade
drainage system, thus reducing hydrostatic
pressure. Water running down the basement
wall surface will travel through the smaller
pores of the soil rather than into any large
cracks in the basement wall—assuming there is
no hydrostatic pressure.

Drain Pipes

Of course, if the free-draining material
permits the flow of groundwater downwards,
a subgrade drainage system must be provided
for removing the water at the base of the wall.
The subgrade drainage system in effect lowers
the groundwater table immediately adjacent to
the foundation.

The subgrade drainage system is usually a
perforated drainage pipe located at the perimeter of the foundation below the basement floor
level (if a basement space is present) on the
exterior of the wall. Locating perimeter
drainage pipe inside the footing under the
basement floor slab can also be effective. To
provide redundancy some builders/designers
install drain pipes both on the exterior and the
interior of the footing.

The perforated drainage pipe is encased in
crushed stone (free from fines) and surrounded
by a filter medium. As groundwater rises, it
rises into the drainage pipe and is carried
away. Drainage pipe should be installed with
holes facing down. Drain pipes should be
sloped to facilitate drainage and should be
connected to daylight, to a sump, or to a storm
sewer. It should be noted that some storm
sewer systems tend to back up during heavy
rains and can pipe water into foundation
assemblies rather than away from them. As a
result some builders install check valves at
storm sewer connections which only allow
groundwater to flow away from the foundation.

Free-Draining Building Materials

If implemented effectively, foundation
assemblies using the drain screen concept
remain dry even if numerous holes, openings,
or cracks exist in the walls. Variations on the
classic drain screen involve the use of free-
draining building materials or exterior foundation insulation with drainage properties rather
than free-draining backfill material.

Free-draining materials often rely on two
concepts: (1) the provision of air spaces or
openings of sufficient size to allow water to
drain through them, and (2) the flow of water

through oriented materials (sometimes referred to as the *thatched-roof effect*). Since it is easier for water to run down fibers under the influence of gravity rather than across fiber layers, materials manufactured with a fiber orientation can be used to control groundwater entry. Examples of free-draining materials include fiberglass insulation, rigid plastic insulations with vertical channels, and drainage mats.

Free-draining materials that replace free-draining backfill in the drain screen approach must also be connected to a perimeter subgrade drainage system (Figure 2-4). They must extend above grade and/or be capped with a flashing to prevent surface water from entering over their top edges.

Drain screens located on the exterior of the wall are generally most effective. However, interior and interstitial drain screens may provide the only option available for ground-water control for some renovation and rehabilitation work. They should only be used with great caution and must address radon and mold concerns as well.

Waterproofing Barriers/Membranes

Control of groundwater entry by elimination of all below-grade openings involves the installation of waterproofing barriers or membranes. These membranes are typically installed on the exterior of the perimeter foundation walls (Figure 2-5). A few applications also involve waterproofing under basement floor slabs, but this is costly and thus highly unlikely in a residential building. If upward water pressure is anticipated, the floor slab should be designed to resist the force. Otherwise, the slab can crack, resulting in greater damage than a flooded basement would cause. Accordingly, drain screens and subgrade drainage systems are typically employed in conjunction with waterproofing systems when continuous hydrostatic pressure must be resisted. In some cases the drainage system can be designed to permanently lower the water table around the structure, thus reducing or eliminating the hydrostatic pressure condition. This raises the question of whether a waterproofing system is necessary if a subgrade drainage system can apparently do the job by itself. Because of the potential for failure with any of these techniques, both systems are recommended to provide a backup system (the concept of redundancy). In some cases, of course, providing redundant systems may not be justified.

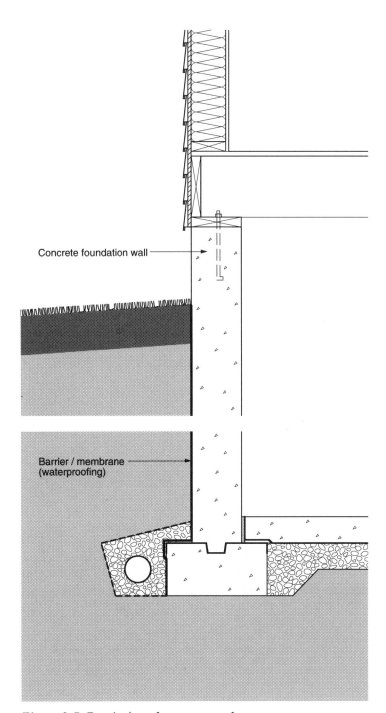

Concrete foundation wall

Barrier / membrane (waterproofing)

Figure 2-5: Barrier/membrane approach.

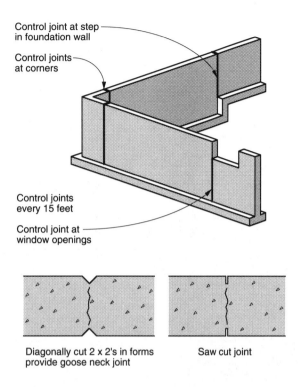

Control joint at step in foundation wall

Control joints at corners

Control joints every 15 feet

Control joint at window openings

Diagonally cut 2 x 2's in forms provide goose neck joint

Saw cut joint

Figure 2-6: Control joints in concrete walls.

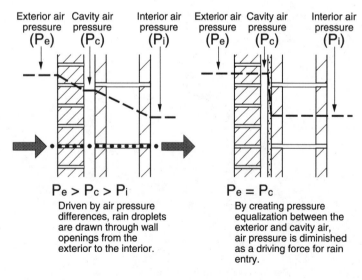

Exterior air pressure (P_e) Cavity air pressure (P_c) Interior air pressure (P_i)

$P_e > P_c > P_i$

Driven by air pressure differences, rain droplets are drawn through wall openings from the exterior to the interior.

Exterior air pressure (P_e) Cavity air pressure (P_c) Interior air pressure (P_i)

$P_e = P_c$

By creating pressure equalization between the exterior and cavity air, air pressure is diminished as a driving force for rain entry.

Figure 2-7: Air pressure difference as a driving force for rain entry.

Control Joints

An alternative to covering the entire wall with a membrane is to use control joints in order to make a cast concrete foundation wall watertight. In most cast concrete foundation wall assemblies, shrinkage cracks appear after backfilling has occurred and subsequently lead to groundwater entry. These cracks are usually repaired during the callback period, but this can be expensive and an aggravation to both the contractor and the occupant.

Rather than attempting to prevent concrete from cracking, the control joints permit the concrete to crack predictably in straight lines at predetermined locations. Control joints basically weaken the wall at preselected locations by providing crack initiators—the straight cracks that result are less upsetting to occupants. These cracks can be repaired or sealed prior to backfilling. Control joints can also be provided by cutting the wall immediately after the forms are stripped or cast into the wall initially (Figure 2-6). A further variation involves applying the drain screen at the control joints only, rather than sealing the joints with mastic or some other sealant. With this approach, as with all foundation assemblies, radon concerns must be addressed.

RAINWATER

To control rainwater entry effectively, two general strategies should be applied: (1) reduce the amount of rainwater deposited on building surfaces and assemblies, and (2) control rainwater deposited on building assemblies. Reducing the amount of rainwater deposited on building surfaces and assemblies has traditionally been a function of siting and architectural design. The following measures have historically proven effective:

1. Place buildings so that they are sheltered from prevailing winds, to reduce exposure to wind-driven rain.

2. Provide roof overhangs to shelter exterior walls from rain deposition.

3. Provide architectural detailing that sheds rainwater from building faces.

Controlling rainwater deposited on building surfaces or assemblies involves the implementation of one or more of these three approaches:

1. Control air pressure differentials across the exterior cladding by using a rain screen.

2. Drain rainwater that enters building assemblies (the drain screen for above-grade assemblies).

3. Control above-grade openings with a weatherproofing barrier/membrane to resist rain entry (building papers, house-wraps) or by sealing openings (face-sealing or barrier wall).

To control rainwater entry, it is necessary to understand the four underlying driving forces that are present: air pressure difference, momentum, surface tension, and gravity. Figure 2-7 illustrates how rain entry from air pressure differences occurs and can be prevented by the use of *pressure equalization* (discussed below). Momentum is controlled by eliminating openings that go straight through the wall assembly (Figure 2-8). The use of drip edges and kerfs is the conventional method of preventing rain entry by surface tension (Figure 2-9). Using flashings and layering the wall assembly elements to drain water to the exterior are typical techniques to keep water from entering by gravity flow (Figure 2-10).

Rain Screens

A rain screen is a technique for controlling rain entry in an exterior wall that involves locating a pressure-equalized air space immediately behind exterior cladding. This reduces the air pressure difference, which is the principle driving force for rain entry (other driving forces are described above). To do this, the air pressure drop across a wall assembly is designed to occur at the sheathing or at some other component of the assembly inside of the exterior cladding.

Wall assembly elements resist air pressures according to their relative airtightness. The greater the resistance of a component to the wind, the greater the air pressure drop across that element. Therefore, the driving force for rain entry across a relatively airtight component will be greater.

If the exterior cladding is tight, then the air pressure drop across the exterior cladding and consequently the driving force for rain entry will be increased. Also, the greater the driving force across the exterior cladding, the more significant any cracks, flaws, or openings become with respect to rain entry. Thus, workmanship, component durability, and/or some provision for moisture removal is critical in preventing rain entry in wall assemblies where the exterior cladding is relatively tight. By reducing the air pressure drop across the

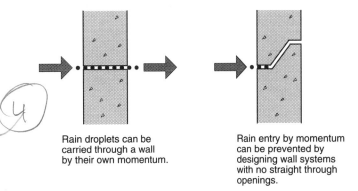

Rain droplets can be carried through a wall by their own momentum.

Rain entry by momentum can be prevented by designing wall systems with no straight through openings.

Figure 2-8: Momentum as a driving force for rain entry.

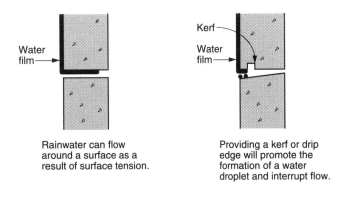

Water film

Kerf

Water film

Rainwater can flow around a surface as a result of surface tension.

Providing a kerf or drip edge will promote the formation of a water droplet and interrupt flow.

Figure 2-9: Surface tension as a driving force for rain entry.

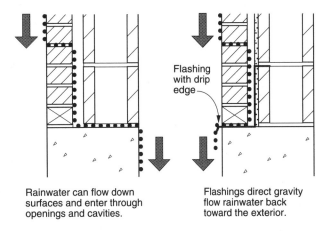

Flashing with drip edge

Rainwater can flow down surfaces and enter through openings and cavities.

Flashings direct gravity flow rainwater back toward the exterior.

Figure 2-10: Gravity as a driving force for rain entry.

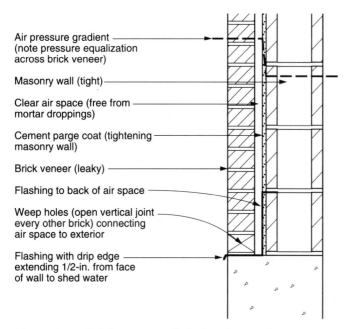

Air pressure gradient (note pressure equalization across brick veneer)

Masonry wall (tight)

Clear air space (free from mortar droppings)

Cement parge coat (tightening masonry wall)

Brick veneer (leaky)

Flashing to back of air space

Weep holes (open vertical joint every other brick) connecting air space to exterior

Flashing with drip edge extending 1/2-in. from face of wall to shed water

Figure 2-11: Brick veneer wall designed as a rain screen.

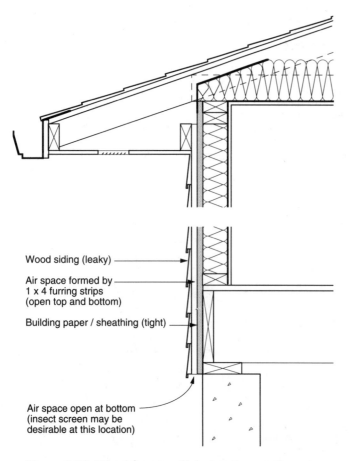

Wood siding (leaky)

Air space formed by 1 x 4 furring strips (open top and bottom)

Building paper / sheathing (tight)

Air space open at bottom (insect screen may be desirable at this location)

Figure 2-12: Wood frame wall designed as a rain screen.

exterior cladding and moving it inward to the sheathing or some other component, workmanship and component durability become less critical. Thus, the entire wall assembly becomes less susceptible to rain entry.

Air pressure drops at exterior claddings are reduced by making the exterior cladding leaky with respect to the rest of the wall. An air space is often provided immediately behind the exterior cladding and connected to the free stream of exterior air. To enhance this effect, the rest of the wall assembly to the back of the air space is tightened. If this approach is taken to its limit, no pressure difference will occur between the free stream of air and the air space behind the exterior cladding—referred to as *pressure equalization* (Garden 1983).

A classic example of the rain screen or pressure equalization concept is a wall consisting of a brick veneer, an air space, and a concrete masonry wall (Figure 2-11). By providing weep openings at the bottom to connect the air space behind the brick veneer to the exterior air, brick veneer is made leaky with respect to the rest of the wall. The weep openings also serve a drainage function. A parge coat of cement is applied on the exterior surface of the masonry back-up wall, making the rest of the wall assembly tighter than the exterior cladding. The air space needs to remain clear (free from mortar droppings) and be at least 3/8-inch wide to allow for drainage. Difficulties in maintaining air spaces clear of mortar droppings have led to recommendations for 1-inch (and in some cases 2-inch) air spaces behind brick veneers, although a clear 3/8-inch air space usually should suffice. The key features in this wall are:

1. A clear air space (free from mortar droppings) of minimum thickness of 3/8 inch (1-inch to 2-inch air space is recommended).

2. Clear weep holes spaced every other brick horizontally at the base course of brick. This should occur in one brick course in each story of the building. If the back of the air space is tight, fewer weep holes are required. Conversely, if the back of the air space is leaky, a greater number of weep holes will be required.

3. A plane of tightness at the back of the clear air space.

4. A flashing at the base of the air space directing water to the exterior.

Another example utilizing the rain screen principle is the installation of horizontal wood lap siding on vertical furring strips over an exterior sheathing (Figure 2-12). Similar to the brick veneer wall, an air space is created behind the cladding. Installing the wood siding on furring makes the siding leaky relative to the sheathing. The sheathing in turn is much tighter than the siding. Thus, the air pressure drop occurs at the sheathing, not at the siding.

A further example of this concept is the installation of vinyl or aluminum siding over a building paper (Figure 2-13). Many vinyl and aluminum sidings either have perforations along their bottom edges or do not lock together in an airtight manner. By installing claddings with this cross section over a relatively tight building paper, the air space pressure is equalized.

For the rain screen to be effective, pressure must be equalized over the surface area of the wall plane as well as across the wall cladding. Significant air pressure drops can occur around exterior corners as a result of wind. This can lead to rain entry even in walls that have air spaces located behind exterior claddings (Figure 2-14). However, this can be avoided if the air spaces are compartmentalized. Where horizontal siding is installed over vertical furring this compartmentalization occurs at each furring strip.

Height compartmentalization also may be required to limit convection. With one- and two-story walls, *capping* the air spaces or compartments at the top of the walls helps equalize pressure. This capping is usually accomplished in brick veneer walls by placing flashings at the drainage openings between stories. However, reducing air flow (convection) also reduces ventilation of the cavity, which diminishes the removal of absorbed moisture in claddings and sheathings.

In climatic zones where wind-driven rain is a major concern (some coastal regions) and in tall buildings, height compartmentalization is usually desired. However, it may be more desirable in some instances to reduce the effect of pressure equalization and gain the effect of ventilation by avoiding height compartmentalization (i.e., leaving air spaces behind exterior claddings open at both the bottom and top). This may be justifiable since far more moisture is likely to be removed by ventilating the cavity than would enter as a result of convection in the undivided cavity.

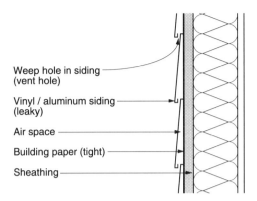

Figure 2-13: Wall using vinyl or aluminum siding designed as a rain screen.

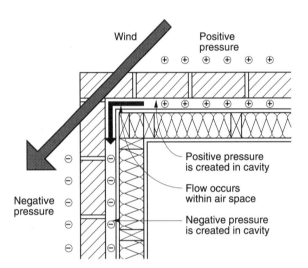

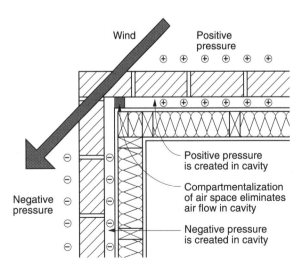

Figure 2-14: Effects of wind around the corner of a brick veneer wall.

Drain Screens Applied Above Grade

An example of the drain screen wall above grade can be found in metal buildings that use metal skins as exterior claddings. These skins and the corresponding wall cavities are often flashed at their base to direct water to the exterior. A free-draining material such as fiberglass batt insulation is located immediately behind an exterior cladding. Flashing at the base of the wall directs water to the exterior of the assembly (Figure 2-15). Any rainwater that enters the building assembly through joints, openings, or flaws will run down the interface between the batt insulation and the back surface of the cladding and out the bottom of the wall.

Using the drain screen approach above grade can also drain any condensed water from the back surface of the cladding which may have migrated to that surface as a result of either air leakage or vapor diffusion from the interior. If this approach is utilized with wood rather than metal cladding, it is necessary to prevent the back surface of the cladding from absorbing moisture by back-priming the siding. This also protects the cladding from moisture that incident solar radiation may drive inward from the exterior.

The effects of wind-washing of thermal insulation as well as convective heat loss must be considered in assemblies using the drain screen principle. In commercial applications higher density fiberglass insulation is usually utilized to address these air movement issues. Another potential problem is that openings in exterior sheathings can increase the exfiltration

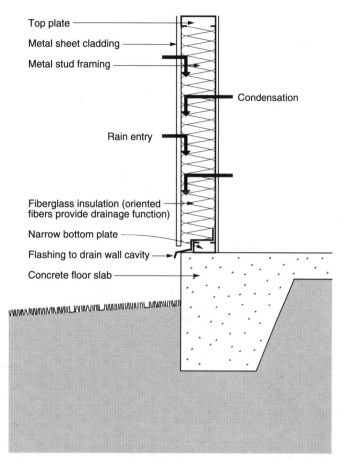

Figure 2-15: Metal building wall designed as a drain screen.

Top plate
Metal sheet cladding
Metal stud framing
Condensation
Rain entry
Fiberglass insulation (oriented fibers provide drainage function)
Narrow bottom plate
Flashing to drain wall cavity
Concrete floor slab

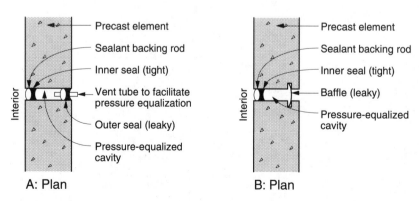
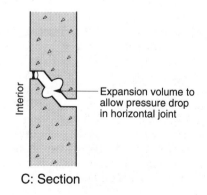

A: Plan

Precast element
Sealant backing rod
Inner seal (tight)
Vent tube to facilitate pressure equalization
Outer seal (leaky)
Pressure-equalized cavity
Interior

B: Plan

Precast element
Sealant backing rod
Inner seal (tight)
Baffle (leaky)
Pressure-equalized cavity
Interior

C: Section

Expansion volume to allow pressure drop in horizontal joint
Interior

Figure 2-16: Rain screen concept applied to precast concrete joint design.

of interior moisture-laden air where openings in the interior sheathing are also present. In spite of these concerns, the drain screen applied above grade is gaining acceptance in commercial applications by virtue of its low cost and powerful rain control capabilities.

Controlling Openings (Weatherproofing or Barrier Wall)

Eliminating exterior openings to control rain entry involves the concept of face-sealing or the provision of a barrier/membrane to resist rain entry (i.e., building papers, housewraps). This approach is more dependent on workmanship and materials than the rain screen—thus, long-term performance may not be as effective. Because all buildings move, it is likely that surfaces that are initially tight will open up, resulting in increased leakage over time (Latta 1973).

Common examples of the face-seal approach include caulking and flashing joints between prefinished exterior plywood sheet siding in housing, or caulking joints between exterior precast concrete cladding elements in commercial construction. A common example of the barrier/membrane approach is the application of building papers and housewraps without openings, installed shingle fashion to shed rain.

Rain Screens Applied to Joints

A hybrid approach to controlling rain entry involves the use of a weatherproof exterior cladding with a rain screen applied at the joints only (since rainwater usually enters building assemblies at the joints). An example of this is the two-stage joint common with precast claddings, which combine a leaky outer seal with a tight inner seal (Figure 2-16). Joint design employing the rain screen is also common for window design. For example, operable windows utilize pairs of weather strips/seals to provide pressure-equalized cavities, and drainage openings between panes of sliding windows equalize the air space pressure between the sliders.

Flashings

Flashings serve several important functions: (1) they direct water out of construction joints, (2) they direct water out of building assemblies, and (3) they prevent water from flowing along wall surfaces by providing a drip edge (Figures 2-17 and 2-18).

The role of flashings should not be con-

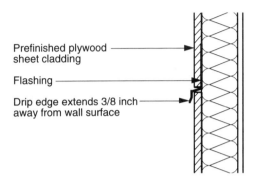

Figure 2-17: Flashing directing water out of a cladding joint.

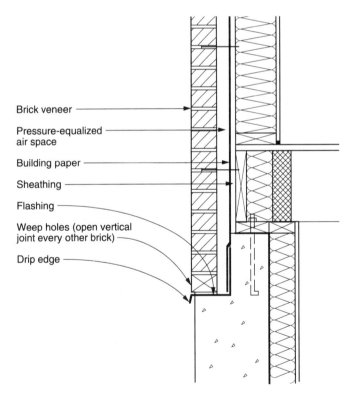

Figure 2-18: Flashing directing water out of a wall assembly.

fused with the role of caulking or sealants. Caulking or sealants eliminate or close off an opening, whereas flashings promote drainage from the opening itself or the entire assembly. In order to work effectively, all flashings should be sealed at lap joints.

An often overlooked function of a flashing is to direct water away from exterior cladding surfaces. In many assemblies flashings do not extend sufficiently outward from the exterior face of a cladding to provide a drip edge, and water can subsequently be drawn back into an assembly under the flashing. Flashings should extend at least 3/8 inch from the exterior face of the cladding.

The protruding exterior edge of a window sill is a common example where flashing is used to keep water away from the exterior cladding. The bottom edges of window sills typically have a kerf cut in them to keep water (driven by surface tension) from entering under the sill. The ends of such window sills should be turned up to prevent water running along the wall, forming moustache-shaped patterns below windows. Similar problems occur where flashings concentrate water at column/shear wall intersections in high-rise buildings.

In wall assemblies where the rain screen is utilized, it is important to extend flashings to the back of the pressure-equalized air space. This is often overlooked, especially above window and door openings with brick veneers and where wood siding is installed over furring. In wall assemblies where building papers and house-wraps are utilized, it is important to extend flashings behind these building papers or behind sheathings where building papers are not utilized.

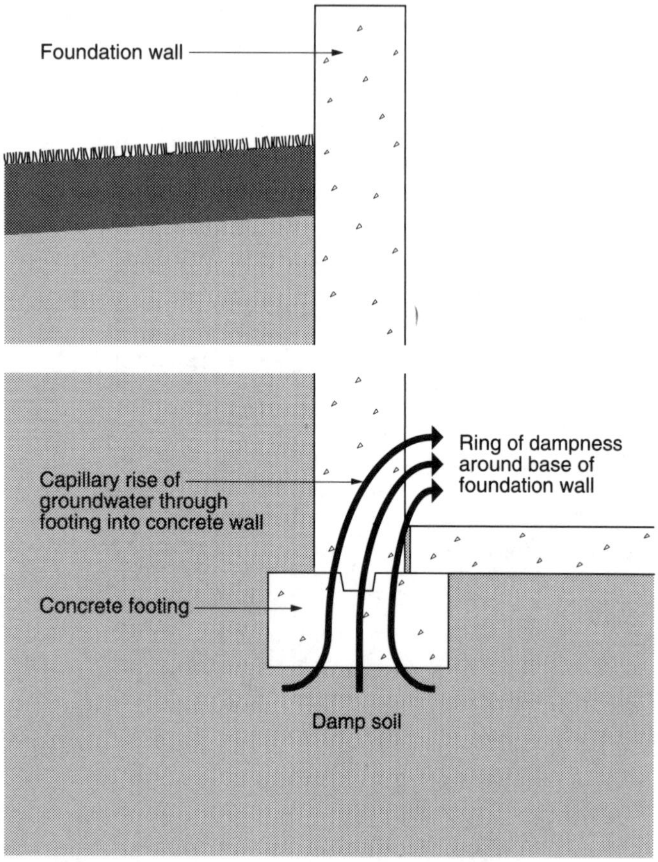

Capillary Suction

The second major moisture transport mechanism is capillary suction. Capillary suction acts primarily to move moisture into porous materials. For example, when one end of a piece of blotting paper is placed in contact with water, capillary suction causes the water to be drawn into the paper. Capillarity is a function of, among other things, pore size and available moisture. If pore size in a material is large, such as in clear gravel and coarse sand, then capillarity will not exist. If pore size in a material is small, such as in concrete, silty clay, and blotting paper, then capillarity is possible.

Naturally, capillarity will not exist in materials that do not have pores such as glass, steel, and most plastics. However, if two materials which do not have any capillary pores are placed closely enough together, such as two panes of glass, the space between them can itself become a capillary pore. Another example of this phenomenon is the migration of solder by capillarity into the tight space between two plumbing pipes when they are joined.

Capillarity can be significant in the portions of building envelopes where they are below grade or where they come in contact with the ground. An example of this is a concrete footing cast on damp soil. Concrete is porous and susceptible to capillarity. Capillary water is drawn up into the footing and then into the perimeter concrete foundation wall. Once in the foundation wall, the capillary

Figure 2-19: Capillary rise through a concrete footing.

Labels: Foundation wall; Capillary rise of groundwater through footing into concrete wall; Concrete footing; Ring of dampness around base of foundation wall; Damp soil water can evaporate to the interior of the basement at the bottom of the foundation wall. This often manifests itself as a ring of dampness visible around the base of the basement foundation wall (Figure 2-19). This mechanism is also referred to as *rising damp.*

Capillary draw, or suction, can also be a factor in building envelopes above grade where a film of water is deposited on the exterior of a building envelope as a result of rain action or dew formation. Even more rainwater can be deposited on the lower portion of the wall because of *splashback*—rainwater bounces off the ground adjacent to the building. Capillary suction may draw this water film into the building envelope. An example of this occurs when water is trapped between the laps in horizontal wood siding in spite of the influence of gravity (Figure 2-20). Thus, joints between materials exposed to water, above and below grade, should be designed with capillarity in mind.

Capillarity can be controlled in the following ways:

1. Controlling the availability of capillary moisture.

2. Sealing capillary pores.

3. Making capillary pores larger.

4. Providing a receptor for capillary moisture.

CAPILLARY CONTROL BELOW GRADE

The availability of capillary moisture below grade can be minimized by site selection as well as effective surface and subsurface drainage techniques. Capillary suction in concrete foundation walls is traditionally controlled by dampproofing the exterior surface of the wall where it is in contact with the surrounding damp soil (Figure 2-21). This dampproofing is usually a bituminous liquid that fills the tiny capillary pores in the concrete. The dampproofing film is typically not meant to span cracks or large openings, and as such it is not a waterproofing membrane. While waterproofing membranes provide an excellent capillary break, dampproofing films are usually poor waterproofing membranes.

Capillary suction under concrete floor slabs is traditionally prevented by placing the floor slab over large-pore gravel (3/4-inch crushed stone with fines removed). Since the pore size in the granular pad is too large to support capillary suction, the granular pad acts as a capillary break (Figure 2-21).

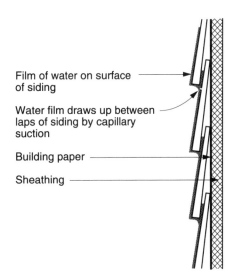

Film of water on surface of siding

Water film draws up between laps of siding by capillary suction

Building paper

Sheathing

Figure 2-20: Capillary rise in wood siding.

Capillary suction in masonry block foundation walls is traditionally controlled by coating the exterior surface of the masonry blocks with a thin coat of mortar (parge coat) and then applying a dampproof coating over it. Applying a dampproof coating directly on the masonry blocks has not always proven successful. The pore size of the mortar joints can be too large for a fluid-applied dampproof coating to span, while at the same time it can be small enough to support capillary suction. The mortar parge coat fills the large capillary pores in the block joints, and the subsequent tiny pores in the mortar parge coat are in turn filled by the fluid-applied bituminous coating (Timusk 1983).

Capillary breaks can be located over the top of the concrete footing prior to the construction of perimeter foundation walls to prevent moisture from entering the foundation wall and evaporating into the basement. A capillary break can also be placed between the sill plate and the top of foundation wall to prevent construction moisture in the foundation wall from migrating into the floor framing (Figure 2-21). These capillary breaks can be a dampproofing fluid-applied film or a sheet of polyethylene, since pores in the polyethylene are too small to support capillary suction.

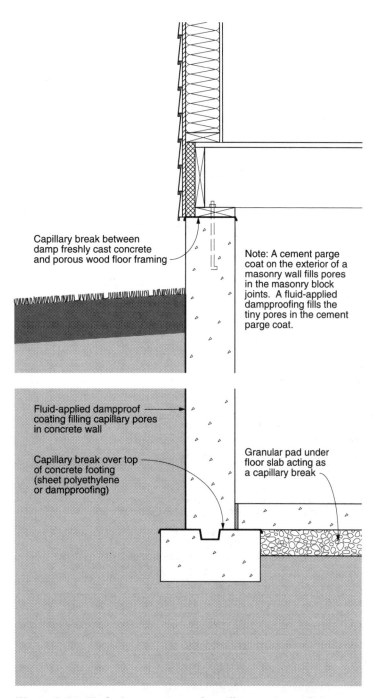

Capillary break between damp freshly cast concrete and porous wood floor framing

Note: A cement parge coat on the exterior of a masonry wall fills pores in the masonry block joints. A fluid-applied dampproofing fills the tiny pores in the cement parge coat.

Fluid-applied dampproof coating filling capillary pores in concrete wall

Capillary break over top of concrete footing (sheet polyethylene or dampproofing)

Granular pad under floor slab acting as a capillary break

Figure 2-21: Techniques to control capillary moisture below grade.

CAPILLARY CONTROL ABOVE GRADE

Capillary suction in porous cladding materials can be minimized by sealing or filling the pores. One of the most common examples of this is the application of a paint film on wood-based siding to reduce the absorption of deposited rainwater. The paint film seals the capillary pores on the surface of the wood (Figure 2-22).

Where capillary suction occurs between the laps of horizontal siding, the seams at the laps can be sealed with caulking, thereby eliminating the capillary pores (Figure 2-23). Although this is a common approach it ultimately fails if the caulking is not maintained. Wood-based siding changes moisture content as ambient relative humidity changes. Thus, the siding expands and contracts regularly, causing the caulking to fail quickly. Consequently, this approach is not recommended.

Alternatively, spacers can be used to separate the siding pieces so that water is not drawn up or held between the overlapping material as a result of capillary forces (Figure 2-24). The spacers are typically wedges, clips, tacks, or oval-headed nails. Another approach is to *back-prime* the siding (paint its back surface), to fill capillary pores at the overlaps (Figure 2-25). Both have proven to be very effective strategies (Lstiburek 1989).

The siding can also be installed on furring strips (Figure 2-26) or over an absorptive building paper (Figure 2-27). Both the air space and the building paper serve as receptors for capillary moisture. Deposited rainwater absorbed by the siding through capillary suction can evaporate into the air space. This moisture can also be driven inward from the siding into the air space (or into the absorptive building paper) as a result of a temperature difference created when the sun warms the siding.

Caution should be exercised where absorptive building paper is used as a receptor for moisture due to its limited amount of moisture storage potential. A related concern is that wet building paper may become saturated and subsequently contribute to rotting of the sheathing material beneath the paper. Alternatively, an absorptive sheathing such as asphalt-impregnated fiberboard can be an effective receptor for moisture since it has far greater moisture storage potential than a building paper (Figure 2-25).

Another example where an air space serves as a capillary break as well as a receptor for

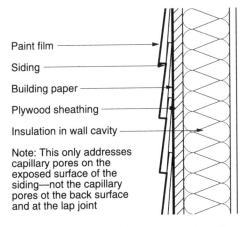

Paint film

Siding

Building paper

Plywood sheathing

Insulation in wall cavity

Note: This only addresses
capillary pores on the
exposed surface of the
siding—not the capillary
pores ot the back surface
and at the lap joint

*Figure 2-22: Paint film to control capillary
moisture in a wood frame wall.*

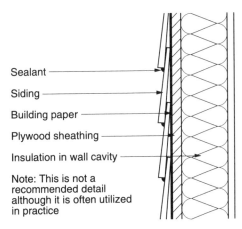

Sealant

Siding

Building paper

Plywood sheathing

Insulation in wall cavity

Note: This is not a
recommended detail
although it is often utilized
in practice

*Figure 2-23: Caulking to control capillary
moisture in a wood frame wall.*

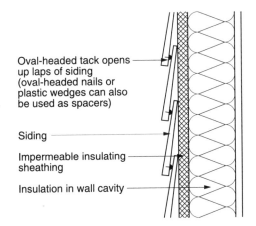

Oval-headed tack opens
up laps of siding
(oval-headed nails or
plastic wedges can also
be used as spacers)

Siding

Impermeable insulating
sheathing

Insulation in wall cavity

*Figure 2-24: Spacers between siding to control
capillary moisture in a wood frame wall.*

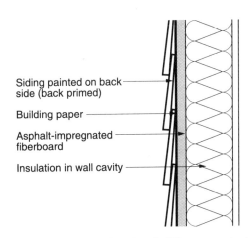

Siding painted on back
side (back primed)

Building paper

Asphalt-impregnated
fiberboard

Insulation in wall cavity

*Figure 2-25: Back-primed siding to control
capillary moisture in a wood frame wall.*

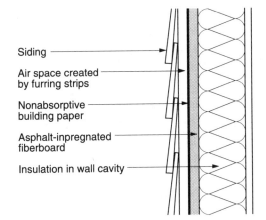

Siding

Air space created
by furring strips

Nonabsorptive
building paper

Asphalt-inpregnated
fiberboard

Insulation in wall cavity

*Figure 2-26: Air space behind siding serves as
a receptor for capillary moisture in a wood
frame wall.*

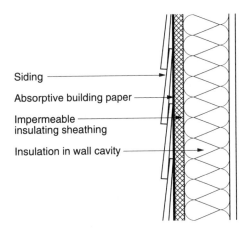

Siding

Absorptive building paper

Impermeable
insulating sheathing

Insulation in wall cavity

*Figure 2-27: Building paper beneath siding
serves as a receptor for capillary moisture in a
wood frame wall.*

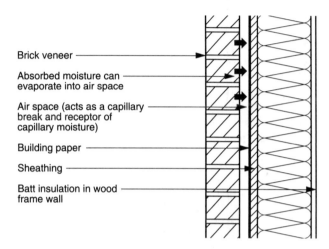

Brick veneer

Absorbed moisture can evaporate into air space

Air space (acts as a capillary break and receptor of capillary moisture)

Building paper

Sheathing

Batt insulation in wood frame wall

Figure 2-28: Capillary break in a brick veneer wall.

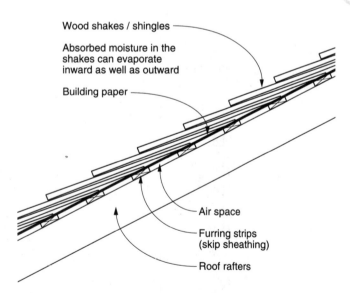

Wood shakes / shingles

Absorbed moisture in the shakes can evaporate inward as well as outward

Building paper

Air space

Furring strips (skip sheathing)

Roof rafters

Figure 2-29: Capillary break in a wood shake roof.

capillary moisture occurs in a typical brick veneer wall (Figure 2-28). The bricks can absorb significant amounts of deposited rainwater. When solar radiation warms the brick veneer, the moisture is driven inward—from the bricks into the air space.

Where wood shingles or shakes are installed over furring strips (*skip-sheathing* on 1 x 4 roof assemblies), the same phenomenon occurs (Figure 2-29). The wood shakes or shingles absorb deposited rainwater due to capillary suction. If the shakes or shingles were placed over a plywood sheathing instead of on furring strips, they could dry to the exterior but inward drying could not occur effectively. This leads to moisture buildup and degradation of materials. Using furring strips, however, they dry in both directions (to the exterior and into the attic space) in the absence of a temperature gradient. Where a temperature gradient exists due to solar radiation, using furring strips instead of plywood sheathing permits the wood shakes or shingles to dry into the attic. The function of the building/roofing paper is to help equalize pressure across the roof assembly. The shakes/shingles are leaky, whereas the building/roofing paper is tight.

Air Movement

The third moisture transport mechanism is air movement. This mechanism can move moisture into building assemblies both from within the conditioned space and from the exterior.

Depending on temperature, air can hold varying amounts of moisture in the vapor state (see Chapter 1). When air moves as a result of an air pressure difference it will carry the moisture held within it. If air containing moisture comes in contact with a surface below the air's dew point temperature, the air may deposit some of its moisture on that surface in the form of condensation. For moisture to be moved into a building assembly as a result of air movement, three conditions are necessary:

1. Air containing moisture must be present.

2. An opening or hole must exist in the assembly.

3. An air pressure difference acting across the opening or hole must exist.

Although moisture may enter a building assembly if these three conditions are met, moisture may not necessarily be deposited within the assembly. Air flow speeds must be slow enough for the air to cool to the dew point temperature before it exits the air leakage path. Fast flowing air can warm the surfaces of the flow path above the dew point temperature of the outflowing air and condensation may not occur.

Controlling moisture movement resulting from air movement involves three approaches: (1) reducing the amount of moisture present in the air; (2) controlling the number, location, and size of openings in the building envelope; and (3) controlling the air pressure differential acting across the building envelope. Although attempting to minimize the openings in a building envelope may be the first approach most commonly pursued, it may be just as practical to reduce the moisture content in the air and to control the pressure differential acting across the building envelope.

CONTROLLING THE AMOUNT OF MOISTURE IN AIR

It is obvious that only interior airborne moisture levels can be controlled, since the local climate controls exterior airborne moisture levels. However, the local climate and hence exterior moisture levels typically influence the approach taken to control interior moisture levels. Interior moisture levels can be controlled three ways: (1) source control, (2) dilution, and (3) dehumidification.

Source Control

One of the most effective approaches for controlling interior airborne moisture levels is to reduce moisture sources. If moisture is not generated within a space, if it is removed at the point of generation, and/or if it is prevented from migrating into a space, it does not have to be removed or controlled after the fact. Source control is effective regardless of climate zone or season and is typically the most cost-effective and energy-efficient approach .

One of the single largest sources of moisture in conditioned spaces, regardless of climate zone or season, is the migration of moisture from the surrounding soil into foundations and subsequently into conditioned spaces (White 1991). Therefore, building dry basements, slabs, and crawl spaces can be one of the single most effective strategies in controlling interior airborne moisture. Leaky basements and the evaporation of moisture from exposed ground into crawl spaces without a polyethylene ground cover continue to remain among the largest contributing factors to moisture-related building problems. Even if a polyethylene ground cover is present, it may move (if there is no ballast on the ground cover and the soil is permeable), thus permitting a significant amount of soil gas to enter.

Unvented clothes dryers and the line drying of clothes indoors can also be major sources of moisture, depending on life style. Clothes dryers should be vented directly to the exterior and indoor line drying should be avoided. Another major source of moisture during heating periods are combustion products from unvented space heaters. The two major by-products of combustion are carbon dioxide and moisture. It is unwise to use unvented combustion devices in any climate zone due to moisture and other health-related concerns. Unvented combustion devices should be avoided, or better yet, removed and replaced with vented combustion devices.

Firewood storage indoors can also be a major source of moisture. In fact, seasonal storage of one cord of green firewood indoors can be equivalent to the moisture produced by a family of four through respiration during the same period.

In cooling climates, the major source of moisture is the exterior ambient air, which is typically warm and humid or cool and wet. The greater the air change with exterior air in cooling climates, the greater the rate of inward moisture migration. Accordingly, in cooling climates source control of exterior moisture-laden air involves reducing infiltration and ventilation rates (in a manner which does not compromise indoor air quality). This is done by reducing leakage openings in building assemblies and sealing ductwork associated with forced air heating systems, which may be located outside of conditioned spaces, or by locating such ductwork within conditioned spaces.

Also in cooling climates, the improper draining of condensate from air conditioning systems, which allows for the re-evaporation of moisture and subsequent migration back into conditioned spaces, has proven to be a major contributing factor to moisture-related health and building problems. Condensate should be drained to the exterior, not into crawl spaces. Standing water should be avoided in condensate pans for moisture and other health-related reasons.

Rooms in which significant moisture can be generated, such as bathrooms and kitchens, should be vented directly to the exterior with a mechanical exhaust system regardless of climate. This mechanical exhaust system, which includes bathroom fans and kitchen range hoods, can be operated on an intermittent basis according to moisture load by utilizing timers or dehumidistat control.

Table 2-1 provides an overview of typical moisture sources. Not all moisture sources lend themselves to source control. However, wherever source control is possible, it is usually the most practical and cost-effective approach for control of interior airborne moisture.

People generate moisture simply by breathing as well as by perspiring. Limiting this source of moisture is not possible, short of specifying family size and time of occupancy. It should be recognized that respiration is a major source of moisture generation, and at night it is often concentrated in one or two bedrooms.

Seasonal absorption/desorption of materials involves moisture pick-up by furnishings, carpets, and building materials within conditioned spaces during summer months in heating climates and the subsequent moisture release from these same materials during the heating season. Source control in this case is also not possible or practical. Air conditioning with dehumidification, however, can be utilized to remove moisture from these sources.

A major moisture source which can lend itself to source control under limited circumstances is construction moisture. Newly constructed buildings give off significant quantities of moisture during their first year as a result of construction moisture trapped within construction materials. Hundreds of gallons of water can be contained in fresh concrete, green lumber, and wet-applied insulations. To reduce this potential, kiln-dried lumber can be specified, and the rate of evaporation of the moisture of construction toward conditioned spaces from concrete and masonry can be reduced by the use of coatings and sealants. In addition, building assemblies utilizing wet materials can be designed to dry to the exterior or permitted to dry before enclosure.

Dilution

Dilution of interior airborne moisture involves air change, or the exchange of interior moisture-laden air with exterior dry air. The greater the air change, the greater the flushing action this air change has on interior airborne moisture levels. Of course this only holds true if the exterior air is dryer than the interior air. In cooling climates or during cooling periods this is often not the case. Under such circumstances the greater the air change, the greater the inward migration of moisture. Thus, dilution and air change are strategies typically utilized in heating climates during heating seasons. In some mild heating climates such as the Pacific Northwest that experience high ambient moisture levels during the heating season, dilution is also not very effective. In heating climates, dilution involving air change is most effective when controlled mechanical ventilation is implemented.

Buildings with combustion heating systems linked to active chimneys have higher rates of air change than do buildings without active chimneys. Chimneys can be described as exhaust fans or *chimney fans* as a direct result of the quantities of air they extract from a building enclosure for draft control and combustion. This high level of air change dilutes interior airborne moisture in buildings located in heating climates. The trend away from active chimneys to electric heating and high efficiency combustion appliances, which extract little or no air from conditioned spaces, has contributed to higher interior moisture levels in many cases.

Dehumidification

Warm air is capable of holding more moisture than cool air. Dehumidification usually involves the cooling of warm, moisture-laden air to reduce its ability to hold moisture, thereby forcing the air to give up moisture in the form of condensation. As such, dehumidification is often coupled with air conditioning and is common in cooling climates or during the cooling season. In some cases dehumidification involves the use of desiccants (materials which are initially dry) that draw moisture out of air and subsequently release this moisture under controlled conditions, usually when the desiccants are deliberately heated.

Since dilution or air change is not effective in controlling interior airborne moisture levels in cooling climates, dehumidification through air conditioning is the most common approach. Dehumidification is most effective when also coupled with source control. In cooling climates a major source of airborne moisture is the infiltration of exterior moisture-laden air. Thus, source control in cooling climates also involves reducing air change. This is achieved by limiting ventilation, controlling leakage openings, and limiting air pressure differentials arising from forced air duct systems.

Table 2-1: Household moisture sources.

MOISTURE SOURCE BY TYPE	ESTIMATED MOISTURE AMOUNT (PINTS)
Household Produced	
Aquariums	Replacement of evaporative loss
Bathing: tub (excludes towels and spillage)	0.12/standard size bath
shower (excludes towels and spillage)	0.52/5-minute shower
Clothes washing (automatic, lid closed, standpipe discharge)	0+/load (usually nil)
Clothes drying: vented outdoors	0+/load (usually nil)
not vented outdoors or indoor drying line	4.68 to 6.18/load (more if gas dryer)
Combustion (unvented kerosene space heater)	7.6/gallon of kerosene burned
Cooking: breakfast (family of four, average)	0.35 (plus 0.58 if gas cooking)
lunch (family of four, average)	0.53 (plus 0.68 if gas cooking)
dinner (family of four, average)	1.22 (plus 1.58 if gas cooking)
simmer at 203 F., 10 minutes, 6-inch pan (plus gas)	less than 0.01 if covered, 0.13 if uncovered
boil 10 minutes, 6-inch pan (plus gas)	0.48 if covered, 0.57 if uncovered
Dishwashing: breakfast (family of four, average)	0.21
(by hand) lunch (family of our, average)	0.16
dinner (family of four, average)	0.68
Firewood storage indoors (cord of green firewood)	400 to 800/6 months
Floor mopping	0.03/square foot
Gas range pilot light (each)	0.37 or less/day
House plants (5 to 7 average plants)	0.86 to 0.96/day
Humidifiers	0 to 120+/day (2.08 average/hour)
Pets	Fraction of human adult weight
Respiration and perspiration (family of four, average)	0.44/hour (family of four, average)
Refrigerator defrost	1.03/day (average)
Saunas, steam baths, and whirlpools	0 to 2.7+/hour
Vegetable storage (large-scale storage is significant)	0+ (not estimated)
Nonhousehold Produced	
Combustion exhaust gas backdrafting or spillage	0 to 6,720+/year
Desorption of materials: seasonal	6.33 to 16.91/average day
new construction	10+/average day
Ground moisture migration	0 to 105/day
Plumbing leaks	0+ (not estimated)
Rain or snowmelt penetration	0+ (not estimated)
Seasonal high outdoor absolute humidity	64 to 249+/day

Source: W. Angell and W. Olson, Cold Climate Housing Information Center, University of Minnesota

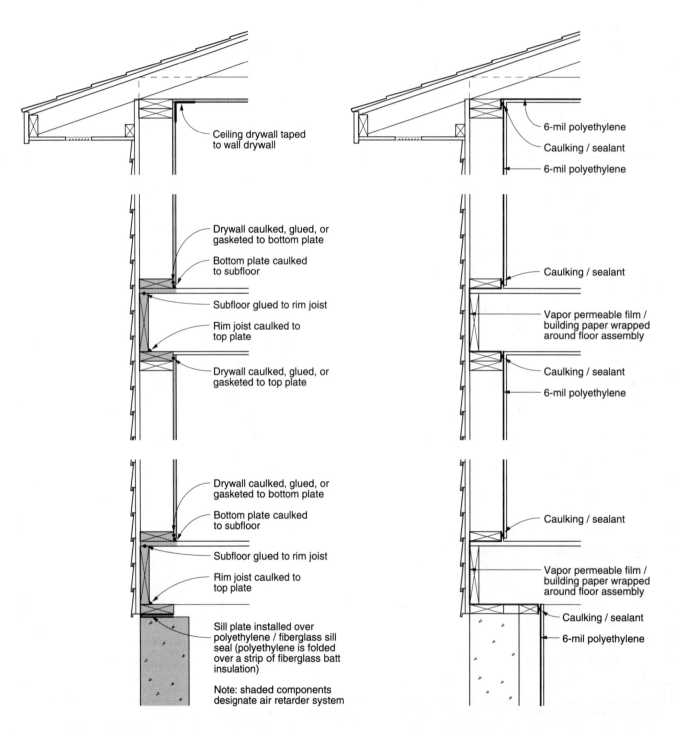

Figure 2-30: Interior air retarder using the air drywall approach (ADA).

Figure 2-31: Interior air retarder using the poly-wrap approach.

CONTROLLING OPENINGS (AIRTIGHTNESS)

If openings in building assemblies are minimized, then air movement through assemblies can also be controlled. The tighter the assembly, the less air movement through the assembly, and therefore the less moisture transported through that assembly. When a set of building assemblies are linked they enclose the conditioned space and form the building envelope. The components of the building envelope that provide tightness characteristics are referred to as the *air retarder system*.

Resistance to air flow can be provided at any location in a building assembly—at the exterior surface, the interior surface, or at any location between. An assembly that is made airtight at the exterior surface is just as effective in reducing exfiltration as an assembly that is airtight at the interior surface. The underlying rationale is that if the air cannot exit the assembly to the exterior, it will not be able to enter from the interior. The same is true when dealing with infiltration. In some cases two air retarders may be required—one to control infiltration/exfiltration and another to stop wind-washing through insulation. In practice, it is generally desirable to provide both interior and exterior air retarders in all climate zones.

Interior Air Retarder

One approach to increasing resistance to air flow (creating airtightness) is to place an air retarder at the interior surface of a building assembly. This is typically achieved by sealing the interior cladding (gypsum board) to framing elements (Figure 2-30), or by installing a continuous, sealed polyethylene film between the interior cladding or gypsum board and the framing elements (Figure 2-31). Using the interior gypsum board as the interior air retarder system is sometimes referred to as the *air drywall approach* to airtightness, or ADA (Lischkoff and Lstiburek 1987). Using a continuous polyethylene film as the interior air retarder system is sometimes referred to as the *poly-wrap approach* to airtightness (Lux and Brown 1989). Both address air leakage concerns at the following critical locations:

1. Exterior walls intersecting floor/roof assemblies (Figures 2-30 and 2-31)

2. Window openings (Figure 2-32)

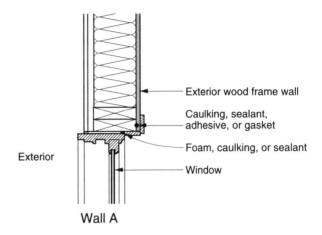

Wall A

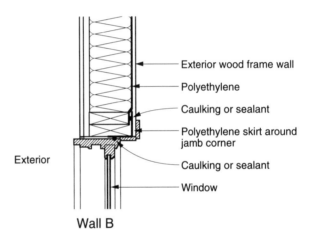

Wall B

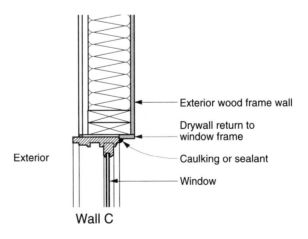

Wall C

Figure 2-32: Interior air retarder details at window jamb.

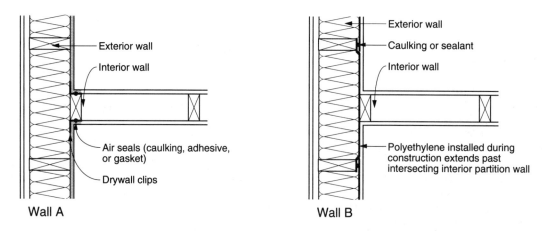

Figure 2-33: Interior air retarder details at intersection of exterior and interior partition walls.

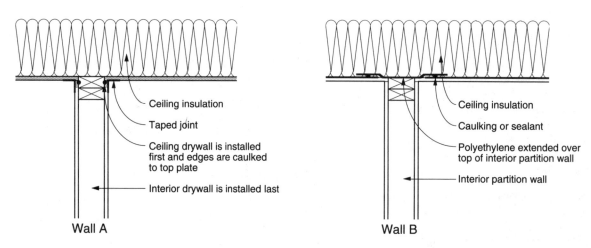

Figure 2-34: Interior air retarder details at intersection of roof and interior partition walls.

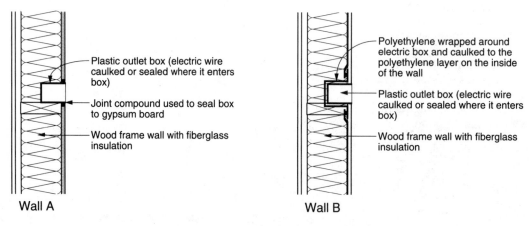

Figure 2-35: Interior air retarder details at electric outlet boxes in exterior walls.

3. Interior partition walls intersecting exterior walls (Figure 2-33)

4. Interior partition walls intersecting attic ceilings (Figure 2-34)

5. Electrical outlet boxes on exterior walls (Figure 2-35)

An advantage of interior air retarder systems over exterior systems is that they also control the entry of interior moisture-laden air into assembly cavities due to air convection or during heating periods. The significant disadvantage of interior air retarder systems is the inability to control wind-washing through insulation.

Interstitial (Cavity) Air Retarder

Airtightness can also be provided within a building assembly. This is typically achieved by utilizing a dense cavity fill insulation that provides significant resistance to air flow (dense-pack blown cellulose) or by constructing a composite wall (Figure 2-36).

The advantage of dense-pack cellulose insulation is that it is an excellent retrofit option for existing buildings; however, the disadvantage is the lack of qualified installers (Fitzgerald et al. 1990).

Exterior Air Retarder

Another approach to creating airtightness is to place an air retarder at the exterior surface of a building assembly. This is typically achieved by sealing the exterior sheathing to framing elements or by installing a continuous, sealed building paper over the exterior sheathing. Using the exterior sheathing as the exterior air retarder system is sometimes referred to as the *air sheathing approach* to airtightness, or ASA (Figure 2-37). Using a continuous building paper as the exterior air retarder system is sometimes referred to as the *house-wrap approach* (Figure 2-38). Other examples of exterior air seals are typically found in stucco-clad buildings, precast concrete buildings, and buildings that utilize face-sealing to control rain entry.

The significant advantage of exterior air retarder systems over interior air retarder systems is the ease of installation and the lack of detailing issues due to intersecting partition walls and service penetrations. However, exterior air retarder systems must deal with transitions where roof assemblies intersect exterior walls. For example, an exterior house-wrap should be sealed to the ceiling air retarder

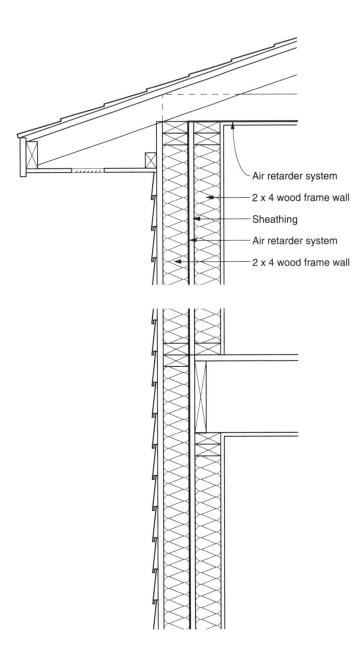

Figure 2-36: Interstitial air retarder in composite wall.

Air retarder system
2 x 4 wood frame wall
Sheathing
Air retarder system
2 x 4 wood frame wall

5/13 vapor permiable

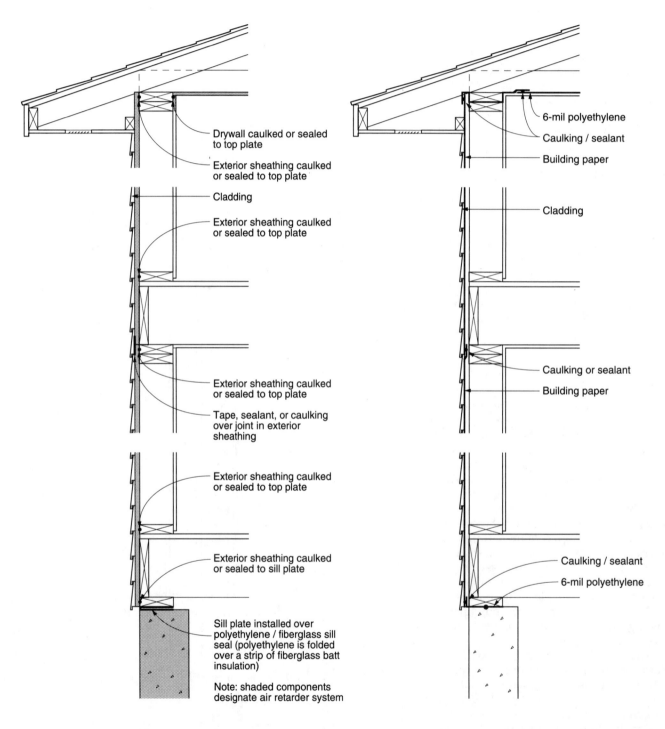

Figure 2-37: Exterior air retarder using the air sheathing approach (ASA).

Figure 2-38: Exterior air retarder using the house-wrap approach.

system through the top of the exterior perimeter wall.

An additional advantage of exterior air retarder systems is the control of wind-washing that an exterior air seal provides. This limits mold and mildew growth on interior surfaces in heating climates or during the heating season. The significant disadvantage of exterior air retarder systems is the inability to drain condensed moisture from within wall cavities. In addition, exterior air retarder systems do not control the entry of air-transported moisture into assembly cavities from the interior. This can result from air convection around poorly installed cavity insulation in heating climates or during heating periods.

Common Air Leakage Problem Sites

Some common air leakage problem sites include the following: (1) bathtubs located on exterior walls, (2) recessed lighting on insulated ceilings, (3) dropped ceilings and cabinet bulkheads, (4) cantilevered floors, and (5) plumbing vent pipes. These locations require specific assembly details. Numerous practices that address these problem sites are outlined in existing literature (Lstiburek 1991).

CONTROLLING AIR PRESSURE

The driving force for air movement is air pressure. Air moves from regions of higher air pressure to regions of lower air pressure. If moisture is present in air, it will be carried along. Air pressure differences across building assemblies are created and influenced by the following: (1) the stack effect, (2) chimneys, (3) wind, and (4) mechanical systems.

The Stack Effect

The stack effect is caused by the tendency of warm heated air to leak out of the upper portions of a building as a result of the natural buoyancy of the heated air (Figure 2-39). A building can be visualized as a hot air balloon that is too heavy to leave the ground. As warm air rises, inside air pressure in the upper portions of the building is greater than outside air pressure, leading to exfiltration. At the lower portion of the building, inside air pressure is lower than outside air pressure, leading to infiltration. The force of exfiltration increases progressively with height reaching its maximum at the top of the building envelope. Conversely, the force of infiltration increases progressively in the lower portions of a

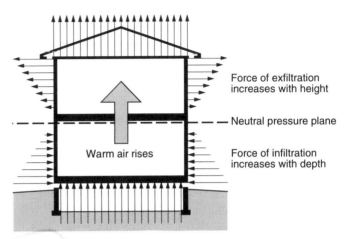

Figure 2-39: Air pressure patterns caused by the stack effect.

building. The plane at which no pressure difference between the interior and the exterior exists is called the *neutral pressure plane*. Air exfiltrates through all openings located above the neutral pressure plane and infiltrates through all openings below the neutral pressure plane. Neither exfiltration nor infiltration would occur through an opening located at the neutral pressure plane (Hutcheon and Handegord 1983).

Approximately half the openings in a building occur above the neutral pressure plane. Sealing openings in the upper portions of a building tends to lower the location of the neutral pressure plane, whereas sealing openings in the lower portion tends to raise it. Also, sealing openings further away from the neutral pressure plane has more effect than sealing those that are close. Sealing the upper openings thus reduces the total area available for flow, but increases the pressure acting over the remaining openings—this diminishes the effectiveness of the sealing action.

In heating climates, the stack effect is responsible for the exfiltration of warm interior air through building assemblies located at the upper portions of building envelopes. If this air also contains moisture, it will be carried along and can potentially be deposited within the building assemblies as the exfiltrating air is cooled. The stack effect explains why moisture problems are likely to be located high up in buildings in heating climates rather than down low.

Chimneys

A conditioned space under a slight negative pressure (a depressurized space) has a neutral pressure plane located above its ceiling. Therefore infiltration occurs through every opening since they are all located below the neutral pressure plane. Exhaust fans can be used to depressurize a conditioned space.

A conditioned space under a slight positive pressure, or pressurized, has a neutral pressure plane located below the basement floor slab. Therefore exfiltration occurs through every opening since they are all located above the neutral pressure plane. Supply fans can be used to pressurize a conditioned space.

An active chimney acts similar to an exhaust fan. In fact, a combustion appliance (furnace) connected to an active chimney can be described as an exhaust-only ventilation system. Active chimneys tend to raise the location of the neutral pressure plane, inducing infiltration over the majority of the surface area of the building envelope (Figure 2-40). Buildings without active chimneys can have neutral pressure planes located well below ceiling height, exposing a great deal of the surface area of the building envelope to exfiltration forces.

Buildings in heating climates with neutral pressure planes located above ceiling levels tend to have fewer air movement moisture problems than buildings with neutral pressure planes located below ceiling levels. In other words, homes with active chimneys have fewer air movement moisture problems than buildings without them (Marshall et al. 1983).

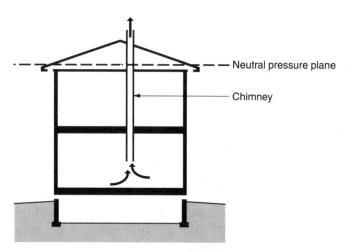

Figure 2-40: Change in the neutral pressure plane caused by the chimney effect.

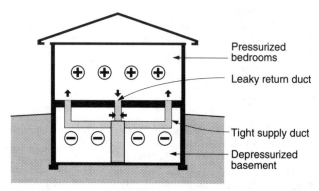

Figure 2-41: Air pressurization patterns in a house with the mechanical system in the basement.

Wind

When wind blows over a building it tends to exert a positive air pressure on the windward side and a negative air pressure on the leeward side. Because wind induces exfiltration on the leeward side and infiltration on the windward side, more moisture problems induced by air movement will occur on the leeward side of buildings in heating climates. When combined with the stack effect, moisture-related problems are most likely up high on the leeward side of buildings rather than down low on the windward side.

Mechanical Systems

Ducted distribution systems in conditioned spaces, under typical design assumptions, have traditionally been thought not to alter interior air pressures. They have been viewed as interior circulation systems which move air from place to place within a conditioned space, with a neutral effect on the pressure differences between interior and exterior. However, ducted distribution systems (forced air heating and cooling systems) often have significant impacts on pressure differences across building assemblies and subsequently on air change rates and interior airborne moisture levels.

A typical ducted, forced air heating system can be viewed as two systems—a supply duct system and a return duct system connected through a fan. In heating climate buildings most supply duct systems and air handlers (furnaces) are located in basement spaces. The supply system is usually relatively tight, with supply ducts usually running to every room in the building.

In contrast, the return system is usually relatively leaky and often utilizes partition wall stud spaces, floor joist space cavities with sheet metal nailed to their lower surfaces (floor joist panned system), and holes cut in floor sheathing with wood blocking as duct openings. Furthermore, there is often only one common return for the whole building. It is rare to find a return register in every room in which a supply register is also located. Accordingly, most of the return air is drawn from the basement through the leaks in the return system. This depressurizes the basement area relative to the exterior and the main level. In addition, rooms with a supply register but no return register, such as bedrooms, are pressurized when doors are closed (Figure 2-41).

When basements are depressurized in heating climates, air made moist by the humid ground will infiltrate. Radon gas is also likely to be carried along with the moisture in the infiltrating air. Basement depressurization can also lead to the spillage of combustion products from water heaters and furnaces with standard chimneys.

In heating climates where the above-grade space is pressurized, interior moisture-laden air may exfiltrate. If this airborne moisture condenses within building assemblies it can lead to moisture-related problems.

By inducing infiltration below grade and forcing exfiltration above grade, the forced air system, in effect, operates as a ventilation system providing outside air change. These elevated levels of outside air change resulting from the pressure effects of forced air systems can have significant impacts on energy consumption. For example, two buildings in the same climate—one with a forced air ducted system and the other a radiant system—will have significantly different levels of energy use even if they have identical levels of insulation and leakage openings. The building with the forced air system typically has much higher energy consumption levels due to the pressure effects of leaky ductwork.

It is recommended that basement spaces have sufficient supply registers to avoid depressurization, and that return ductwork be as tight as the supply ductwork. In addition, it may be desirable to match return registers with supply registers in conditioned spaces to avoid pressurization in heating climates or during heating periods.

In cooling climates supply ductwork is often located outside of conditioned spaces in attics and vented, unconditioned crawl spaces. These ducts tend to depressurize the condi-

tioned space, inducing the infiltration of exterior hot, humid air (Figures 2-42 and 2-43). They also dump cool conditioned air into the attic or crawl space, reducing the efficiency of the cooling systems. Leaky return ducts in crawl spaces can also draw radon and pesticides into the enclosure. Where both leaky supply and leaky return ducts are located outside of conditioned spaces, air pressure differences in the conditioned space may not be present (Figure 2-44) and yet serious problems may still exist.

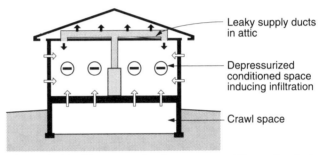

Figure 2-42: Air pressurization pattern with mechanical system ducts in the attic.

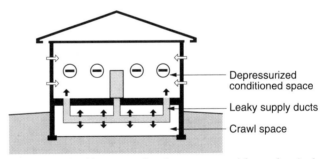

Figure 2-43: Air pressurization pattern with mechanical system ducts in the crawl space.

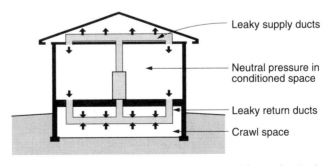

Figure 2-44: Air pressurization pattern with mechanical system ducts in the attic and the crawl space.

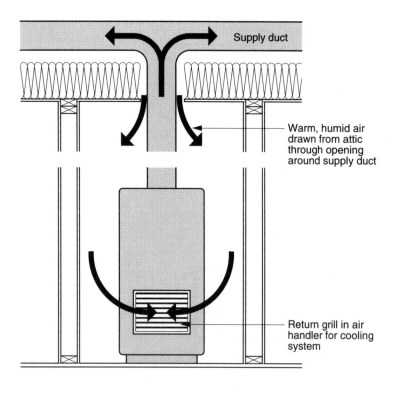

Supply duct

Warm, humid air drawn from attic through opening around supply duct

Return grill in air handler for cooling system

Figure 2-45: Warm, humid air drawn from attic through opening around supply duct.

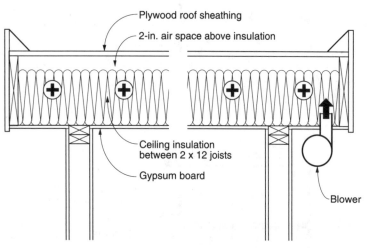

Plywood roof sheathing

2-in. air space above insulation

Ceiling insulation between 2 x 12 joists

Gypsum board

Blower

Figure 2-46: Pressurization of flat roof assembly to control exfiltration.

A common example of an air pressure related moisture problem in a cooling climate occurs where the air handler for a forced air cooling system is located in a closet/utility room. A large unsealed opening exists between the supply ductwork, which is located in the attic space, and the ceiling of the closet/utility room where the supply duct penetrates (Figure 2-45). Return air for the system is drawn from the hot, humid attic space into the utility room through the opening around the ductwork and into the return grill of the air handler. There are cases where the temperature of the conditioned space has actually gone up when the air conditioner was turned on in similar installations. The cooling load increase that occurs from drawing the hot, humid air into the system is actually greater than the capacity of the cooling system. Thus, ductwork for forced air heating and cooling systems installed within conditioned spaces is preferred. Ductwork should never be installed in attics or vented crawl spaces unless it is sealed airtight with mastic and then tested for leakage.

It may be desirable to utilize air handling systems, exhaust systems, and supply systems to deliberately pressurize and depressurize conditioned spaces. This approach could control the exfiltration of warm, interior moisture-laden air during heating periods; the infiltration of warm, humid exterior air during cooling periods; and the infiltration of soil gas, moisture, radon, and pesticides below grade.

Pressurizing Building Assemblies

Air pressures in flat roof assemblies can be actively controlled to reduce the exfiltration of interior air. Exterior air can be used to pressurize a flat roof assembly to prevent the migration of airborne moisture from the conditioned space into the flat roof assembly (Figure 2-46). Pressurization can be maintained with a fan/blower, which need only operate when the exterior temperature drops below the dew point temperature of the conditioned space (Handegord 1991). In cold climates, caution should be exercised to prevent overpressurization and the potential of freezing pipes in interior partition walls or promoting mold and mildew on cooled interior surfaces. *This approach should be avoided in cooling climates where hot, humid exterior air blown into the building assembly is undesirable.*

Vapor Diffusion

The fourth, and final, moisture transport mechanism is vapor diffusion. It can move moisture into building assemblies both from within the conditioned space as well as from the exterior. Vapor diffusion is the movement of moisture in the vapor state through a material. Materials are not able to stop vapor diffusion, they are only able to slow the process down, or retard it. Hence, the term *vapor diffusion retarder* is appropriate, not *vapor barrier*.

Vapor diffusion is a function of the vapor permeability of a material and the driving force or vapor pressure differential acting across the material. If no vapor pressure difference exists across a material, then no moisture will move as a result of vapor diffusion.

When a building is being heated in a cold climate, the vapor pressure is higher inside the building than outside. Thus, vapor diffusion typically moves moisture from within the conditioned space toward the outside and into building assemblies. It is possible in heating climates to reduce the diffusion driving force by reducing interior moisture levels. However, since some moisture-generating sources are always present, it is usually necessary to provide vapor diffusion retarders to minimize problems.

The opposite occurs when a building is being cooled in a warm climate with high ambient vapor pressures. Vapor diffusion typically moves moisture from the exterior into building assemblies and subsequently into the conditioned space.

It is important to note, however, that exceptions to the above two generalizations are common and often overlooked. One example occurs in foundations and below-grade building assemblies, where vapor diffusion can move moisture into the wall assembly from both directions—the surrounding soil as well as the conditioned space.

Another example of vapor pressure behaving contrary to general rules occurs in a heating climate when a sunlit wall with a brick veneer has absorbed moisture from deposited rain. A similar case is a wall with wood cladding that has absorbed moisture during the evening due to high ambient relative humidities, from rain, or from surface condensation. In both cases, moisture can be driven inward from the cladding material into the wall cavity as a result of high exterior surface temperatures from incident solar radiation. The vapor pressure gradient, under these circumstances, can move moisture by vapor diffusion from the exterior cladding into the building envelope during sunny periods.

Vapor diffusion is also a function of surface area. For instance, if 90 percent of a building envelope surface area is covered with a vapor diffusion retarder, that vapor diffusion retarder is 90 percent effective. Continuity of a vapor diffusion retarder is not a critical factor. For instance, a paint film of an appropriate per-

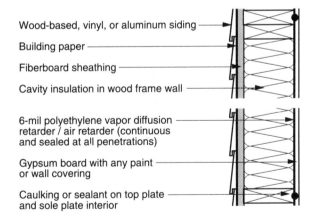

Wood-based, vinyl, or aluminum siding

Building paper

Fiberboard sheathing

Cavity insulation in wood frame wall

6-mil polyethylene vapor diffusion retarder / air retarder (continuous and sealed at all penetrations)

Gypsum board with any paint or wall covering

Caulking or sealant on top plate and sole plate interior

Figure 2-47: Vapor diffusion retarder on the interior of an above-grade wood frame wall—typical heating climate application.

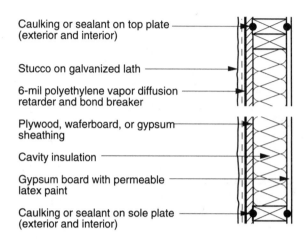

Caulking or sealant on top plate (exterior and interior)

Stucco on galvanized lath

6-mil polyethylene vapor diffusion retarder and bond breaker

Plywood, waferboard, or gypsum sheathing

Cavity insulation

Gypsum board with permeable latex paint

Caulking or sealant on sole plate (exterior and interior)

Figure 2-48: Vapor diffusion retarder on the exterior of an above grade wood frame wall—typical cooling climate application.

meance, applied only on the interior exposed surface of a building envelope, will typically act as an effective vapor diffusion retarder. However, this paint film vapor diffusion retarder does not deal with air-transported moisture which can leak through joints between the interior cladding (typically gypsum board) and wood framing elements, nor does it deal with vapor diffusion from the exterior migrating inwards due to incident solar radiation, or other climatic effects.

CONTROL OF VAPOR DIFFUSION ABOVE GRADE

Vapor diffusion is controlled above grade by selecting the appropriate vapor permeability of building assembly components. Materials that have a high resistance to vapor flow (low vapor permeability) are referred to as *vapor diffusion retarders*. In general, vapor diffusion retarders are located to the interior of building assemblies in heating climates (Figure 2-47), and to the exterior of building assemblies in cooling climates (Figure 2-48). However, in a heating climate where cladding elements which store a great deal of moisture are utilized, it may also be desirable to locate a vapor diffusion retarder behind the cladding. This prevents the inward flow of vapor resulting from a solar-radiation-induced temperature gradient. Commonly used vapor diffusion

retarders are: polyethylene films, aluminum foils, low permeability paints, vinyl wall coverings, impermeable rigid insulations, sheet metal, dampproofing, plywood, and waferboard.

CONTROL OF VAPOR DIFFUSION BELOW GRADE

In general, vapor diffusion retarders are located on the exterior of building assemblies below grade to retard the inward movement of water vapor from the surrounding soil into the basement space. Dampproofing coatings or films typically have very high resistance to vapor flow and therefore act as effective vapor diffusion retarders on the exterior of concrete and masonry foundation walls (Figure 2-49). Vapor diffusion under floor slabs is typically controlled by installing a polyethylene sheet between the concrete slab and the granular capillary break (Figure 2-49).

In many cases an insulated wood frame wall is built inside a concrete or masonry foundation wall. Vapor diffusion from the basement space into this wall framing is minimized by locating a vapor diffusion retarder to the interior of the framing (Figure 2-50). Diffusion of construction moisture from concrete and from masonry foundation walls into basement wall framing can be avoided by locating a vapor diffusion retarder at the interior surface of the concrete and masonry foundation walls (Figure 2-50).

Vapor diffusion into foundation walls from the surrounding soil can also be minimized by placing rigid insulation on the foundation wall exterior. By insulating on the exterior, the average temperature of the foundation wall will rise relative to the soil, thereby reducing the equilibrium relative humidity in the foundation wall. The foundation wall, by being appreciably warmer than the surrounding soil, will tend to dry into the soil. In other words, moisture will tend to migrate by diffusion out of the concrete and masonry foundation wall into the soil, rather than migrate from the soil into the foundation wall.

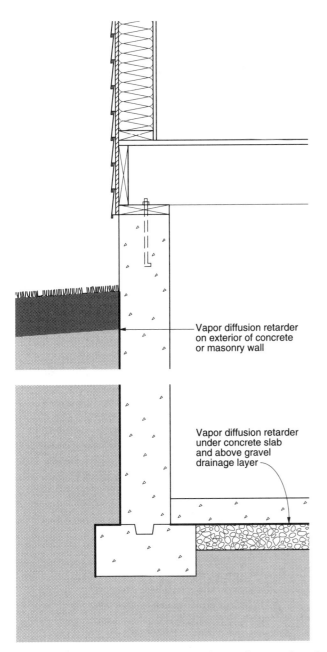

Figure 2-49: Vapor diffusion retarder on the exterior of a concrete or masonry foundation wall and beneath the concrete slab.

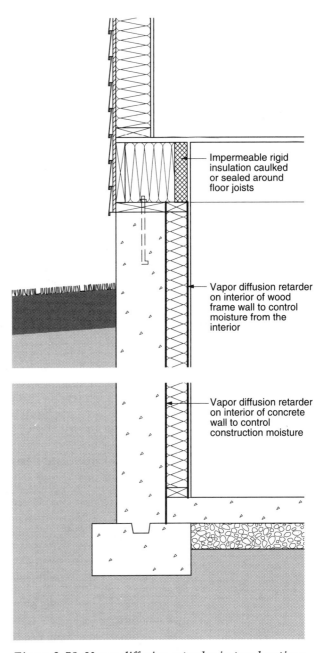

Figure 2-50: Vapor diffusion retarder in two locations inside of the foundation wall—on the interior of a wood frame wall and on the interior of a concrete or masonry foundation wall.

CHAPTER 3

Design Considerations for Building Assemblies

This chapter describes moisture behavior in building assemblies and summarizes the strategies to prevent moisture problems. In the remainder of this introduction, some key concepts and definitions underlying effective design are introduced. These include: moisture sources and movement mechanisms, moisture balance, and wetting and drying of building assemblies. The chapter includes three main sections: (1) wall assemblies in heating climates, (2) wall assemblies in cooling climates, and (3) roof assemblies in both heating and cooling climates. While foundations are not directly addressed here, many of the concepts and strategies are similar. In Chapters 4, 5, and 6, the U.S. climate zones are defined and recommended wall, roof, and foundation assemblies are presented.

Moisture Sources and Movement Mechanisms

In order to effectively design building assemblies to control moisture, the entire set of moisture sources and movement mechanisms must be considered. To begin with, building assemblies can become wet in three ways: (1) moisture can enter from the interior, (2) moisture can enter from the exterior, or (3) the assembly can start out wet as a result of using wet building materials or building under wet conditions. Moisture can enter from the interior by air movement or vapor diffusion, while moisture can enter from the exterior through four mechanisms: liquid flow, capillary suction, air movement, and vapor diffu-

sion (see Chapter 2). Moisture can be redistributed within an assembly by these same four mechanisms. Finally, moisture can be removed (dried) to the exterior or to the interior in three ways: (1) liquid flow due to gravity (drainage), (2) air movement (ventilation), and (3) vapor diffusion (vapor pressure differences). All of these mechanisms can act singly or in combination.

Moisture typically enters an assembly in a liquid or vapor state. Under some limited circumstances moisture can also enter in the solid form, such as wind-deposited snow in ventilated roof assemblies. When moisture enters an assembly in a liquid state, or when it changes to liquid from a vapor state by condensing, its movement is principally governed by liquid flow due to gravity and capillarity. When moisture enters an assembly in a vapor state, or evaporates from the liquid state within an assembly, its movement is principally governed by air movement and vapor diffusion.

Moisture Balance

Numerous strategies can be implemented to minimize the risk of moisture damage. The strategies fall into the following three groups: (1) control of moisture entry, (2) control of moisture accumulation, and (3) removal of moisture (drying). Strategies in the three groupings have proven to be most effective when utilized in combination, but they must be applied appropriately to avoid negative consequences. For example, controlling moisture entry is often not effective if building assemblies start out wet, and in fact can be detrimental. If an assembly is designed to prevent moisture from entering, it is likely that the assembly will be effective in preventing moisture from leaving. Conversely, a design that is effective at removing moisture may also allow moisture to enter.

In designing building assemblies, it is critical to consider the combined effect of all the moisture control strategies being employed. The key concept is to maintain a balance between the moisture entry and removal in a building assembly. For example, moisture accumulates when the rate of moisture entry into an assembly exceeds the rate of moisture removal. This can be mitigated by the ability of the assembly materials to store the moisture without significantly degrading performance or long-term service life. When the accumulation exceeds the combined effects of the storage capacity of the materials and the removal rate, moisture problems may result.

Wetting and Drying of Building Assemblies

Ideally, building assemblies would always be built with dry materials under dry conditions, and would never get wet from imperfect design, poor workmanship, or occupants. Unfortunately, these conditions do not exist.

It has been accepted by many in the building industry that building assemblies often become wet during service, and in many cases start out wet. In many circumstances it may be impractical to design and build assemblies so that they never get wet. This has given

rise to the concept of *acceptable performance*. Acceptable performance implies the design and construction of building assemblies which may periodically get wet, or start out wet, but yet are still durable and provide a long, useful service life. Repeated wetting followed by repeated drying can provide acceptable performance if during the wet period, materials do not stay wet long enough to deteriorate.

In order to successfully apply the concept of acceptable performance, the wetting of building assemblies must be controlled. Then, should an assembly become wet, it should be designed to permit drying.

Wall Assemblies in Heating Climates

The behavior of moisture in wall assemblies transported by vapor diffusion or air transport is discussed in the beginning of this section. This is followed by a graphical analysis method that identifies the potential for condensation. Then, schematic diagrams of moisture mechanisms in wall assemblies are presented. Finally, there is a summary of moisture control strategies for wall design in heating climate conditions.

VAPOR DIFFUSION IN HEATING CLIMATE WALL ASSEMBLIES

Figure 3-1 illustrates a wood frame wall in a heating climate with unfaced fiberglass batt insulation installed within the cavities. Gyp-

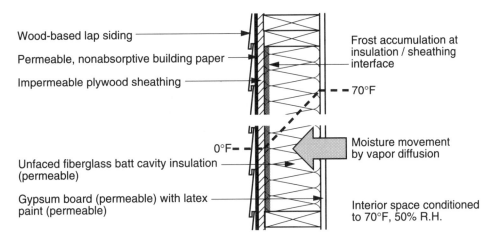

Figure 3-1: Moisture movement in a wood frame wall in a heating climate.

---

sum board covered with a relatively vapor permeable latex paint is installed to the interior. Relatively impermeable plywood sheathing is placed on the exterior. Wood-based lap siding over a permeable, nonabsorptive building paper is installed over the exterior plywood sheathing. The conditioned space operates at a high interior vapor pressure (50 percent relative humidity at 70 degrees Fahrenheit), and a typical exterior temperature during the month of January is 0 degrees Fahrenheit. To simplify matters, assume that the wall is constructed airtight and that no air pressure difference exists between the interior and exterior of the wall—this eliminates air movement as a moisture transport mechanism. In addition, wall convection effects will be ignored.

In this example, vapor diffusion will move moisture from the interior conditioned space through the painted gypsum wall board and the fiberglass cavity insulation to the interior surface of the exterior plywood sheathing. If this surface—the insulation/sheathing interface—is below the dew point temperature of the air/vapor mix at the interface, the vapor may condense to a liquid. If the insulation/sheathing interface temperature is below the freezing point of water, the vapor may freeze.

In this particular example, the dew point temperature of the interior air/vapor mix is approximately 50 degrees Fahrenheit. Condensation will typically be found at the first surface below the dew point temperature, in this case the cavity side of the exterior plywood sheathing.

The permeance of the sheathing is not as significant in determining whether condensation will occur at the insulation/sheathing interface as is the temperature of the interior surface of the sheathing. For example, if the exterior plywood sheathing were eliminated, leaving only the permeable nonabsorptive building paper at the exterior of the wall behind the wood-based siding, condensation might still occur on the cavity side of the permeable building paper (permeable compared to the plywood sheathing, but impermeable compared to air). This is because the building paper is below the dew point temperature of the air/vapor mix in the cavity.

Once moisture condenses or freezes on the interior surface of the sheathing or building paper, the permeance and moisture storage capability of the material will affect the rate and quantity of moisture that subsequently passes through by diffusion and/or capillarity to the back of the siding. Moisture may accumulate and become visible in the form of water or frost if the rate of moisture movement to the insulation/sheathing interface is greater than the rate at which moisture is absorbed or passes through the sheathing.

Effect of Insulation Material

In Figure 3-1, moisture from the interior conditioned space migrates by vapor diffusion to the insulation/sheathing interface and accumulates in the form of frost. As the temperature of the sheathing rises due to incident solar radiation or a rise in the outside

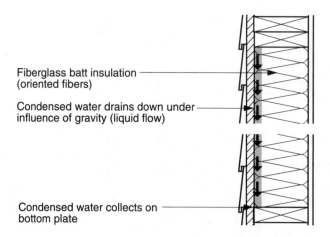

Fiberglass batt insulation (oriented fibers)

Condensed water drains down under influence of gravity (liquid flow)

Condensed water collects on bottom plate

Figure 3-2: Condensation pattern with fiberglass cavity insulation.

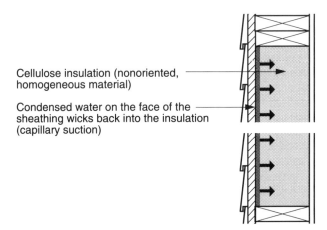

Cellulose insulation (nonoriented, homogeneous material)

Condensed water on the face of the sheathing wicks back into the insulation (capillary suction)

Figure 3-3: Condensation pattern with cellulose cavity insulation.

temperature, the frost melts and water drains down the sheathing to the bottom plate of the wall as shown in Figure 3-2. The condensed water does not wick back by capillary suction into the fiberglass batt insulation due to the oriented nature of the insulation fibers (the layered structure of the insulation emulates the *thatched-roof effect*). However, if the wall cavity were insulated with a nonoriented insulation such as cellulose, then capillary suction would draw the condensed water from the insulation/sheathing interface into the insulation (Figure 3-3).

With oriented fiberglass batt insulation, the insulation remains dry and its thermal resistance is not noticeably altered when interstitial condensation occurs. This is because condensation and moisture/frost accumulation occur at the insulation/sheathing interface, not within the insulation, and also because of the lack of inward capillary moisture movement. However, with cellulose cavity insulation, the wicking of condensed water into the insulation from the insulation/sheathing interface reduces the thermal resistance of the wall.

Effect of Sheathing Material

In walls where the exterior sheathing is vapor impermeable and nonabsorptive, such as foil-faced sheathings or plastic sheathings (extruded and expanded polystyrenes), condensed water will either run down the interior face of the sheathings toward the bottom plate (wall cavities insulated with

oriented fiberglass batts) or be wicked back into the cavity insulation and held there (wall cavities insulated with cellulose). Moisture is not absorbed by the sheathings nor does it migrate through the sheathings to influence the exterior siding.

Vapor impermeable, nonabsorptive sheathings basically disconnect or uncouple the exterior siding from interior moisture-related problems. A benefit to using an impermeable, nonabsorptive sheathing is that wood-based sidings and their painted or stained surfaces are not affected by interior moisture. A drawback is that cavity moisture problems do not demonstrate visible exterior symptoms on the exterior siding. Where the impermeable sheathing also has an insulating value, however, the wall cavity is often free from condensation problems due to elevated cavity temperatures.

It is necessary to consider, however, that with impermeable sheathings (both insulating and noninsulating), the dwell time for moisture that has entered wood-based sidings from the exterior increases. This can lead to paint failures and other material deterioration problems in the cladding.

Since the vapor impermeable and nonabsorptive sheathings do not absorb or transmit moisture, they do not deteriorate when exposed to moisture. In walls insulated with fiberglass batt insulation, condensed water runs down the sheathing to the bottom plate of the wall. Serious problems can develop, however, if the amount of moisture reaching the wood bottom plate (1) exceeds the plate's ability to absorb moisture without decaying (that is, reaching the fiber saturation point—30 percent moisture content by oven-dry weight), and (2) remains there long enough under conditions that support decay (between 32 and 100 degrees Fahrenheit with spores present). In this type of wall (with fiberglass batt insulation), the bottom plate and floor/rim joist assembly may deteriorate first. In walls insulated with cellulose, the condensed water on the sheathing is held within the insulation and may not reach the bottom plate.

In walls where the exterior sheathing is vapor impermeable, absorptive, and wood-based, such as plywood, waferboard, or OSB sheathing (as in Figure 3-1), the sheathings will absorb some condensed water. Where oriented fiberglass batt insulation is used in wall cavities, the remaining condensed water will run down the interior face of the sheathing toward the bottom plate. In wall cavities insulated with cellulose, it will be wicked back into the cavity insulation and held there.

Similar to impermeable, nonabsorptive sheathings, serious problems can occur from the amount of moisture accumulating at the exterior sheathing and bottom plate. In walls with plywood, waferboard, or OSB sheathing, the sheathing material itself may deteriorate along with the studs, bottom plates, and floor/rim joist assemblies. Although these wood-based sheathings are impermeable when dry, as they absorb moisture they begin to transfer moisture through them to the exterior. Consequently, some visible symptoms of interior cavity moisture problems may be present on exterior sidings, such as peeling paint and buckled siding. This moisture "diode" effect of some wood-based sheathings (specifically plywood) provides a degree of forgiveness in many wall assemblies.

In walls where the exterior sheathing is vapor permeable and absorptive, such as asphalt-impregnated fiberboard or gypsum board, condensed water will be absorbed by the sheathings and transferred to the exterior building paper and cladding. The permeance of the sheathing and the building paper (if present) determines the rate at which moisture can migrate to the cladding. If the rate of moisture supply from the interior conditioned space to the cavity side of the sheathing is greater than the rate of moisture removal through the sheathing to the building paper and the cladding, moisture accumulates within the sheathing. This can cause serious problems if the amount of moisture accumulating within

the sheathing exceeds its capacity. The result is either long-term strength deterioration in the case of gypsum board, or potential decay and strength deterioration in the case of asphalt-impregnated fiberboard.

With vapor permeable sheathings, visible symptoms of interior cavity moisture problems are often readily apparent on exterior sidings. Since these exterior sheathings are vapor permeable, the rate of moisture migration from the interior to the sheathing has to be rather high before significant moisture accumulation at the sheathing can occur. With respect to permitting the wall assembly to dry, these sheathings tend to be more forgiving than vapor impermeable sheathings.

Effect of Building Paper and Siding

Where moisture is transferred through the sheathing to the building paper, three characteristics of the building paper—temperature, permeability, and moisture storage capacity—determine the amount of condensation, absorption, drainage, and moisture transfer that occurs at the sheathing/building paper interface. Due to the relatively high permeance and lack of storage capacity of most building papers, moisture is easily transferred to the back of the exterior cladding/siding. Once moisture has travelled to the back of the exterior cladding/siding, condensation, absorption, drainage, diffusion, and evaporation can all occur at this location, depending on the nature of the exterior cladding.

Moisture absorbed in the back of wood-based cladding tends to migrate through the wood toward the exterior cladding/paint film interface where it halts. How much moisture passes through the paint film depends on the film's permeance. The more permeable the paint film, the more moisture it will allow to pass. Condensation at the cladding/paint film interface may not occur unless a void or air space (blister) also exists.

It is speculated that blisters and paint peeling are caused by the expansion and contraction of the wood cladding substrate due to changing or cycling of the moisture contents in the wood cladding (Lstiburek 1989). The expansion and contraction of the wood substrate causes the paint film to lift or separate from the wood as the paint film attempts to stretch with the wood. In other words, the moisture does not push the paint off the siding, rather the mechanical stresses on the paint film caused by the expansion and contraction of the wood substrate due to changing moisture content cause the paint to fail.

Surfaces exposed to solar radiation are prone to more severe peeling and blistering as the sun warms the siding during the day, pushing the moisture from the siding back into the wall, thus drying out the siding. Of course at night the siding gets wet from the inside again. This repeated wetting and drying of the siding swells and shrinks the wood substrate and stresses the paint film, ultimately leading to failure. Paints that are vapor permeable, with substantial adhesive and cohesive properties tend to be more durable than those that are not. Of course the paints also must be resistant to solar radiation, prevent water absorption (act as an exterior capillary break for the wood-based siding), and have good aesthetic properties. Unfortunately, some of these properties can be mutually exclusive.

Location of Vapor Retarder

Traditionally in heating climates, vapor diffusion into wall assemblies from interior moisture sources is controlled by installing a vapor diffusion retarder on the warm side of the dew point location within the wall. In practice, the vapor diffusion retarder is located at the interior wall surface at one or more of the following locations:

1. Between the gypsum wall board and the wall framing (sheet polyethylene, aluminum foil)

2. On the interior surface of the cavity insulation (backed batt insulation)

3. On the cavity side of the interior gypsum board (foil-backed gypsum board)

4. Within the interior gypsum board (vapor barrier gypsum board)

5. On the interior surface of the interior gypsum board (vapor barrier paint, low permeability wall coverings)

These vapor diffusion retarders are often specified by building codes to have a permeability of 1 perm or less (ASHRAE 1989a). A more obscure recommendation specifies that the permeability of the exterior sheathing/ building paper/cladding assembly should be five times the permeability of the interior sheathing/cladding assembly where dew point temperatures of the air/vapor mix of the interior conditioned space are reached within wall cavities (Joy 1951). This gives builders and designers the option of manipulating both interior and exterior permeability. Unfortu-

nately, this recommendation is not recognized in most codes and standards. Furthermore, it is important to note that these recommendations are for controlling moisture transport by vapor diffusion from the interior only, and not for air-transported moisture.

AIR MOVEMENT IN HEATING CLIMATE WALL ASSEMBLIES

Up to this point, only vapor diffusion as a moisture transport wetting mechanism has been considered. When air movement from the interior toward the exterior is introduced, its effects are combined with those of vapor diffusion.

When flaws or openings exist in a wall assembly coupled with an air pressure difference, air will move through the assembly. If the interior conditioned space is at a greater air pressure than the exterior, the air flow is from the interior toward the exterior. This exfiltrating air will carry moisture into the wall assembly assuming the interior air contains moisture. Whether moisture is deposited within the wall depends on the moisture content and the surface temperature of each material inside the wall. An example of this can occur where an electrical outlet box is placed in an exterior wall (Figure 3-4).

When air movement occurs within wall assemblies, moisture condenses and accumulates in a manner similar to the vapor diffusion examples described previously. Specifically, moisture condenses and accumulates at the interfaces between materials. However, there are differences between vapor diffusion and air movement. Where air movement exists it tends to dominate vapor diffusion, and has a significantly greater effect on moisture transfer into building assemblies than vapor diffusion when both are present (Quirouette 1985).

In the majority of cases, for air to get into a wall assembly, air must also leave the wall assembly. Thus, both an inlet opening and an outlet opening typically must exist. Air inlet openings are usually unsealed electrical outlet boxes, the bottom edges of interior gypsum board cladding, or openings, gaps, and joints in interior air retarder systems. Air outlet openings are usually the joints between sheets of exterior sheathings and the joints between top plates, bottom plates, and exterior sheathings, in addition to any construction flaws or service penetrations.

In some cases, openings are intentionally created in the exterior sheathing to permit a wall to dry to the exterior. The interior surface

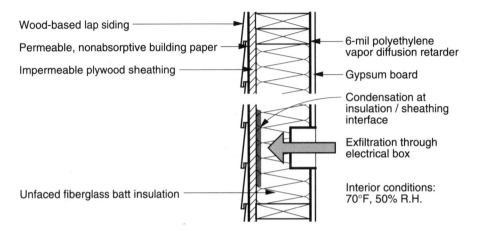

Wood-based lap siding

Permeable, nonabsorptive building paper

Impermeable plywood sheathing

6-mil polyethylene
vapor diffusion retarder

Gypsum board

Condensation at
insulation / sheathing
interface

Exfiltration through
electrical box

Unfaced fiberglass batt insulation

Interior conditions:
70°F, 50% R.H.

Figure 3-4: Moisture transport wetting mechanisms in a heating climate wall assembly with an electrical outlet box.

of the wall assembly must be airtight in these cases or moisture problems related to outward air flow will increase.

Variables Influencing Condensation

Assuming flaws or openings (both inlet and outlet) exist in a wall assembly, as well as an outward-acting air pressure difference, indoor air will flow outward, coming in contact with surfaces (interfaces) at progressively lower temperatures. Condensation may occur whenever the temperature of a surface is below the dew point of the air/vapor mixture arriving at that surface.

There are a number of complex variables that influence whether condensation will occur. The sensible heat available in the flowing air must be considered as it can heat the surfaces along the flow path, potentially raising their temperatures above the dew point. Also, as soon as condensation takes place, latent heat is available to slow down subsequent condensation. Of course, this condensation may improve material conductivity allowing further chilling. In simple, straight openings through moderately insulating materials, all surfaces along the flow path may warm above the dew point temperature and no condensation will occur.

If condensation occurs at a surface, the exfiltrating air leaves that condensing surface at 100 percent relative humidity, but the air is at a lower moisture content (less the condensed

moisture). In this manner, each successive surface can dehumidify the moving air stream as it flows through the wall to the outside. The amount of condensation at each interface will be dependent on the rate of air flow and the difference in moisture content between the air arriving and leaving each interface.

ANALYSIS OF CONDENSATION POTENTIAL IN HEATING CLIMATE WALLS

In order to understand the potential for condensation in an particular climate, a simple graphical analysis method is described in this section (Handegord 1985). The wall assembly shown in Figure 3-4 illustrates a potential condensation problem. It is a wood frame wall with unfaced fiberglass batt insulation installed within the cavities. Gypsum board covered with a relatively vapor permeable latex paint is installed over a 6-mil polyethylene vapor diffusion retarder to the interior. Relatively impermeable plywood sheathing is installed to the exterior. Wood-based lap siding over a permeable, nonabsorptive building paper is installed over the exterior plywood sheathing.

In this example, the wall is located in a heating climate—Chicago, Illinois. The conditioned space operates at a high interior vapor pressure (50 percent relative humidity at 70 degrees Fahrenheit). As shown in Figure 3-4, the wall is not airtight and contains an unsealed electrical outlet box. Assume that this electrical outlet box is located above the neutral pressure plane in the building so that an outward-acting air pressure exists across this opening, providing the driving force for the exfiltration of warm, moist interior air.

Figure 3-5 plots mean daily ambient temperature over a one-year period in Chicago. To simplify matters, assume that the temperature of the insulation/sheathing interface is approximately equivalent to the mean daily ambient temperature, since the thermal resistance values of the siding, building paper, and sheathing are small compared with the thermal resistance of the insulation in the wall cavity. The dew point temperature of the interior air/vapor mix is approximately 50 degrees Fahrenheit (this can be found on the psychrometric chart in Chapter 1). In other words, whenever the insulation/sheathing interface drops below 50 degrees Fahrenheit, the potential for condensation exists at that interface should moisture migrate from the interior conditioned space via vapor diffusion and/or air movement.

From the plot it is clear that the mean daily insulation/sheathing interface temperature drops below the dew point temperature during early October and does not go above the dew point temperature until late March. The

shaded area under the dew point line is the potential for condensation, or *wetting potential* for this assembly should moisture from the interior reach the insulation/sheathing interface. From the description of the wall assembly it is clear that moisture from the interior is in fact reaching the insulation/sheathing interface via air movement through the electrical outlet box.

Vapor diffusion is also occurring, but only through the electrical outlet box, as the balance of the wall assembly is covered with a very effective vapor diffusion retarder—the 6-mil sheet polyethylene. Since the surface area of this flaw (with respect to diffusion only) is small compared to the total surface area covered with the 6-mil vapor diffusion retarder, vapor diffusion can be effectively discounted as a major moisture transport problem in this assembly. However, air movement cannot be discounted, and this wall assembly, *under these conditions*, in this particular climate will likely suffer distress.

In the following section, eight strategies for moisture control in wall assemblies are described. This graphical analysis of condensation will illustrate how some of the strategies minimize or eliminate the potential for condensation.

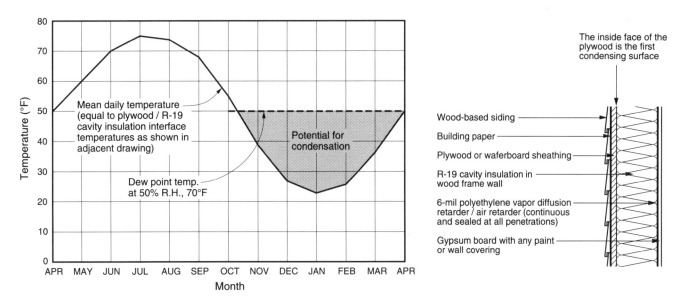

Figure 3-5: Potential for condensation in a wood frame wall cavity in Chicago, Illinois (Handegord 1985).

Raise dew pt by insulating

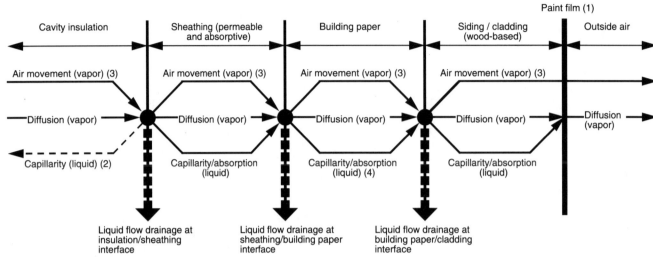

Notes:
1. Condensation at siding/paint interface may not occur unless void or air space is present.
2. Some cavity insulations are not susceptible to capillarity.
3. Air movement only occurs through openings/gaps in sheathing, building paper, and cladding.
4. Some building papers are not susceptible to capillarity and are nonabsorptive.

Figure 3-6: Schematic of moisture transport wetting mechanisms in a heating climate wall with wood siding.

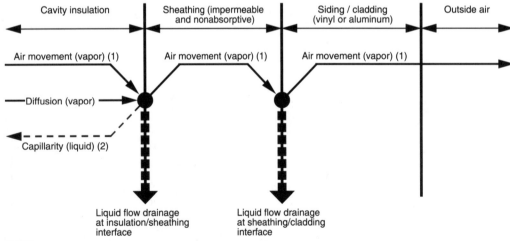

Notes:
1. Air movement only occurs through openings/gaps in sheathing, building paper, and cladding.
2. Some cavity insulations are not susceptible to capillarity.

Figure 3-7: Schematic of moisture transport wetting mechanisms in a heating climate wall with vinyl or aluminum siding.

SCHEMATIC DIAGRAMS OF MOISTURE BEHAVIOR IN HEATING CLIMATE WALLS

In summary, considering both vapor diffusion and air movement as moisture transport wetting mechanisms from the interior, it is clear that condensation, capillarity/absorption (storage), liquid flow (drainage), air movement (re-evaporation), and diffusion can all occur (singly or in concert) at each of the following interfaces:

1. The insulation/sheathing interface

2. The sheathing/building paper interface

3. The building paper/cladding interface

This is presented schematically in Figure 3-6. What actually happens at each interface depends on many factors, not least of which are the material properties of the components of the wall assembly, the geometry of the assembly itself, the interior and exterior environmental conditions (temperature, vapor pressure, and air pressure differences or driving forces), and the length of time being considered. It is also important to note that the interior and exterior environmental conditions are dynamic, not static, which further complicates matters .

In the case of a wall with vinyl or aluminum siding over a foil-faced sheathing, the schematic is simplified considerably (Figure 3-7). The vapor diffusion and capillary/absorptive components of the cladding and sheathing can be ignored, and the building paper is absent.

The key to understanding, predicting, and controlling moisture redistribution and accumulation within building assemblies are the conditions existing at material interfaces. Basically, if moisture appears it will appear at an interface. Thus, if the properties of the interfaces are controlled, the design of the entire assembly is controlled (Lischkoff and Timusk 1984).

MOISTURE CONTROL STRATEGIES FOR WALLS IN HEATING CLIMATES

As shown in Table 3-1, control strategies for alleviating moisture problems in heating climate wall assemblies fall into three groups: (1) control of moisture entry, (2) control of moisture accumulation, and (3) removal of moisture. Of these three groups, control of moisture entry has traditionally proven to be

the most effective. Obviously, if moisture never gets into a building assembly, concerns about its accumulation and removal are eliminated. The importance of the control of moisture entry cannot be overstated.

The development of new materials and the increasing complexity of building designs have led to the greater acceptance of the strategy of controlling moisture accumulation within building assemblies. This is an effective strategy where the practitioner understands the moisture transport mechanisms involved, the influence of climate, the limitations of workmanship, and the impact of occupants. Techniques arising from this strategy may conflict with traditional practice, requiring careful consideration by both practitioners and code officials.

The strategy of moisture removal once it has entered the building assembly has a long historical basis. Attic and crawl space ventilation techniques can be traced back over several decades. Permeable exterior and interior sheathings along with various attempts at wall ventilation also have a long history. More recently, drainage techniques for removing moisture from building assemblies have been developed. Attic and crawl space ventilation as well as permeable sheathings have a proven track record of performance in the removal of moisture from building assemblies.

Table 3-1: Moisture control strategies for wall assemblies in heating climates.

Control of Moisture Entry

1. Reduce moisture in the interior air.

2. Install vapor diffusion retarder on the interior (warm side).

3. Eliminate air inlet/outlet openings.

4. Control air pressure differentials.

Control of Moisture Accumulation

5. Raise the temperature of interstitial condensing surfaces located on the exterior.

Removal of Moisture

6. Remove moisture by vapor diffusion.

7. Remove moisture by air movement (ventilation).

8. Drain condensed moisture.

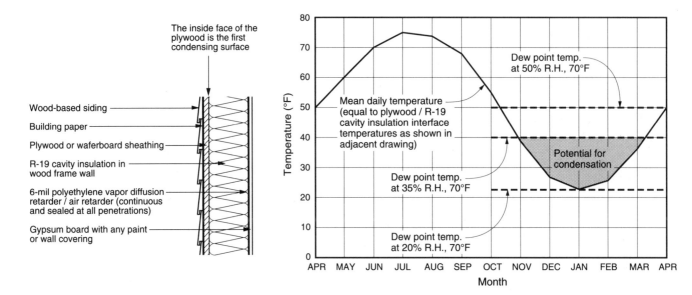

The inside face of the plywood is the first condensing surface

Wood-based siding

Building paper

Plywood or waferboard sheathing

R-19 cavity insulation in wood frame wall

6-mil polyethylene vapor diffusion retarder / air retarder (continuous and sealed at all penetrations)

Gypsum board with any paint or wall covering

Dew point temp. at 50% R.H., 70°F

Mean daily temperature (equal to plywood / R-19 cavity insulation interface temperatures as shown in adjacent drawing)

Dew point temp. at 35% R.H., 70°F

Potential for condensation

Dew point temp. at 20% R.H., 70°F

Figure 3-8: Potential for condensation in a wood frame wall cavity in Chicago, Illinois (Handegord 1985). By reducing interior moisture levels, the potential condensation is reduced or eliminated.

Wall cavity ventilation is discussed in this section not because it is necessarily a recommended practice but because it is often viewed as a potential solution to wall cavity moisture problems. Likewise, wall cavity drainage is discussed in this section because it is beginning to be utilized in commercial high-rise applications as a cost-effective alternative to the rain screen approach and face-sealing (barrier wall construction). Consequently, the technique of wall cavity drainage is being adapted to residential applications.

In this section, the strategies are illustrated with heating climate examples. In some cases, the wall design strategies for mixed climates are similar in concept to these heating climate approaches, although they may differ slightly in actual practice.

Approach 1: Reduce moisture in the interior air

The first approach is to control the amount of moisture in the interior air. Referring back to the wall assembly and the graph of potential condensation shown in Figure 3-5, it can be demonstrated that reducing interior moisture levels reduces or even eliminates the potential for condensation in the wall. If the relative humidity of the interior conditioned space is reduced to 35 percent at 70 degrees Fahrenheit (Figure 3-8), the dew point temperature of this

air/vapor mixture is lowered to 40 degrees Fahrenheit, thus reducing the period of the year and the temperature conditions when condensation may occur.

As Figure 3-8 also illustrates, if the relative humidity of the interior conditioned space is maintained below 20 percent at 70 degrees Fahrenheit, the dew point temperature of this air/vapor mixture is below the mean daily insulation/sheathing temperature for the year. This approach, which guarantees no condensation, can be accomplished in Chicago with source control of moisture and with dilution (air change via controlled ventilation). Of course this may prove to be uncomfortable, since 20 percent relative humidity is uncomfortably low for many individuals. It may also be expensive to implement, if the operating cost of mechanical ventilation is considered.

Approach 2: Install vapor diffusion retarder

Other than plumbing leaks and water spills, moisture can enter a wall from the interior in only two ways: (1) by vapor diffusion and (2) by air movement. Vapor diffusion is controlled by installing a 6-mil polyethylene vapor diffusion retarder (Figure 3-9). However, the vapor diffusion retarder does not eliminate the air movement problem.

NW -Drywall & PVA paint

Approach 3: Eliminate air inlet/outlet openings

The third approach is to eliminate the inlet and outlet openings. A typical approach is to seal the gypsum board and/or a polyethylene air retarder to the inside face of the wood frame wall. An electrical outlet box, which creates an opening in this system, should be sealed to the gypsum board or polyethylene sheet to maintain the interior air retarder. Alternatively, the exterior sheathing can be sealed to the frame assembly (Figure 3-9), and/or the assembly can be filled with a cavity insulation that completely fills the voids with density sufficient to eliminate air movement. If there are no openings for the air to pass through, the air will not carry moisture into the assembly. (See Chapter 2 for some outlet sealing details).

Approach 4: Control air pressure differential

The fourth approach is to control the pressure differential across the wall assembly. The enclosure can be depressurized by installing exhaust-only ventilation, causing infiltration under all conditions. Where depressurization strategies are employed, however, spillage and backdrafting in combustion appliances and potential radon gas entry must be addressed. For example, sealed combustion appliances should be used. Conversely the wall assembly itself can be mechanically pressurized with exterior air. Although this is not typically practical in wall assemblies, it is an option available for roof/attic assemblies (see Chapter 2). This air pressure control would only be necessary during the period when the insulation/sheathing interface is below the interior dew point temperature (Handegord 1991).

Approach 5: Raise the temperatures of interstitial condensing surfaces

The fifth approach is to control the temperature of the first condensing surface, namely the insulation/sheathing interface. If the temperature of this interface is raised above the interior dew point temperature, condensation is not possible. For example, using the wall assembly illustrated in Figure 3-5, the plywood sheathing, which has a negligible thermal resistance, can be replaced with insulating sheathing.

Figures 3-10 and 3-11 illustrate two walls with insulated sheathing on the exterior. The sheathing in the first wall has a thermal resistance of R-12, while in the second wall, the sheathing has a thermal resistance of R-7. In the first case where the sheathing R-value is R-12 or greater, and the cavity insulation is R-11 or less, the insulation/sheathing interface remains above the interior dew point temperature (Figure 3-10). The temperature of this interface is calculated in the following manner. Divide the thermal resistance to the exterior of the interface by the total thermal resistance of the wall. Then multiply this ratio by the temperature difference between the interior

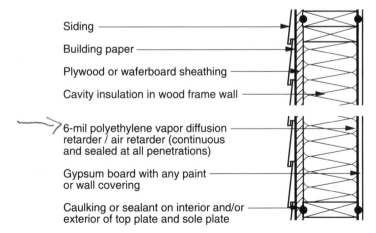

Siding

Building paper

Plywood or waferboard sheathing

Cavity insulation in wood frame wall

6-mil polyethylene vapor diffusion retarder / air retarder (continuous and sealed at all penetrations)

Gypsum board with any paint or wall covering

Caulking or sealant on interior and/or exterior of top plate and sole plate

Figure 3-9: A vapor diffusion retarder is typically located on the interior of a wall assembly in a heating climate. Air movement is controlled by sealing the exterior sheathing to the framing, the interior air retarder to the framing, or by filling the cavity with dense pack cellulose which serves as an interstitial air retarder.

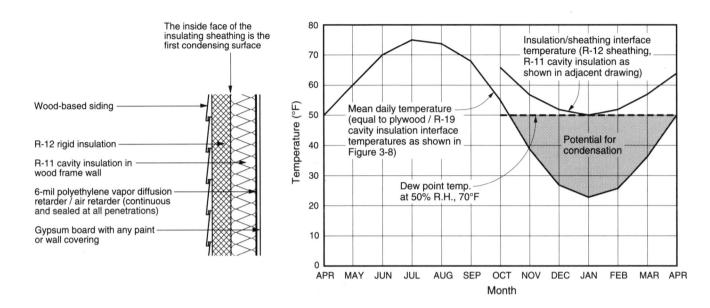

Figure 3-10: Potential for condensation in a wood frame wall cavity in Chicago, Illinois (Handegord 1985). The R-12 insulating sheathing raises the dew point temperature at the first condensing surface so that no condensation will occur with interior conditions of 50 percent relative humidity at 70 degrees Fahrenheit.

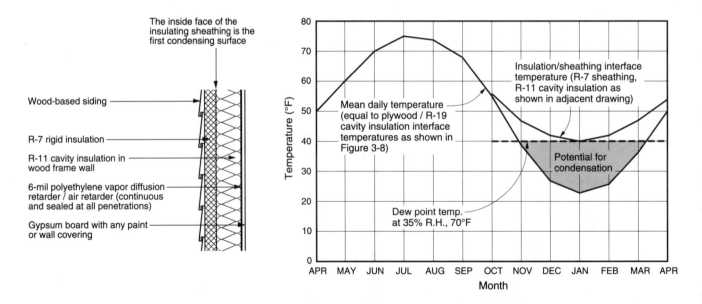

Figure 3-11: Potential for condensation in a wood frame wall cavity in Chicago, Illinois (Handegord 1985). The R-7 insulating sheathing raises the dew point temperature at the first condensing surface so that no condensation will occur with interior conditions of 35 percent relative humidity at 70 degrees Fahrenheit.

and the exterior. Finally, add this to the outside base temperature. Thus, the points forming the line plotted in Figure 3-10 are based on the following calculation:

$$T_{interface} = (R_{ext}/R_{total} \times (T_{int} - T_{ext})) + T_{ext}$$

$$T_{interface} = (12/23 \times (70° - 23°)) + 23°$$

$$T_{interface} = 47.5°$$

Where:

$T_{interface}$ = Interface temperature for January

R_{ext} = Thermal resistance to the exterior of the interface

R_{total} = Total thermal resistance of the wall

T_{int} = Interior temperature

T_{ext} = Mean daily temperature for January

This wall assembly typically would be built as a 2 x 4 wall with 2-1/2 to 3 inches of rigid insulation to the exterior. With this type of wall assembly, an interior vapor diffusion retarder/air retarder is not necessary since the temperature of the first condensing surface is controlled. This may not be the most economical wall assembly to build, but it does control condensation under the conditions specified. A more economical approach would be to construct a wall with sheathing of thermal resistance of R-7, and cavity insulation of thermal resistance of R-11 or less (as shown in Figure 3-11). Then, interior moisture levels should be limited to 35 percent relative humid-ity at 70 degrees (a dew point temperature of approximately 40 degrees), resulting in no potential condensation.

Approach 6: Remove moisture by vapor diffusion

The sixth approach is to remove any condensed moisture by relying on vapor diffusion. The exterior plywood sheathing can be replaced with vapor permeable, asphalt-impregnated fiberboard, which will allow the transfer of moisture to the building paper and ultimately to the cladding. The nature of the cladding system and its associated geometry will determine the rate of moisture removal from the building paper/cladding and sheathing/building paper interfaces. Vinyl and aluminum sidings allow more moisture to migrate to the exterior (due to the air spaces and air circulation behind these claddings) than wood-based claddings, unless the wood-based claddings are installed over furring (Figure 3-12).

It is desirable to paint the back of wood-based claddings (back-priming) to protect the siding from absorbing moisture that passes through the vapor permeable sheathing. This also limits capillary effects at siding laps. Installing the cladding on furring, in effect, ventilates both the back of the siding and front face of the sheathing. This approach, which links ventilation of the siding with diffusion through the sheathing, is much more effective than relying on diffusion acting alone through the sheathing, building paper, and cladding.

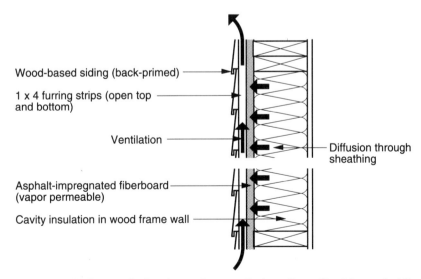

Wood-based siding (back-primed)

1 x 4 furring strips (open top and bottom)

Ventilation

Diffusion through sheathing

Asphalt-impregnated fiberboard (vapor permeable)

Cavity insulation in wood frame wall

Figure 3-12: Removal of moisture by ventilation of a wall with wood siding.

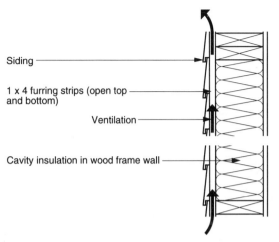

Siding

1 x 4 furring strips (open top and bottom)

Ventilation

Cavity insulation in wood frame wall

Figure 3-13: By using no sheathing or building paper, moisture freely moves into the air space behind the siding and is removed by ventilation.

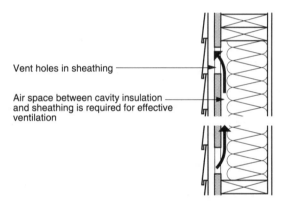

Vent holes in sheathing

Air space between cavity insulation and sheathing is required for effective ventilation

Figure 3-14: Openings in the sheathing permit ventilation to enter the wall cavity. With this approach, the interior surface of the wall assembly must be airtight.

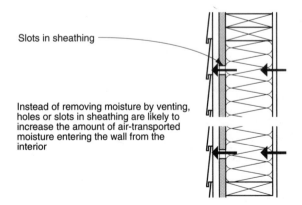

Slots in sheathing

Instead of removing moisture by venting, holes or slots in sheathing are likely to increase the amount of air-transported moisture entering the wall from the interior

Figure 3-15: If the interior surface of the wall assembly is not airtight, exfiltration of moist interior air can cause moisture problems within the wall.

Approach 7: Remove moisture by air movement

The seventh approach is to utilize air movement (ventilation) to remove moisture from the wall assembly. There are several basic strategies for providing ventilation to wall assemblies. The first has already been described in Figure 3-12, which links the ventilation of siding with diffusion through a vapor permeable sheathing. A variation of this approach is to install only a vapor permeable building paper in place of a vapor permeable sheathing. This approach also works well. However, provisions for wall racking strength and cladding support may need to be provided when replacing the exterior sheathing with a building paper.

An alternative strategy is not to install any sheathing or building paper and provide air flow over the outer surface of the cavity insulation between the insulation and the exterior cladding (Figure 3-13). The arguments against this approach are that it will increase exfiltration/infiltration through the wall assembly if openings or flaws are present at the interior surface, and significantly reduce the thermal effectiveness of low density cavity insulations due to wind-washing. Furthermore, with no exterior sheathing, provisions for racking strength and cladding support may be necessary. However, with dense cavity insulation (or a building paper over typical cavity insulation), a tight interior cladding, and an appropriate method to resist racking, the approach can be effective. This approach is typically utilized in commercial wall systems—a high density rigid fiberglass sheet insulation is used in curtain wall assemblies as well as in many veneer and rain screen assemblies.

Another strategy is to provide openings in the sheathing (Figure 3-14). This approach will only be effective if an air space exists between the sheathing and the exterior face of the cavity insulation and an airtight interior cladding is provided. In practice this is rarely the case, and more often than not the openings in the sheathing lead to either rain entry or greater exfiltration of interior air (Figure 3-15). If greater exfiltration is the result, and provisions for drainage and protection against moisture absorption by the exterior sheathing are not present, serious moisture accumulation problems may result.

Approach 8: Drain condensed moisture

The eighth approach is to allow the condensation to occur, but to drain it from the wall assembly before deterioration in performance or durability occurs. Since condensation will occur at the insulation/sheathing interface, the back of the plywood sheathing can be sealed to prevent capillarity and absorption of condensed water into the plywood. Then, drainage at the bottom of the wall assembly can be provided with an appropriate opening and flashing (Figure 3-16). Protection of wood studs is also necessary.

The drainage strategy is successfully utilized in commercial metal buildings. It is important to note that drainage will not remove absorbed water from a material. It will only remove condensed water from nonabsorbent materials. Drainage will not work with nonoriented cavity insulations such as cellulose, or with non-back-primed or sealed wood-based sheathings. In addition, drainage will not remove absorbed moisture from asphalt-impregnated fiberboard or gypsum board.

The principle argument against drainage is that by providing drainage openings, exfiltration of air through the wall assembly increases. If flaws or openings are present at the interior surfaces of a wall assembly, providing openings at the exterior of the assembly will increase the through-flow of air. An overriding advantage of this approach, however, is that although condensation may be increased at the insulation/sheathing interface, drainage will be sufficient to alleviate the problem. However, thermal performance will likely be reduced with increased air flow. Another significant advantage of this approach is that the same drainage mechanism removes both condensed moisture as well as any rainwater that enters the wall assembly. This dual benefit makes the drainage approach attractive in the design of many commercial wall assemblies.

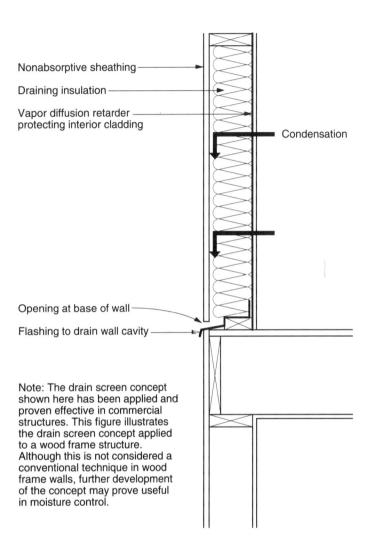

Nonabsorptive sheathing

Draining insulation

Vapor diffusion retarder protecting interior cladding

Condensation

Opening at base of wall

Flashing to drain wall cavity

Note: The drain screen concept shown here has been applied and proven effective in commercial structures. This figure illustrates the drain screen concept applied to a wood frame structure. Although this is not considered a conventional technique in wood frame walls, further development of the concept may prove useful in moisture control.

Figure 3-16: Conceptual illustration of the drain screen technique applied to a wood frame wall.

Wall Assemblies in Cooling Climates

The behavior of moisture in wall assemblies in cooling climates transported by vapor diffusion, rain, capillarity, and air movement is discussed in the beginning of this section. This is followed by a graphical analysis method that identifies the potential for condensation. Then, schematic diagrams of moisture mechanisms in wall assemblies are presented. Finally, there is a summary of moisture control strategies for wall design in cooling climate conditions.

VAPOR DIFFUSION IN COOLING CLIMATE WALL ASSEMBLIES

In cooling climates, vapor diffusion as a moisture transport mechanism should be a major concern to builders and designers. Vapor pressure differences between conditioned spaces and the exterior are often greater than those typically found in heating climates. For example, the vapor pressure difference between the exterior design dew point temperature in Miami (79 degrees Fahrenheit, 2.49 kPa) and an interior air conditioned space (55 degree Fahrenheit dew point temperature, 1.50 kPa) is 0.97 kPa. In Minneapolis, with a heating design temperature of minus 16 degrees Fahrenheit (0.06 kPa) and an interior space conditioned to 70 degrees Fahrenheit at 35 percent relative humidity (0.93 kPa), the vapor pressure difference is 0.87 kPa. The cooling

climate vapor pressure difference is 15 percent larger than the vapor pressure difference in the heating climate. While the cooling climate vapor pressures are more significant, measures to control vapor diffusion are more commonly accepted by the building community in heating climates.

Figure 3-17 illustrates a concrete masonry wall with a brick veneer. Gypsum board covered with a relatively permeable latex paint is installed over furring to the interior of the masonry. The conditioned space is cooled by an air conditioning system and operates at a temperature of 75 degrees Fahrenheit and a relative humidity of 60 percent (a 60 degree Fahrenheit dew point). Assume exterior conditions during the month of July to be 80 degrees Fahrenheit and 75 percent relative humidity (a 71 degree Fahrenheit dew point temperature). To simplify matters, assume that the wall is constructed airtight and that no air pressure difference exists between the interior and exterior of the wall—this eliminates air movement as a moisture transport mechanism. In addition, wall convection effects will be ignored.

In this example, vapor diffusion will move moisture from the vented air space behind the brick veneer on the exterior through the concrete masonry block to the furring strip side of the interior gypsum board. To further simplify matters, assume that temperature and moisture conditions in the air space behind the brick veneer are approximated by exterior conditions as a result of the vented nature of the cavity. If the exterior surface (furring strip

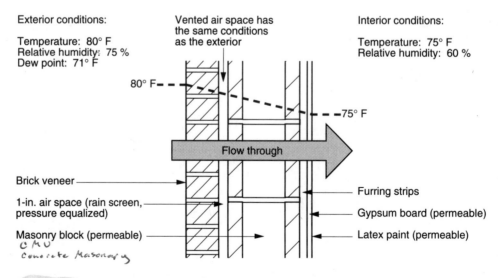

Figure 3-17: Moisture movement by diffusion in a cooling climate masonry wall.

side) of the gypsum board is below the dew point temperature of the air/vapor mix at the surface, the vapor may condense to liquid.

In this particular example, the dew point temperature of the exterior air/vapor mix is approximately 71 degrees Fahrenheit. Condensation is not likely, as the interior space is conditioned to 75 degrees Fahrenheit and the gypsum board interior sheathing will likely be slightly higher in temperature. However, if a supply air diffuser is positioned such that air conditioned air below 71 degrees Fahrenheit is blown against the gypsum board surface, localized cooling may be sufficient to cause condensation.

Vapor diffusion will transport moisture across the furring strip air space, through the gypsum board to the interior paint film. If the rate of moisture transmission across the interior paint film is greater than the rate of moisture transmission through the gypsum board to the paint film, moisture will not accumulate at the gypsum board/paint film interface. Under the conditions described, assuming a vapor permeable interior latex paint, moisture is not likely to accumulate at the paint film. The moisture will "flow through" the wall assembly into the conditioned space and be removed from the building by the dehumidification capabilities of the air conditioning system.

Effect of Interior Temperature and Moisture Conditions

If the interior space is operated at drier conditions, such as an interior temperature of 75 degrees Fahrenheit and 50 percent relative humidity, the rate at which moisture will migrate inward under the action of vapor diffusion will increase. Although the interior paint film is relatively vapor permeable, the rate at which moisture arrives at the paint film through the gypsum board may be greater than the rate at which it passes through the paint film. This becomes more of a concern as the exterior temperature and relative humidity rise (increasing the exterior vapor pressure), thus increasing the dew point temperature of the exterior air.

If the interior space is cooled such that interior conditions are now 70 degrees Fahrenheit and 50 percent relative humidity, the temperature of the gypsum board itself will approach the dew point temperature of the exterior air, and condensation may be possible at the furring strip side of the gypsum board.

Overcooling of conditioned spaces in cooling climates typically occurs as occupants

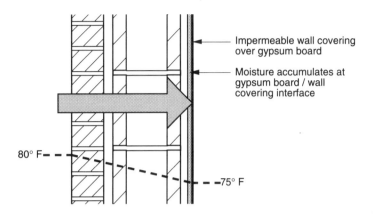

Figure 3-18: Moisture accumulation within wall assembly caused by impermeable interior surface finish material.

attempt to increase the moisture removal capability of air conditioning systems by increasing run time. Although this does result in greater removal of moisture from the air within the conditioned space, it also results in an increased rate at which moisture is drawn into the conditioned space through the building envelope. As interior surfaces drop below exterior dew point temperatures, condensation becomes likely. Problems will also occur if interior surface finishes are not sufficiently vapor permeable to permit the increased moisture to flow through the assembly.

Effect of Permeability of Interior Finishes

If the interior permeable latex paint finish in Figure 3-17 is replaced with an impermeable surface finish such as a vinyl wall covering (Figure 3-18), "flow through" of water vapor by diffusion will not occur and moisture will accumulate at the interface of the wall covering and the gypsum board. Mold and other biological growth can occur under these conditions. Excretions from some forms of growth can react with vinyl wall coverings, resulting in pink "blotches" that show through the finished surfaces.

Reducing the rate of moisture passing through the assembly from the exterior can limit the deleterious effects of impermeable interior surface finishes. This is often attempted by locating vapor diffusion retarders toward the exterior of the wall assembly. In heating climates, the rule of thumb for creating an effective vapor diffusion retarder is that the

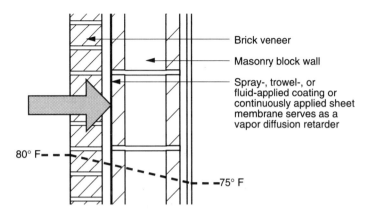

Figure 3-19: Coating or membrane on the exterior of a masonry wall acts as a vapor diffusion retarder.

Brick veneer

Masonry block wall

Spray-, trowel-, or fluid-applied coating or continuously applied sheet membrane serves as a vapor diffusion retarder

80° F

75° F

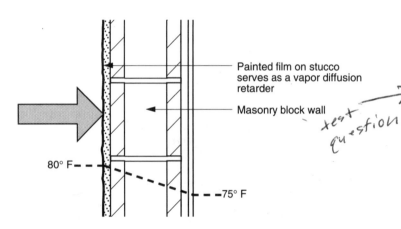

Figure 3-20: Painted film on the exterior surface of stucco applied to a masonry wall acts as a vapor diffusion retarder.

Painted film on stucco serves as a vapor diffusion retarder

Masonry block wall

80° F

75° F

test question

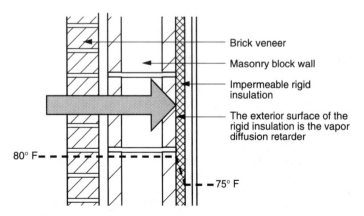

Figure 3-21: Impermeable rigid insulation on the interior of a masonry wall acts as a vapor diffusion retarder.

Brick veneer

Masonry block wall

Impermeable rigid insulation

The exterior surface of the rigid insulation is the vapor diffusion retarder

80° F

75° F

permeability of the cold side of the wall must be five times the permeability of the warm side. Applying this ratio in a cooling climate becomes a daunting task if the proper materials are not used on the interior (cold side). For example, vinyl wall coverings typically have permeabilities of 0.5 perm or less. An exterior vapor diffusion retarder with a permeability of less than 0.1 perm is necessary to maintain the five-to-one ratio. A material applied over the masonry that meets this specification may require proprietary products and application techniques. Even if the ratio is successfully achieved, vapor diffusion from the exterior is only one mechanism of moisture transport to consider. Air-transported moisture is often more significant and also should be considered. Installing impermeable interior surface finishes may not be worth the risk when all factors are considered.

Location of Vapor Retarder

Vapor diffusion into wall assemblies from the exterior in cooling climates can be controlled by installing a vapor diffusion retarder on the warm side of the dew point location within the wall. In practice, the vapor diffusion retarder is typically located to the exterior of the wall on the exterior surface of the concrete masonry block in the form of a spray- or trowel-applied mastic, or an adhered membrane similar to roofing and waterproofing systems (Figure 3-19). One of the most common manifestations of exterior vapor diffusion retarders in southern climates are paint films applied on the exterior of stucco/masonry wall assemblies (Figure 3-20).

The vapor diffusion retarder can also be located to the interior of the concrete masonry block as long as it is still on the warm side of the dew point location. This requirement is met by using an impermeable rigid insulation installed on the interior of a concrete masonry block wall as the vapor diffusion retarder (Figure 3-21). The exterior surface of the rigid insulation (the masonry/rigid insulation interface) is on the warm side of the wall as a result of the thermal resistance characteristics of the rigid insulation. This exterior surface of the rigid insulation acts as the vapor diffusion retarder in this wall assembly.

Effect of Rain and Sun

Wall performance can alter dramatically when an absorptive exterior cladding becomes saturated from rainwater. Consider the effect of rain on the wall in Figure 3-17. Assume the brick veneer becomes saturated from rainwater. The conditions in the air space behind the brick can be approximated by air at a temperature of 80 degrees Fahrenheit and a relative humidity of 100 percent (vapor pressure of 3.56 kPa). This raises the dew point temperature to 80 degrees Fahrenheit and results in more than a 40 percent increase in the effective exterior vapor pressure when the cavity is compared to outside air.

The effect of incident solar radiation on a rain saturated cladding is even more dramatic. Consider that the brick veneer can be readily warmed by the sun well above 120 degrees Fahrenheit. The air in the air space is similarly warmed and can be considered to be at saturated conditions (vapor pressure of 11.74 kPa). This results in an increase of almost 500 percent in the effective exterior vapor pressure (Figure 3-22). Solar radiation is a powerful force that drives moisture in rain-saturated cladding inwards. This force can be ten times greater than the vapor diffusion driving moisture outwards in the most hostile conditions experienced in heating climates.

EFFECT OF CAPILLARITY AND RAIN LEAKAGE

Consider the effect of rain penetration on the wall in Figure 3-17. Assume that due to the lack of a properly functioning rain screen,

rainwater is deposited on the exterior surface of the concrete masonry block. Capillarity will draw water toward the interior. This effect will be superimposed over the inward acting vapor diffusion driving force described earlier and any gravity flow of rainwater which may also be occurring.

When hydrophobic coatings are applied over masonry and brick exterior claddings, they can reduce the amount of rainwater absorbed by the exposed exterior surfaces of the claddings. These coatings, however, are unable to span large pores and openings. Consequently, they are unable to prevent rain penetration at these openings. Rain absorption by exposed surfaces is reduced, but rain entry still occurs. The rainwater which bypasses the hydrophobic coating is driven inwards by solar radiation and vapor pressure differences as well as pulled inwards by capillarity. Hydrophobic coatings are rarely the solution to rain leakage and rain absorption problems.

AIR MOVEMENT IN COOLING CLIMATE WALL ASSEMBLIES

Up to this point, only vapor diffusion, rain leakage, and capillarity as moisture transport wetting mechanisms have been considered. When air movement from the exterior toward the interior is introduced, its effects are combined with those of the other mechanisms.

As in heating climates, when flaws or

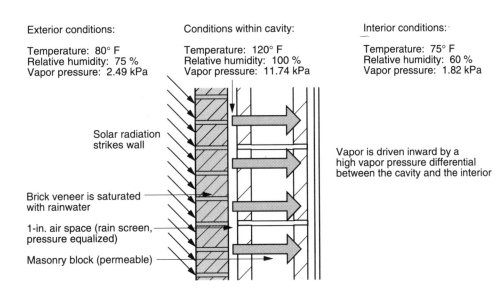

Figure 3-22: Inward moisture movement is increased by solar radiation in a cooling climate.

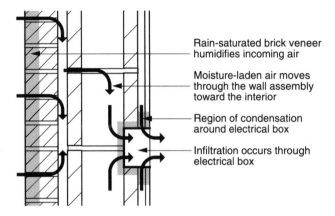

Rain-saturated brick veneer humidifies incoming air

Moisture-laden air moves through the wall assembly toward the interior

Region of condensation around electrical box

Infiltration occurs through electrical box

Figure 3-23: Moisture transport by air movement through a masonry wall with an electrical outlet box.

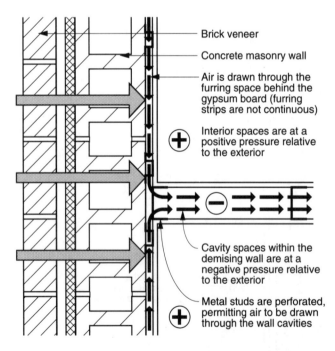

Brick veneer

Concrete masonry wall

Air is drawn through the furring space behind the gypsum board (furring strips are not continuous)

Interior spaces are at a positive pressure relative to the exterior

Cavity spaces within the demising wall are at a negative pressure relative to the exterior

Metal studs are perforated, permitting air to be drawn through the wall cavities

Figure 3-24: Moist outside air can be drawn into the cavities within buildings even though the interior space is positively pressurized. This is caused by negative pressures within wall cavities created by an air handling system with leaky return ducts.

openings exist in a wall assembly coupled with an air pressure difference, air will move through the assembly. If the interior conditioned space is at a lower air pressure than the exterior, the air flow is from the exterior toward the interior. This infiltrating air will carry moisture into the wall assembly assuming the exterior air contains moisture. Whether moisture is deposited within the wall depends on the moisture content and the surface temperature of each material in the wall assembly.

When air movement occurs within wall assemblies, moisture condenses and accumulates in a manner similar to the vapor diffusion examples described previously. As in the heating climate examples, where air movement exists it tends to dominate vapor diffusion, and has a significantly greater effect on moisture transfer into building assemblies than vapor diffusion when both are present.

Figure 3-23 illustrates the effect of infiltrating air through an electrical outlet box in a concrete masonry block wall assembly. The effect of air leakage on the wetting of the wall assembly is significantly magnified as a result of rain wetting the exterior cladding. The rain-saturated building elements "humidify" the infiltrating air as it passes through, over, or around them.

In an effort to reduce the effect of infiltrating moisture-laden air, designers and builders attempt to pressurize building enclosures relative to the exterior. In concept, this strategy is a good one. Unfortunately, field experience has shown numerous examples where even though building enclosures have been pressurized relative to the exterior, building envelope interstitial spaces have been depressurized (Figure 3-24).

Building mechanical systems can succeed in pressurizing building enclosures relative to the exterior with conditioned air. However, duct leakage from return systems and air handlers enclosed in building cavities and service chases can succeed in depressurizing demising walls and other interstitial cavities. If these cavities are connected to the exterior they become pathways for infiltrating hot, humid air. As this air is cooled on its inward journey, moisture can be deposited on the surfaces within these cavities. Once moisture is deposited on these surfaces, vapor diffusion attempts to pull the moisture into the conditioned spaces. If interior surface finishes retard this inward migration, serious problems can occur.

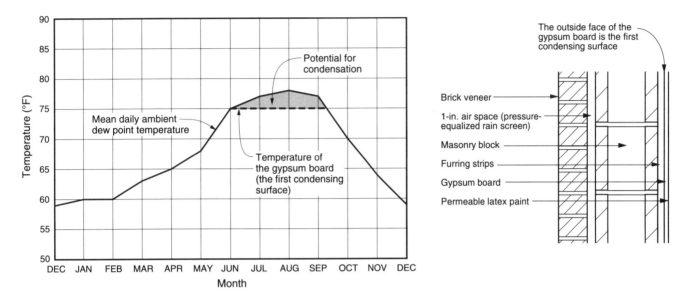

Figure 3-25: Potential for condensation in a masonry wall in Miami, Florida.

ANALYSIS OF CONDENSATION POTENTIAL IN COOLING CLIMATE WALLS

In order to understand the potential for condensation in this climate, a graphical analysis method is presented. This is similar to the method described previously for heating climates. The masonry wall with a brick veneer shown in Figure 3-17 can be used to illustrate a potential condensation problem. Gypsum board covered with a relatively permeable latex paint is installed over furring to the interior of the masonry.

In this example, the wall is located in Miami, Florida. Figure 3-25 plots mean daily ambient dew point temperature over a one-year period in Miami. To simplify matters, assume that the temperature of the interior gypsum board is approximately equivalent to the interior temperature of the conditioned space, and that the temperature of the gypsum board is uniform through its thickness. The horizontal line in Figure 3-25 plots the temperature of the gypsum board. The exterior surface (furring strip side) of the gypsum board represents the location of the first condensing surface in the wall assembly. In other words, whenever the exterior surface of the gypsum board is below the temperature of the mean

daily ambient dew point temperature, the potential for condensation exists at this surface (should moisture be permitted to migrate from the exterior via vapor diffusion and/or air movement).

Figure 3-25 is similar to Figure 3-5 in the previous section which illustrates the potential for condensation in a wood frame wall cavity in Chicago, Illinois. There are some key differences, however. For cooling climates, the mean ambient dew point temperature is plotted rather than the mean daily ambient temperature. The condensing surface is the exterior surface of interior sheathing (gypsum board) and is approximated by the interior temperature, rather than the interior surface of the exterior sheathing approximated by the exterior temperature as was the case in the heating climate example. Finally, the shaded area above the horizontal line (the temperature of the condensing surface, typically the exterior surface of the interior gypsum board) represents the potential for condensation in cooling climates, whereas in heating climates it is the shaded area below the horizontal line (dew point temperature of the interior air/vapor mix).

In both approaches the potential for condensation is represented by shaded areas located between a line corresponding to dew point temperatures of an air/vapor mix and a line corresponding to a condensing surface temperature. In cooling climates the air/vapor mix representing the moisture source is found exterior to the conditioned space. In heating climates the air/vapor mix representing the moisture source is found within the conditioned space.

In Figure 3-25 it is clear that the dew point temperature of the ambient air rises above the temperature of the interior gypsum board in early June and does not drop below it until late September. The shaded area represents the potential for condensation should moisture from the exterior reach the exterior surface of the interior gypsum board. If openings exist in this wall assembly and if an air pressure difference exists to draw exterior moisture inwards, this wall with likely suffer serious distress.

In the following section, strategies for moisture control in wall assemblies in cooling climates are described. This graphical analysis of condensation will illustrate how some of the strategies minimize or eliminate the potential for condensation.

SCHEMATIC DIAGRAM OF MOISTURE BEHAVIOR IN COOLING CLIMATE WALLS

In summary, considering rain, capillarity, vapor diffusion, and air leakage as moisture transport wetting mechanisms, it is clear that condensation, capillarity/absorption (storage), liquid flow (drainage), air movement (re-evaporation), and diffusion can all occur (singly or in concert) at each of the following interfaces:

1. Exterior face of the brick veneer

2. Interior face of the brick veneer

3. Exterior face of the masonry block

4. Interior face of the masonry block

5. Cavity face of the interior gypsum board

6. Interior paint film/gypsum board interface

This is presented schematically in Figure 3-26. What happens at each interface depends on many factors including: (1) the material

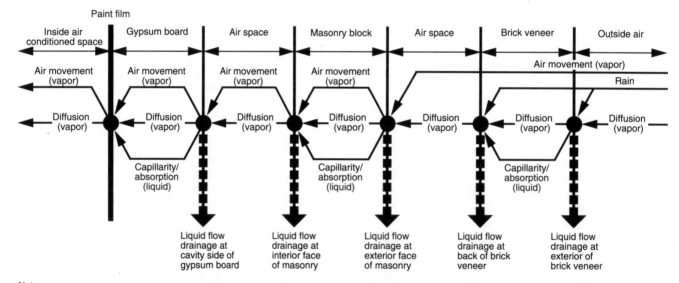

Notes:
1. The rain screen in this example is assumed to function effectively—there is no rain leakage to the masonry block.
2. An exterior vapor retarder is not installed on the exterior of the masonry block.

Figure 3-26: Schematic of moisture transport wetting mechanisms in a masonry wall with brick veneer in a cooling climate.

properties of the components of the wall assembly, (2) the geometry of the assembly itself, (3) the interior and exterior environmental conditions (temperature, vapor pressure, rain, solar radiation, and air pressure differences or driving forces), and (4) the length of time being considered. It is also important to note that the interior and exterior environmental conditions are dynamic, not static, which further complicates matters.

MOISTURE CONTROL STRATEGIES FOR WALLS IN COOLING CLIMATES

As shown in Table 3-2, control strategies for alleviating moisture problems in wall assemblies in cooling climates (as in heating climates) fall into three groups: (1) control of moisture entry, (2) control of moisture accumulation, and (3) removal of moisture. As in heating climates, control of moisture entry has traditionally proven to be the most effective. However, both control of moisture accumulation and removal of moisture have also proven successful.

In this section, the wall design strategies are illustrated with cooling climate examples. In some cases, the wall design strategies for mixed climates are similar in concept to these cooling climate approaches; however, they may differ slightly in actual practice.

Approach 1: Control rain via rain screen or barrier wall

The first approach is to keep rainwater out of building assemblies. The most successful rain control mechanism is the rain screen. To be effective, the rain screen requires a clear air space behind a cladding connected to the free stream air. Furthermore, the back of the air space must be substantially tighter than the cladding so that the air pressure drop across the wall assembly occurs at a location inward of the cladding. In order to facilitate this air pressure drop, the exterior cladding is vented or connected to the air space immediately behind it. Finally, the air space must be drained (usually with the use of flashings) to the exterior. Figure 3-27 illustrates the key elements of this approach. The cement parge coat is a significant component in the success of this strategy. The masonry wall can be tightened by other means such as adhered, trowelled-on, or torched-on sheet membranes. Where sheet membranes are used, provision

Table 3-2: Moisture control strategies for wall assemblies in cooling climates.

Control of Moisture Entry

1. Control rain via rain screen or barrier wall.

2. Provide a capillary break.

3. Install vapor diffusion retarder on the exterior (warm side).

4. Eliminate air inlet openings.

5. Control air pressure differentials.

Control of Moisture Accumulation

6. Raise the temperature of interstitial condensing surfaces located on the interior.

Removal of Moisture

7. Remove moisture by vapor diffusion (permit vapor to flow through and be removed by dehumidification capability of air conditioning system).

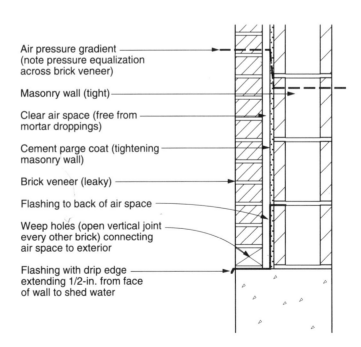

Air pressure gradient (note pressure equalization across brick veneer)

Masonry wall (tight)

Clear air space (free from mortar droppings)

Cement parge coat (tightening masonry wall)

Brick veneer (leaky)

Flashing to back of air space

Weep holes (open vertical joint every other brick) connecting air space to exterior

Flashing with drip edge extending 1/2-in. from face of wall to shed water

Figure 3-27: Rain screen approach to control rain entry in a brick veneer wall.

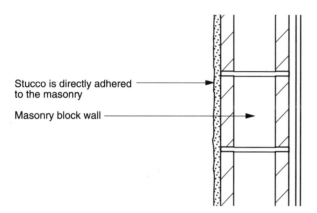

Stucco is directly adhered to the masonry

Masonry block wall

Figure 3-28: Barrier approach to control rain entry by use of traditional stucco.

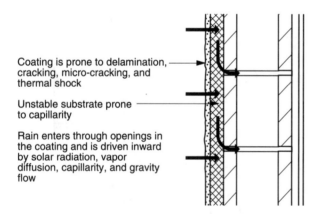

Coating is prone to delamination, cracking, micro-cracking, and thermal shock

Unstable substrate prone to capillarity

Rain enters through openings in the coating and is driven inward by solar radiation, vapor diffusion, capillarity, and gravity flow

Figure 3-29: Barrier approach to control rain entry using an external insulated finish system (EIFS).

for brick ties becomes a consideration. Building papers have proven woefully inadequate in this application, and should be avoided.

The barrier wall approach (face-sealing, weatherproofing) has been traditionally employed in cooling climates in the form of a masonry wall clad with a traditional stucco (Figure 3-28). The key to performance is eliminating all openings where rainwater may enter. This approach is more dependent on workmanship, materials, and maintenance than the rain screen.

A variation of the traditional stucco cladding/masonry wall is the use of proprietary synthetic stuccos over rigid insulation. These systems are commonly referred to as external insulated finish systems or EIFS. Generally, they have not proven successful in controlling rain. One of the principle attractive features of EIFS to designers and builders has been the thermal performance benefits of the exterior rigid insulation. The irony is that the external rigid insulation is one of the major contributing flaws to most EIFS problems. The rigid insulation in most EIFS installations is not as stable a substrate as masonry block in traditional stucco installations.

The EIFS coatings allow rain entry through poor control joints, sealant failures, micro-cracking, and thermal shock coating failure. Coatings are also prone to delamination as a result of their vapor permeability/impermeability characteristics. Once rainwater penetrates coating surfaces, many rigid insulations are susceptible to capillary transport. Capillary transport coupled with gravity flow of rainwater at delamination locations allows major movement of moisture into building assemblies (Figure 3-29). Where such systems are installed over gypsum board in place of masonry, catastrophic failure occurs. Face-sealed or barrier wall EIFS installations should be avoided where it rains.

Approach 2: Provide a capillary break

The second approach involves provision of a capillary break. In brick veneer installations, the air space behind the brick veneer is an effective capillary break (Figure 3-30). In stucco installations the paint coating applied over the stucco can act as a capillary break (Figure 3-31). Finally, rigid insulation installed in a continuous manner to the interior of an assembly can also act as a capillary break (Figure 3-32).

Approach 3: Install vapor diffusion retarder

The third approach involves installing a vapor diffusion retarder. Vapor diffusion into wall assemblies from the exterior in cooling climates can be controlled by installing a vapor diffusion retarder on the warm side of the dew point location within the wall. In brick veneer systems, a coating can be applied on the exterior of the masonry block wall over the cement parge coat (Figure 3-30). As an alternative, a spray- or trowel-applied mastic, or an adhered membrane similar to roofing and waterproofing systems, can be used in place of the cement parge coat and coating. Paint films applied on the exterior of stucco/masonry wall assemblies also can act as vapor diffusion retarders (Figure 3-31). The vapor diffusion retarder can also be located to the interior of the concrete masonry block as long as it is still on the warm side of the dew point location. This requirement is met by using an impermeable rigid insulation installed on the interior of a concrete masonry block wall as the vapor diffusion retarder (Figure 3-32). The exterior surface of the rigid insulation (the masonry/rigid insulation interface) is on the warm side of the wall as a result of the thermal resistance characteristics of the rigid insulation. This exterior surface of the rigid insulation acts as the vapor diffusion retarder in this wall assembly.

Approach 4: Eliminate air inlet openings

The fourth approach is to eliminate the air inlet openings. One method is to seal the exterior of masonry walls with a stucco finish and to connect this stucco finish to air leakage control strategies employed at roofs and/or ceilings. Another approach is to install air retarder systems (air barrier membranes) on the exterior of masonry walls. In wood frame construction, sealing the exterior sheathing to wall framing has proven successful. If there are no openings for the exterior air to pass through, the air will not carry moisture into the assembly.

In cooling climates, control of air transported moisture through the elimination of openings has not been successful if air pressure differences are not also controlled. Even under the most stringent workmanship requirements, all openings in a building envelope cannot be eliminated. When the realities of long-term performance and maintenance requirements of building envelope seals are considered, air

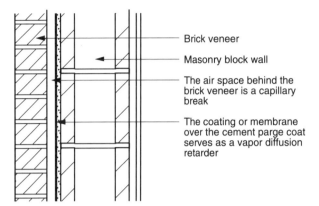

Figure 3-30: Capillary break and vapor diffusion retarder in an uninsulated masonry wall with brick veneer.

Brick veneer

Masonry block wall

The air space behind the brick veneer is a capillary break

The coating or membrane over the cement parge coat serves as a vapor diffusion retarder

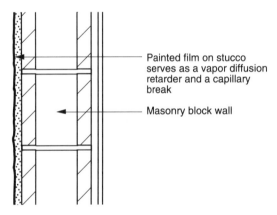

Figure 3-31: Capillary break and vapor diffusion retarder in an uninsulated masonry wall with stucco.

Painted film on stucco serves as a vapor diffusion retarder and a capillary break

Masonry block wall

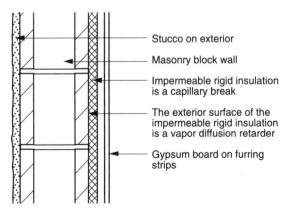

Figure 3-32: Capillary break and vapor diffusion retarder in a masonry wall with stucco and interior insulation.

Stucco on exterior

Masonry block wall

Impermeable rigid insulation is a capillary break

The exterior surface of the impermeable rigid insulation is a vapor diffusion retarder

Gypsum board on furring strips

leakage control must be implemented along with strategies to control air pressure differences in order to have effective performance.

Approach 5: Control air pressure differential

The fifth approach is to control the pressure differential across the wall assembly. Building enclosures can be pressurized by introducing more air from the exterior than is extracted from conditioned spaces. This make-up air should be conditioned (cooled and dehumidified) prior to introduction into the conditioned space, and should more than replace air extracted by other enclosure exhaust systems or air consuming devices. Building enclosure conditioning strategies which rely on central exhaust systems and make-up air introduced via through-the-wall units (packaged terminal heat pumps—PTHP's) should be avoided.

Negative air pressures within interstitial spaces can occur as a result of leakage of both return and supply ductwork of air handling systems. Leaky supply system ductwork located in unconditioned spaces can lead to negative air pressures in utility rooms or chases which contain air handling equipment. These chases and utility rooms are typically connected to demising walls and other interstitial building cavities. Negative air pressure fields in interstitial spaces can extend great distances away from air handling equipment due to the perforated nature of most framing systems coupled with electrical, plumbing, and mechanical servicing.

Since traditional air balancing testing is limited to the measurement of air flows into and out of supply and return registers, it is ineffectual at identifying duct leakage and air pressure relationships in building conditioned spaces and cavities. Air pressures are not measured in this process. Furthermore, subtracting the sum of return flows from the sum of supply flows will not determine quantities of outside air or air pressure relationships since duct leakage is not considered.

Due to the major impact on durability, health, and performance that adverse pressure relationships can create, building envelopes and mechanical systems should be commissioned prior to occupancy. Air pressure measurements of building cavities and conditioned spaces should occur.

Approach 6: Raise the temperatures of interstitial condensing surfaces

The sixth approach is to control the temperatures of the interstitial condensing surfaces. In cooling climates, condensing surfaces are typically the interior gypsum board. If the temperature of the interior gypsum board is raised above exterior dew point temperature, condensation can be controlled. This can be done in two ways—by raising the interior air temperature, or by installing insulation in the wall assembly to raise the temperature of the first condensing surface.

Figure 3-33 illustrates the case of a wall experiencing condensation as a result of overcooling. By raising the interior conditioned space temperature, the temperature of the first condensing surface is raised. Consequently, as the graph in Figure 3-33 shows, the potential for condensation is eliminated in this climate.

Figure 3-34 illustrates the case of a wall experiencing condensation as a result of diffusion in a particularly severe cooling climate (Miami, Florida). By using impermeable rigid insulation (approximately R-7) on the interior of the masonry wall, the temperature of the first condensing surface is raised. As shown in the graph in Figure 3-34, condensation potential is eliminated since the temperature of the exterior face of the rigid insulation (the first condensing surface) is above the ambient range throughout the year.

Approach 7: Remove moisture by vapor diffusion

The seventh approach is to remove moisture from wall assemblies by relying on vapor diffusion. This strategy is referred to as *flow through*. If the rate of moisture transmission across the interior cladding (gypsum board) and interior finish is greater than the rate of moisture supply to the gypsum board, moisture will not accumulate in the gypsum board or at the interior finish. The moisture will "flow through" the wall assembly into the conditioned space and be removed from the building by the dehumidification capabilities of the air conditioning system. This strategy relies on permeable interior surface finishes and a low rate of moisture entry. When used with the previously discussed approaches for moisture entry control, this approach can be very effective.

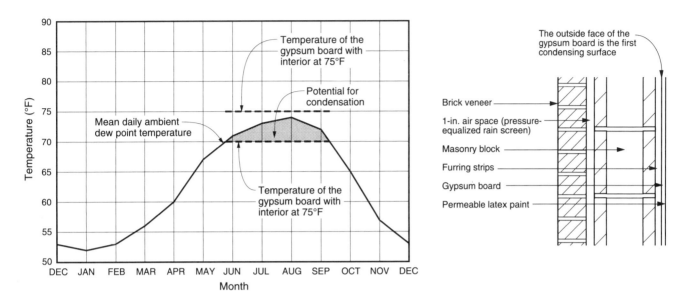

Figure 3-33: Potential for condensation in a masonry wall cavity in Tampa, Florida. By raising the temperature of the interior conditioned space from 70° F to 75° F, the temperature of the first condensing surface (the outside surface of the gypsum board) is raised above the mean daily ambient dew point temperature so that no condensation will occur.

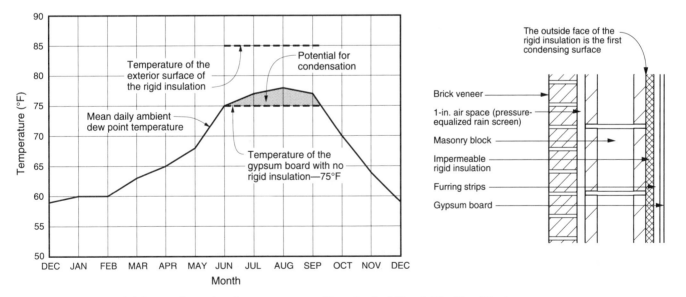

Figure 3-34: Potential for condensation in a masonry wall cavity in Miami, Florida. Placing rigid insulation on the interior of the masonry wall raises the temperature of the first condensing surface above the mean daily ambient dew point temperature so that no condensation will occur. The outside surface of the rigid insulation becomes the first condensing surface in this assembly.

Moisture Behavior in Roof Assemblies

This section describes the key moisture transport mechanisms that may affect roof assemblies—vapor diffusion and air movement. Examples in this section are mostly based on heating climate conditions, although some cooling climate examples and conditions are also addressed. Chapters 5 and 6 illustrate mixed and cooling climate roof assembly designs.

VAPOR DIFFUSION

Figure 3-35 illustrates an attic assembly located in a heating climate (Chicago). Gypsum board covered with a relatively vapor permeable latex paint is installed to the underside of the bottom chords of wood roof trusses. Ceiling insulation consists of unfaced fiberglass batts of thermal resistance R-30. The roof sheathing is plywood, and the roof assembly is not deliberately vented. The conditioned space operates at a high interior vapor pressure (50 percent relative humidity at 70 degrees Fahrenheit). Assume that the ceiling gypsum board has been installed in an airtight manner, and that no attic bypasses exist. Thus, no flaws or openings between the conditioned space and the unconditioned attic are present which would allow for air movement through the attic ceiling. Furthermore, assume that no air pressure difference exists between the interior conditioned space and the unconditioned attic in order to eliminate air movement as a moisture transport mechanism.

Vapor diffusion, during the heating season, will move moisture from the interior conditioned space through the painted ceiling gypsum board and into the ceiling fiberglass batt insulation. The first surface below the dew point temperature that this vapor comes in contact with is the underside of the roof sheathing (Figure 3-35).

If the roof sheathing is wood, this moisture is absorbed by the wood sheathing until the storage capability of the wood is exceeded and

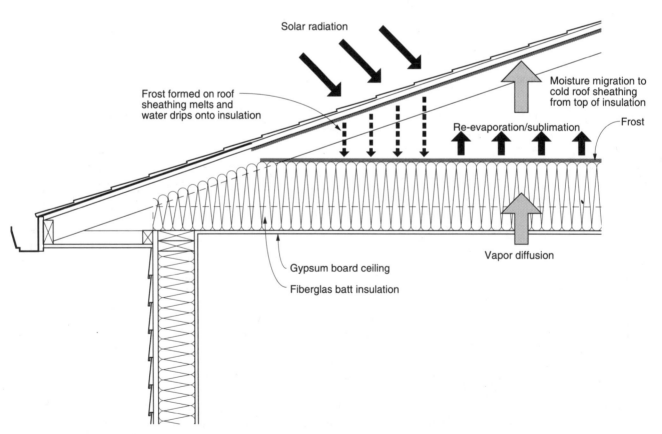

Figure 3-35: Moisture transport wetting mechanisms in a roof assembly.

the moisture subsequently accumulates on the interior surface of the roof sheathing in the form of frost or condensation. Dripping of condensed moisture (or frost melted by solar radiation) from the underside of the roof sheathing is common, and the wetting of ceiling insulation follows (Marshall 1983). It is interesting to note that this wetting of the insulation is from above (the dripping of condensed moisture from the underside of roof sheathing) rather than from below (vapor diffusion from the interior), although in this case the original moisture source was from the interior conditioned space below. When solar radiation elevates the temperature of the sheathing so that it is above the temperature of the upper surface of the ceiling insulation, moisture can also be driven from the underside of the roof sheathing into the attic space.

Serious problems can occur if the amount of moisture reaching the roof sheathing and roof framing members (1) exceeds the ability of these members to absorb moisture without the potential for decay (greater than 30 percent moisture content by weight), and (2) remains there long enough under conditions which will support decay.

Attic Ventilation

The most traditional and widespread vapor diffusion control strategy is roof/attic ventilation. In this approach, moisture enters the attic from below, mixes with the air in the attic space, and is removed by ventilation. Specific air inlet and outlet openings are provided for this ventilation air flow. The size and location of the ventilation openings are typically specified in standards and codes. The requirements are usually presented as a ratio of free vent area to insulated ceiling area, with half the vent area located at the upper portion of the attic and the remainder at the soffit areas. The most common value specified is 1 square foot of vent area for every 300 square feet of insulated ceiling area, or a ratio of 1:300. No additional measure is introduced in most cases to provide for an operative pressure difference across these openings to ensure flow, other than the effect of wind or the difference in height, and the inferred stack effect when the attic space and the outdoor air are at different temperatures.

Location of Vapor Retarder

A further traditional vapor diffusion control strategy, as in the wall example, is the

installation of a vapor diffusion retarder. In practice, this ceiling vapor diffusion retarder can be installed at one or more of the following locations:

1. Between the ceiling gypsum board and the bottom cords of roof trusses or the underside of the roof rafters (sheet polyethylene, aluminum foil, rigid impermeable insulation)

2. On the interior surface of the roof insulation (backed batt insulation)

3. On the attic side of the ceiling gypsum board (foil-backed gypsum board)

4. Within the ceiling gypsum board (vapor barrier gypsum board)

5. On the interior surface of the ceiling gypsum board (vapor barrier paint, low permeability wall coverings)

These vapor diffusion retarders are usually required by building codes to have a permeability of 1 perm or less.

AIR MOVEMENT

When air movement from the interior is introduced to the roof assembly described in Figure 3-35, its effects can be superimposed over those of vapor diffusion in a manner similar to the previous wall examples. Like the wall examples, where air movement exists as a moisture transport mechanism, it tends to dominate vapor diffusion. Moisture deposition/accumulation from air movement is usually concentrated at surfaces adjacent or opposite to flaws and openings.

MOISTURE CONTROL STRATEGIES FOR ROOFS

The key to understanding, predicting, and controlling moisture accumulation in roof assemblies, as in wall assemblies, is understanding the moisture balance, or the rate of moisture entry compared with the rate of moisture removal. Eight basic moisture control strategies for roof assemblies are shown in Table 3-3. As with other building assemblies, the control strategies which can be implemented to alleviate the roof moisture problems fall into three groups: (1) control of moisture entry, (2) control of moisture accumulation, and (3) removal of moisture.

Moisture can enter a roof assembly in four ways: (1) from the exterior by gravity (roof leaks), (2) from the exterior by air transport (ventilation), (3) from the interior by vapor diffusion, and (4) from the interior by air transport.

The strategies in this section are illustrated primarily with heating climate examples. While similar in concept to heating climate approaches, the strategies for mixed and cooling climates may be different in actual practice. Chapter 4 shows a series of roof assembly designs appropriate for heating climates, while Chapters 5 and 6 show assembly designs for mixed and cooling climates.

Approach 1: Prevent roof leaks

The most obvious and most significant approach to roof moisture control is to prevent roof leakage. Roof leaks are typically addressed as the first priority, and they make other moisture entry mechanisms comparatively insignificant. For example, ventilation or any other moisture removal mechanism designed to control moisture accumulation from roof leaks is not practical. This is because the rate of moisture entry through leaks is typically much greater than the rate of removal by ventilation.

Table 3-3: Moisture control strategies for roof assemblies.

Control of Moisture Entry

1. Eliminate roof leaks (gravity).

2. Reduce moisture entry by not ventilating roof assemblies in extreme climates.

3. Reduce moisture entry by vapor diffusion (installing an interior vapor diffusion retarder).

4. Eliminate air inlet, outlet or air flow paths/openings.

5. Reduce moisture in the interior air.

6. Control air pressure differentials.

Control of Moisture Accumulation

7. Raise the temperatures of potential condensing surfaces in roof assemblies.

Removal of Moisture

8. Remove moisture by air movement (ventilation).

Approach 2: Avoid roof assembly ventilation in extreme climates

The second approach to roof moisture control is to avoid ventilating roof assemblies under conditions where ventilation brings moisture from the exterior. Such conditions may be prevalent in extreme climates, such as hot, humid coastal regions where extensive mechanical cooling occurs, and cold, hostile, arctic, and subarctic climates with heavily insulated roof assemblies.

In hot, humid climates the ambient air often contains more moisture than the air within the roof assembly or cavity during cooling periods, especially during evenings or cloudy, overcast days. When this is the case, roof ventilation can bring moisture into the roof assembly or cavity rather than remove it, and it can be a significant causal factor relating to mold and mildew problems on interior gypsum board surfaces. Similarly, crawl space ventilation in hot, humid climates also often brings moisture into crawl spaces. In mixed climates (where both heating and cooling occur for extended periods) and heating climates, ambient humid conditions can also reduce the removal rate from roof assemblies or cavities.

Where attics are framed with wood sheathing, wood rafters, and trusses, these wood materials absorb moisture according to the relative humidity present in the attic, rather than the vapor pressure. Although cold air typically has a low vapor pressure (making it dry in the absolute sense), it normally has a high relative humidity. When exterior cold, dry, low vapor pressure air with a high relative humidity comes in contact with cold roof wood framing, the wood framing absorbs moisture— it does not dry out. In heavily insulated roof assemblies in heating climates, low heat loss results in attic spaces which operate close to exterior temperatures. In this case, both the exterior air entering the attic space (ventilation air) and the roof sheathing are cold. Thus, the ventilation air (with a high relative humidity) is bringing moisture into the attic space.

In roof spaces, regardless of the sheathing or framing materials (wood, steel, or other), night sky radiation on a clear winter night can cool roof surfaces and roof decking 10 degrees Fahrenheit or more below exterior ambient conditions (often below the dew point). In such cases, it is typical for moisture to be added to the roof space by air movement from the exterior. For example, the exterior air may be at 15 degrees Fahrenheit with a relative humidity of 80 percent. This corresponds to a vapor pressure of approximately 0.210 kPa. The roof sheathing can be at 0 degrees Fahrenheit due to night sky radiation, and at saturation this temperature corresponds to vapor pressure of approximately 0.110 kPa. This is a lower vapor pressure than the ambient, so air movement from the exterior is actually moving moisture into the attic space, rather than out.

Approach 3: Install vapor diffusion retarder

The third approach to roof moisture control is to install an interior vapor diffusion retarder in a heating climate (Figure 3-36). Moisture from the interior can enter by air transport and vapor diffusion. Although air transport is more significant than vapor diffusion, in many cases vapor diffusion by itself can move sufficient moisture into a roof assembly to create problems.

Vapor diffusion retarders are typically sheet polyethylene (visqueen); however, they may take many other forms such as low permeance paint-on surfaces, backing on insulation batts, foil backing on gypsum board, and low permeance wall and ceiling coverings. The effectiveness of a vapor diffusion retarder is dependent on both its resistance to moisture flow by diffusion (permeability) and its coverage (surface area). In other words, it is a direct or linear function of both surface area and permeability (Fick's Law).

Traditionally, the permeability of a vapor diffusion retarder has been limited to 1 perm or less. Regarding surface area, Fick's Law can be interpreted such that if 95 percent of the surface area of a ceiling or roof assembly is covered with a vapor diffusion retarder, then that vapor diffusion retarder is 95 percent effective. Hence, vapor diffusion retarders need not be perfect to control vapor diffusion. Holes, rips, tears, punctures, and gaps in vapor diffusion retarders need not lead to catastrophic failure if their surface area is small relative to the total surface area of the retarder.

Several coats of paint on the exposed

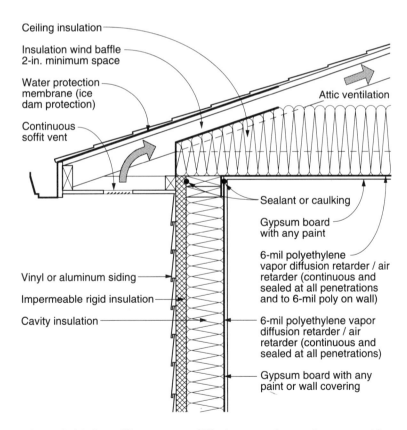

Figure 3-36: Installing a vapor diffusion retarder on the warm side of a roof assembly is a traditional moisture control strategy in heating climates. Air movement is controlled by sealing the interior air retarder to the framing.

surfaces of ceilings are typically satisfactory to control vapor diffusion into roof assemblies in mixed and heating climates. However, paint does not control air-transported moisture into roof assemblies. Paint can act as an effective vapor diffusion retarder, but it cannot act as an air retarder.

Vapor diffusion retarders are often not installed in mixed climates. However, the trends toward higher levels of roof assembly insulation and the subsequent reduction of available energy to evaporate moisture has increased the number of vapor diffusion retarder installations in these climates.

Vapor diffusion retarders are rarely installed in the ceilings of cooling climate enclosures to control moisture entry into roof assemblies from the interior. This is because the moisture flow by diffusion is in the opposite direction. Air movement (attic ventilation) is often responsible for moving moisture from the exterior into the roof assembly (attic). Vapor diffusion and air transport can subsequently move the moisture from within the roof assembly to the interior conditioned space. Vapor moves from the attic to the conditioned space only if the space is air conditioned or otherwise dehumidified.

The recognition that moisture flows from the ventilated attic cavity into the enclosure (and increases the latent cooling load) makes

the installation of ceiling vapor diffusion retarders in cooling climates desirable. Problems can occur, however, if ceiling vapor diffusion retarders are located where they fall below the dew point temperature of the air/vapor mixture in the roof assembly. A traditional heating climate installation with a polyethylene sheet just above the ceiling gypsum board is inappropriate under these conditions. When the interior space is air conditioned, the polyethylene sheet is on the cold side of the assembly—not the warm side as it is in a heating climate installation. This problem can be alleviated by replacing the polyethylene with impermeable rigid insulation. The insulation still acts as a vapor diffusion retarder on the interior side of the assembly; however, it also raises the temperature of the first condensing surface—making condensation less likely. This technique is discussed further and illustrated under Approach 7 in this section.

Approach 4: Eliminate air inlet/outlet openings

The fourth approach to roof moisture control is to eliminate openings that allow air flow from the conditioned space through the ceiling into the roof assembly. Control of openings between the interior conditioned

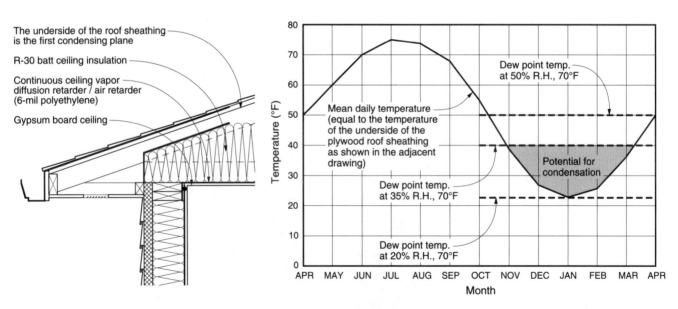

Figure 3-37: Potential for condensation in a roof assembly in Chicago, Illinois. The roof assembly has R-30 fiberglass batt insulation and an unvented attic space. By reducing interior moisture levels, the potential condensation is reduced or eliminated.

Chapter 3—Wetting and Drying of Building Assemblies

space and the roof assembly is one of the most common and most effective techniques for the control of moisture entry from the interior by air transport. Openings are often closed using continuous, sealed, sheet polyethylene and/or continuous sealed gypsum board in new construction (Figure 3-36). In existing construction they are closed with caulks, sealants, and spray foams. Recently, significant success has been reported by utilizing dry blown dense pack cellulose to fill cavities completely in flat roofs (Fitzgerald et al. 1990).

Openings are best controlled at the design stage for new construction. Almost all roof assembly penetrations can be eliminated by relocation (electrical, ductwork) or identified and accommodated (plumbing vents) for sealing during the construction process.

Control of openings in existing roof assemblies is much more difficult than at the design stage for new construction. Success is often determined by roof assembly geometry. If there is access into a roof assembly, then closing openings is possible, but if access is difficult, effective elimination of openings is unlikely. Roof assemblies that have attics of sufficient volume to accommodate tradesmen are readily airtightened from within with simple tools and techniques. The most successful strategies employ fan depressurization/pressurization equipment to identify air leakage sites.

Approach 5: Control moisture in the interior air

The fifth approach to roof moisture control is to control interior moisture levels. Control of interior conditioned space moisture levels can be a very powerful strategy with respect to both vapor diffusion and air transport. If moisture is not present in the first place then there is no moisture for vapor diffusion or air movement to transport. Referring back to the roof assembly shown in Figure 3-35, it is possible to graph the potential condensation (Figure 3-37). If the relative humidity of the interior conditioned space is maintained below 20 percent at 70 degrees Fahrenheit, the dew point temperature of this air/vapor mixture is below the mean daily insulation/sheathing temperature for the year. Similar to the analysis of wall assemblies in the previous section, this approach guarantees no condensation.

Figure 3-37 also indicates the dew point temperature when the space is maintained below 35 percent relative humidity at 70

degrees Fahrenheit. In this case the condensation potential is reduced but not eliminated. This graphical analysis is a simplification that does not take into account night sky radiation or solar heat gain, thus resulting in a conservative set of assumptions.

Maintaining low interior moisture levels can be accomplished in Chicago with control of moisture sources and with dilution (air change via controlled ventilation). Dilution is more energy intensive than source control. Thus, a significant component of any energy conservation program should be the source control of moisture. The alternatives—uncontrolled ventilation, controlled ventilation, and high evaporation energies (high drying potentials through low insulation levels)—all consume significant amounts of energy.

Approach 6: Control air pressure differentials

The sixth approach to roof moisture control is to control air pressure differentials which act across ceilings. Most building enclosures in heating climates today operate at a positive air pressure relative to roof assemblies due to the stack effect and the pressurization that often occurs with forced air ductwork systems. This positive air pressure difference acts as a driving force for air transport into roof assemblies from the conditioned space. When this conditioned air contains sufficient moisture and roof assembly surfaces are below the dew point temperature of the interior air, moisture problems can occur when the moisture storage capacity of roof assembly materials is finally exceeded. If the air pressure driving force is eliminated, air-transported moisture between the conditioned space and the roof assembly can also be eliminated.

Historically, in building enclosures with fuel-fired combustion appliances coupled to active chimneys, neutral pressure planes were often located above insulated ceilings in roof assemblies, and the conditioned space operated at a negative air pressure relative to the roof assembly. The trend away from active chimneys has eliminated this source of enclosure depressurization. Consequently there has been an increase in roof assembly air-transported moisture problems.

A building enclosure can be deliberately maintained at a slight negative air pressure relative to the roof assembly to control air-transported moisture by the use of exhaust ventilation. However, this is often only practical when the building enclosure is relatively tight. In leaky building enclosures, this strategy would result in excessive exhaust air volume in order to maintain negative pressures in the enclosure and be very wasteful of energy. As mentioned earlier, depressurization strategies must also consider impacts on fuel-fired appliances and the ingress of radon gas.

It is also possible to deliberately maintain a roof assembly at a slight positive air pressure relative to the conditioned space by the use of supply ventilation directly from the exterior into roof assembly cavities. This strategy has proven effective with flat roof cavities where roof vents have been sealed and exterior air is used to pressurize the cavities (see Chapter 2). The pressurization fan typically operates only when the exterior air temperature drops the moisture accumulation surface (usually the roof sheathing) temperatures below the conditioned space dew point temperature. This strategy is not dependent on total enclosure leakiness. However, if overpressurization of the roof cavities leads to significant air flow from the roof cavities into the enclosure, interior enclosure surfaces may be cooled sufficiently to lead to mold, mildew, and surface condensation. Furthermore, it is possible to freeze plumbing within interior partition walls under extreme conditions. Finally, care must be taken not to blow insulation material into the living space.

In building enclosures which contain forced air ductwork, and where supply ducts are not matched to return ducts on a room by room basis, supply air ducts tend to pressurize

conditioned spaces relative to the exterior and roof assemblies. Balancing ductwork and sealing leaky ducts can lead to significant reductions in the air pressure driving forces influencing air-transported moisture.

Approach 7: Control temperatures of condensing surfaces within roof assembly

The seventh approach is to control the temperature of condensing surfaces in roof assemblies. If moisture accumulation surface temperatures do not fall below the interior air dew point temperature, air moisture transport and vapor diffusion are not concerns regardless of interior moisture levels, openings, and air pressures.

Surface relative humidities of 100 percent are typically necessary for wood to decay, and surface relative humidities of greater than 70 percent over an extended period of time are required for surface mold, mildew, and corrosion. Therefore if condensation can be prevented or at least limited in roof assemblies, wood decay can also be prevented. Furthermore, if surface relative humidities can be limited to 70 percent, corrosion and surface mold growth can also be avoided. Condensation on a surface (and surface relative humidity) can be controlled by either limiting the amount of moisture available to that surface, or by controlling the surface temperatures such that condensation does not occur (or occurs in such limited quantities that moisture problems do not occur).

Using thermal insulation to increase roof assembly moisture accumulation surface temperatures can be effective in the prevention of moisture-induced roof deterioration. The most common example of this strategy is the installation of thermal insulation above roof sheathing in flat roofs and cathedral ceiling construction. The insulation raises the surface temperature of the sheathing, which is typically the principle moisture accumulation surface in a roof assembly. The roof membrane is installed either over the top of this thermal insulation or under the thermal insulation directly on the sheathing or structural deck. This last approach, shown in Figure 3-38, is referred to as an inverted roof membrane.

The temperature of the principle moisture accumulation surface in a roof assembly is determined by two characteristics: (1) the temperature difference between the interior conditioned space and the exterior, and (2) the ratio of the amount of thermal insulation

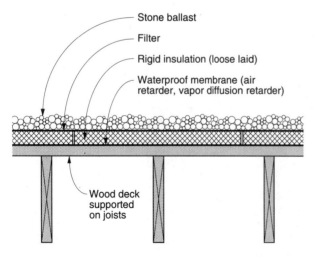

Stone ballast

Filter

Rigid insulation (loose laid)

Waterproof membrane (air retarder, vapor diffusion retarder)

Wood deck supported on joists

Figure 3-38: Inverted roof membrane.

(thermal resistance) to the exterior of the surface compared to the total thermal resistance of the assembly. Surfaces become warmer as the amount of thermal resistance to the exterior of the surface increases, compared to the interior. Condensation will not occur at the roof sheathing if all the thermal insulation is above it. Where all the thermal insulation is below the roof sheathing, condensation can occur if exterior temperatures are sufficiently low and sufficient moisture can reach the sheathing surfaces.

The greater the temperature difference between the interior conditioned space and the exterior, the greater the possibility of surface condensation. Therefore, the possibility of surface condensation on roof assembly surfaces is greater in more hostile climates. Conversely, the more moderate the climate, the less likely surface condensation will occur. Controlling temperatures within assemblies is effective regardless of whether the moisture transport mechanism is vapor diffusion or air transport.

For example, Figure 3-39 illustrates an unvented cathedral ceiling constructed in Chicago, Illinois exposed to the following interior conditions: 70 degrees Fahrenheit with 50 percent relative humidity. The temperature of the insulation/sheathing interface is proportional to the thermal resistance to the exterior of the interface compared with the thermal resistance to the interior of the interface for any given temperature difference. The calculation for determining the dew point temperature at this interface was described in the previous section on wall assemblies.

Figure 3-39 graphically illustrates how the potential for condensation is eliminated at this interface in the wall cavity. If the insulation above the sheathing has a thermal resistance of R-20 or greater, and the cavity insulation is R-19 or less, the insulation/sheathing interface remains above the interior dew point temperature. This roof assembly typically would be constructed as 2 x 6 rafters with 4 inches of rigid insulation to the exterior.

With this type of cathedral ceiling assembly, an interior vapor diffusion retarder or air retarder is not necessary since the temperature of the first condensing surface is controlled. This may not be the most economical cathedral ceiling assembly to build, but it does control condensation under the conditions specified.

A more economical approach may be to limit interior moisture levels to 35 percent relative humidity at 70 degrees (a dew point temperature of approximately 40 degrees) and couple this with an insulating sheathing of

thermal resistance of R-12 or greater, and cavity insulation of thermal resistance of R-28 or less. Figure 3-40 illustrates this roof construction assembly and indicates graphically how the potential condensation in the cavity is eliminated when interior moisture levels are lowered.

The same principle of controlling temperatures of condensing surfaces within roof assemblies in heating climates can be applied in cooling climates. In cooling climates, moisture moves from the hot, humid attic space toward the cooler, air conditioned interior space. Under these conditions, the first condensing surface is typically the attic side of the ceiling gypsum board. The temperature of this condensing surface can be raised by installing impermeable rigid insulation between the ceiling gypsum board and the underside of the roof framing (see Figure 3-41).

Approach 8: Remove moisture by ventilation

Roof ventilation is the most common means of removing moisture from roof assemblies and controlling moisture accumulation. With this approach, ambient air from the exterior enters the roof assembly or cavity and subsequently leaves the roof cavity (Figure 3-42). This approach relies on the ability of exterior ambient air to pick up moisture when it is within the roof assembly and carry it to the exterior. For this approach to be successful, the following conditions must prevail:

1. The ambient, exterior air must be able to pick up moisture when it is within the roof assembly or cavity.

2. The rate of removal of moisture from the roof assembly or cavity must be greater than the rate of moisture accumulation.

The first condition implies that the ambient air is drier than the air within the roof assembly or cavity. When this is the case, and when this is coupled with the second condition, roof ventilation is successful. However, the ambient air is not always drier than the air within the roof assembly or cavity, and ventilation air entering roof assemblies may actually carry moisture into the roof assemblies as discussed previously (see Approach 2).

In well-insulated roofs, sufficient energy may not be available to facilitate moisture evaporation from roof assembly materials. The ability of ambient air to pick up moisture depends on both the amount of moisture already contained in the ambient air and the

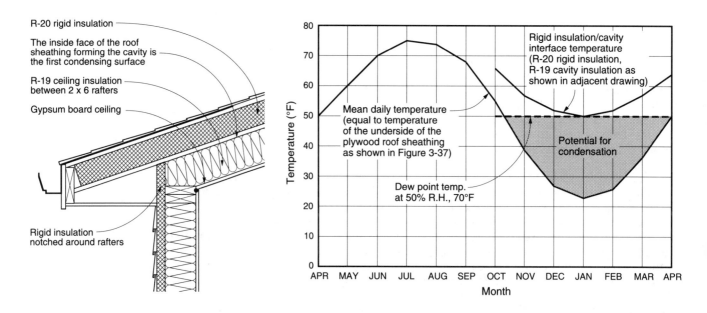

Figure 3-39: Potential for condensation in a roof assembly in Chicago, Illinois. The unvented cathedral ceiling has R-20 rigid insulation above R-19 batt insulation. The R-20 insulating sheathing raises the dew point temperature at the first condensing surface so that no condensation will occur with interior conditions of 50 percent relative humidity at 70 degrees Fahrenheit.

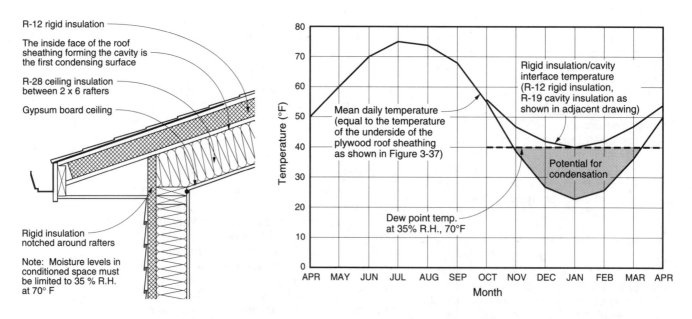

Figure 3-40: Potential for condensation in a roof assembly in Chicago, Illinois. The unvented cathedral ceiling has R-12 rigid insulation above R-28 batt insulation. The R-12 insulating sheathing raises the dew point temperature at the first condensing surface so that no condensation will occur with interior conditions of 35 percent relative humidity at 70 degrees Fahrenheit.

temperature of the ambient air. The colder air is, the less moisture it can hold. Historically, roof assemblies have not contained significant levels of insulation and during heating periods, heat loss from within the conditioned space has warmed roof assemblies and cavities. When cold, ambient air entered these roof assemblies and cavities, it was warmed by the heat loss from the conditioned space, enhancing its ability to pick up moisture. The trend toward higher levels of insulation has reduced the heat or energy flow from the conditioned space and therefore reduced the effectiveness of ventilation in removing moisture from roof assemblies and cavities.

Solar radiation can raise roof cavity and assembly surface temperatures and provide energy for the evaporation of moisture. Roof assemblies that receive direct solar radiation (south-facing surfaces and unshaded roofs) are therefore less prone to moisture problems than other roofs. Similarly, roof assemblies in climatic regions that get a great deal of solar radiation are less prone to moisture problems than those that do not. The same argument holds for roofs constructed with dark surfaces (therefore warmer) compared with light-colored surfaces.

Ventilation is more effective in removing moisture from roof assemblies and cavities where insulation levels are low, or during periods when the ambient air is sufficiently warm and dry to pick up moisture, or when incident solar radiation is intense. Ventilation may not be effective in removing significant amounts of moisture from well-insulated assemblies where the ventilation air remains cold and unable to pick up moisture, or where ambient air is humid and already saturated with moisture. Examples of this can be found in hot humid climates and during humid periods in mixed and heating climates during cloudy or overcast periods.

The second condition listed above relates to moisture balance. Where the rate of moisture entry into a roof assembly or cavity exceeds the rate of moisture removal, moisture accumulates.

If roof assemblies are initially constructed dry and prevented from getting wet during

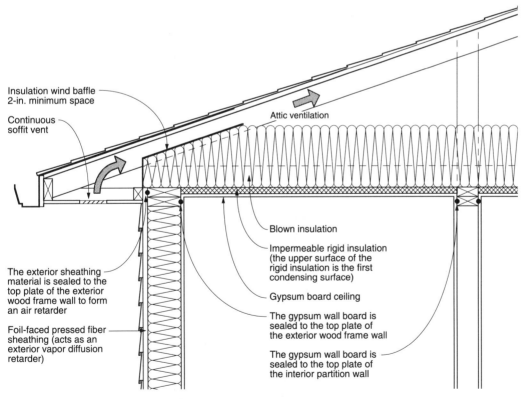

Insulation wind baffle 2-in. minimum space

Continuous soffit vent

Attic ventilation

The exterior sheathing material is sealed to the top plate of the exterior wood frame wall to form an air retarder

Foil-faced pressed fiber sheathing (acts as an exterior vapor diffusion retarder)

Blown insulation

Impermeable rigid insulation (the upper surface of the rigid insulation is the first condensing surface)

Gypsum board ceiling

The gypsum wall board is sealed to the top plate of the exterior wood frame wall

The gypsum wall board is sealed to the top plate of the interior partition wall

Figure 3-41: Roof assembly in a cooling climate utilizing impermeable rigid insulation above the ceiling gypsum board. The rigid insulation acts as a vapor diffusion retarder and raises the temperature of the first condensing surface (the upper surface of the rigid insulation).

service, then the rate of moisture entry is zero, and removal of moisture is not necessary. Unvented roof assemblies have historically proven successful when the moisture entry mechanisms—gravity, vapor diffusion, and air transport (either exterior/ventilation or interior/air leakage)—have been controlled. It is common practice to build unvented flat roof assemblies with air and vapor retarder systems. It is also possible to build unvented cathedral ceilings where air-transported moisture and vapor diffusion are controlled.

Varying degrees of success have been reported where not all the moisture entry mechanisms have been controlled, but moisture removal (ventilation) is used to offset or balance moisture entry (Cleary 1984). Experience has shown that ventilation cannot be relied upon to balance the gravity moisture entry mechanism (roof assemblies leaking rainwater). However, ventilation can balance the vapor diffusion and air transport (interior) moisture entry mechanisms, where the rates of moisture entry and accumulation are low and the rate of moisture removal is high. This is often the case in roof assemblies located in mixed climates. In such climates it has been common to build successfully performing roof assemblies without vapor diffusion retarders and relatively leaky (to air) ceilings. It is important to note that these roof assemblies have typically been constructed with relatively low levels of insulation and that as insulation levels increase, moisture problems may appear.

Experience has shown that where vapor diffusion retarders have been installed, roof assemblies do not need to be ventilated to control vapor diffusion. Experience has also shown that where roof assemblies are constructed tight, roof assemblies do not need to be ventilated to control air-transported moisture from the interior. The question of how "tight" is necessary is important. A psychrometric mixing model can be utilized to indicate the amount of cavity ventilation needed for a given climate when roof assembly leakage areas are known and interior moisture levels are specified (Handegord and Giroux 1984). Unfortunately, roof assembly leakage areas are rarely known, and interior moisture levels are often not limited or controlled.

Several arguments against roof ventilation can be made because of the potential for creating rather than alleviating moisture problems. It should be noted, however, that most local building codes require roof ventilation, and that builders omitting ventilation may be in violation of local code requirements.

Ventilation of well-insulated roof spaces that are over leaky ceilings can actually draw moisture-laden air out of the building enclosure into the cold roof cavity. This is analogous to the problems experienced with the ventilation of wall assemblies. In such a case if

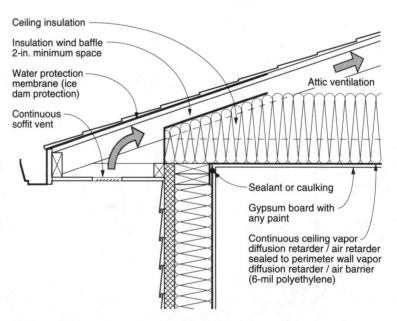

Ceiling insulation

Insulation wind baffle
2-in. minimum space

Water protection
membrane (ice
dam protection)

Continuous
soffit vent

Attic ventilation

Sealant or caulking

Gypsum board with
any paint

Continuous ceiling vapor
diffusion retarder / air retarder
sealed to perimeter wall vapor
diffusion retarder / air barrier
(6-mil polyethylene)

Figure 3-42: Attic ventilation is a traditional moisture control strategy in heating climates.

ventilation were not present, moisture would not be moved into the space due to air movement. If the attic space remains cold due to attic insulation, more moisture will be carried into the attic space as a result of the air pressure difference between the interior conditioned space and attic space. The resultant exfiltration of moisture-laden air through the leaky ceiling will not be removed from the attic by ventilation due to the ineffectiveness of ventilation in cold attics.

Of course, should the ceiling be extremely leaky and the exfiltrating air flow large, the air flow may carry sufficient heat with it to warm the attic to such an extent that the attic ventilation may now be effective. This usually explains the fairly common phenomenon of homeowners' heating bills increasing after the installation of additional attic insulation coupled with attic ventilation and a leaky ceiling. The new attic vents dramatically increase the air leakage into the attic from the house through the leaky ceiling and hence increase the total house air change (Blasnik 1990). The increased energy cost due to the increased air change is often greater than the energy savings from a reduced conductive heat loss.

The magnitude of this effect is even greater if powered or turbine vents are installed. These devices can vent the entire house through the attic if ceilings are leaky. The heat loss is often so great that the house furnace is not large enough to heat the house when the wind is blowing. As a result it is not uncommon to see plastic bags placed over these vents in the winter to stop them from operating. To make these turbine vents cost-effective from an operating perspective, the ceiling has to be tight and additional openings or vents may be necessary to provide make-up air from the exterior for the attic. The irony is that if these two requirements are implemented, a turbine vent is no longer necessary. Powered attic vents, although not practical for heating season moisture control, are often practical for summertime cooling of poorly insulated attics as long as the attic ceiling remains leaky.

Where the turbine vents are coupled with a leaky ceiling during the summer conditions, the turbine vents increase the air change by ventilating the house through the leaky ceiling. Power ventilation in an attic during the summer to reduce cooling loads is not very effective in a house with a tight ceiling, as most of the heat gain in a summer attic is due to radiation. There is poor coupling with the thermal mass of the attic air and the thermal mass of the shingle/sheathing complex. The hot roof sheathing (160 degrees Fahrenheit plus) radiates heat to the top of the attic insulation. High attic air change through turbine ventilation does not provide a significant cooling effect.

ADDITIONAL CONSIDERATIONS RELATED TO ROOF ASSEMBLY VENTILATION

Roofs and roof cavities traditionally have been vented for four reasons:

1. Removal of moisture from assembly cavities, structural members, sheathings, and insulation

2. Enhancement of roofing life span by a reduction of roofing and roof sheathing temperatures

3. Reduction of cooling loads and increased occupant comfort during the cooling season

4. Control of ice damming

Moisture removal has already been examined. Enhancement of roofing life span, cooling load reduction, occupant comfort, and control of ice damming are discussed below.

Enhancement of Roofing Life Span

The surface temperatures of roof membranes, shingles, and sheathings directly influence their service lives. Generally, the higher the surface temperature, the shorter the service life. Roof ventilation has traditionally been employed to control roof membrane, shingle, and sheathing temperatures. Unfortunately, traditional physics and recent evidence question this practice. It has been known for some time (but only recently accepted) that the operating surface temperatures of roof membranes, shingles, and sheathings are far more dependent on their color, orientation, solar intensity, and wind exposure than on roof ventilation (Rose 1991).

Roof membranes and shingles are warmed directly by solar radiation, and transfer heat to sheathings and rigid insulation by conduction. In cavity roof assemblies, the underside of the roof sheathing transfers heat principally by radiation to the top of the insulation. The intervening air in the cavity is typically much cooler than the underside of the sheathing or the upper surface of the insulation due to the radiant heat transfer.

Cavity ventilation can only remove significant heat from the roof assembly and lower shingle, membrane, and sheathing temperatures if good thermal coupling exists between the underside of the sheathing and the air in the cavity. However, this is not the case. A ventilation rate of anywhere from 1 to 15 air changes per hour has a small effect on membrane, shingle, and sheathing temperatures. Typical average air change rates in ventilated roof assemblies range from 3 to 6 air changes per hour over the year (Rose 1991).

Consequently, it does not make sense to ventilate roof assemblies to enhance service life. If service life is a concern, lighter-colored roof membranes and shingles have been shown to have much longer service lives since they maintain lower surface temperatures.

Reduction of Cooling Loads

In some regions, roofs and roof cavities have traditionally been vented to reduce cooling loads during the cooling season. Although roof ventilation has a negligible impact on membrane, shingle, and sheathing operating surface temperatures, roof ventila-tion does affect roof assembly cavity air temperatures and to a lesser extent, the upper surface temperature of cavity insulation. This also affects cooling loads. However, the impact is reduced when the amount of roof insulation and ceiling airtightness are increased.

In roof cavity assemblies which are poorly insulated (less than R-10), ventilation can reduce cooling loads by 25 percent. However, when these assemblies have thermal resis-tances of greater than R-25, ventilation has a negligible effect (Rose 1991). Furthermore, the sensations of comfort that are felt by occupants when roof assemblies are ventilated has been attributed to leaky ceiling assemblies. This occurs where the roof ventilation, in effect, draws warm air out of the conditioned space into the roof cavity. It also chills the ceiling surface.

Ventilation of roof assemblies also has a negligible impact on cooling loads, where roof assemblies are tight and well insulated. Ventilation of roof assemblies that are leaky and poorly insulated has a significant effect on reducing cooling loads, because coupling between the conditioned space and the roof assembly exists. Consequently, this same

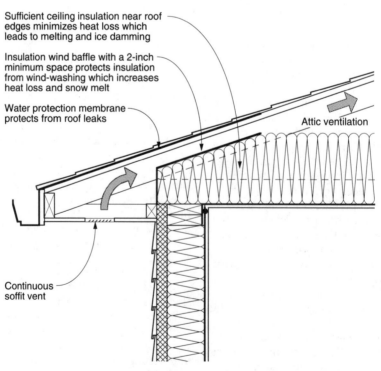

Sufficient ceiling insulation near roof edges minimizes heat loss which leads to melting and ice damming

Insulation wind baffle with a 2-inch minimum space protects insulation from wind-washing which increases heat loss and snow melt

Water protection membrane protects from roof leaks

Attic ventilation

Continuous soffit vent

Figure 3-43: Ice damming can be controlled by providing soffit ventilation with a clear path combined with sufficient insulation at the roof edge.

ventilation is likely to be responsible for drawing warm, interior moisture-laden air from the conditioned space into the roof assembly during the heating season, leading to potential moisture problems if the space is well insulated (low drying potential) and if interior moisture levels are high.

The most effective strategy to reduce cooling loads through a roof assembly is to select reflective roof membranes or shingles, insulate the roof assembly well, and construct the assembly in an airtight manner.

Control of Ice Damming

In heating climates, where sufficient heat loss occurs at the roof perimeter above insulated wall assemblies, ice damming can occur. The heat loss can melt snow on the roof, causing water to run down over the roof overhang, where it can freeze to form a *dam*.

The ice dam causes the water to back up and potentially leak under overlapped shingles and through roof sheathing. This heat loss can occur from either a lack of thermal insulation where exterior walls intersect roof and attic assemblies, or from air leakage up and out of exterior walls.

Continuous soffit ventilation has traditionally been used in heating climates to flush this heat away from the underside of the roof assembly, preventing it from melting accumulated snow on the roof and thus controlling the formation of ice dams. This strategy has proven to be very effective where a clear, continuous 2-inch air space has been provided over the entire roof eave perimeter (Figure 3-43). Ice damming can also be controlled by providing sufficient thermal insulation at the intersection of perimeter walls and ceilings, coupled with controlling air leakage up and out of walls.

CHAPTER 4

Moisture Control Practices for Heating Climates

This chapter includes four major sections that address moisture control practices for heating climates in the United States. First, an introductory section defines the climate, identifies key moisture problems found there, and discusses some general approaches to solving these problems. The last three sections of the chapter address wall, foundation, and roof assemblies. For each component, several construction assemblies designed to control moisture in this climate are shown. There are detailed construction drawings, a list of the key characteristics for each assembly, and a summary discussion of the control strategies for this climate.

Introduction

This climate zone is defined as a heating climate with 4000 heating degree days or greater. Intermittent cooling (air conditioning) typically is necessary. The design/construction practice recommendations in this section pertain to humid heating climates, not to dry heating climates, although no distinction is made between the two in the accompanying map (Figure 4-1). The recommendations in this section will perform satisfactorily in both types of heating climates.

The climate zone specified is broad and general for simplicity. For a specific location, designers and builders should consider weather records, local experience, and the microclimate around a building. Incident solar radiation, nearby water and wetlands, vegetation, and undergrowth can all affect the microclimate.

For residential buildings in this climate, wood frame construction is predominate. The presence of relatively deep ground frost in this climate has led to the widespread use of basement foundations, since footings typically must be located below frost penetration depth. Crawl spaces are utilized in the more moderate regions of heating climates. Concrete and masonry foundations are most common, with some limited use of wood foundations.

KEY MOISTURE CONCERNS

In heating climates the principle moisture concerns are rain penetration, groundwater, ice damming on roofs, interstitial condensation (condensation within building assemblies), and interior mold and mildew linked to high interior levels of humidity. These are discussed below along with some other problems related to mechanical systems and the use of combustion appliances.

Rain and Groundwater

Controlling rain penetration and groundwater is a common concern to builders in all climates. Rain that is permitted to penetrate the exterior cladding of a building can cause material deterioration as well as contribute to other moisture problems within the building assemblies. Basement spaces are often conditioned and occupied in this climate, further raising the level of concern with groundwater penetration and infiltration of soil gas (including radon).

Ice Damming

Heat loss at the perimeter of roof and attic assemblies during heating months can lead to ice damming. This is caused by (1) a lack of thermal insulation where exterior walls intersect roof and attic assemblies, (2) air leakage up and out of exterior walls, and (3) insufficient or discontinuous soffit ventilation.

Condensation in Building Assemblies

Conditioned spaces are typically heated by either electric or fuel-fired appliances. Negative interior air pressures (a traditional characteristic of a cold climate house with a chimney), have been reduced as active chimneys are replaced by high efficiency combustion appliances and electric heat sources. Other important changes in building construction are to create tighter enclosures and reduce air changes, which lead to higher levels of interior moisture. These trends combine to raise concerns about exfiltration of interior moisture-laden air causing condensation within insulated assemblies.

Air leakage into insulated attics during heating months, coupled with insufficient attic ventilation, can lead to roof sheathing decay. Air leakage into insulated wall cavities during the heating months, coupled with an insufficient or limited drying ability, can cause the decay of structural framing members.

Cladding systems that can absorb significant amounts of moisture when exposed to rain, such as brick, masonry, wood, and stucco, should only be incorporated in wall assemblies designed and built to deal with the inward migration of moisture. Solar radiation warms exterior wall surfaces, and this warming creates temperature gradients from the exterior to the interior. Along with the air conditioning of interior surfaces, this can cause problems if not taken into account.

An example of this is the installation of gypsum board covered with vinyl wallpaper on the interior of a masonry block wall without provision for an appropriate vapor diffusion retarder and air barrier system. Without these, the gypsum wall board is not protected from exterior moisture or from construction moisture which may be trapped in the masonry units. Thus, wherever vinyl interior wall coverings are used in this climate zone, precautions must be taken to prevent gypsum wall board from absorbing moisture either from the exterior or from construction moisture.

Building assemblies constructed with wet lumber (greater than 19 percent moisture content by weight) or employing wet-applied

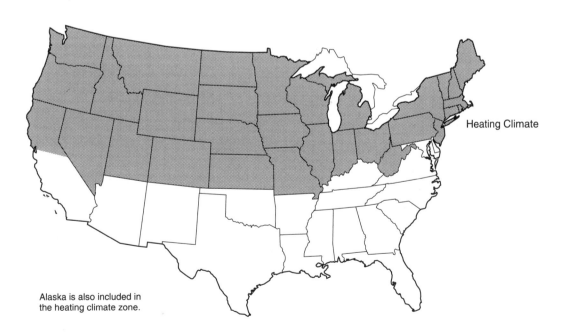

Heating Climate

Alaska is also included in the heating climate zone.

Figure 4-1: Map of heating climate zone in the United States.

insulation (wet spray cellulose or wet blown fiberglass) merit special attention. These assemblies must be designed and built so that they can dry to the exterior or interior, or the materials must be allowed to dry prior to enclosure.

High Interior Humidity Resulting in Mold, Mildew, and Condensation

Low air change during the heating season due to the construction of tight enclosures can lead to elevated interior levels of moisture. These elevated levels can cause condensation on window surfaces and give rise to surface mold and mildew, as well as concealed condensation within walls and roof spaces (discussed above).

Cold interior surfaces during the heating months arising from thermal bridges or other thermal defects (wind blowing through insulation) create high interior surface relative humidities and often lead to mold and mildew at these locations. Most common locations are where exterior walls intersect insulated ceilings, exterior corners, and uninsulated (or poorly insulated) window lintels or headers.

Air change (infiltration/exfiltration combined with controlled ventilation) removes interior moisture from within building enclosures during the heating season. The greater the air change rate, the greater the removal rate of interior moisture. However, typical construction practice results in building enclosures which have air change rates from random leakage that are inadequate to control interior moisture levels.

Mechanical System Concerns

Leaky return ducts located in attics draw significant amounts of cold air into conditioned spaces during heating months, increasing heating loads. They also draw significant amounts of warm, moisture-laden air into the conditioned space from the attic during cooling periods, increasing cooling loads. Leaky return ducts located in vented crawl spaces draw significant amounts of soil gas, moisture, pesticides, radon, and other pollutants into the conditioned spaces. This often creates moisture problems, increases heating and cooling loads, and risks occupant health and safety.

Leaky supply ducts located in attics or vented crawl spaces depressurize the conditioned space. Cold air thus infiltrates excessively during heating periods, heating loads increase, and sufficient interior moisture is potentially supplied to attic and roof assemblies to create roof sheathing moisture and decay problems. During cooling periods, the same mechanism can induce infiltration of exterior, warm, moisture-laden air, increasing cooling loads.

Many building enclosures in heating climates are now built airtight. Where forced air systems with minimal returns (a single return is common) are installed in tight building enclosures, pressurization of bedrooms and depressurization of basement spaces can occur. This can lead to the spillage and backdrafting of combustion appliances, infiltration of soil gas, and exfiltration of moisture-laden air into building assembly cavities.

Combustion Appliances

Unvented combustion appliances such as gas stoves with standing pilot lights and room space heaters are significant sources of moisture as well as sources for other pollutants.

GENERAL STRATEGIES TO CONTROL MOISTURE PROBLEMS

For the potential moisture problems identified above for buildings in this climate, there are several control strategies. The control strategies generally fall into two groups: (1) those applying to the building envelope assemblies, and (2) those related to the overall building and its mechanical systems. To be effective, all of these strategies must be applied as a complete system.

Building Envelope Strategies

Detailed presentations of building envelope strategies are found in the last three sections of the chapter for wall, foundation, and roof assemblies. Some of the key principles are:

- Control rain penetration in walls using rain screens, building papers, and appropriate placement of flashings.

- Direct water away from foundations using gutters and downspouts as well as careful site grading.

- Control groundwater with a subgrade drainage system.

- Control moisture movement by air leakage (the exfiltration of interior moisture-laden air) by limiting air leakage openings and installing air retarder systems in all assemblies.

- Place vapor diffusion retarders in walls, roofs, and foundations to control moisture movement by vapor diffusion from the interior.

- If possible, permit wall assemblies to dry if they become wet. Wall design and construction in this climate typically locates vapor diffusion retarders and measures to control air leakage toward the interior. Thus, it is convenient to allow walls to dry to the exterior in the direction of typical vapor flow during the heating season. Drying to the interior is possible, but more difficult to facilitate and typically intermittent.

- Ventilate roof assemblies to remove moisture in all but heavily insulated assemblies in the harshest climates.

Whole Building System Strategies

The second group of strategies pertains to the overall design and operation of the building and its mechanical system in particular. These include:

- Minimize interior moisture sources by direct venting of clothes dryers, and providing kitchen and bath exhaust systems.

- To control air leakage, design the mechanical system to maintain basement spaces at a positive air pressure relative to the exterior, while above-grade spaces are maintained at a negative air pressure relative to the exterior. Positive pressurization of the basement eliminates the infiltration of soil gas, radon, and other pollutants. Depressurization of the above-grade conditioned spaces eliminates the exfiltration of interior moisture-laden air. This principle is shown in Figure 4-2 for three typical building configurations appropriate for this climate. All three buildings have basement foundations while each illustrates a different roof assembly: (1) a vented attic, (2) a vented cathedral ceiling, and (3) an unvented cathedral ceiling.

- Ventilate enclosures in a controlled manner to limit interior moisture levels and to alleviate other indoor air quality problems. An effective controlled ventilation system

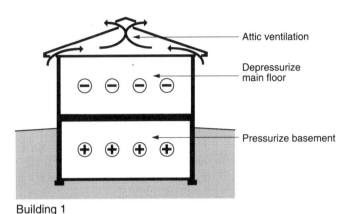

Building 1

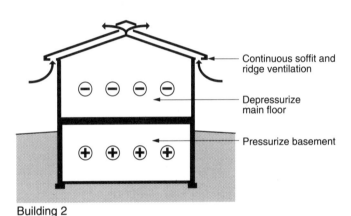

Building 2

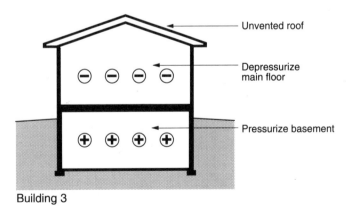

Building 3

Figure 4-2: Recommended air pressure distribution to reduce moisture problems in heating climate buildings.

must do the following: (1) exhaust stale air, (2) supply fresh outside air, (3) operate continuously when occupants are present, and (4) provide effective distribution. A schematic of such a system is shown in Figure 4-3 with notes describing its components, operation, and control. This type of system is essential with tight construction to control both health and moisture problems. The HVAC system, central exhaust, and fresh air supply must be balanced and commissioned in order to maintain the pressure relationships shown in Figure 4-2.

• In the more moderate heating regions with high exterior vapor pressures during the heating season, such as the Pacific Northwest, mechanical dehumidification is practical.

• Install ductwork for forced air heating and cooling systems only within conditioned spaces, not in attics or vented crawl spaces. Where ductwork is located in dropped ceilings adjacent to attics and exterior walls, it is important that air barrier continuity is maintained above the dropped ceiling or at the exterior wall.

• Seal all ductwork with mastic. Of particular concern are return systems utilizing floor joist and stud wall cavities to form return air ducts. Utilize multiple return registers (particularly located in bedrooms), and transfer grills between bedrooms and interior corridors to prevent pressurization of above-grade rooms.

• Avoid unvented combustion appliances. Gas stoves and cook tops without standing pilot lights should be installed in conjunction with vented range hoods or some other vent provision.

• Make sure that combustion appliances are aerodynamically uncoupled (not influenced by enclosure air pressures or supply air availability) from the conditioned space. In other words, use combustion devices that are sealed, power vented, induced draft, condensing, or pulse. Devices with traditional draft hoods should be avoided.

• Provide fireplaces with their own air supply (correctly sized) from the exterior as well as tight-fitting glass doors. Wood stoves should also have their own supply of exterior air ducted directly to their firebox.

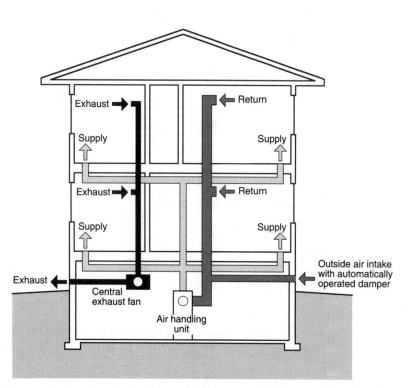

Figure 4-3: Controlled ventilation system for a house in a heating climate.

Notes for Figure 4-3:
An effective controlled ventilation system in a heating climate should have the following characteristics:

• *Stale air is removed through a central exhaust system. Exhaust vents are located in the kitchen and bathrooms.*
• *The central exhaust system operates continuously – at least 15 minutes per hour whenever occupants are present.*
• *The outside air supply is connected to the return side of the air handling unit. An automatically operated damper covers the outside air intake.*
• *The forced air system provides effective distribution of fresh air throughout the house.*
• *The control system is designed so that the central exhaust system only operates when the outside air damper is open and the air handling unit is running.*
• *The overall system must be designed, balanced, and commissioned so that the pressure relationships recommended for heating climate buildings are maintained (see Figure 4-2).*
• *The outside air damper need not be open when only the air handler is operating.*

Wall Construction in Heating Climates

In this section six wall assemblies are shown that can be used successfully in heating climates. There are four wood frame walls with siding, and a fifth wood frame wall with brick veneer. A final case illustrates a concrete block wall with brick veneer. A key difference between the wood frame walls is the type of sheathing used and, in some cases, the type of siding. The basic characteristics of the wall assemblies are summarized in Table 4-1.

First, each wall assembly is illustrated and briefly described. Text adjacent to each drawing indicates how the assembly is designed to handle each of the critical moisture problems in this climate: (1) rain penetration, (2) rain absorption, (3) air movement, and (4) vapor diffusion. In addition, comments concerning the ability of the wall to dry and other limitations of each wall assembly are included. Following the drawings is a summary discussion of key moisture control strategies for wall assemblies in this climate.

Insulation levels in wall assemblies, except where specifically noted to control moisture accumulation on condensing surfaces, are left to the judgement of the reader.

Table 4-1: Characteristics of wall assemblies for heating climates.

	WALL TYPE	EXTERIOR COMPONENT	SHEATHING	OTHER FEATURES	DRYING
WALL 1	Wood frame	Wood, vinyl, or aluminum siding	Plywood or waferboard (Impermeable)	Polyethylene vapor diffusion retarder (Interior)	Limited
WALL 2	Wood frame	Aluminum or vinyl siding	Rigid insulation (Impermeable)	Polyethylene vapor diffusion retarder (Interior)	Limited
WALL 3	Wood frame	Wood, vinyl, or aluminum siding	Rigid fiberglass insulation (Permeable)	Polyethylene vapor diffusion retarder (Interior)	To the exterior
WALL 4	Wood frame	Wood siding over air space	Rigid insulation (Impermeable)	Low permeability paint acts as a vapor diffusion retarder	Limited
WALL 5	Wood frame	Brick veneer over cavity	Asphalt-impregnated fiberboard or gypsum (Permeable)	Polyethylene vapor diffusion retarder (Interior)	To the exterior
WALL 6	Concrete block	Brick veneer over cavity	Rigid insulation	Air/vapor retarder on exterior of masonry block	Limited to the interior

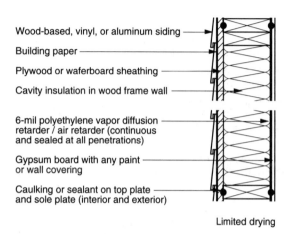

Wood-based, vinyl, or aluminum siding
Building paper
Plywood or waferboard sheathing
Cavity insulation in wood frame wall

6-mil polyethylene vapor diffusion retarder / air retarder (continuous and sealed at all penetrations)
Gypsum board with any paint or wall covering
Caulking or sealant on top plate and sole plate (interior and exterior)

Limited drying

Figure 4-4: Wall 1—heating climate.

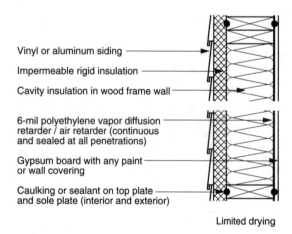

Vinyl or aluminum siding
Impermeable rigid insulation
Cavity insulation in wood frame wall

6-mil polyethylene vapor diffusion retarder / air retarder (continuous and sealed at all penetrations)
Gypsum board with any paint or wall covering
Caulking or sealant on top plate and sole plate (interior and exterior)

Limited drying

Figure 4-5: Wall 2—heating climate.

Wall 1—Heating Climate: This conventional wood frame wall assembly utilizes an impermeable, noninsulating sheathing material consisting of plywood or waferboard covered by building paper. Any type of siding—wood-based, vinyl, or aluminum—can be applied. A polyethylene vapor diffusion retarder is placed on the inside of the wall beneath the gypsum board.

Key characteristics:
- *The rain screen principle controls rain penetration when vinyl or aluminum siding are used. With wood siding, the barrier approach (sealing all openings) is used.*
- *Building paper controls rain absorption into the sheathing.*
- *To control air movement, the exterior sheathing and the polyethylene on the interior are sealed to the framing to form air retarders.*
- *The polyethylene sheet placed beneath the gypsum board acts as a vapor diffusion retarder.*
- *Drying toward the interior or exterior of the wall is limited. Therefore, framing and insulation materials should be dry or permitted to dry before enclosure.*
- *Interior relative humidity should not exceed 35 percent at 70 degrees F during heating periods.*
- *Vapor permeable or impermeable interior surface finishes may be used.*
- *Where wood-based siding is utilized over plywood, waferboard, or OSB sheathing, utilize dry materials, back-prime the siding, and nail according to manufacturers' recommended installation practices. Using spacers, wedges, or installing siding over furring should be considered.*

Wall 2—Heating Climate: Impermeable rigid insulation is used as the sheathing material in this wood frame wall assembly. Vinyl or aluminum siding is applied over the sheathing. Similar to Wall 1, a polyethylene vapor diffusion retarder is placed on the inside of the wall beneath the gypsum board.

Key characteristics:
- *The rain screen principle controls rain penetration.*
- *No building paper is required to control rain absorption since rigid insulation is impermeable.*
- *To control air movement, the exterior sheathing and the polyethylene on the interior are sealed to the framing to form air retarders.*
- *The polyethylene sheet placed beneath the gypsum board acts as a vapor diffusion retarder.*
- *Insulating sheathing raises the wall cavity temperature and limits potential condensation.*
- *Drying toward the interior or exterior of the wall is limited. Therefore, framing and insulation materials should be dry or permitted to dry before enclosure.*
- *Interior relative humidity should not exceed 35 percent at 70 degrees F during heating periods.*
- *Vapor permeable or impermeable interior surface finishes may be used.*

Wall 3—Heating Climate: Rigid fiberglass insulating board is used as a permeable exterior sheathing material in this wood frame wall assembly. This permeable sheathing permits the wall assembly to dry toward the exterior. A polyethylene vapor diffusion retarder is placed on the inside of the wall beneath the gypsum board.

Key characteristics:
- *The rigid fiberglass sheathing serves as a drainage path (the drain screen principle) to control rain penetration.*
- *Permeable rigid insulating sheathing acts as a receptor for capillary moisture and absorbed moisture driven inward by solar radiation.*
- *The polyethylene sheet placed beneath the gypsum board acts as an air retarder to control air movement, and acts as a vapor diffusion retarder.*
- *Insulating sheathing raises the wall cavity temperature and limits potential condensation.*
- *Vapor permeable sheathing permits drying toward the exterior.*
- *Vapor permeable or impermeable interior surface finishes may be used.*
- *Where wood-based siding is utilized over plywood, waferboard, or OSB sheathing, utilize dry materials, back-prime the siding, and nail according to manufacturers' recommended installation practices. Using spacers, wedges, or installing siding over furring should be considered.*

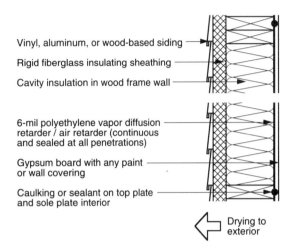

Vinyl, aluminum, or wood-based siding
Rigid fiberglass insulating sheathing
Cavity insulation in wood frame wall

6-mil polyethylene vapor diffusion retarder / air retarder (continuous and sealed at all penetrations)
Gypsum board with any paint or wall covering
Caulking or sealant on top plate and sole plate interior

Drying to exterior

Figure 4-6: Wall 3—heating climate.

Wall 4—Heating Climate: Similar to Wall 2, an impermeable rigid insulation is used as the exterior sheathing material in this wood frame wall assembly. Unlike Wall 2, however, wood-based siding is applied and an air space behind the siding is a receptor for moisture. In contrast to the polyethylene used in the previous three wall assemblies, a low permeability paint or wall covering serves as the vapor diffusion retarder.

Key characteristics:
- *The rain screen principle controls rain penetration.*
- *The air space beneath the wood siding acts as a receptor for capillary moisture and absorbed moisture driven inward by solar radiation.*
- *No building paper is required to control rain absorption since rigid insulation is impermeable.*
- *To control air movement, the exterior sheathing and the gypsum board on the interior are sealed to the framing to form air retarders.*
- *Low permeability paint or wall covering acts as a vapor diffusion retarder. Vapor impermeable interior surface finishes must be used. Alternatively, batt insulation with vapor diffusion retarder backing can be used.*
- *Drying toward the interior or exterior of the wall is limited. Therefore, framing and insulation materials should be dry or permitted to dry before enclosure.*
- *Interior relative humidity should not exceed 35 percent at 70 degrees F during heating periods.*
- *Back-prime the siding and utilize dry materials.*

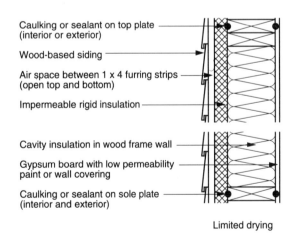

Caulking or sealant on top plate (interior or exterior)
Wood-based siding
Air space between 1 x 4 furring strips (open top and bottom)
Impermeable rigid insulation

Cavity insulation in wood frame wall
Gypsum board with low permeability paint or wall covering
Caulking or sealant on sole plate (interior and exterior)

Limited drying

Figure 4-7: Wall 4—heating climate.

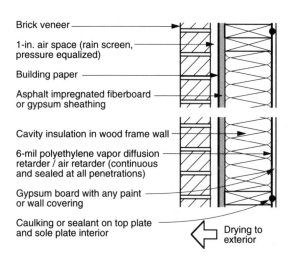

Brick veneer

1-in. air space (rain screen, pressure equalized)

Building paper

Asphalt impregnated fiberboard or gypsum sheathing

Cavity insulation in wood frame wall

6-mil polyethylene vapor diffusion retarder / air retarder (continuous and sealed at all penetrations)

Gypsum board with any paint or wall covering

Caulking or sealant on top plate and sole plate interior

Drying to exterior

Figure 4-8: Wall 5—heating climate.

Wall 5—Heating Climate: This wood frame wall is covered on the exterior by a brick veneer. An air space between the brick and the wood frame assembly is a receptor for moisture. The permeable noninsulating sheathing (asphalt-impregnated fiberboard or gypsum) permits the wall assembly to dry toward the exterior. Like most other wood frame wall assemblies, a polyethylene vapor diffusion retarder is placed on the inside of the wall beneath the gypsum board.

Key characteristics:
- *The rain screen principle controls rain penetration.*
- *The air space behind the brick veneer acts as a receptor for capillary moisture and absorbed moisture driven inward by solar radiation.*
- *Building paper controls rain absorption into the sheathing. It must be continuous and fastened.*
- *The polyethylene sheet placed beneath the gypsum board acts as an air retarder to control air movement, and acts as a vapor diffusion retarder.*
- *Vapor permeable sheathing permits drying toward the exterior.*
- *Vapor permeable or impermeable interior surface finishes may be used.*

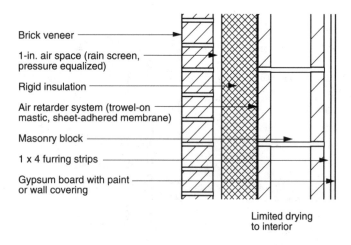

Brick veneer

1-in. air space (rain screen, pressure equalized)

Rigid insulation

Air retarder system (trowel-on mastic, sheet-adhered membrane)

Masonry block

1 x 4 furring strips

Gypsum board with paint or wall covering

Limited drying to interior

Figure 4-9: Wall 6—heating climate.

Wall 6—Heating Climate: This concrete block wall assembly with brick veneer is the only one that is not wood frame construction. Either permeable or impermeable rigid insulation is placed in the cavity between the block wall and brick veneer. An air space between the brick and the insulation is a receptor for moisture. An air retarder system (trowel-on mastic or a sheet-adhered membrane) is applied to the exterior face of the masonry wall to control vapor diffusion and air leakage.

Key characteristics:
- *The rain screen principle controls rain penetration.*
- *The air space behind the brick veneer acts as a receptor for capillary moisture and absorbed moisture driven inward by solar radiation.*
- *An air retarder system (mastic or membrane) controls air movement, and acts as a vapor diffusion retarder.*
- *A vapor permeable paint finish on the gypsum board permits some drying to the interior.*
- *If an impermeable interior finish is used instead, then a polyethylene vapor barrier should be installed beneath the gypsum board. In this case, framing and insulation materials should be dry or permitted to dry before enclosure.*

Chapter 4—Moisture Control Practices for Heating Climates

SUMMARY: WALL ASSEMBLIES IN HEATING CLIMATES

Rain Penetration

All but one of the six wall assemblies recommended for this climate utilize the rain screen principle to control rain penetration. Wall 3 utilizes the drain screen principle (discussed below).

The rain screen principle requires a pressure-equalized cavity behind the cladding. In Walls 1 and 2, vinyl or aluminum siding is installed over a tight sheathing. The cavities created behind vinyl or aluminum siding serve this purpose and they should not be filled with insulation material. For pressure to be equalized in these cavities, the exterior sheathing must be significantly tighter than the cladding. It should be installed vertically, with all joints falling on framing members, with the option of utilizing a sealant or adhesive at sheathing joints and edges.

Alternatively, a tightly installed building paper (lapped or taped joints) may be utilized to equalize pressure. In Wall 1, wood-based siding may be used instead of vinyl or aluminum, but all exterior holes in the building paper and sheathing then must be eliminated to prevent rain penetration.

In Wall 4, the rain screen principle is utilized by installing wood-based siding on furring strips to create an air space open at the top and bottom of the wall.

In Walls 5 and 6, the rain screen is created using a brick veneer over a minimum 1-inch air space. This air space must be clear of mortar droppings and should be open at the top of the brick veneer wall as well as vented at its base. Such brick veneer walls should be vented at their base by leaving open every other vertical mortar joint in the first course of brick.

These vertical open joints serve two functions, first to allow inward air movement to equalize pressure and second to provide a weep or drainage function. As in all rain screen systems, the sheathing must be significantly tighter than the cladding for pressure equalization in the cavity to occur. This is accomplished by both tightening the sheathing and making the brick veneer deliberately leaky. Venting the air space at the top and bottom make the brick veneer sufficiently leaky. The asphalt-impregnated fiberboard or gypsum sheathing should be installed airtight as described above for Wall 1.

The sheathing is sometimes further tightened relative to the brick veneer by the installation of a building paper in a continuous manner. This building paper must be extensively fastened to prevent flexing under wind action which could pump moisture into the assembly. Flashings at the base of brick veneer walls are also critical so that cavity moisture can be directed to the exterior through the weep holes under the influence of gravity. These base flashings must extend to the back of the rain screen cavity and be placed behind the sheathing or building paper.

Wall 3 is the only assembly shown here that does not use the rain screen approach. Instead the drain screen principle is applied by providing a drainage medium behind the exterior cladding. In this case a permeable rigid fiberglass insulating sheathing is installed so that its fiber orientation drains incident rainwater. This approach is compatible with wood-based siding where the wood-based siding does not provide for a pressure-equalized cavity (rain screen). The approach is also compatible with vinyl or aluminum siding.

Appropriate installation of flashings over window and door openings is critical in all rain screen assemblies, ideally tucking in behind exterior sheathings or building papers. In drain screen assemblies, flashings over window and door openings are also critical to direct rainwater to the exterior of the assembly.

Rain Absorption/Capillary Suction

In the six wall assemblies shown here, there are two basic concepts to control moisture from rain absorption and capillary suction: (1) impermeable materials are used to keep moisture out of the wall assembly, and (2) a space or permeable material acts as a receptor for this moisture, providing a path for it to leave the wall assembly.

Rain absorption by vinyl or aluminum siding (as shown in Walls 1, 2, and 3) and siding capillarity effects are not a concern as a result of the inherent material properties of the vinyl and aluminum. Where wood-based siding is utilized (in Walls 1 and 4, for example), back-priming (painting or coating the back surfaces) is recommended to limit capillary and vapor absorption by the siding. Installing the wood siding on furring strips, or using spacers or wedges to create openings between siding pieces is also recommended. It is important to use dry materials and nail according to the manufacturers' recommended installation practices.

In Wall 1, building paper inhibits capillarity effects and rain absorption by the exterior structural use panels (plywood, waferboard, or OSB sheathing). In this assembly a vapor permeable, nonabsorptive building paper should be used. In Walls 2 and 4, where the sheathing material is impermeable rigid insulation, building paper is not required to prevent water absorption by the sheathing.

The second concept of creating a receptor for moisture from rain absorption and capillarity is demonstrated in Walls 3, 4, 5, and 6. In Wall 3, the permeable rigid fiberglass insulating sheathing provides a receptor for both siding capillary moisture and siding absorbed moisture driven inward by incident solar radiation.

In Wall 4, an air space behind the wood-based siding controls rain absorption by the siding itself, as well as capillarity effects. Similarly, in Walls 5 and 6, an air space behind the brick veneer controls rain absorption and brick veneer capillarity effects. In all three cases, the air space also acts as a receptor for both capillary moisture and absorbed moisture driven inward by incident solar radiation. In Wall 5, a building paper may be installed in some assemblies to limit rain absorption by the asphalt-impregnated fiberboard or gypsum sheathing. In such cases a vapor permeable, nonabsorptive building paper should be used.

Air Movement

In this climate, an air seal (air retarder) at either the interior or exterior of a wall assembly controls air-transported moisture from the interior. This means that either the interior gypsum wall board, polyethylene vapor diffusion retarder, or exterior sheathing is sealed to the wall framing. This air sealing can be accomplished with adhesive, caulk, or some other sealant. To ensure effectiveness, it is desirable to create both an interior and exterior air retarder when materials permit.

In Walls 1, 2, 3, and 5, the interior air retarder is a continuous 6-mil polyethylene sheet. In Wall 4, the gypsum board is sealed to the wall framing and acts as the interior air retarder. Since polyethylene often serves the dual function of air and vapor retarder in this climate, the air retarder frequently occurs at the interior face of the wall.

An exterior air retarder is shown in Walls 1, 2, and 4. This has the added advantage of facilitating pressure equalization of the exterior cladding to create the rain screen. Exterior air seals over permeable sheathing usually feature a continuous exterior building paper (vapor permeable and nonabsorptive). Over impermeable sheathing, the building paper is not

required and the rigid board is simply sealed to the framing.

In Wall 6, an air retarder system on the exterior of the masonry block wall controls air-transported moisture from the interior in this wall assembly. Utilizing the rigid insulation as an integral air retarder system has in practice proven to be difficult due to the dimensional instability of rigid insulations. The air retarder also controls air-transported moisture from the exterior (infiltration of warm, humid air during the cooling season) in this wall assembly. This moisture transport mechanism can lead to moisture damage where significant moisture has been stored in the brick veneer.

Vapor Diffusion

To control vapor diffusion from the interior during heating periods in this climate, a vapor diffusion retarder is generally installed at the interior of the wall. As shown in Walls 1, 2, 3, and 5, the vapor diffusion retarder consists of a continuous polyethylene sheet installed beneath the interior gypsum board.

In Wall 4, there is no polyethylene sheet in the wall assembly. In this case, a low permeability paint or wall covering acts as the vapor diffusion retarder.

During heating periods, moisture accumulation within walls due to vapor diffusion can also be controlled by elevating the temperature of the first condensing surface within the wall assembly—the cavity side of the exterior sheathing. This is accomplished in Walls 2, 3, and 4 by installing an insulating sheathing which limits periods of potential condensation.

During cooling periods and under the action of incident solar radiation, vapor diffusion from the exterior can occur in some wall assemblies. For example, in Walls 3 and 5 this can occur because of the permeable exterior sheathing materials. In both cases, the vapor diffusion retarder at the interior of the wall assembly controls the problem. Although installing a vapor diffusion retarder at this location does not prevent moisture from entering the wall, the vapor diffusion retarder effectively protects the interior gypsum board and any interior finishes from moisture damage.

This interior vapor diffusion retarder can get wet on the cavity side during the day as a result of exterior absorbed moisture driven inward by incident solar radiation and the air conditioned interior. This moisture then typically migrates outward in the evening when the temperature gradient reverses.

Walls 3 and 5 can get intermittently wet

from the exterior as well as dry intermittently to the exterior. Since intermittent wetting of the vapor diffusion retarder may occur in these assemblies, the interior vapor diffusion retarder should be continuous to provide satisfactory performance. Foil-backed interior gypsum board and vapor diffusion retarder-backed cavity insulation may not be effective due to discontinuities at joints. A continuous polyethylene vapor diffusion retarder has proven to be effective in this type of assembly.

In Wall 6, a vapor diffusion retarder on the exterior of the masonry block wall between the masonry and the rigid insulation controls vapor diffusion from the interior during heating periods. Moisture accumulation within the wall assembly is further controlled by using insulating sheathing which elevates the temperature of the first condensing surface within the wall assembly—the masonry block wall. The vapor diffusion retarder on the exterior of the masonry block in Wall 6 controls vapor diffusion from the exterior as well.

Drying of Wall Assemblies

In Walls 1, 2, and 4, drying toward either the interior or exterior is limited by a vapor impermeable exterior sheathing and an interior vapor diffusion retarder. Should the wall assembly become wet during service, or be built wet due to wet framing materials or wet-applied cavity insulations (wet spray cellulose or blown fiberglass), it may not dry. Accordingly, dry framing materials (wood at a moisture content of 19 percent by weight or lower) and dry-applied insulations are recommended. Alternatively, wall assemblies must be allowed to dry prior to enclosure.

For these same three wall assemblies (Walls 1, 2, and 4), interior moisture levels should be limited to 35 percent relative humidity at 70 degrees Fahrenheit during heating periods. This will further control air-transported moisture and vapor diffusion with these wall assemblies, since only limited drying can occur.

In Wall 3, a vapor permeable sheathing on the exterior of the wall framing helps dry the wall toward the exterior. Since the rigid insulating sheathing is close to the permeability of air, the exterior cladding in essence "sees" the wall cavity and framing members. When the cladding is cold, it attracts interior cavity and framing moisture, effectively freeze drying the wall. Should the wall assembly become wet during service or be built wet due to wet framing materials or wet-applied cavity insulations (wet spray cellulose or blown

fiberglass), it dries rapidly to the exterior during the heating season or during evenings. Once the interior cavity moisture has migrated to the exterior cladding it can either drain to the exterior or evaporate. Where wood-based sidings are used, they should be protected from this moisture migration toward their back surfaces from the interior by back-priming.

Similar to Wall 3, Wall 5 utilizes a vapor permeable sheathing on the exterior of the wall framing to help dry the wall toward the exterior. An air space between the cladding (brick veneer) and the sheathing acts as a receptor for interior cavity moisture.

In Wall 6, a vapor permeable paint finish on the interior gypsum wall board promotes wall drying toward the interior from within the masonry block wall assembly. Should the masonry block wall assembly become wet during service or be built wet through the use of wet masonry, it can dry to the interior due to an inward temperature and vapor pressure gradient present as a result of air conditioning the enclosure during the cooling season. However, it should be noted that only limited drying toward the interior may occur.

In cases where impermeable interior surface treatments are utilized, such as wall coverings and impermeable paints, the masonry block wall assembly should be allowed to dry prior to enclosure. Alternatively, an additional vapor diffusion retarder may be installed between the interior gypsum wall board and the interior surface of the masonry wall to retard the inward migration of construction moisture and reduce the possible damage to interior surface finishes.

Interior Finishes

Either vapor permeable or vapor impermeable interior surface finishes may be used in conjunction with Walls 1, 2, 3, and 5 since there is no drying to the interior and a polyethylene sheet serves as a vapor diffusion retarder. In Wall 4, however, a vapor impermeable interior surface finish must be used since the interior finish must serve as the vapor diffusion retarder. In Wall 6, a vapor permeable interior surface finish is required to permit some drying to the interior. If a polyethylene vapor retarder is installed in Wall 6, however, then any type of interior finish is acceptable.

Where wall assemblies with permeable interior surface treatments have been performing satisfactorily and are subsequently covered with impermeable interior surface treatments, mold and mildew problems may appear at the gypsum board/surface treatment interface.

Foundation Construction in Heating Climates

In this section nine foundation assemblies are shown that can be used successfully in heating climates. There are eight basement wall assemblies and one slab-on-grade foundation. Six of the basement walls are concrete or masonry construction, while the remaining two utilize pressure-treated wood walls. A key difference between the basement walls is the type and placement of insulation on either the interior or exterior of the wall, as well as in the rim joist area and under or above the floor slab. The basic characteristics of the foundation assemblies are summarized in Table 4-2.

First, each foundation assembly is illustrated and briefly described. Text adjacent to each drawing indicates how the assembly is designed to handle each of the critical moisture problems in this climate: (1) rain and groundwater, (2) capillary suction, (3) air movement, and (4) vapor diffusion. In addition, comments concerning the ability of the wall to dry and other limitations of each foundation assembly are summarized. Following the drawings is a summary discussion of key moisture control strategies for foundation assemblies in this climate.

Insulation levels in foundation assemblies, except where specifically noted to control moisture accumulation on condensing surfaces, are left to the judgement of the reader. Guidance regarding optimum insulation levels for foundation assemblies can be found in the *Builder's Foundation Handbook* (Carmody et al. 1991).

Table 4-2: Characteristics of foundation assemblies for heating climates.

	FOUNDATION TYPE	FOUNDATION WALL INSULATION	FLOOR INSULATION	DRYING
BASEMENT 1	Concrete	Cavity insulation in wood frame wall (Interior)	Rigid insulation beneath slab	Limited
BASEMENT 2	Concrete	Rigid insulation (Interior)	Rigid insulation above slab	To the interior
BASEMENT 3	Concrete	Draining rigid fiberglass insulation (Exterior)	None	To the exterior
BASEMENT 4	Concrete masonry	Cavity insulation in wood frame wall (Interior)	None	Limited
BASEMENT 5	Concrete masonry	Rigid insulation (Exterior)	None	Limited
BASEMENT 6	Concrete supporting brick veneer	Cavity insulation in wood frame wall (Interior)	Rigid insulation beneath slab	Limited
BASEMENT 7	Pressure-treated wood frame	Cavity insulation in wood frame wall— Exterior draining rigid fiberglass insulation	Rigid insulation beneath wood floor	Limited
BASEMENT 8	Pressure-treated wood frame	Cavity insulation in wood frame wall— Exterior draining rigid fiberglass insulation	Rigid insulation beneath wood floor	Limited
SLAB 1	Slab with grade beam	Rigid insulation covers grade beam and extends horizontally into soil	Rigid insulation beneath slab	Limited

Basement 1—Heating Climate: This concrete basement wall assembly illustrates cavity insulation in a wood frame wall on the interior of the foundation wall. Cavity insulation is placed between joists on the rim joist interior, and rigid insulation covers the rim joist on the exterior as well. A layer of rigid insulation is also shown beneath the concrete floor slab. The above-grade wall shown here corresponds to Wall 2 in the previous section.

Key characteristics:
- *Rainwater is controlled by gutters and downspouts, impermeable soil cap over backfill, and grade sloping away from the building.*
- *Groundwater is controlled by free-draining backfill and a drain pipe at the footing.*
- *Capillary suction is controlled by a dampproof coating on the exterior wall, a break over the footing, a break over the top of the concrete wall, and a layer of gravel under the slab.*
- *Air movement is controlled by sealing the sill/rim joist area, and sealing the polyethylene air retarder under the floor slab to the gypsum board on the basement wall.*
- *Vapor diffusion from the surrounding soil is controlled by the dampproof coating on the wall exterior and the polyethylene sheet beneath the floor slab.*
- *Vapor diffusion from the interior space is prevented from entering the construction assemblies by a vapor diffusion retarder backing on the cavity insulation and by polyethylene covering the insulation in the rim joist area.*
- *A dampproof coating (low perm or elastomeric paint) on the interior of the concrete wall prevents construction moisture contained in the concrete wall from entering the wall assembly. This can be eliminated if the concrete wall is permitted to dry.*
- *Insulation outside the rim joist raises the wall cavity temperature and limits potential condensation.*
- *Drying toward the interior or exterior of the wall is limited. Therefore, framing and insulation materials should be dry or permitted to dry before enclosure.*
- *Interior relative humidity should not exceed 35 percent at 70 degrees F during heating periods.*
- *Vapor permeable or impermeable interior surface finishes may be used on walls.*

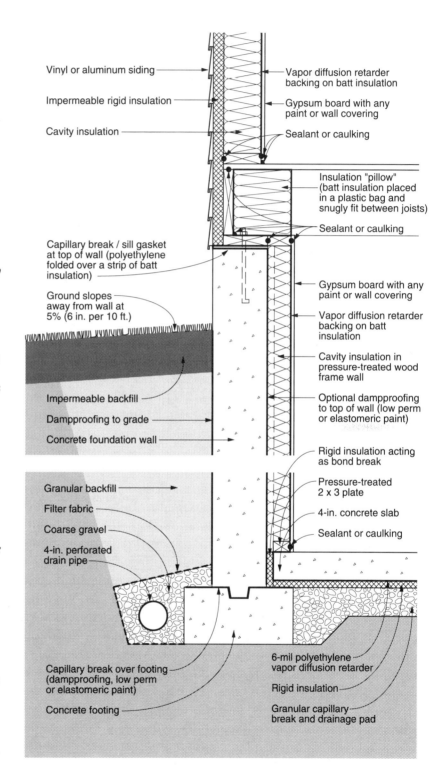

Figure 4-10: Basement 1—heating climate.

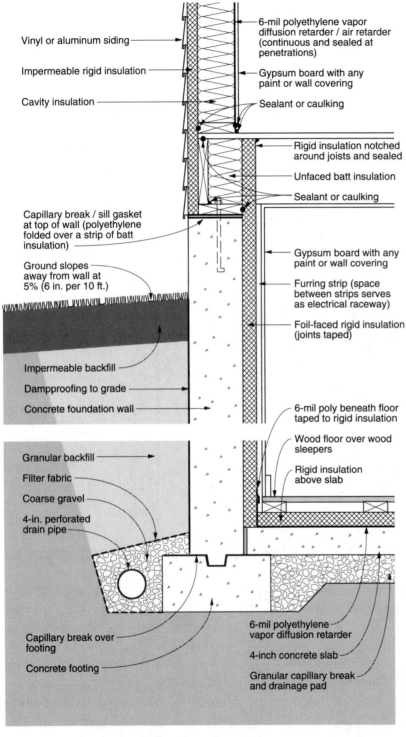

Vinyl or aluminum siding

Impermeable rigid insulation

Cavity insulation

6-mil polyethylene vapor diffusion retarder / air retarder (continuous and sealed at penetrations)

Gypsum board with any paint or wall covering

Sealant or caulking

Rigid insulation notched around joists and sealed

Unfaced batt insulation

Sealant or caulking

Capillary break / sill gasket at top of wall (polyethylene folded over a strip of batt insulation)

Ground slopes away from wall at 5% (6 in. per 10 ft.)

Gypsum board with any paint or wall covering

Furring strip (space between strips serves as electrical raceway)

Foil-faced rigid insulation (joints taped)

Impermeable backfill

Dampproofing to grade

Concrete foundation wall

6-mil poly beneath floor taped to rigid insulation

Wood floor over wood sleepers

Rigid insulation above slab

Granular backfill

Filter fabric

Coarse gravel

4-in. perforated drain pipe

6-mil polyethylene vapor diffusion retarder

4-inch concrete slab

Granular capillary break and drainage pad

Capillary break over footing

Concrete footing

Figure 4-11: Basement 2—heating climate.

Basement 2—Heating Climate: This concrete basement wall assembly illustrates rigid insulation on the interior of the foundation wall. The rigid insulation extends up between joists on the interior, and rigid insulation covers the rim joist on the exterior as well. A floating floor resting on a layer of rigid insulation is placed over the concrete floor slab. This approach raises the floor temperature reducing condensation and relative humidities near surfaces thereby minimizing potential dust mite growth. The above-grade wall shown here corresponds to Wall 2 in the previous section.

Key characteristics:

• *Rainwater is controlled by gutters and downspouts, impermeable soil cap over backfill, and grade sloping away from the building.*

• *Groundwater is controlled by free-draining backfill and a drain pipe at the footing.*

• *Capillary suction is controlled by a dampproof coating on the exterior wall, a break over the footing, a break over the top of the concrete wall, and a layer of gravel under the slab.*

• *Air movement is controlled by sealing the rigid insulation to the wall and in the sill/rim joist area. Also, the polyethylene air retarder over the floor slab is sealed to the rigid insulation on the basement wall.*

• *Vapor diffusion from the surrounding soil is controlled by the dampproof coating on the wall exterior, the impermeable rigid insulation on the wall interior, and the polyethylene sheet over the floor slab.*

• *Vapor diffusion from the interior space is prevented from entering the construction assemblies by polyethylene covering the insulation in the rim joist area, and by the impermeable rigid insulation.*

• *Insulation outside the rim joist raises the wall cavity temperature and limits potential condensation.*

• *Wood framing dries toward the interior.*

• *Carpet installed over the floating wood floor will be dry and warm, significantly reducing the potential for dust mite and mold growth. Wood flooring or tile further reduces this potential.*

• *Interior relative humidity should not exceed 35 percent at 70 degrees F during heating periods.*

• *Vapor permeable or impermeable interior surface finishes may be used on walls or floors.*

Basement 3—Heating Climate: Draining rigid fiberglass insulation board covers the exterior of this concrete basement wall. Rigid insulation covers the exterior of the rim joist, and cavity insulation (with a vapor diffusion retarder) is placed between joists on the rim joist interior. This is the only foundation wall assembly that dries to the exterior. The above-grade wall shown here corresponds to Wall 4 in the previous section.

Key characteristics:
- *Rainwater is controlled by gutters and downspouts, and grade sloping away from the building.*
- *Groundwater is controlled by free-draining insulation board and a drain pipe at the footing (the drain screen principle).*
- *Capillary suction is controlled by the rigid draining fiberglass insulation on the exterior wall, a break over the footing, and a layer of gravel under the slab.*
- *Air movement into the space is controlled by sealing the concrete slab to the concrete foundation wall with caulking, limiting or sealing all penetrations, sealing the sill/rim joist area, and placing a polyethylene sheet (air retarder) under the floor slab.*
- *Vapor diffusion from the surrounding soil is controlled by the polyethylene sheet beneath the floor slab, and the rigid insulation on the exterior of the wall. In this case, the rigid, vapor permeable insulation permits the wall to dry to the exterior since its temperature is raised by the insulation.*
- *Vapor diffusion from the interior space is prevented from entering the rim joist assembly by polyethylene covering the insulation in the rim joist area.*
- *Insulation on the outside of the basement wall and the rim joist raises the wall temperature and limits potential condensation.*
- *Vapor permeable sheathing below grade permits drying toward the exterior.*
- *A low permeability paint or dampproof coating can be applied to the foundation wall interior as protection from construction moisture that is held within the concrete foundation wall.*

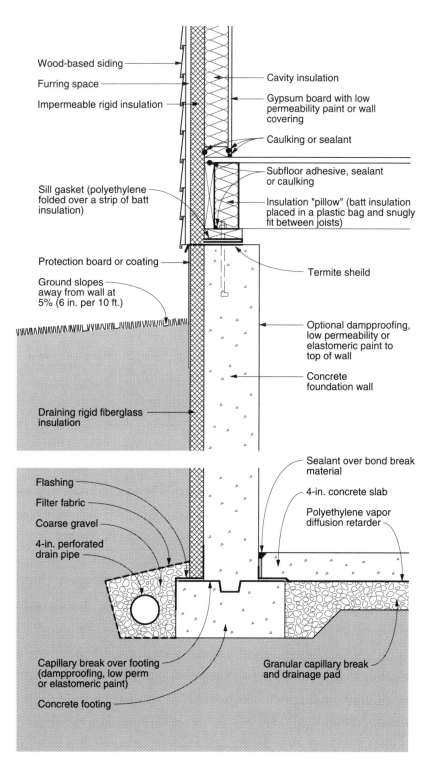

Figure 4-12: Basement 3—heating climate.

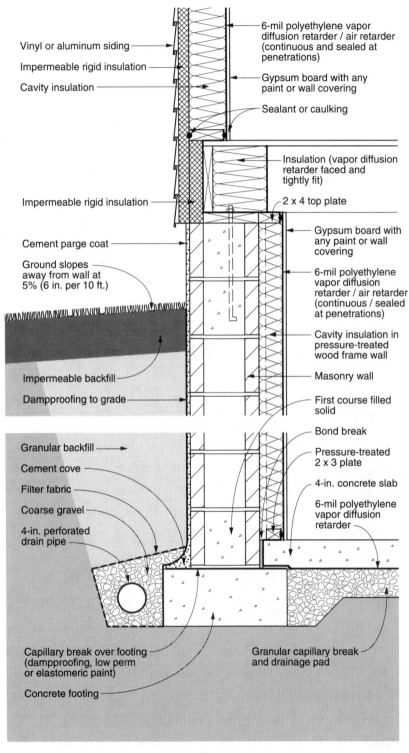

Vinyl or aluminum siding

Impermeable rigid insulation

Cavity insulation

Impermeable rigid insulation

Cement parge coat

Ground slopes away from wall at 5% (6 in. per 10 ft.)

Impermeable backfill

Dampproofing to grade

Granular backfill

Cement cove

Filter fabric

Coarse gravel

4-in. perforated drain pipe

Capillary break over footing (dampproofing, low perm or elastomeric paint)

Concrete footing

6-mil polyethylene vapor diffusion retarder / air retarder (continuous and sealed at penetrations)

Gypsum board with any paint or wall covering

Sealant or caulking

Insulation (vapor diffusion retarder faced and tightly fit)

2 x 4 top plate

Gypsum board with any paint or wall covering

6-mil polyethylene vapor diffusion retarder / air retarder (continuous / sealed at penetrations)

Cavity insulation in pressure-treated wood frame wall

Masonry wall

First course filled solid

Bond break

Pressure-treated 2 x 3 plate

4-in. concrete slab

6-mil polyethylene vapor diffusion retarder

Granular capillary break and drainage pad

Figure 4-13: Basement 4—heating climate.

Basement 4—Heating Climate: This foundation assembly illustrates a concrete masonry basement wall. Similar to Basement 1, cavity insulation is placed in a wood frame wall on the interior of the foundation wall. Cavity insulation is placed between joists on the rim joist interior, and rigid insulation covers the rim joist on the exterior as well. The polyethylene vapor diffusion retarder is continuous from the above-grade wall interior, through the rim joist area, extending over the basement wall interior, and then beneath the slab. The above-grade wall shown here corresponds to Wall 2 in the previous section.

Key characteristics:

• Rainwater is controlled by gutters and downspouts, impermeable soil cap over backfill, and grade sloping away from the building.

• Groundwater is controlled by free-draining backfill and a drain pipe at the footing.

• Capillary suction is controlled by a dampproof coating on the exterior wall, a break over the footing, and a layer of gravel under the slab.

• Air movement is controlled by sealing the polyethylene air retarder under the floor slab to the polyethylene sheet air retarder beneath the gypsum board on the basement wall. In addition, a polyethylene sheet is wrapped around the rim joist assembly and is sealed to the polyethylene air retarders on the basement and above-grade walls.

• Vapor diffusion from the surrounding soil is controlled by the dampproof coating on the wall exterior and the polyethylene sheet beneath the floor slab.

• Vapor diffusion from the interior space is prevented from entering the construction assemblies by a polyethylene sheet beneath the gypsum board on the interior wall and a vapor diffusion retarder covering the insulation in the rim joist area.

• Insulation outside the rim joist raises the wall cavity temperature and limits potential condensation.

• Drying toward the interior or exterior of the wall is limited. Therefore, framing and insulation materials should be dry or permitted to dry before enclosure.

• Interior relative humidity should not exceed 35 percent at 70 degrees F during heating periods.

• Vapor permeable or impermeable interior surface finishes may be used on walls.

Basement 5—Heating Climate: This concrete masonry basement wall assembly illustrates rigid insulation board on the exterior. This is somewhat similar to Basement 2 where a rigid draining fiberglass board is used on the exterior, however granular backfill is necessary in this case (Basement 4) since the rigid insulation has no drainage characteristics. Like all previous foundation assemblies, rigid insulation covers the exterior of the rim joist, and cavity insulation (with a vapor diffusion retarder) is placed between joists on the rim joist interior. The above-grade wall shown here corresponds to Wall 4 in the previous section.

Key characteristics:

- *Rainwater is controlled by gutters and downspouts, impermeable soil cap over backfill, and grade sloping away from the building.*
- *Groundwater is controlled by free-draining backfill and a drain pipe at the footing.*
- *Capillary suction is controlled by a dampproof coating on the exterior wall, a break over the footing, and a layer of gravel under the slab.*
- *Air movement into the space is controlled by sealing the concrete slab to the concrete foundation wall with caulking, filling the first course of masonry with mortar, sealing the sill/rim joist area, and placing a polyethylene air retarder under the floor slab that extends over the footing.*
- *Vapor diffusion from the surrounding soil is controlled by the dampproof coating on the wall exterior and the polyethylene sheet beneath the floor slab.*
- *Vapor diffusion from the interior space is prevented from entering the construction assemblies by polyethylene covering the insulation in the rim joist area.*
- *Insulation on the outside of the basement wall and the rim joist raises the wall temperature and limits potential condensation.*
- *Exposed concrete masonry wall can dry toward the interior.*

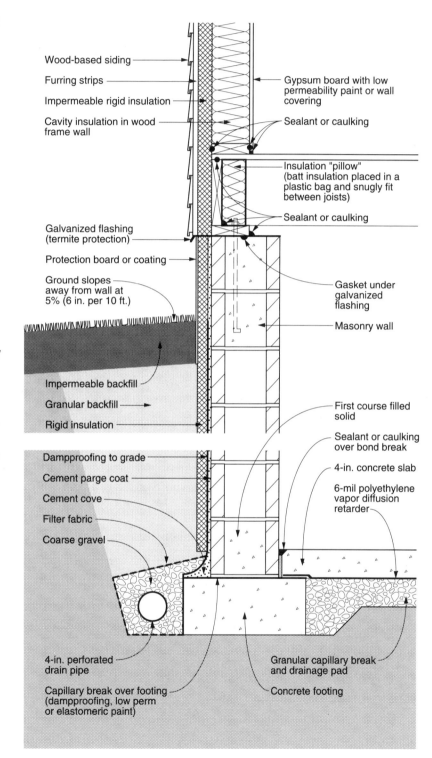

Figure 4-14: Basement 5—heating climate.

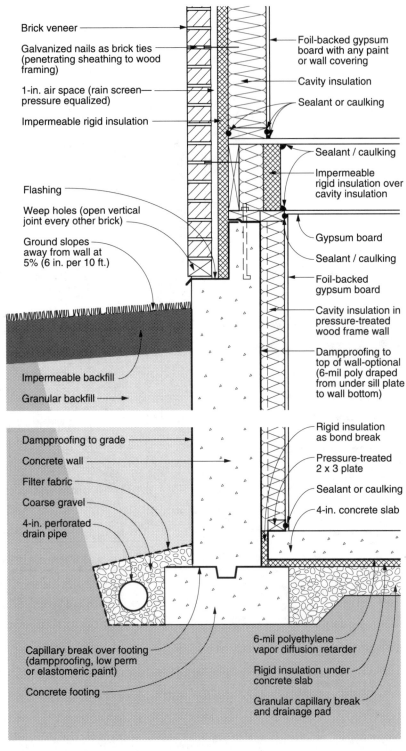

Brick veneer

Galvanized nails as brick ties (penetrating sheathing to wood framing)

1-in. air space (rain screen—pressure equalized)

Impermeable rigid insulation

Flashing

Weep holes (open vertical joint every other brick)

Ground slopes away from wall at 5% (6 in. per 10 ft.)

Impermeable backfill

Granular backfill

Dampproofing to grade

Concrete wall

Filter fabric

Coarse gravel

4-in. perforated drain pipe

Capillary break over footing (dampproofing, low perm or elastomeric paint)

Concrete footing

Foil-backed gypsum board with any paint or wall covering

Cavity insulation

Sealant or caulking

Sealant / caulking

Impermeable rigid insulation over cavity insulation

Gypsum board

Sealant / caulking

Foil-backed gypsum board

Cavity insulation in pressure-treated wood frame wall

Dampproofing to top of wall-optional (6-mil poly draped from under sill plate to wall bottom)

Rigid insulation as bond break

Pressure-treated 2 x 3 plate

Sealant or caulking

4-in. concrete slab

6-mil polyethylene vapor diffusion retarder

Rigid insulation under concrete slab

Granular capillary break and drainage pad

Figure 4-15: Basement 6—heating climate.

Basement 6—Heating Climate: In this example, a concrete basement wall assembly supports a wood frame wall with brick veneer. Similar to Basement 1, there is cavity insulation in a wood frame wall on the interior of the foundation wall. Also, a layer of rigid insulation is shown beneath the concrete floor slab. The above-grade wall shown here is similar to Wall 5 in the previous section, except for the impermeable insulating sheathing and foil-backed gypsum board.

Key characteristics:
- Rainwater is controlled by gutters and downspouts, impermeable soil cap over backfill, and grade sloping away from the building. Flashing at the base of the brick veneer directs water outward.
- Groundwater is controlled by free-draining backfill and a drain pipe at the footing.
- Capillary suction is controlled by a dampproof coating on the exterior wall, a break over the footing, a break over the top of the concrete wall, and a layer of gravel under the slab.
- Air movement into the space is controlled by sealing the polyethylene air retarder under the floor slab to the gypsum board on the basement wall. The gypsum board is sealed to the perimeter framing, and rigid insulation blocks are sealed into the joist spaces at the top of the wall.
- Vapor diffusion from the surrounding soil is controlled by the dampproof coating on the wall exterior and the polyethylene sheet beneath the floor slab.
- Vapor diffusion from the interior space is prevented from entering the construction assemblies by foil-backed gypsum board on the interior wall and impermeable insulation in the rim joist area.
- A dampproof coating on the interior of the concrete wall prevents construction moisture contained in the concrete wall from entering the wall assembly. This can be eliminated if the concrete wall is permitted to dry.
- Insulation outside the rim joist raises the wall cavity temperature and limits potential condensation.
- Drying toward the interior or exterior of the wall is limited. Therefore, framing and insulation materials should be dry or permitted to dry before enclosure.
- Interior relative humidity should not exceed 35 percent at 70 degrees F during heating periods.
- Vapor permeable or impermeable interior surface finishes may be used on walls.

Basement 7—Heating Climate: This pressure-treated wood foundation wall rests on a concrete footing. Cavity insulation is placed within the wood frame wall and draining rigid fiberglass board covers the exterior. A layer of rigid insulation is placed beneath the wood floor. Because of the balloon-style framing at the rim joist, the insulated wood foundation wall extends over the rim joist on the exterior. Rigid insulation covers the rim joist on the exterior as well. Gypsum board with low permeability paint or wall covering serves as a vapor diffusion retarder on the interior side of the wall assembly. The above-grade wall shown here corresponds to Wall 4 in the previous section.

Key characteristics:
- *Rainwater is controlled by gutters and downspouts, and grade sloping away from the building.*
- *Groundwater is controlled by free-draining insulation board and a drain pipe at the footing (the drain screen principle).*
- *Capillary suction is controlled by the rigid draining fiberglass insulation on the exterior wall, a break over the footing, and a layer of gravel under the floor.*
- *Air movement into the space is controlled by sealing the polyethylene air retarder under the floor assembly to the plywood subfloor. The subfloor is sealed to the perimeter wall framing, and the rim joist area is sealed as well.*
- *Vapor diffusion from the surrounding soil is controlled by the polyethylene sheets on the wall exterior and beneath the floor slab.*
- *Low permeability paint or wall covering acts as a vapor diffusion retarder. Vapor impermeable interior surface finishes must be used.*
- *Insulation on the outside of the basement wall and the rim joist raises the wall temperature and limits potential condensation. Similarly, insulation beneath the floor assembly raises the temperature in the floor cavity.*
- *Drying toward the interior or exterior of the wall is limited. Therefore, framing and insulation materials should be dry or permitted to dry before enclosure.*
- *Interior relative humidity should not exceed 35 percent at 70 degrees F during heating periods.*

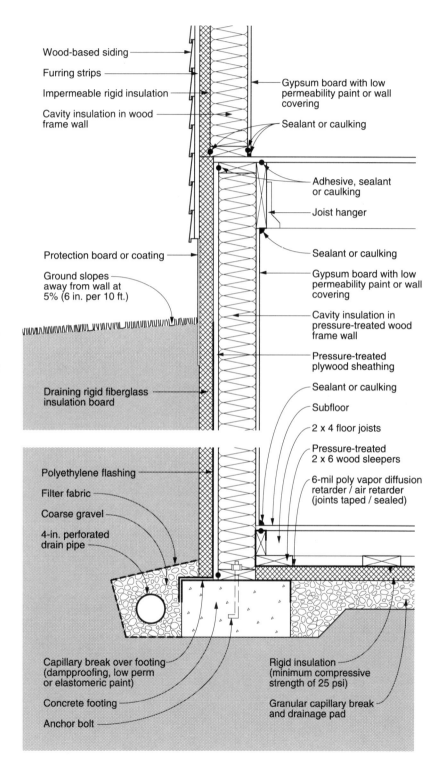

Wood-based siding
Furring strips
Impermeable rigid insulation
Cavity insulation in wood frame wall

Gypsum board with low permeability paint or wall covering
Sealant or caulking
Adhesive, sealant or caulking
Joist hanger
Sealant or caulking
Gypsum board with low permeability paint or wall covering
Cavity insulation in pressure-treated wood frame wall
Pressure-treated plywood sheathing
Sealant or caulking
Subfloor
2 x 4 floor joists
Pressure-treated 2 x 6 wood sleepers
6-mil poly vapor diffusion retarder / air retarder (joints taped / sealed)

Protection board or coating
Ground slopes away from wall at 5% (6 in. per 10 ft.)
Draining rigid fiberglass insulation board

Polyethylene flashing
Filter fabric
Coarse gravel
4-in. perforated drain pipe

Capillary break over footing (dampproofing, low perm or elastomeric paint)
Concrete footing
Anchor bolt

Rigid insulation (minimum compressive strength of 25 psi)
Granular capillary break and drainage pad

Figure 4-16: Basement 7—heating climate.

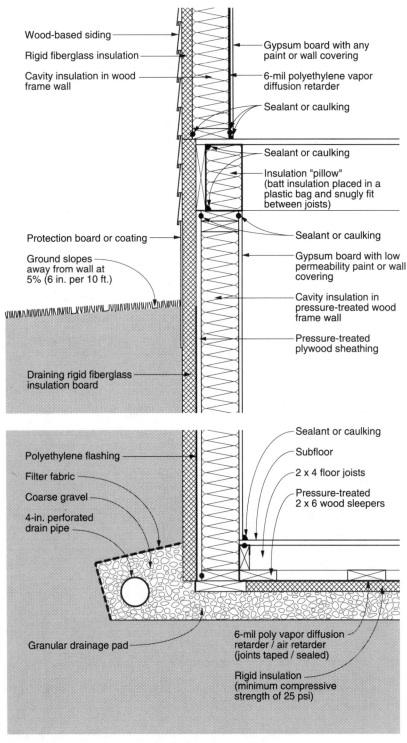

Wood-based siding

Rigid fiberglass insulation

Cavity insulation in wood frame wall

Gypsum board with any paint or wall covering

6-mil polyethylene vapor diffusion retarder

Sealant or caulking

Sealant or caulking

Insulation "pillow" (batt insulation placed in a plastic bag and snugly fit between joists)

Sealant or caulking

Protection board or coating

Ground slopes away from wall at 5% (6 in. per 10 ft.)

Gypsum board with low permeability paint or wall covering

Cavity insulation in pressure-treated wood frame wall

Pressure-treated plywood sheathing

Draining rigid fiberglass insulation board

Polyethylene flashing

Filter fabric

Coarse gravel

4-in. perforated drain pipe

Sealant or caulking

Subfloor

2 x 4 floor joists

Pressure-treated 2 x 6 wood sleepers

Granular drainage pad

6-mil poly vapor diffusion retarder / air retarder (joints taped / sealed)

Rigid insulation (minimum compressive strength of 25 psi)

Figure 4-17: Basement 8—heating climate.

Basement 8—Heating Climate: Similar to Basement 7, this is a pressure-treated wood foundation wall. Cavity insulation is placed within the wood frame wall and draining rigid fiberglass board covers the exterior. A layer of rigid insulation is placed beneath the wood floor. Unlike Basement 6, this assembly illustrates the wood wall resting directly on a gravel drainage pad rather than on a concrete footing. Another difference is that the rim joist insulation shown here is conventional platform framing rather than the balloon framing of Basement 6. Cavity insulation is placed between joists on the rim joist interior, and rigid insulation covers the rim joist on the exterior as well. Gypsum board with low permeability paint or wall covering serves as a vapor diffusion retarder on the interior side of the basement wall assembly. The above-grade wall shown here corresponds to Wall 3 in the previous section.

Key characteristics:
- *Rainwater is controlled by gutters and downspouts, and grade sloping away from the building.*
- *Groundwater is controlled by free-draining insulation board and a drain pipe at the footing (the drain screen principle).*
- *Capillary suction is controlled by the rigid draining fiberglass insulation on the exterior wall, and a layer of gravel under the slab and the wood footing.*
- *Air movement into the space is controlled by sealing the polyethylene air retarder under the wooden floor to the framing at the base of the basement wall. The gypsum board is sealed to the perimeter framing, and the rim joist area is sealed as well.*
- *Vapor diffusion from the surrounding soil is controlled by the polyethylene sheets on the wall exterior and beneath the floor.*
- *Low permeability paint or wall covering acts as a vapor diffusion retarder. Vapor impermeable interior surface finishes must be used.*
- *Insulation on the outside of the basement wall and the rim joist raises the wall temperature and limits potential condensation.*
- *Drying toward the interior or exterior of the wall is limited. Therefore, framing and insulation materials should be dry or permitted to dry before enclosure.*
- *Interior relative humidity should not exceed 35 percent at 70 degrees F during heating periods.*

Slab 1—Heating Climate: This slab-on-grade foundation assembly illustrates a shallow grade beam insulated for protection from frost penetration. Rigid insulation covers the vertical face of the grade beam and then extends horizontally into the soil surrounding the foundation perimeter. Additional rigid insulation is placed beneath the floor slab. The above-grade wood frame wall with stucco cladding does not correspond to any of the wall assemblies shown in the previous section.

Key characteristics:
- *Rainwater is controlled by gutters and downspouts, and grade sloping away from the building.*
- *Air movement into the space from the ground is controlled by a polyethylene sheet placed beneath the floor slab and grade beam.*
- *Vapor diffusion from the surrounding soil is also controlled by the polyethylene sheet placed beneath the floor slab and grade beam.*
- *Avoid ductwork beneath the slab and minimize other slab penetrations to control air movement and diffusion.*
- *Capillary suction is controlled by a dampproof coating on the exterior face of the grade beam, the polyethylene sheet beneath the grade beam, and a layer of gravel under the slab.*

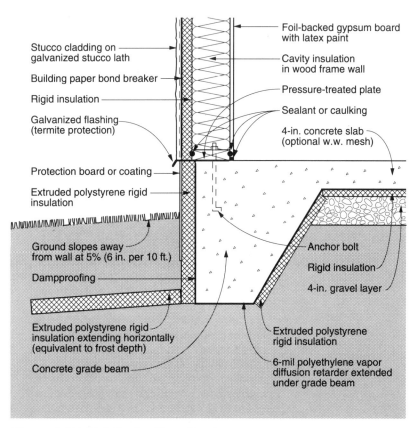

Stucco cladding on galvanized stucco lath
Building paper bond breaker
Rigid insulation
Galvanized flashing (termite protection)
Protection board or coating
Extruded polystyrene rigid insulation
Ground slopes away from wall at 5% (6 in. per 10 ft.)
Dampproofing
Extruded polystyrene rigid insulation extending horizontally (equivalent to frost depth)
Concrete grade beam

Foil-backed gypsum board with latex paint
Cavity insulation in wood frame wall
Pressure-treated plate
Sealant or caulking
4-in. concrete slab (optional w.w. mesh)
Anchor bolt
Rigid insulation
4-in. gravel layer
Extruded polystyrene rigid insulation
6-mil polyethylene vapor diffusion retarder extended under grade beam

Figure 4-18: Slab 1—heating climate.

SUMMARY: FOUNDATION ASSEMBLIES IN HEATING CLIMATES

Rain and Groundwater

To reduce the entry of rainwater into the foundation, all buildings in this climate should utilize gutters and downspouts, along with careful site grading, which direct water away from the structure. Surface water penetration into the ground immediately adjacent to basements should be limited by a cap of impermeable backfill material.

The brick veneer construction shown in Basement 6 introduces an additional rain penetration concern. In this case, rainwater from the above-grade wall assembly controlled by the rain screen must be prevented from draining into the top of the perimeter concrete foundation wall. To do so, flashing is installed at the base of the brick veneer wall extending to the back of the rain screen cavity and up over the top of the concrete foundation wall. This flashing directs water to the exterior of the assembly.

A subgrade drainage system is necessary to inhibit groundwater entry into basements. Two types of subsurface drainage systems are shown in this section. The first type (Basements 1, 2, 4, 5, and 6) consists of a drain pipe located at the perimeter of the concrete footings coupled with free-draining backfill material. The second type (Basements 3, 7, and 8) utilizes a free-draining insulation board instead of the backfill. The drain pipe and the free-draining backfill material (or insulation board) act together to provide a drain screen.

The drain pipe is connected to a sump, storm sewer, or to daylight. Perforations in the perimeter drain pipe should be installed with the holes down to allow groundwater to rise up into the drain pipe and be carried away.

Coarse gravel should surround the perimeter drain pipe and in turn be surrounded by a filter fabric. Filter fabric should be located both below and above the perimeter drain pipe, as drain pipe perforations face down and often clog from underneath. Drain tile should have at least 2 inches of gravel underneath, yet still be below the bottom surface of the basement floor slab.

Capillary Suction

Capillary moisture may move into a concrete or masonry foundation wall, a concrete floor slab, and the sill/rim joist area. Several methods are used to control moisture movement by capillarity into the foundation wall. In Basements 1, 2, 4, 5, and 6, the concrete foundation wall is protected by a dampproof coating on the exterior. In Basements 3, 7, and 8, rigid draining fiberglass insulation acts as a capillary break on the exterior of the concrete foundation wall.

In all basements shown here, a capillary break (dampproofing, low permeability paint, or elastomeric paint) covers the top of the concrete footing. It should be noted that dampproofing applied to footings presents a greater clean-up problem than paint products. A granular pad beneath the footing (shown in Basement 8) also can serve as a capillary break.

Where the concrete foundation wall is in direct contact with the sill plate (Basements 1 through 6), capillary moisture can move into the sill/rim joist area. This moisture movement into the sill/rim joist assembly can be controlled by a capillary break at the top of the perimeter concrete foundation wall. In Basement 6, capillary moisture from the concrete foundation wall can migrate into the brick veneer. This is controlled by an impermeable flashing at the base of the brick veneer and the rain screen cavity.

In all basements as well as the slab assembly, capillary moisture movement into the floor slab is controlled by a granular capillary break under the slab. The break is a 4-inch- to 6-inch-thick layer of 3/4-inch gravel with fines removed.

Where slab construction is utilized with a perimeter concrete grade beam (Slab 1), the slab vapor diffusion retarder is extended under the concrete grade beam to act as a capillary break at this location. Furthermore, dampproofing is installed on the exterior of the perimeter of the grade beam also to act as a capillary break. This dampproofing, if it is fluid or spray applied, must be chemically compatible with any rigid insulation installed over it.

Air Movement

In basement assemblies it is important to eliminate air flow between the surrounding soil and the basement space. To control air-transported moisture infiltrating into the basement space, the basement should be pressurized relative to the surrounding soil and air leakage openings should be limited (tight construction). Pipe penetrations and electrical conduits through concrete floor slabs and perimeter concrete walls, floor drains, and sump openings should be sealed or closed with tight covers.

Where perimeter concrete foundation walls are insulated on the interior, it is also important to prevent warm, interior, moisture-laden air from the basement space from coming in contact with cold, concrete surfaces during both heating and cooling periods.

Air leakage through the floor slab can be controlled by placing a polyethylene sheet beneath the slab and sealing it to the foundation wall assembly in various ways. Often it is sealed to the polyethylene or the gypsum board in wall assemblies with interior insulation (Basements 1, 4, and 6). In a similar fashion, the polyethylene beneath wooden floor assemblies in Basements 2, 7, and 8 is sealed to the wall. In Basements 3 and 5, the concrete floor slab is sealed directly to the foundation wall with caulking. In Basement 5, the first course of masonry is filled with mortar, and the basement floor slab vapor retarder is extended over the top of the concrete footing.

Air movement through the wall assembly is typically controlled by a polyethylene sheet on the interior (Basement 4), or by sealing the gypsum board to the framing (Basements 1, 6, 7, and 8). This interior air barrier is particularly important in insulated wood foundation wall cavities to prevent warm, moisture-laden air from the basement from coming in contact with cold sheathing surfaces. In Basement 2, the impermeable rigid insulation acts as an interior air barrier.

In almost all cases, the elements that form the sill/rim joist/floor assembly should be sealed to control air movement in this area. There are many variations in rim joist construction practice. For example, the structural elements of the rim joist assembly are not sealed in Basement 4. Instead, the rim joist/floor assembly is wrapped by polyethylene and this polyethylene is sealed to both the foundation wall perimeter vapor diffusion retarder and the above-grade wall vapor diffusion retarder.

In Basement 6, air leakage in the rim joist/floor assembly is minimized by installing blocks of rigid insulation between floor joists and sealing them to the top of the perimeter basement frame wall and the underside of the subfloor sheathing. Similarly, rigid insulation forms the air retarder in the rim joist area of Basement 2.

In Basements 1, 3, 5, and 8, a tight-fitting, insulation "pillow" is installed at the interior of the rim joist assembly between floor joists. The insulation pillow is formed by placing batt insulation in a plastic bag and snugly fitting the bag containing the insulation between the floor joists. Gaps at this location around the insulation pillow need to be minimized to control potential convective moisture transfer from the interior basement space to the interior surface of the rim joist.

Vapor Diffusion

Moisture movement by vapor diffusion can be controlled in several ways. When moisture moves from the surrounding soil into the concrete foundation wall, it is controlled by installing a vapor diffusion retarder on the exterior of the foundation wall. In Basements 1, 2, 4, 5, and 6, the dampproof coating on the exterior of the foundation wall acts as a vapor diffusion retarder.

Similarly, in Basements 7 and 8, a vapor diffusion retarder on the exterior controls moisture entering the wood foundation wall from the surrounding soil. The impermeable sheathing on the exterior of the wood foundation wall also acts as a vapor diffusion retarder.

In Basement 3, rigid insulation on the exterior of the concrete foundation wall controls moisture entering from the surrounding soil. The rigid insulation raises the temperature of the concrete, lowers its equilibrium relative humidity, and thereby allows the concrete foundation wall to dry into the surrounding soil. A vapor diffusion retarder on the exterior of this foundation wall is therefore not necessary.

For all foundations, vapor diffusion through the floor slab assembly from the surrounding soil can be controlled with a polyethylene vapor diffusion retarder under the slab (or wooden floor).

Where there is interior insulation, moisture from the basement space is typically prevented from diffusing into the perimeter foundation wall framing by installing insulation with a vapor diffusion retarder backing or a polyethylene vapor diffusion retarder on the interior of the framing (Basements 1 and 4). Another approach shown in Basement 6, utilizes foil-backed gypsum board as the interior vapor diffusion retarder, while in Basements 7 and 8, a low permeability paint serves this purpose. The rigid insulation in Basement 2 is a vapor diffusion retarder.

In Basements 1 and 6, construction moisture contained in the perimeter concrete foundation wall is prevented from diffusing into the perimeter foundation frame wall cavity by applying dampproofing, low permeability paint, or elastomeric paint on the interior of the perimeter foundation wall. Alternatively, the wall can be allowed to dry prior to enclosure. Where interior dampproofing is used, consideration should be given to potential odors and other indoor environment concerns.

There are a number of approaches to controlling moisture diffusing from the interior basement space into the perimeter rim joist assembly during the heating season. In Basements 1, 3, 5, and 8, the plastic bag facing on the batt insulation controls vapor diffusion.

In all basement examples, moisture accumulation from vapor diffusion migrating from the interior space at the rim joist assembly is limited by installing insulating sheathing at the exterior of the rim joist. This elevates the temperature of the first condensing surface at this location (the interior surface of the rim joist).

In slab assemblies (Slab 1) it is important to eliminate the moisture flow from the exterior into the enclosure by air flow and vapor diffusion. To do this, a vapor diffusion retarder is installed under the slab and construction is tight. Ductwork should be avoided in slabs, because groundwater and soil gas seepage into ducts and diffusion and capillarity into concrete slabs from surrounding soil transferred to the ducts often become significant sources of moisture to the enclosure.

Drying of Foundation Assemblies

Basement 3 dries to the exterior and Basement 5 can dry to the interior. In most cases, however (Basements 1, 2, 4, 6, 7, and 8), drying toward either the interior or exterior is limited by an impermeable coating on the exterior of the wall and the interior vapor diffusion retarder. Should the wall assembly become wet during service or be built wet due to wet framing materials or wet-applied cavity insulations (wet spray cellulose or blown fiberglass), it may not dry. Accordingly, dry framing materials (wood at a moisture content of 19 percent by weight or lower) and dry-applied insulations are recommended. Alternatively, wall assemblies must be allowed to dry prior to enclosure.

For these basements with limited drying (Basements 1, 2, 4, 6, 7, and 8), interior basement moisture levels should be limited to 35 percent relative humidity at 70 degrees Fahrenheit during heating periods. This is needed to further control air-transported moisture and vapor diffusion with this wall assembly, since only limited drying of the assembly occurs.

Interior Finishes

Either vapor permeable or vapor impermeable interior surface finishes may be used in conjunction with any foundation wall assembly except for Basements 7 and 8 where an impermeable paint must be used to act as a vapor diffusion retarder.

Concrete floor slabs contain significant quantities of moisture when initially placed. Covering this surface with an impermeable surface finish or floor covering may lead to deterioration of these surfaces if the construction moisture is not allowed to dry. Initial drying of the construction moisture contained in concrete may also lead to elevated interior moisture levels during the first few months of occupancy.

Installing carpets on cold, damp, concrete floor slabs can lead to serious allergenic reactions in sensitive individuals and other health-related consequences. It is not recommended that carpets be installed on concrete slabs unless the carpets can be kept dry and warm; that is, carpet relative humidities should be kept below 70 percent (Godish 1989). In practice this is typically not possible unless floor slab assemblies are insulated and basement areas are conditioned. The wooden floors shown in Basements 2, 7, and 8 avoid this problem.

Details

In several cases (Basements 3, 5, 7, 8 and Slab 1), rigid insulation is installed on the exterior of the perimeter concrete foundation wall to reduce heating and cooling loads and is protected above grade on its exterior from mechanical damage. Appropriate below grade flashings or other protection may be necessary, since this rigid insulation can act as a conduit

for insects to enter the enclosure.

In Basements 1, 4, and 6, the perimeter foundation frame wall is held away from the concrete in order to enhance the durability of the wood members. This is accomplished by using a 2 x 4 top plate with 2 x 3 studs and a 2 x 3 bottom plate. The cavity insulation, however, fills the entire void and touches the interior face of the concrete foundation wall. Fiberglass batt insulation is recommended as the cavity insulation by virtue of its draining characteristics and nonhygroscopic nature.

In Basement 4, tight-fitting faced insulation should be installed at the interior of the rim joist assembly between floor joists. Gaps at this location in the insulation need to be minimized to control potential convective moisture transfer from the interior basement space to the interior surface of the rim joist. If convective moisture transfer is inhibited at this location and the facing on the insulation acts as an interior vapor diffusion retarder, the thermal resistance of the rigid insulation on the exterior of the rim joist can be reduced and the thermal resistance of the insulation at the interior of the rim joist can be increased.

The granular drainage pad located under basement floors can be integrated into a subslab ventilation system to control radon migration by adding a vent pipe connected to the surface and an exhaust fan. In all construction, it is good practice to install a passive vent pipe connecting this subslab gravel layer to the exterior through the roof. An exhaust fan can be added later if necessary.

In Basements 2, 7, and 8, the rigid insulation under the basement floor framing requires a compressive strength of 25 psi to control settling. Regarding the two wood foundation assemblies, publications of the National Forest Products Association should be consulted including *Permanent Wood Foundation System: Design, Fabrication and Installation Manual* (NFPA 1987).

In the slab-on-grade assembly, perimeter rigid insulation installed horizontally protects this foundation from frost. The rigid insulation should extend horizontally a distance equivalent to the depth of local frost penetration and have a minimum thermal resistance determined by the local freezing degree days (NAHB 1988). In addition, the rigid insulation should resist capillarity effects and be sufficiently protected from mechanical damage during construction and during service. Specific information regarding frost-protected slab foundations should be obtained from local authorities.

Roof Construction in Heating Climates

In this section five roof assemblies are shown that can be used successfully in heating climates. There is one wood roof truss with a vented attic, and four examples of cathedral ceilings. Two of the cathedral ceiling assemblies are ventilated and the remaining two are unvented. The basic characteristics of the roof assemblies are summarized in Table 4-3.

First, each roof assembly is illustrated and briefly described. Text adjacent to each drawing indicates how the assembly is designed to handle each of the critical moisture problems in this climate: (1) ventilation, (2) air movement, and (3) vapor diffusion. In addition, comments related to special concerns such as ice damming are summarized for each assembly. Following the drawings is a summary discussion of key moisture control strategies for roof assemblies in this climate.

Insulation levels in roof assemblies, except where specifically noted to control moisture accumulation on condensing surfaces, are left to the judgement of the reader.

Table 4-3: Characteristics of roof assemblies for heating climates.

	ROOF TYPE	VENTILATION	CEILING INSULATION	OTHER FEATURES	DRYING
ROOF 1	Wood truss with flat ceiling	Vented attic	Cavity insulation	Polyethylene vapor diffusion retarder (Interior)	To the exterior
ROOF 2	Cathedral ceiling	Vented	Cavity insulation	Polyethylene vapor diffusion retarder (Interior)	To the exterior
ROOF 3	Cathedral ceiling	Vented	Cavity insulation with rigid insulation on the interior	Polyethylene vapor diffusion retarder (Interior)	To the exterior
ROOF 4	Cathedral ceiling	Unvented	Cavity insulation with rigid insulation on the exterior	Low perm paint is vapor diffusion retarder (Interior)	Limited
ROOF 5	Cathedral ceiling	Unvented	Rigid insulation	Polyethylene vapor diffusion retarder (Interior)	Rafters dry to the interior

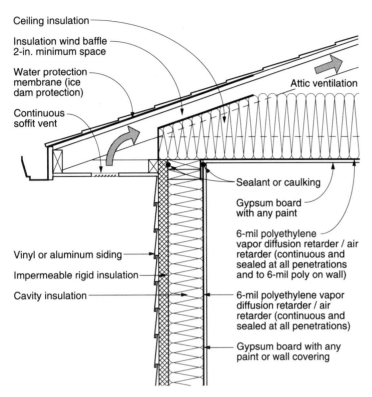

Ceiling insulation

Insulation wind baffle 2-in. minimum space

Water protection membrane (ice dam protection)

Continuous soffit vent

Attic ventilation

Sealant or caulking

Gypsum board with any paint

6-mil polyethylene vapor diffusion retarder / air retarder (continuous and sealed at all penetrations and to 6-mil poly on wall)

Vinyl or aluminum siding

Impermeable rigid insulation

Cavity insulation

6-mil polyethylene vapor diffusion retarder / air retarder (continuous and sealed at all penetrations)

Gypsum board with any paint or wall covering

Figure 4-19: Roof 1—heating climate.

Roof 1—Heating Climate: This conventional wood truss roof system is insulated above the flat ceiling. The attic space is ventilated. A polyethylene vapor diffusion retarder is placed above the ceiling gypsum board on the interior side of the insulation. The wall shown here corresponds to Wall 2 in a previous section of this chapter.

Key characteristics:
- *The attic is ventilated permitting drying to the exterior.*
- *The polyethylene sheet placed beneath the gypsum board acts as an air retarder to control air movement, and acts as a vapor diffusion retarder.*
- *Air movement is further controlled by limiting and sealing all penetrations between the conditioned space and the attic.*
- *The conditioned space should be depressurized relative to the attic.*
- *The wind baffle prevents wind-washing of the perimeter insulation.*
- *A membrane over the roof sheathing protects against moisture damage from ice damming.*

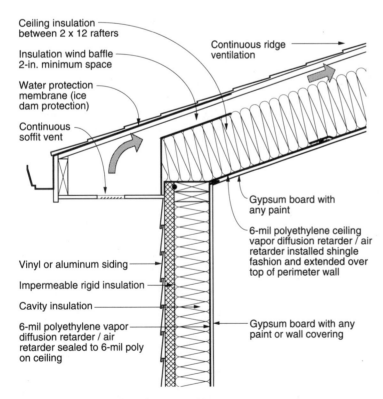

Ceiling insulation between 2 x 12 rafters

Insulation wind baffle 2-in. minimum space

Continuous ridge ventilation

Water protection membrane (ice dam protection)

Continuous soffit vent

Gypsum board with any paint

6-mil polyethylene ceiling vapor diffusion retarder / air retarder installed shingle fashion and extended over top of perimeter wall

Vinyl or aluminum siding

Impermeable rigid insulation

Cavity insulation

6-mil polyethylene vapor diffusion retarder / air retarder sealed to 6-mil poly on ceiling

Gypsum board with any paint or wall covering

Figure 4-20: Roof 2—heating climate.

Roof 2—Heating Climate: In this roof assembly with a cathedral ceiling, cavity insulation is placed between 2 x 12 rafters. Ventilation is provided through a 2-inch air space above the insulation. A polyethylene vapor diffusion retarder is placed above the ceiling gypsum board on the interior side of the insulation. The wall shown here corresponds to Wall 2 in a previous section of this chapter.

Key characteristics:
- *Ventilation is provided by a 2-inch air space above the insulation with continuous soffit and ridge vents. This permits drying to the exterior.*
- *The polyethylene sheet placed beneath the gypsum board acts as an air retarder to control air movement, and acts as a vapor diffusion retarder.*
- *Air movement is further controlled by limiting and sealing all roof penetrations.*
- *The conditioned space should be depressurized relative to the attic.*
- *The wind baffle prevents wind-washing of the perimeter insulation.*
- *A membrane over the roof sheathing protects against moisture damage from ice damming.*

Roof 3—Heating Climate: Similar to Roof 2, this is a roof assembly with a ventilated cathedral ceiling. Cavity insulation is placed between 2 x 10 rafters and ventilation is provided through a 2-inch air space above the insulation. The key difference between this and Roof 2 is the rigid insulation placed beneath the rafters. The wall shown here corresponds to Wall 2 in a previous section of this chapter.

Key characteristics:
- Ventilation is provided by a 2-inch air space above the insulation with continuous soffit and ridge vents. This permits drying to the exterior.
- The polyethylene sheet, placed between the rigid board and cavity insulation layers, acts as an air retarder to control air movement, and acts as a vapor diffusion retarder.
- Air movement is further controlled by limiting and sealing all roof penetrations.
- The conditioned space should be depressurized relative to the attic.
- The wind baffle prevents wind-washing of the perimeter insulation.
- A membrane over the roof sheathing protects against moisture damage from ice damming.

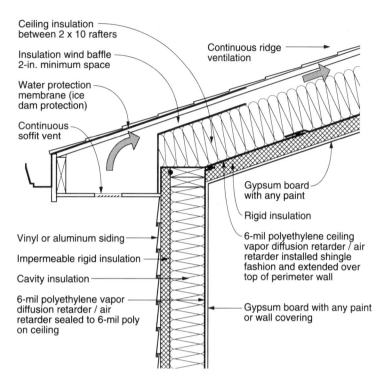

Figure 4-21: Roof 3—heating climate.

Roof 4—Heating Climate: This roof assembly illustrates a cathedral ceiling that is unvented. Cavity insulation is placed between 2 x 8 rafters. Above the roof sheathing is a layer of rigid insulation. The wall shown here corresponds to Wall 2 in a previous section of this chapter, except for the type of vapor diffusion retarder used.

Key characteristics:
- Drying in this roof assembly is limited. Therefore, framing and insulation materials should be dry or permitted to dry before enclosure.
- Air movement is controlled by the rigid insulation installed with staggered joints, and sealing all roof penetrations.
- The conditioned space should be depressurized relative to the attic.
- Low permeability paint acts as a vapor diffusion retarder on the interior.
- Insulation board raises the roof cavity temperature and limits potential condensation.
- Interior relative humidity should not exceed 35 percent at 70 degrees F during heating periods.
- The wind baffle (rigid insulation) prevents wind-washing of the perimeter insulation.
- A membrane over the roof sheathing protects against moisture damage from ice damming.

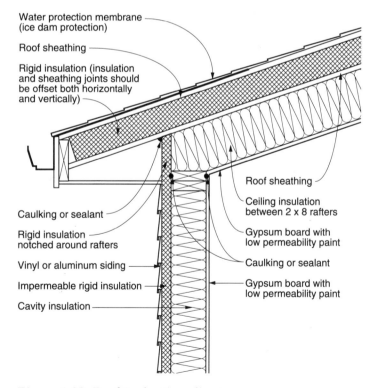

Figure 4-22: Roof 4—heating climate.

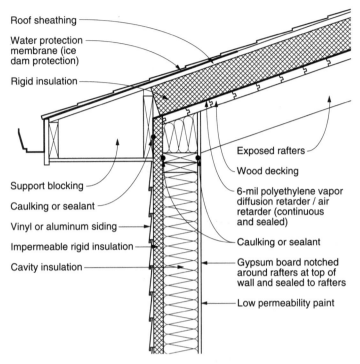

Roof sheathing

Water protection
membrane (ice
dam protection)

Rigid insulation

Support blocking

Caulking or sealant

Vinyl or aluminum siding

Impermeable rigid insulation

Cavity insulation

Exposed rafters

Wood decking

6-mil polyethylene vapor
diffusion retarder / air
retarder (continuous
and sealed)

Caulking or sealant

Gypsum board notched
around rafters at top of
wall and sealed to rafters

Low permeability paint

Figure 4-23: Roof 5—heating climate.

Roof 5—Heating Climate: Similar to Roof 4, this roof assembly illustrates a cathedral ceiling that is unvented. In this case, rafters and wood decking are exposed on the interior of the space and a layer of rigid insulation is placed above the decking. A polyethylene vapor diffusion retarder is placed beneath the rigid insulation. The wall shown here corresponds to Wall 2 in a previous section of this chapter, except for the use of low permeability paint as a vapor diffusion retarder.

Key characteristics:
- *The exposed rafters and decking can dry to the interior.*
- *The polyethylene sheet placed beneath the gypsum board acts as an air retarder to control air movement, and acts as a vapor diffusion retarder.*
- *Air movement is further controlled by limiting and sealing all roof penetrations.*
- *A membrane over the roof sheathing protects against moisture damage from ice damming.*
- *The construction sequence for this roof assembly is as follows: (1) install wood decking over rafters, (2) place polyethylene over wood decking, (3) install edge and support blocking to keep rigid insulation from sliding off the roof, and (4) place rigid insulation and roof sheathing over the polyethylene so that vertical and horizontal joints are offset.*

SUMMARY: ROOF ASSEMBLIES IN HEATING CLIMATES

Ventilation

Roofs 1, 2, and 3 are ventilated while Roofs 4 and 5 are not. Where roof assemblies are ventilated in this climate, it is done to remove moisture from attic spaces and, to a limited extent, to reduce cooling loads by reducing solar heat gain. Where there is an open attic space (as in Roof 1), a minimum of 1 square foot of vent area should be provided for every 300 square feet of insulated ceiling area. In addition, vents should be distributed between the soffit and ridge to prevent zones of dead or stagnant air and should not be blocked by roof assembly insulation or other obstructions.

If cathedral ceiling assemblies are ventilated (as are Roofs 2 and 3), a minimum of 1 square foot of vent area should be provided for every 150 square feet of insulated ceiling area. Continuous soffit and ridge vents should be installed with a minimum 2-inch space be-

tween the top of the insulation and the underside of the roof sheathing.

In unvented cathedral ceiling assemblies (such as Roofs 4 and 5), as in most wall assemblies, the emphasis is on the prevention of moisture movement into the assembly rather than the removal of moisture once it has entered the assembly by ventilation.

Air Movement

During the heating season, airborne moisture exfiltrates from the conditioned space into the attic or roof assembly cavities under typical conditions. To control this, the conditioned space should be depressurized relative to the attic or roof assembly cavities. In addition, penetrations through the ceiling where air leakage can occur should be limited as much as possible. This applies to Roofs 1, 2, 3, and 4.

In vented roof assemblies such as Roof 1, it is important to eliminate air flow between conditioned spaces and the attic. The attic needs to be uncoupled from the conditioned space so that conditions within the building enclosure influence the attic to a minimum. This is best accomplished by not installing any forced air ductwork, furnaces, or air conditioners in attics. In addition, penetrations for plumbing, wiring, dropped ceilings, and kitchen cabinet bulkheads should be sealed.

In an unvented cathedral ceiling assembly such as Roof 4, the exfiltration of warm, moisture-laden air during the heating season is controlled by sealing the interior gypsum wall board to the roof joist framing, as well as sealing the exterior rigid insulation to the roof joists. This air sealing can be with an adhesive, caulk, or some other sealant. Experience has shown that some exterior rigid insulations are thermally unstable, and may not be compatible with sealing techniques which provide little allowance for movement. The joints in the layers of rigid insulation should be staggered horizontally and vertically to form an effective air retarder.

Roof 5 contains no cavity within the roof assembly making air movement easier to control. To minimize movement of airborne moisture from the interior, a sheet polyethylene vapor diffusion retarder/air retarder is installed in Roof 5 that extends from the ridge to the eave. The joints in the sheet polyethylene should be taped or sealed to provide air retarder continuity. In both Roofs 4 and 5, the joints in the roof sheathing installed over the rigid insulation should be staggered over the joints in the rigid insulation to enhance air tightness.

Vapor Diffusion

During heating periods, vapor diffusion from the interior may carry moisture into the roof assembly, where it accumulates. In Roofs 1, 2, 3, and 5, outward moisture movement by diffusion is controlled by a continuous polyethylene vapor diffusion retarder. The polyethylene sheet is sealed to the perimeter wall vapor diffusion retarder in Roofs 1, 2, and 3.

In Roofs 2 and 3, the continuous ceiling vapor diffusion retarder is installed shingle fashion and extended over the top of the exterior perimeter wall to allow for drainage of any condensed moisture on the top surface and to provide secondary protection for roof rainwater leakage.

In Roof 4, low permeability paint on the ceiling gypsum board acts as the vapor diffusion retarder on the interior. Vapor diffusion is further controlled by elevating the temperature

of the first condensing surface within the cathedral ceiling assembly, namely, the cavity side of the roof sheathing. In Roof 4, rigid insulation is installed to limit periods of potential condensation.

Drying of Roof Assemblies

Roofs 1, 2, and 3 all permit drying to the exterior since they are vented. In Roof 4, however, drying toward either the interior or exterior is limited by the vapor impermeable rigid insulation and an interior vapor diffusion retarder.

Should the cathedral ceiling assembly in Roof 4 be built wet through the use of wet framing materials or wet-applied cavity insulations (wet spray cellulose or blown fiberglass), it may not dry. Accordingly, dry framing materials (wood at a moisture content of 19 percent by weight or lower) and dry-applied insulations are recommended. Alternatively, cathedral ceiling assemblies should be allowed to dry prior to enclosure.

If Roof 4 is used, interior moisture levels should be limited to 35 percent relative humidity at 70 degrees Fahrenheit during heating periods. This is needed to further control airborne moisture and vapor diffusion with this cathedral ceiling assembly, since only limited drying of the assembly occurs.

In Roof 5, the rafters are exposed to facilitate drying of the wood framing toward the interior.

Comments

In Roofs 1, 2, 3, and 4, a wind baffle is installed at the perimeter of the attic or cathedral ceiling area where the insulated ceiling intersects the exterior wall. This prevents thermal short-circuiting of the insulation by wind (wind-washing). In this climate, wind-washing during the heating season can cool the perimeter wall top plate and ceiling gypsum board surfaces, subsequently causing interior mold and mildew growth.

Where exterior ventilation air enters soffit assemblies, it experiences a pressure drop, as the soffit assembly acts as an expansion space. This is due to the combination of a narrow soffit vent opening up to a relatively large volume soffit assembly and then being squeezed into a narrow space between the underside of the roof sheathing and the wind baffle. This pressure drop induces the ventilation air to deposit airborne rain droplets and snow in the soffit assembly rather than transport them farther into the roof assembly. Accordingly, it may be desirable to back-prime wood soffit materials.

Ice damming for all roofs in this climate is controlled by installing a water protection membrane over the sheathing at the eave. In addition, sufficient thermal insulation (along with air tightening) should be provided at the intersection of the perimeter wall and ceiling to reduce heat loss, which can lead to snow melt. Also, where the soffit assembly is vented, it flushes heat from the conditioned space away from the roof sheathing to maintain a cold deck.

In the vented cathedral ceiling shown in Roof 3, rigid insulation on the interior side of the roof rafters (beneath the sheet polyethylene vapor diffusion retarder) provides additional thermal resistance. In cases where the rigid insulation is impermeable, the sheet polyethylene ceiling vapor retarder can be replaced by the rigid insulation alone. It must be installed in a continuous fashion (edges sealed), and sealed to the perimeter wall vapor diffusion retarder.

In cases where attachment of the interior-applied rigid insulation and ceiling gypsum board is a concern, the rigid insulation can be held in place by furring (installed to the interior of the rigid insulation), and the gypsum board subsequently fastened to the furring.

The rigid insulation installed in the roof assembly is typically fastened with long wood screws passing through the upper roof sheathing.

Some unvented roof assemblies have led to an elevation of shingle/shake/sheathing temperatures and subsequently to premature degradation of shingles/shakes/sheathings and a reduced service life. Accordingly, light-colored shakes and shingles should be utilized. In addition, it may be desirable to install roofing papers to provide additional protection against rainwater entry should shakes and shingles deteriorate prematurely. Rigid insulation placed over the roof sheathing should be fastened with 5- to 6-inch wood screws penetrating into the rafters.

CHAPTER 5

Moisture Control Practices for Mixed Climates

This chapter includes four major sections that address moisture control practices for mixed heating and cooling climates in the United States. First, an introductory section defines the climate, identifies key moisture problems found there, and discusses some general approaches to solving these problems. The last three sections of the chapter address wall, foundation, and roof assemblies. For each component, several construction assemblies designed to control moisture in this climate are shown. There are detailed construction drawings, a list of the key characteristics for each assembly, and a summary discussion of the control strategies for this climate.

Introduction *Mixed Climate Defined*

This climate zone is defined as a heating climate with up to 4000 heating degree days combined with a significant number of cooling (air conditioning) hours. This is in essence a mixed climate where both heating and cooling are needed for significant periods of time. The design/construction practice recommendations in this section are geared to mixed, humid climates, not to mixed, dry climates, although no distinction is made between the two in the accompanying map (Figure 5-1). The recommendations in this section will perform satisfactorily in both types of mixed climates. It also should be noted that the recommended practices in this section will result in satisfactory performance in warm, dry climates.

The climate zone specified is broad and general for simplicity. For a specific location, designers and builders should consider weather records, local experience, and the microclimate around a building. Incident solar radiation, nearby water and wetlands, vegetation, and undergrowth can all affect the microclimate.

For residential buildings in this climate, wood frame construction is predominate. Due to shallow ground frost penetration, this climate includes a mixture of basement foundations and frost-protected crawl spaces. Concrete and masonry foundations are common, with some limited use of wood foundations and wood crawl spaces.

KEY MOISTURE CONCERNS

In mixed climates where both heating and cooling occur for significant periods of time, the principle moisture concerns are rain penetration, groundwater, concealed condensation within wall and roof spaces, and interior mold and mildew. High interior levels of humidity during heating periods encourage mold and mildew growth, as do high exterior levels of humidity and cool interior surfaces due to the air conditioning of enclosures during cooling periods. These are discussed below along with some other problems related to mechanical systems and the use of combustion appliances.

Rain and Groundwater

Controlling rain penetration and groundwater is a common concern to builders in all climates. Rain that is permitted to penetrate the exterior cladding of a building can cause material deterioration as well as contribute to other moisture problems within the building assemblies. Basement spaces are often conditioned and occupied in this climate, further raising the level of concern with groundwater penetration and infiltration of soil gas (including radon).

Condensation in Building Assemblies

Conditioned spaces are typically heated by either electric or fuel-fired appliances. Negative interior air pressures have been reduced as active chimneys are replaced by high efficiency combustion appliances and electric heat sources. Other important changes in building construction are the creation of tighter enclosures and the reduction of outside air changes, which lead to higher levels of interior moisture. These trends combine to raise concerns about exfiltration of interior moisture-laden air causing condensation within insulated assemblies.

During cooling periods, mechanical cooling coupled with dehumidification is widespread. Air movement and vapor diffusion thus carry moisture from the exterior to the interior cooled area, because the vapor pressure is higher outdoors than it is indoors. These vapor pressure differences during cooling periods in this climate can be more significant than those found during heating periods. High inward flow of moisture during cooling periods can increase energy costs due to high cooling loads, as well as increase building deterioration.

Air leakage into insulated attics during heating months, coupled with insufficient attic ventilation, can lead to roof sheathing decay. Air leakage into insulated wall cavities during the heating months, coupled with an insufficient or limited drying ability, can cause the decay of structural framing members.

Cladding systems that can absorb significant amounts of moisture when exposed to rain, such as brick, masonry, wood, and stucco, should only be incorporated in wall assemblies designed and built to deal with the inward migration of moisture. Solar radiation warms exterior wall surfaces, and this warming creates temperature gradients from the exterior to the interior. Along with the air conditioning of interior surfaces, this can cause problems if not taken into account.

An example of this is the installation of gypsum board covered with vinyl wallpaper

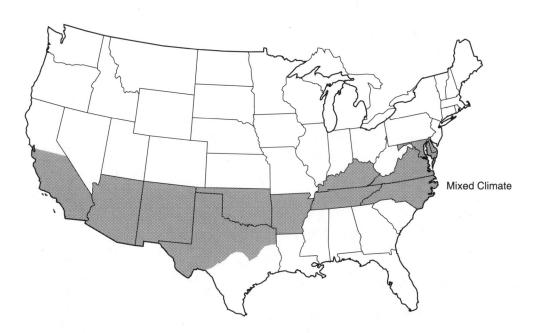

Figure 5-1: Map of mixed climate zone in the United States.

on the interior of a masonry block wall without provision for an appropriate vapor diffusion retarder and air barrier system. Without these, the gypsum wall board is not protected from exterior moisture or from construction moisture which may be trapped in the masonry units. Thus, wherever vinyl interior wall coverings are used in this climate zone, precautions must be taken to prevent gypsum wall board from absorbing moisture either from the exterior or from construction moisture.

Building assemblies constructed with wet lumber (greater than 19 percent moisture content by weight) or employing wet-applied insulation (wet spray cellulose or wet blown fiberglass) merit special attention. These assemblies must be designed and built so that they can dry to the exterior or interior, or the materials must be allowed to dry prior to enclosure.

High Interior Humidity Resulting in Mold, Mildew, and Condensation

Low air change during the heating season due to the construction of tight enclosures can lead to elevated interior levels of moisture. These elevated levels can lead to condensation on window surfaces and give rise to surface mold and mildew, as well as concealed condensation within walls and roof spaces (discussed above).

Cold interior surfaces during the heating months arising from thermal bridges or other thermal defects (wind blowing through insulation) create high interior surface relative humidities and often lead to mold and mildew at these locations. Most common locations are where exterior walls intersect insulated ceilings, exterior corners, and uninsulated (or poorly insulated) window lintels or headers.

Air change (infiltration/exfiltration combined with controlled ventilation) removes interior moisture from within building enclosures during the heating season. The greater the air change rate, the greater the removal rate of interior moisture. However, typical construction practice results in building enclosures which have air change rates from random leakage that are inadequate to control interior moisture levels.

During cooling periods, elevated interior moisture levels can result from high air change due to infiltration/exfiltration, duct leakage, and excessive ventilation. Naturally, interior moisture levels increase as the amount of hot, humid exterior air brought into an enclosure increases.

Mechanical System Concerns

During hot, humid cooling periods, leaky return ducts located in attics draw significant amounts of warm, moisture-laden air into the conditioned space from the attic, often creating moisture problems and increasing cooling loads. During heating periods these same leaky return ducts draw cold air into the conditioned space, increasing heating loads. Leaky return ducts in vented crawl spaces draw significant amounts of soil gas, moisture, possibly pesticides, radon, and other pollutants into the conditioned spaces. This often creates moisture problems, increases cooling and heating loads, and risks occupant health and safety.

Leaky supply ducts in attics or vented crawl spaces during cooling periods depressurize the conditioned space, leading to the infiltration of exterior warm air, often creating moisture problems and increasing cooling loads. During heating periods the same mechanism can deposit sufficient interior moisture into attic assemblies to create roof sheathing moisture and decay problems. It may also depressurize the conditioned space, leading to infiltration and increasing heating loads.

Many building enclosures in mixed climates are now built airtight. Where forced air systems with minimal returns (a single return is common) are installed in tight building enclosures, bedrooms can be pressurized and basement spaces can be depressurized. This can lead to the spillage and backdrafting of combustion appliances, infiltration of soil gas, and exfiltration of moisture-laden air into building assembly cavities.

Combustion Appliances

Unvented combustion appliances such as gas stoves with standing pilot lights and room space heaters are significant sources of moisture as well as sources for other pollutants.

GENERAL STRATEGIES TO CONTROL MOISTURE PROBLEMS

For the potential moisture problems identified above for buildings in this climate, there are several control strategies. The control strategies generally fall into two groups: (1) those applying to the building envelope assemblies, and (2) those related to the overall building and its mechanical systems. To be

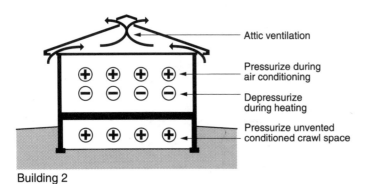

Building 1

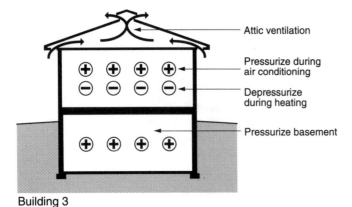

Building 2

Building 3

Figure 5-2: Recommended air pressure distribution to reduce moisture problems in mixed climate buildings.

effective, all of these strategies must be applied as a complete system.

Building Envelope Strategies

Detailed presentations of building envelope strategies are found in the last three sections of the chapter for wall, foundation, and roof assemblies. Some of the key principles are:

- Control rain penetration in walls using rain screens, building papers, and appropriate placement of flashings.

- Direct water away from foundations using gutters and downspouts as well as careful site grading.

- Control groundwater with a subgrade drainage system.

- Control moisture movement by air leakage (the exfiltration of interior moisture-laden air) by limiting air leakage openings and installing air retarder systems in all assemblies.

- Place vapor diffusion retarders in walls, roofs, and foundations to control moisture movement by vapor diffusion from the interior.

- If possible, permit wall assemblies to dry if they become wet. Wall design and construction in this climate locates vapor diffusion retarders and air retarders on either the exterior or the interior of the assembly. Thus, it is convenient to allow walls to dry in either direction.

- Ventilate roof assemblies to remove moisture. Removal will occur continuously during the heating season and intermittently during cooling periods.

Whole Building System Strategies

The second group of strategies pertains to the overall design and operation of the building and its mechanical system in particular. These include:

- Minimize interior moisture sources by direct venting of clothes dryers, and providing kitchen and bath exhaust systems.

- To control air leakage, design the mechanical system to maintain basement and unvented crawl spaces at a positive air pressure relative to the exterior throughout the year. In addition, above-grade spaces should be maintained at a negative air pressure relative to the exterior during the heating season, and at a positive air pressure during cooling periods. Positive pressurization of the basement spaces and crawl spaces eliminates the infiltration of soil gas, radon, and other pollutants. Depressurization of the above-grade conditioned spaces during heating periods eliminates the exfiltration of interior moisture-laden air. Pressurization of the above-grade conditioned space during cooling periods eliminates the infiltration of exterior moisture-laden air. This principle is shown in Figure 5-2 for three typical building configurations appropriate for this climate. All three buildings have vented attics while each illustrates a different foundation assembly: (1) a vented crawl space, (2) an unvented crawl space, and (3) a basement.

• Ventilate enclosures in a controlled manner to limit interior moisture levels. During cooling periods, limit controlled ventilation to minimum levels while maintaining indoor air quality. These levels are established by ASHRAE guidelines, the strength of pollutant sources within enclosures, and/or local authorities (ASHRAE 1989b). An effective controlled ventilation system must do the following: (1) exhaust stale air, (2) supply fresh outside air, (3) operate continuously when occupants are present, and (4) provide effective distribution. A schematic of such a system is shown in Figure 5-3 with notes describing its components, operation, and control. This type of system is essential with tight construction to control both health and moisture problems. The HVAC system, central exhaust, and fresh air supply

Notes for Figure 5-3:
An effective controlled ventilation system in a heating climate should have the following characteristics:

• *Stale air is removed through a central exhaust system. Exhaust vents are located in the kitchen and bathrooms.*
• *The central exhaust system operates continuously — at least 15 minutes per hour whenever occupants are present.*
• *The outside air supply is connected to the return side of the air handling unit. An automatically operated damper covers the outside air intake.*
• *The forced air system provides effective distribution of fresh air throughout the house.*
• *The control system is designed so that the central exhaust system only operates when the outside air damper is open and the air handling unit is running.*
• *The overall system must be designed, balanced, and commissioned so that the pressure relationships recommended for mixed climate buildings are maintained (see Figure 5-2).*
• *To maintain the air pressure relationships for mixed climate buildings during cooling, the outside air damper should be open when the air handler is operating. The air handling unit fan must operate at a higher speed during cooling periods than it does during heating periods to create positive pressurization.*

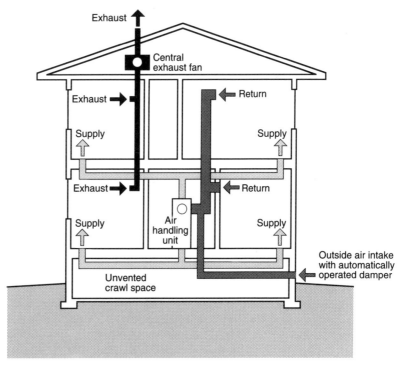

Figure 5-3: Controlled ventilation system for a house in a mixed climate.

must be balanced and commissioned in order to maintain the pressure relationships shown in Figure 5-2.

- In the more moderate heating regions with high exterior vapor pressures during the heating season, mechanical dehumidification is practical.

- It is preferable to install ductwork for forced air heating and cooling systems only within conditioned spaces. If possible, avoid attics or vented crawl spaces. Where ductwork is located in dropped ceilings adjacent to attics and exterior walls, it is important that air barrier continuity is maintained above the dropped ceiling or at the exterior wall.

- Seal all ductwork with mastic. Of particular concern are return systems utilizing floor joist and stud wall cavities to form return air ducts. Utilize multiple return registers (particularly located in bedrooms), and transfer grills between bedrooms and interior corridors to prevent pressurization of above-grade rooms.

- During cooling periods, utilize the dehumidification capabilities of the air conditioning system to control interior humidity. Since latent cooling loads on air conditioning systems can be higher than sensible cooling loads, proper sizing of air conditioning systems is important. Oversizing of air conditioning equipment can lead to high interior humidity problems since oversized equipment will not operate as often, and therefore will dehumidify less than properly sized equipment.

- Locate air conditioning supply air registers so that cold air is not blown directly across wall and ceiling surfaces, potentially chilling the surfaces below dew point temperatures. This could cause condensation or high surface relative humidities and potential mold and mildew growth.

- Insulate and protect air conditioning supply ductwork with an exterior vapor diffusion retarder to control condensation on cold duct surfaces.

- Insulate cold water piping if exposed to warm, humid air during the cooling season.

- Avoid unvented combustion appliances. Gas stoves and cook tops without standing pilot lights should be installed in conjunction with vented range hoods or some other vent provision.

- Use combustion appliances that are aerodynamically uncoupled (not influenced by enclosure air pressures or supply air availability) from the conditioned space. In other words, combustion devices that are sealed, power vented, induced draft, condensing, or pulse should be used. Devices with traditional draft hoods should be avoided.

- Provide fireplaces with their own air supply (correctly sized) from the exterior as well as tight-fitting glass doors. Wood stoves should also have their own supply of exterior air ducted directly to their firebox.

Wall Construction in Mixed Climates

In this section six wall assemblies are shown that can be used successfully in mixed climates. All six examples are wood frame walls—four with siding, one with brick veneer, and one with stucco cladding. Other differences between the wood frame walls include the type of sheathing and whether an interior vapor diffusion retarder is used. The basic characteristics of the wall assemblies are summarized in Table 5-1.

First, each wall assembly is illustrated and briefly described. Text adjacent to each drawing indicates how the assembly is designed to handle each of the critical moisture problems in this climate: (1) rain penetration, (2) rain absorption, (3) air movement, and (4) vapor diffusion. In addition, comments concerning the ability of the wall to dry and other limitations of each wall assembly are included. Following the drawings is a summary discussion of key moisture control strategies for wall assemblies in this climate.

Insulation levels in wall assemblies, except where specifically noted to control moisture accumulation on condensing surfaces, are left to the judgement of the reader.

Table 5-1: Characteristics of wall assemblies for mixed climates.

	WALL TYPE	EXTERIOR COMPONENT	SHEATHING	OTHER FEATURES	DRYING
WALL 1	Wood frame	Wood, vinyl, or aluminum siding	Plywood or waferboard (Impermeable)	Polyethylene vapor diffusion retarder (Interior)	Limited
WALL 2	Wood frame	Aluminum or vinyl siding	Asphalt-impregnated fiberboard or gypsum (Permeable)	Polyethylene vapor diffusion retarder (Interior)	To the exterior
WALL 3	Wood frame	Brick veneer over cavity	Asphalt-impregnated fiberboard or gypsum (Permeable)	Polyethylene vapor diffusion retarder (Interior)	To the exterior
WALL 4	Wood frame	Aluminum or vinyl siding	Rigid insulation (Impermeable)	Rigid insulation acts as vapor diffusion retarder (Exterior)	To the interior
WALL 5	Wood frame	Stucco cladding	Rigid insulation (Impermeable)	Rigid insulation acts as vapor diffusion retarder (Exterior)	To the interior
WALL 6	Wood frame	Wood, vinyl, or aluminum siding	Rigid insulation (Impermeable)	Vapor diffusion retarder backing on insulation (Interior)	Limited

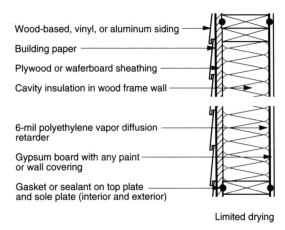

Wood-based, vinyl, or aluminum siding

Building paper

Plywood or waferboard sheathing

Cavity insulation in wood frame wall

6-mil polyethylene vapor diffusion retarder

Gypsum board with any paint or wall covering

Gasket or sealant on top plate and sole plate (interior and exterior)

Limited drying

Figure 5-4: Wall 1—mixed climate.

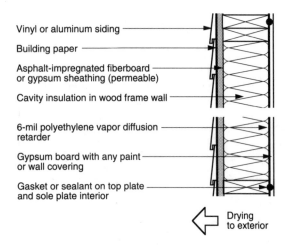

Vinyl or aluminum siding

Building paper

Asphalt-impregnated fiberboard or gypsum sheathing (permeable)

Cavity insulation in wood frame wall

6-mil polyethylene vapor diffusion retarder

Gypsum board with any paint or wall covering

Gasket or sealant on top plate and sole plate interior

Drying to exterior

Figure 5-5: Wall 2—mixed climate.

Wall 1—Mixed Climate: *This conventional wood frame wall assembly utilizes an impermeable, noninsulating sheathing material consisting of plywood or waferboard covered by building paper. Any type of siding—wood-based, vinyl, or aluminum—can be applied. A polyethylene vapor diffusion retarder is placed on the inside of the wall beneath the gypsum board. This wall assembly is identical to Wall 1 for heating climates.*

Key characteristics:
- *The rain screen principle controls rain penetration when vinyl or aluminum siding are used. With wood siding, the barrier approach (sealing all openings) is used.*
- *Building paper controls rain absorption into the sheathing.*
- *To control air movement, the exterior sheathing and the polyethylene on the interior are sealed to the framing to form air retarders.*
- *The polyethylene sheet placed beneath the gypsum board acts as a vapor diffusion retarder.*
- *Drying toward the interior or exterior of the wall is limited. Therefore, framing and insulation materials should be dry or permitted to dry before enclosure.*
- *Vapor permeable or impermeable interior surface finishes may be used.*
- *Where wood-based siding is utilized over plywood, waferboard, or OSB sheathing, utilize dry materials, back-prime the siding, and nail according to manufacturers' recommended installation practices. Using spacers, wedges, or installing siding over furring should be considered.*

Wall 2—Mixed Climate: *In this wood frame wall, permeable noninsulating sheathing (asphalt-impregnated fiberboard or gypsum covered with building paper) permits the wall assembly to dry toward the exterior. Vinyl or aluminum siding is applied over the sheathing. Similar to Wall 1, a polyethylene vapor diffusion retarder is placed on the inside of the wall beneath the gypsum board.*

Key characteristics:
- *The rain screen principle controls rain penetration.*
- *Building paper controls rain absorption into the sheathing.*
- *The polyethylene sheet placed beneath the gypsum board acts as an air retarder to control air movement, and acts as a vapor diffusion retarder.*
- *Vapor permeable sheathing and building paper combined with the openings in vinyl and aluminum siding, permit drying toward the exterior.*
- *Vapor permeable or impermeable interior surface finishes may be used.*

Wall 3—Mixed Climate: This wood frame wall is covered on the exterior by a brick veneer. An air space between the brick and the wood frame assembly is a receptor for moisture. The permeable noninsulating sheathing (asphalt-impregnated fiberboard or gypsum) permits the wall assembly to dry toward the exterior. Like the two previous wood frame wall assemblies, a polyethylene vapor diffusion retarder is placed on the inside of the wall beneath the gypsum board. This wall assembly is identical to Wall 5 for heating climates.

Key characteristics:
- *The rain screen principle controls rain penetration.*
- *The air space behind the brick veneer acts as a receptor for capillary moisture and absorbed moisture driven inward by solar radiation.*
- *Building paper controls rain absorption into the sheathing. It must be continuous and fastened.*
- *The polyethylene sheet placed beneath the gypsum board acts as an air retarder to control air movement, and acts as a vapor diffusion retarder.*
- *Vapor permeable sheathing permits drying toward the exterior.*
- *Vapor permeable or impermeable interior surface finishes may be used.*

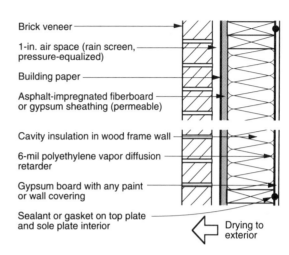

Brick veneer

1-in. air space (rain screen, pressure-equalized)

Building paper

Asphalt-impregnated fiberboard or gypsum sheathing (permeable)

Cavity insulation in wood frame wall

6-mil polyethylene vapor diffusion retarder

Gypsum board with any paint or wall covering

Sealant or gasket on top plate and sole plate interior

Drying to exterior

Figure 5-6: Wall 3—mixed climate.

Wall 4—Mixed Climate: Impermeable rigid insulation is used as the sheathing material in this wood frame wall assembly. Vinyl or aluminum siding is applied over the sheathing. The rigid insulation serves as a vapor diffusion retarder on the exterior. Unlike the previous wall assemblies, there is no vapor diffusion retarder on the inside of the wall. Instead, permeable latex paint on gypsum board permits vapor to enter the wall and then dry to the interior. This approach is dependent on limiting the cavity insulation to R-11, while installing at least R-7 rigid insulation.

Key characteristics:
- *The rain screen principle controls rain penetration.*
- *No building paper is required to control rain absorption since rigid insulation is impermeable.*
- *To control air movement, the exterior sheathing and the interior gypsum board are sealed to the framing to form air retarders.*
- *Impermeable rigid insulation acts as a vapor diffusion retarder for vapor entering from the exterior during cooling periods.*
- *Insulating sheathing raises the wall cavity temperature and limits potential condensation.*
- *A vapor permeable paint finish on the gypsum board permits this wall to dry toward the interior.*
- *Vapor permeable interior surface finishes must be used.*
- *Interior relative humidity should not exceed 35 percent at 70 degrees F during heating periods.*

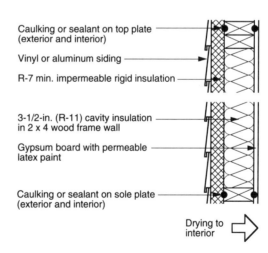

Caulking or sealant on top plate (exterior and interior)

Vinyl or aluminum siding

R-7 min. impermeable rigid insulation

3-1/2-in. (R-11) cavity insulation in 2 x 4 wood frame wall

Gypsum board with permeable latex paint

Caulking or sealant on sole plate (exterior and interior)

Drying to interior

Figure 5-7: Wall 4—mixed climate.

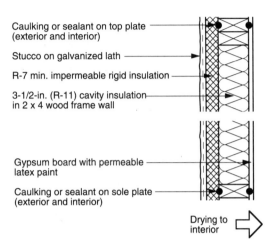

Caulking or sealant on top plate (exterior and interior)

Stucco on galvanized lath

R-7 min. impermeable rigid insulation

3-1/2-in. (R-11) cavity insulation in 2 x 4 wood frame wall

Gypsum board with permeable latex paint

Caulking or sealant on sole plate (exterior and interior)

Drying to interior

Figure 5-8: Wall 5—mixed climate.

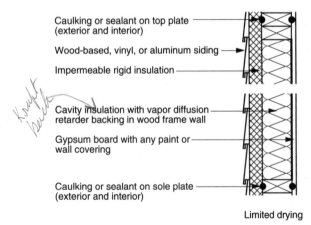

Caulking or sealant on top plate (exterior and interior)

Wood-based, vinyl, or aluminum siding

Impermeable rigid insulation

Cavity insulation with vapor diffusion retarder backing in wood frame wall

Gypsum board with any paint or wall covering

Caulking or sealant on sole plate (exterior and interior)

Limited drying

Figure 5-9: Wall 6—mixed climate.

Vapor drive induced by solar radiation

Wall 5—Mixed Climate: Impermeable rigid insulation is used as the sheathing material in this wood frame wall assembly. Stucco over galvanized lath is applied over the sheathing. The rigid insulation serves as a vapor diffusion retarder on the exterior. Similar to Wall 4, there is no vapor diffusion retarder on the inside of the wall. Instead, permeable latex paint on gypsum board permits vapor to enter the wall and then dry to the interior. This approach is dependent on limiting the cavity insulation to R-11, while installing at least R-7 rigid insulation.

Key characteristics:
- *Stucco cladding forms a barrier to control rain penetration.*
- *Rain absorption and capillary suction through the stucco are controlled by the impermeable rigid insulation.*
- *To control air movement, the exterior sheathing and the interior gypsum board are sealed to the framing to form air retarders.*
- *Impermeable rigid insulation acts as a vapor diffusion retarder for vapor entering from the exterior during cooling periods.*
- *Insulating sheathing raises the wall cavity temperature and limits potential condensation.*
- *A vapor permeable paint finish on the gypsum board permits this wall to dry toward the interior.*
- *Vapor permeable interior surface finishes must be used.*
- *Interior relative humidity should not exceed 35 percent at 70 degrees F during heating periods.*

Wall 6—Mixed Climate: Impermeable rigid insulation is used as the sheathing material in this wood frame wall assembly. Vinyl or aluminum siding is applied over the sheathing. The rigid insulation serves as a vapor diffusion retarder on the exterior. Batt cavity insulation is used with a vapor diffusion retarder backing toward the interior.

Key characteristics:
- *The rain screen principle controls rain penetration.*
- *No building paper is required to control rain absorption since rigid insulation is impermeable.*
- *To control air movement, the exterior sheathing and the interior gypsum board are sealed to the framing to form air retarders.*
- *Impermeable rigid insulation acts as a vapor diffusion retarder for vapor entering from the exterior during cooling periods.*
- *The facing material on the cavity insulation acts as a vapor diffusion retarder on the interior.*
- *Insulating sheathing raises the wall cavity temperature and limits potential condensation.*
- *Drying toward the interior or exterior of the wall is limited. Therefore, framing and insulation materials should be dry or permitted to dry before enclosure.*
- *Vapor permeable or impermeable interior surface finishes may be used.*
- *With wood-based siding, utilize dry materials, back-prime the siding, and nail according to manufacturers' recommended installation practices.*

SUMMARY: WALL ASSEMBLIES IN MIXED CLIMATES

Rain Penetration

All but one of the six wall assemblies recommended for this climate utilize the rain screen principle to control rain penetration. Wall 5 utilizes the barrier approach (discussed below).

The rain screen principle requires a pressure-equalized cavity behind the cladding. In Walls 1, 2, 4, and 6, vinyl or aluminum siding is installed over a tight sheathing. The cavities created behind vinyl or aluminum siding serve this purpose and they should not be filled with insulation material. For pressure to be equalized in these cavities, the exterior sheathing must be significantly tighter than the cladding. It should be installed vertically, with all joints falling on framing members, with the option of utilizing a sealant or adhesive at sheathing joints and edges. Alternatively, a tightly installed building paper (lapped or taped joints) may be utilized to equalize pressure. In Wall 1, wood-based siding may be used instead of vinyl or aluminum, but all exterior holes in the building paper and sheathing then must be eliminated to control rain penetration.

In Wall 3, the rain screen is created using a brick veneer over a minimum 1-inch air space. This air space must be clear of mortar droppings and should be open at the top of the brick veneer wall as well as vented at its base. Such brick veneer walls should be vented at their base by leaving open every other vertical mortar joint in the first course of brick.

These vertical open joints serve two functions, first to allow inward air movement to equalize pressure and second to provide a weep or drainage function. As in all rain screen systems, the sheathing must be significantly tighter than the cladding for pressure to be equalized in the cavity. This is accomplished by both tightening the sheathing and making the brick veneer deliberately leaky. Venting the air space at the top and bottom make the brick veneer sufficiently leaky. The asphalt-impregnated fiberboard or gypsum sheathing should be installed airtight as described above for Wall 1.

The sheathing is sometimes further tightened relative to the brick veneer by the installation of a building paper in a continuous manner. This building paper must be extensively fastened to prevent flexing under wind action, which could pump moisture into the assembly. Flashings at the base of brick veneer walls are also critical so that cavity moisture can be directed to the exterior through the weep holes under the influence of gravity. These base flashings must extend to the back of the rain screen cavity and be placed behind the sheathing or building paper.

Appropriate installation of flashings over window and door openings is critical in all rain screen assemblies, ideally tucking in behind exterior sheathings or building papers. In drain screen assemblies, flashings over window and door openings are also critical to direct rainwater to the exterior of the assembly.

A barrier approach (or face-sealing) controls rain penetration in Wall 5 where an exterior stucco cladding is installed. In order to eliminate all exterior openings, the stucco cladding needs to be continuous and sealed at all penetrations such as at window and door openings.

Uncontrolled cracking of the exterior stucco cladding can lead to significant rain penetration, so control joints are often utilized. The effectiveness of stucco control joints is often dependent on an effective bond breaker placed between the stucco cladding and any sheathing material. Where a bond breaker is not utilized, control joints need to be spaced closer together. Control joint detailing is important since they often provide entry points for rainwater. Thus, selection of appropriate sealants and/or flashings for use at these locations is critical. In this wall assembly (Wall 5), the bond breaker is the face of the impermeable rigid insulating sheathing itself. Other effective bond breakers are sheet polyethylene, as well as both absorptive and nonabsorptive building papers.

Rain Absorption/Capillary Suction

In the six wall assemblies shown here, there are two basic concepts to control moisture from rain absorption and capillary suction: (1) impermeable materials are used to keep moisture out of the wall assembly, and (2) a space or permeable material acts as a receptor for this moisture, providing a path for it to leave the wall assembly.

Rain absorption by vinyl or aluminum siding (as shown in Walls 1, 2, 4, and 6) and siding capillarity effects are not a concern as a result of the inherent material properties of the vinyl and aluminum. Where wood-based siding may be utilized (in Walls 1 and 6, for example), back-priming (painting or coating the back surfaces) is recommended to limit

2 different ways of rain screen

---

capillary and vapor absorption by the siding. Installing the wood siding on furring strips, or using spacers or wedges to create openings between siding pieces, is also recommended. It is important to use dry materials and nail according to the manufacturers' recommended installation practices.

In Walls 1 and 2, building paper controls capillarity effects and rain absorption by the exterior sheathing material. In these assemblies a vapor permeable, nonabsorptive building paper should be used. In Walls 4 and 6, where the sheathing material is impermeable rigid insulation, building paper is not required to prevent water absorption by the sheathing.

In Wall 5, rain absorption by the stucco cladding and stucco capillarity effects are controlled by the impermeable rigid insulation (a capillary break) installed behind the stucco. The formulation and material properties of the stucco cladding itself are also important. Traditional stuccos, which have provided the best service life, have been composed of three layers, where each successive layer to the exterior has been weaker and more permeable than the layer under it. In other words, the base coat is the thickest and has the lowest water to cement ratio, and therefore is the most impermeable. The second coat is thinner and weaker (more permeable) than the base coat, and the finish coat is the thinnest, weakest, and most permeable of the three.

The result of this three-layer stucco application is that the farther that water penetrates into the wall, the more resistance it meets. A further advantage is that once water has penetrated the stucco it is always easier for it to migrate toward the exterior than to penetrate any farther to the interior. Thus, any paint finishes or hydrophobic sealants installed over the outermost surface of a stucco cladding should be more permeable than the outermost surface of the stucco cladding. This is typically very difficult to achieve in practice. Consequently, stains or colorants added to stuccos during application are often more successful than paint films applied to the stucco at a later time.

Rain absorption by the stucco cladding and stucco capillarity effects can also be controlled by exterior paint films and hydrophobic coatings. However, caution and judgement need to be exercised in the application of this control strategy. Although these coatings reduce rain absorption and capillarity, they also often retard the drying of the wall assembly to the exterior if it gets wet through other mechanisms such as interior moisture or failure at control joints.

The second concept of creating a receptor for moisture from rain absorption and capillarity is demonstrated in Wall 3. In this assembly, an air space behind the brick veneer controls rain absorption and brick veneer capillarity effects. The air space also acts as a receptor for both capillary moisture and absorbed moisture driven inward by incident solar radiation. In Wall 3, a building paper may be installed in some assemblies to limit rain absorption by the asphalt-impregnated fiberboard or gypsum sheathing. In such cases a vapor permeable, nonabsorptive building paper should be used.

Air Movement

In this climate, air may transport moisture from the exterior during the cooling season (infiltration of warm humid air) or from the interior during the heating season (exfiltration of warm moisture-laden interior air). To control this moisture, an air seal (air retarder) is installed at either the interior or exterior of the wall. This means that either the interior gypsum wall board, polyethylene vapor diffusion retarder, or exterior sheathing is sealed to the wall framing. This air sealing can be accomplished with adhesive, caulk, or some other sealant. To ensure effectiveness, it is desirable to create both an interior and exterior air retarder when possible.

In Walls 1, 2, and 3, the interior air retarder is a continuous 6-mil polyethylene sheet. In Walls 4, 5, and 6, the gypsum board is sealed to the wall framing and acts as the interior air retarder. An exterior air retarder is shown in Walls 1, 4, 5, and 6—the exterior sheathing is sealed to the framing. This has the added advantage of equalizing the pressure behind the exterior cladding to create the rain screen. Exterior air seals over permeable sheathing usually feature a continuous exterior building paper (vapor permeable and nonabsorptive). Over impermeable sheathing, the building paper is not required and the rigid board is simply sealed to the framing.

An exterior air seal at the asphalt-impregnated fiberboard is not shown for Walls 2 and 3. It has proven difficult in practice to seal asphalt-impregnated fiberboard sheathing. Consequently, in wall assemblies with asphalt-impregnated fiberboard sheathing, the plane of airtightness is often located to the interior of the wall assembly. Alternatively, a tightly sealed exterior building paper in this climate can also be effective in reducing air-transported moisture.

Vapor Diffusion

Similar to air-transported moisture in this climate, vapor diffusion may enter a wall assembly from the exterior during the cooling season (infiltration of warm humid air) or from the interior during the heating season (exfiltration of warm moisture-laden interior air). There are two approaches to controlling vapor diffusion from the interior during heating periods in this climate. As shown in Walls 1, 2, and 3, the vapor diffusion retarder can be installed at the interior of the wall. In all three cases, it consists of a continuous polyethylene sheet installed beneath the interior gypsum board. In Wall 6, the facing on the batt insulation serves as a vapor diffusion retarder on the interior. As an alternative, a low permeability paint or wall covering can act as the vapor diffusion retarder.

Walls 4 and 5 illustrate a different approach to controlling vapor diffusion during heating periods. Instead of creating a barrier, permeable materials permit vapor from the interior to enter the wall assembly where it can accumulate. To reduce this accumulation, the temperature of the first condensing surface within the wall assembly is elevated. In a wood frame wall, the first condensing surface during the heating season is the cavity side of the exterior sheathing.

In Walls 4 and 5, an insulating sheathing of sufficient thermal resistance is installed to limit periods of potential condensation to acceptable levels. An acceptable period would be sufficiently brief so that wood decay does not begin or interior surface water stain marks or mold or mildew do not appear. This period is determined by the temperature of the first condensing surface and the interior moisture level. The temperature of the first condensing surface is determined by the ratio of the amount of thermal insulation installed to the exterior of the condensing surface compared with the amount of thermal insulation installed to the interior of the condensing surface. For Walls 4 and 5 in this climate zone, the thermal resistance of insulating sheathings should be R-7 or greater, and the thermal resistance of cavity insulation should be R-11 or less, where an interior vapor diffusion retarder is not utilized. Furthermore, interior moisture levels during heating periods should be limited to 35 percent relative humidity at 70 degrees Fahrenheit.

During cooling periods, vapor diffusion from the exterior can also be controlled by two methods. Walls 1, 4, 5, and 6 utilize a vapor diffusion retarder on the exterior of the assembly. In Wall 1, structural use panels such as plywood, waferboard, or OSB sheathings are impermeable and act as an effective vapor diffusion retarder. In Walls 4, 5, and 6, an impermeable rigid insulation is installed as the exterior wall sheathing and acts as the exterior vapor diffusion retarder.

An alternative approach to controlling vapor diffusion from the exterior is shown in Walls 2 and 3. In both cases, the vapor diffusion retarder at the interior of the wall assembly controls the problem. Although installing a vapor diffusion retarder at this location does not prevent moisture from entering the wall, the vapor diffusion retarder effectively protects the interior gypsum board and any interior finishes from moisture damage.

This interior vapor diffusion retarder can get wet on the cavity side during the day as a result of exterior absorbed moisture driven inward by incident solar radiation and the air conditioned interior. This moisture then typically migrates outward in the evening when the temperature gradient reverses.

Walls 2 and 3 can get intermittently wet from the exterior as well as dry intermittently to the exterior. Since intermittent wetting of the vapor diffusion retarder may occur in these assemblies, the interior vapor diffusion retarder should be continuous to provide satisfactory performance. Foil-backed interior gypsum board and vapor diffusion retarder-backed cavity insulation may not be effective due to discontinuities at joints. A continuous polyethylene vapor diffusion retarder has proven to be effective in this type of assembly.

Drying of Wall Assemblies

In Walls 1 and 6, drying toward either the interior or exterior is limited by a vapor impermeable exterior sheathing and an interior vapor diffusion retarder. In Wall 2, drying toward the exterior through the vapor permeable exterior sheathing (asphalt-impregnated fiberboard or gypsum board) occurs but is limited somewhat by a vapor impermeable exterior cladding (vinyl or aluminum siding). Drying toward the interior is limited by an interior vapor diffusion retarder. In both cases, should the wall assembly become wet during service, or be built wet due to wet framing materials or wet-applied cavity insulations (wet spray cellulose or blown fiberglass), it may not dry. Accordingly, dry framing materials (wood at a moisture content of 19 percent by weight or lower) and dry-applied insulations are recommended. Alternatively, wall assemblies must be allowed to dry prior to enclosure.

Wall 3 utilizes a vapor permeable sheathing on the exterior of the wall framing to help dry the wall toward the exterior. An air space between the cladding (brick veneer) and the sheathing acts as a receptor for interior cavity moisture.

In Walls 4 and 5, a vapor permeable paint finish on the interior gypsum wall board promotes wall drying toward the interior. Drying will occur due to (1) an inward temperature and vapor pressure gradient present as a result of air conditioning the enclosure during the cooling season, and (2) ambient climatic conditions during the spring and fall.

Interior Finishes

Either vapor permeable or vapor impermeable interior surface finishes may be used in conjunction with Walls 1, 2, and 3, since there is no drying to the interior and a polyethylene sheet serves as a vapor diffusion retarder. In Walls 4 and 5, a vapor permeable interior surface finish is required to permit drying to the interior. Where wall assemblies with permeable interior surface treatments have been performing satisfactorily and are subsequently covered with impermeable interior surface treatments, mold and mildew problems may appear at the gypsum board/surface treatment interface.

Foundation Construction in Mixed Climates

In this section eight foundation assemblies are shown that can be used successfully in mixed climates. There are four basement wall assemblies and four crawl spaces. Three of the basement walls are concrete or masonry construction, while the other utilizes pressure-treated wood walls. All four crawl spaces are unvented—two utilize concrete or masonry walls, and two are pressure-treated wood construction. A key difference between the foundation assemblies is the type and placement of insulation on either the interior or exterior of the wall, as well as in the rim joist area and the floor. The basic characteristics of the foundation assemblies are summarized in Table 5-2.

First, each foundation assembly is illustrated and briefly described. Text adjacent to each drawing indicates how the assembly is designed to handle each of the critical moisture problems in this climate: (1) rain and ground-water, (2) capillary suction, (3) air movement, and (4) vapor diffusion. In addition, comments concerning the ability of the wall to dry and other limitations of each foundation assembly are summarized. Following the drawings is a summary discussion of key moisture control strategies for foundation assemblies in this climate.

In addition to the basements and unvented crawl spaces shown in this section, vented crawl spaces and slab-on-grade foundations are utilized in this climate zone. For these foundation types, see the foundation assemblies presented for cooling climates in Chapter 6.

Insulation levels in foundation assemblies, except where specifically noted to control moisture accumulation on condensing surfaces, are left to the judgement of the reader. Guidance regarding optimum insulation levels for foundation assemblies can be found in the *Builder's Foundation Handbook* (Carmody et al. 1991).

Table 5-2: Characteristics of foundation assemblies for mixed climates.

	FOUNDATION TYPE	FOUNDATION WALL INSULATION	FLOOR INSULATION	DRYING
BASEMENT 1	Concrete	Rigid insulation (Exterior)	None	To the interior
BASEMENT 2	Concrete	Cavity insulation in wood frame wall (Interior)	None	Limited
BASEMENT 3	Concrete masonry supporting brick	Cavity insulation in wood frame wall (Interior)	None	Limited
BASEMENT 4	Pressure-treated wood frame	Cavity insulation in wood frame wall— Rigid insulation (Exterior)	Rigid insulation beneath wood floor	Limited
CRAWL SPACE 1	Concrete	Rigid insulation (Exterior)	None	To the interior
CRAWL SPACE 2	Concrete masonry	Faced batt insulation over wall (Interior)	Faced batt insulation extends onto floor perimeter	Limited
CRAWL SPACE 3	Pressure-treated wood frame	Cavity insulation in wood frame wall— Rigid insulation (Exterior)	None	Limited
CRAWL SPACE 4	Pressure-treated wood frame	Cavity insulation in wood frame wall— Rigid insulation (Exterior)	Faced batt insulation extends onto floor perimeter	Limited

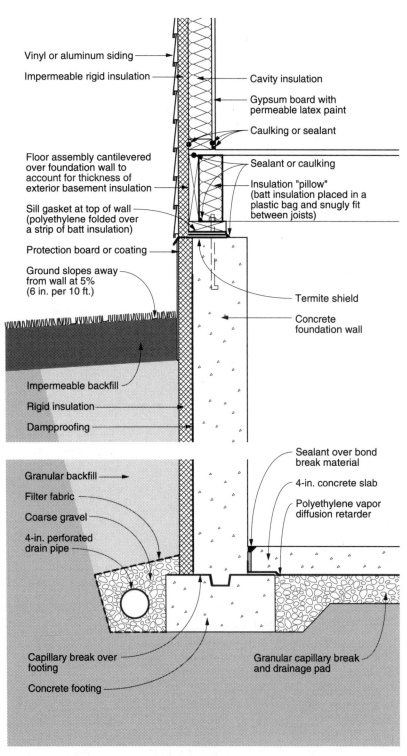

Vinyl or aluminum siding

Impermeable rigid insulation

Cavity insulation

Gypsum board with permeable latex paint

Caulking or sealant

Floor assembly cantilevered over foundation wall to account for thickness of exterior basement insulation

Sealant or caulking

Insulation "pillow" (batt insulation placed in a plastic bag and snugly fit between joists)

Sill gasket at top of wall (polyethylene folded over a strip of batt insulation)

Protection board or coating

Ground slopes away from wall at 5% (6 in. per 10 ft.)

Termite shield

Concrete foundation wall

Impermeable backfill

Rigid insulation

Dampproofing

Granular backfill

Filter fabric

Coarse gravel

4-in. perforated drain pipe

Sealant over bond break material

4-in. concrete slab

Polyethylene vapor diffusion retarder

Capillary break over footing

Concrete footing

Granular capillary break and drainage pad

Figure 5-10: Basement 1—mixed climate.

Basement 1—Mixed Climate: This concrete basement wall assembly illustrates rigid insulation board on the exterior. Rigid insulation covers the exterior of the rim joist, and cavity insulation (with a vapor diffusion retarder) is placed between joists on the rim joist interior. The above-grade wall shown here corresponds to Wall 4 in the previous section.

Key characteristics:
- *Rainwater is controlled by gutters and downspouts, impermeable soil cap over backfill, and grade sloping away from the building.*
- *Groundwater is controlled by free-draining backfill and a drain pipe at the footing.*
- *Capillary suction is controlled by a dampproof coating on the exterior wall, a break over the footing, and a layer of gravel under the slab.*
- *Air movement into the space is controlled by sealing the concrete slab to the concrete foundation wall with caulking, limiting or sealing all penetrations, sealing the sill/ rim joist area, and placing a polyethylene sheet (air retarder) under the floor slab.*
- *Vapor diffusion from the surrounding soil is controlled by the dampproof coating on the wall exterior and the polyethylene sheet beneath the floor slab.*
- *Vapor diffusion from the interior space is prevented from entering the construction assemblies by polyethylene covering the insulation in the rim joist area.*
- *Insulation on the outside of the basement wall and the rim joist raises the wall temperature and limits potential condensation.*
- *Exposed concrete wall can dry toward the interior.*

Basement 2—Mixed Climate: This concrete basement wall assembly illustrates the use of cavity insulation in a wood frame wall on the interior of the foundation wall. Cavity insulation is placed between joists on the rim joist interior, and rigid insulation covers the rim joist on the exterior as well. Unlike other basement wall assemblies, the vapor diffusion retarder is continuous from the above-grade wall interior, through the rim joist area, extending over the basement wall interior, and then beneath the slab. The above-grade wall shown here corresponds to Wall 1 in the previous section.

Key characteristics:
- *Rainwater is controlled by gutters and downspouts, impermeable soil cap over backfill, and grade sloping away from the building.*
- *Groundwater is controlled by free-draining backfill and a drain pipe at the footing.*
- *Capillary suction is controlled by a dampproof coating on the exterior wall, a break over the footing, and a layer of gravel under the slab.*
- *Air movement is controlled by sealing the polyethylene air retarder under the floor slab to the polyethylene sheet air retarder beneath the gypsum board on the basement wall. In addition, a polyethylene sheet is wrapped around the rim joist assembly and is sealed to the polyethylene air retarders on the basement and above-grade walls.*
- *Vapor diffusion from the surrounding soil is controlled by the dampproof coating on the wall exterior and the polyethylene sheet beneath the floor slab.*
- *Vapor diffusion from the interior space is prevented from entering the construction assemblies by a polyethylene sheet beneath the gypsum board on the interior wall and a vapor diffusion retarder covering the insulation in the rim joist area.*
- *Insulation outside the rim joist raises the wall cavity temperature and limits potential condensation.*
- *Drying toward the interior or exterior of the wall is limited. Therefore, framing and insulation materials should be dry or permitted to dry before enclosure.*
- *Interior relative humidity should not exceed 35 percent at 70 degrees F during heating periods.*
- *Vapor permeable or impermeable interior surface finishes may be used on walls.*

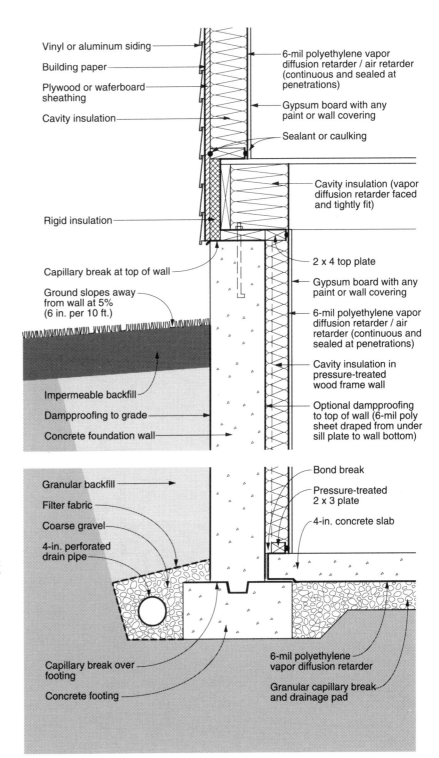

Figure 5-11: Basement 2—mixed climate.

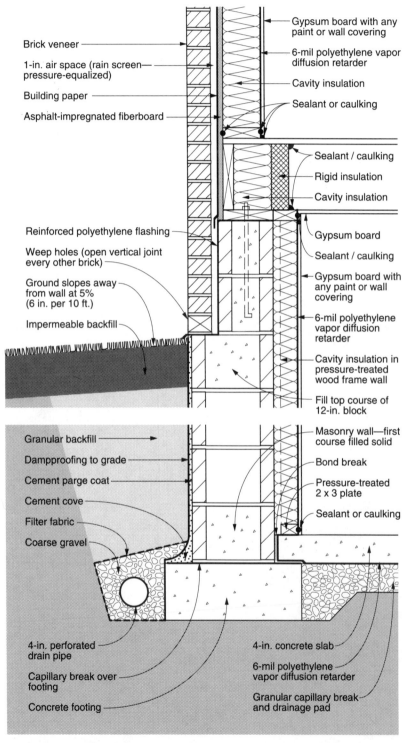

Brick veneer

1-in. air space (rain screen—pressure-equalized)

Building paper

Asphalt-impregnated fiberboard

Reinforced polyethylene flashing

Weep holes (open vertical joint every other brick)

Ground slopes away from wall at 5% (6 in. per 10 ft.)

Impermeable backfill

Granular backfill

Dampproofing to grade

Cement parge coat

Cement cove

Filter fabric

Coarse gravel

4-in. perforated drain pipe

Capillary break over footing

Concrete footing

Gypsum board with any paint or wall covering

6-mil polyethylene vapor diffusion retarder

Cavity insulation

Sealant or caulking

Sealant / caulking

Rigid insulation

Cavity insulation

Gypsum board

Sealant / caulking

Gypsum board with any paint or wall covering

6-mil polyethylene vapor diffusion retarder

Cavity insulation in pressure-treated wood frame wall

Fill top course of 12-in. block

Masonry wall—first course filled solid

Bond break

Pressure-treated 2 x 3 plate

Sealant or caulking

4-in. concrete slab

6-mil polyethylene vapor diffusion retarder

Granular capillary break and drainage pad

Figure 5-12: Basement 3—mixed climate.

Basement 3—Mixed Climate: In this example, a concrete masonry basement wall assembly supports a wood frame wall with brick veneer. Similar to Basement 2, there is cavity insulation in a wood frame wall on the interior of the foundation wall. Unlike the previous foundation assemblies, there is no rigid insulation covering the exterior of the rim joist, although cavity insulation is still placed between joists on the rim joist interior. A variation shown here, however, is the use of impermeable rigid insulation as a vapor diffusion retarder inside the rim joist cavity insulation (in place of faced cavity insulation). A vapor diffusion retarder covers the interior side of the above- and below-grade walls. The above-grade wall shown here corresponds to Wall 3 in the previous section.

Key characteristics:

• Rainwater is controlled by gutters and downspouts, impermeable soil cap over backfill, and grade sloping away from the building. Flashing at the base of the brick veneer directs water outward.

• Groundwater is controlled by free-draining backfill and a drain pipe at the footing.

• Capillary suction is controlled by a cement parge and dampproof coating on the exterior wall, a break over the footing, a break over the top of the foundation wall, and a layer of gravel under the slab.

• Air movement into the space is controlled by sealing the polyethylene air retarder under the floor slab to the gypsum board on the basement wall. The gypsum board is sealed to the perimeter framing, and rigid insulation blocks are sealed into the joist spaces at the top of the wall.

• Vapor diffusion from the surrounding soil is controlled by the dampproof coating on the wall exterior and the polyethylene sheet beneath the floor slab.

• Vapor diffusion from the interior space is prevented from entering the construction assemblies by polyethylene on the interior wall and impermeable insulation in the rim joist area.

• Drying toward the interior or exterior of the wall is limited. Therefore, framing and insulation materials should be dry or permitted to dry before enclosure.

• Interior relative humidity should not exceed 35 percent at 70 degrees F during heating periods.

• Vapor permeable or impermeable interior surface finishes may be used on walls.

Basement 4—Mixed Climate: This pressure-treated wood foundation wall rests on a concrete footing. Cavity insulation is placed within the wood frame wall and rigid insulation board covers the exterior. A layer of rigid insulation is placed beneath the wood floor. Because of the balloon-style framing at the rim joist, the insulated wood foundation wall extends over the rim joist on the exterior. Rigid insulation covers the rim joist on the exterior as well. Gypsum board with low permeability paint or wall covering serves as a vapor diffusion retarder on the interior side of the wall assembly. The above-grade wall shown here is similar to Wall 4 in the previous section, except that wood siding with an air space behind it is shown instead of vinyl or aluminum siding.

Key characteristics:
- Rainwater is controlled by gutters and downspouts, and grade sloping away from the building.
- Groundwater is controlled by free-draining backfill and a drain pipe at the footing.
- Capillary suction is controlled by the polyethylene sheet on the exterior wall, a break over the footing, and a layer of gravel under the floor.
- Air movement into the space is controlled by sealing the polyethylene air retarder under the floor assembly to the plywood subfloor. The subfloor is sealed to the perimeter wall framing, and the rim joist area is sealed as well.
- Vapor diffusion from the surrounding soil is controlled by the polyethylene sheets on the wall exterior and beneath the floor slab.
- Low permeability paint or wall covering acts as a vapor diffusion retarder. Vapor impermeable interior surface finishes must be used.
- Insulation on the outside of the basement wall and the rim joist raises the wall temperature and limits potential condensation. Similarly, insulation beneath the floor assembly raises the temperature in the floor cavity.
- Drying toward the interior or exterior of the wall is limited. Therefore, framing and insulation materials should be dry or permitted to dry before enclosure.
- Interior relative humidity should not exceed 35 percent at 70 degrees F during heating periods.

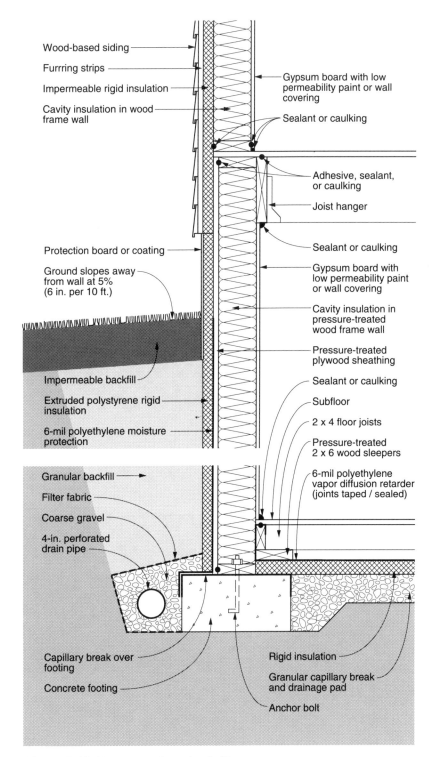

Figure 5-13: Basement 4—mixed climate.

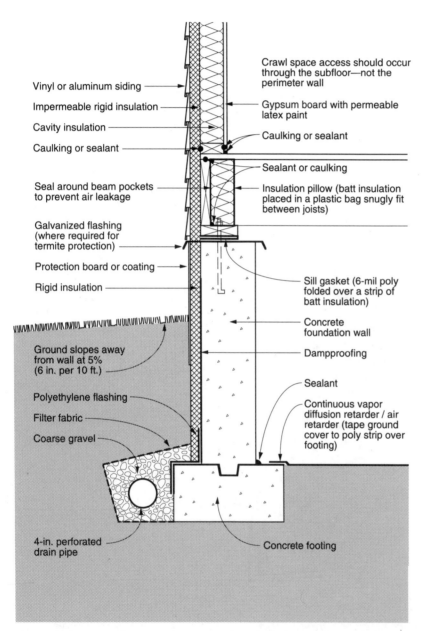

Vinyl or aluminum siding

Impermeable rigid insulation

Cavity insulation

Caulking or sealant

Seal around beam pockets to prevent air leakage

Galvanized flashing (where required for termite protection)

Protection board or coating

Rigid insulation

Ground slopes away from wall at 5% (6 in. per 10 ft.)

Polyethylene flashing

Filter fabric

Coarse gravel

4-in. perforated drain pipe

Crawl space access should occur through the subfloor—not the perimeter wall

Gypsum board with permeable latex paint

Caulking or sealant

Sealant or caulking

Insulation pillow (batt insulation placed in a plastic bag snugly fit between joists)

Sill gasket (6-mil poly folded over a strip of batt insulation)

Concrete foundation wall

Dampproofing

Sealant

Continuous vapor diffusion retarder / air retarder (tape ground cover to poly strip over footing)

Concrete footing

Figure 5-14: Crawl Space 1—mixed climate.

Crawl Space 1—Mixed Climate: This unvented crawl space illustrates a concrete foundation wall with rigid insulation board on the exterior. Rigid insulation covers the exterior of the rim joist, and cavity insulation (with a vapor diffusion retarder) is placed between joists on the rim joist interior. A continuous vapor diffusion retarder/air retarder is placed on the floor of the crawl space and extends over the top of the footing. The above-grade wall shown here corresponds to Wall 4 in the previous section.

Key characteristics:
- Rainwater is controlled by gutters and downspouts, impermeable soil cap over backfill, and grade sloping away from the building.
- Groundwater is controlled by a drain pipe at the footing.
- Capillary suction is controlled by a dampproof coating on the exterior wall, a break over the footing, and a break over the top of the foundation wall.
- Air movement into the space is controlled by pressurizing the crawl space, limiting or sealing all penetrations, sealing the sill/rim joist area, and placing a polyethylene sheet over the crawl space floor. The polyethylene ground cover must extend over the top of the footing with all joints sealed.
- Vapor diffusion from the surrounding soil is controlled by the dampproof coating on the wall exterior and the polyethylene ground cover.
- Vapor diffusion from the interior space is prevented from entering the construction assemblies by polyethylene covering the insulation in the rim joist area.
- Insulation on the outside of the foundation wall and the rim joist raises the wall temperature and limits potential condensation.
- The exposed concrete wall can dry toward the interior.

Crawl Space 2—Mixed Climate: This unvented crawl space illustrates a concrete masonry foundation wall with faced batt insulation covering the interior wall and extending over the floor perimeter. Rigid insulation covers the exterior of the rim joist, and cavity insulation (with a vapor diffusion retarder) is placed between joists on the rim joist interior. A continuous vapor diffusion retarder is placed on the floor of the crawl space and extends over the interior face and top of the foundation wall. The above-grade wall shown here is similar to Wall 4 in the previous section, except that wood siding with an air space behind it is shown instead of vinyl or aluminum siding.

Key characteristics:
- *Rainwater is controlled by gutters and downspouts, impermeable soil cap over backfill, and grade sloping away from the building.*
- *Groundwater is controlled by a drain pipe at the footing.*
- *Capillary suction is controlled by a cement parge coat and dampproofing on the exterior wall. In addition, the polyethylene ground cover is taped to the polyethylene on the wall interior which extends over the top of the foundation wall.*
- *Air movement into the space is controlled by pressurizing the crawl space, limiting or sealing all penetrations, sealing the sill/rim joist area, and placing a polyethylene sheet over the crawl space floor. All joints of the polyethylene ground cover are sealed and it is taped to the polyethylene on the wall to form an air retarder.*
- *Vapor diffusion from the surrounding soil is controlled by the dampproof coating on the wall exterior and the polyethylene ground cover.*
- *Vapor diffusion from the interior space is prevented from entering the construction assemblies by polyethylene covering the insulation in the rim joist area, and the foil facing on the batt insulation.*
- *Insulation on the outside of the rim joist raises the wall temperature and limits potential condensation.*
- *Drying toward the interior or exterior of the wall is limited. Therefore, framing and insulation materials should be dry or permitted to dry before enclosure.*

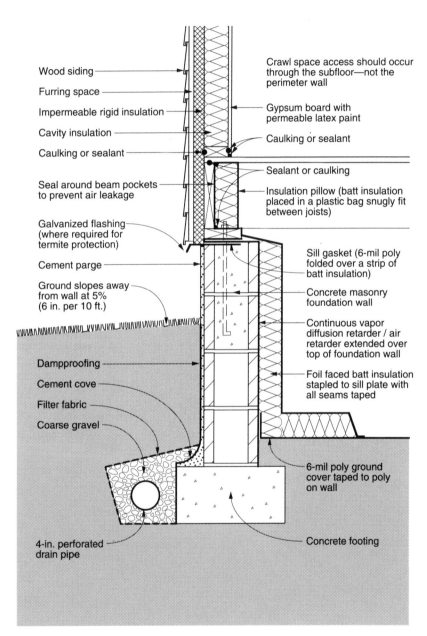

Wood siding

Furring space

Impermeable rigid insulation

Cavity insulation

Caulking or sealant

Seal around beam pockets to prevent air leakage

Galvanized flashing (where required for termite protection)

Cement parge

Ground slopes away from wall at 5% (6 in. per 10 ft.)

Dampproofing

Cement cove

Filter fabric

Coarse gravel

4-in. perforated drain pipe

Crawl space access should occur through the subfloor—not the perimeter wall

Gypsum board with permeable latex paint

Caulking or sealant

Sealant or caulking

Insulation pillow (batt insulation placed in a plastic bag snugly fit between joists)

Sill gasket (6-mil poly folded over a strip of batt insulation)

Concrete masonry foundation wall

Continuous vapor diffusion retarder / air retarder extended over top of foundation wall

Foil faced batt insulation stapled to sill plate with all seams taped

6-mil poly ground cover taped to poly on wall

Concrete footing

Figure 5-15: Crawl Space 2—mixed climate.

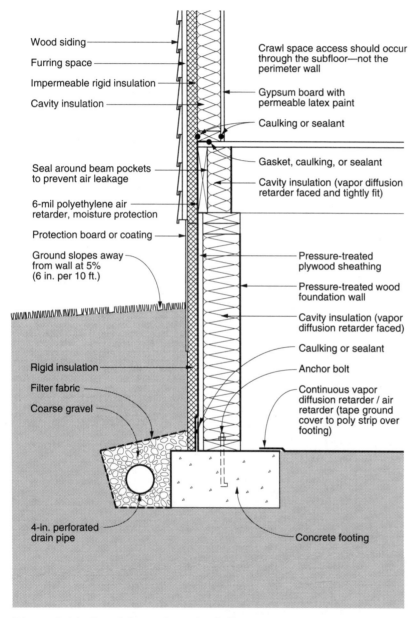

Wood siding

Furring space

Impermeable rigid insulation

Cavity insulation

Crawl space access should occur through the subfloor—not the perimeter wall

Gypsum board with permeable latex paint

Caulking or sealant

Seal around beam pockets to prevent air leakage

Gasket, caulking, or sealant

Cavity insulation (vapor diffusion retarder faced and tightly fit)

6-mil polyethylene air retarder, moisture protection

Protection board or coating

Ground slopes away from wall at 5% (6 in. per 10 ft.)

Pressure-treated plywood sheathing

Pressure-treated wood foundation wall

Cavity insulation (vapor diffusion retarder faced)

Caulking or sealant

Anchor bolt

Rigid insulation

Filter fabric

Coarse gravel

Continuous vapor diffusion retarder / air retarder (tape ground cover to poly strip over footing)

4-in. perforated drain pipe

Concrete footing

Figure 5-16: Crawl Space 3—mixed climate.

Crawl Space 3—Mixed Climate: This unvented crawl space illustrates a pressure-treated wood foundation wall on a concrete footing. Cavity insulation (faced with a vapor diffusion retarder) is placed within the wood frame wall and rigid insulation board covers the exterior. Rigid insulation covers the exterior of the rim joist, and cavity insulation (with a vapor diffusion retarder) is placed between joists on the rim joist interior. A continuous vapor diffusion retarder is placed on the floor of the crawl space and extends over the top of the footing. The above-grade wall shown here is similar to Wall 4 in the previous section, except that wood siding with an air space behind it is shown instead of vinyl or aluminum siding.

Key characteristics:
• Rainwater is controlled by gutters and downspouts, impermeable soil cap over backfill, and grade sloping away from the building.
• Groundwater is controlled by a drain pipe at the footing.
• Capillary suction is controlled by a polyethylene sheet on the exterior wall, and a break over the footing.
• Air movement into the space is controlled by pressurizing the crawl space, limiting or sealing all penetrations, sealing the sill/rim joist area, and placing a polyethylene sheet over the crawl space floor. The polyethylene ground cover must extend over the top of the footing with all joints sealed.
• Vapor diffusion from the surrounding soil is controlled by the polyethylene on the wall exterior and the polyethylene ground cover.
• Insulation on the outside of the foundation wall and the rim joist raises the wall temperature and limits potential condensation.
• Vapor diffusion from the interior space is prevented from entering the construction assemblies by the backing on the insulation which acts as a vapor diffusion retarder in the rim joist area and the foundation wall.
• If unfaced insulation batts are used in the wall cavity, vapor from the interior can enter the wall cavity but the assembly can then dry toward the interior as well.

Crawl Space 4—Mixed Climate: Similar to Crawl Space 3, this unvented crawl space illustrates a pressure-treated wood foundation wall on a concrete footing. Cavity insulation (faced with a vapor diffusion retarder) is placed within the wood frame wall and rigid insulation board covers the exterior. Rigid insulation covers the exterior of the rim joist, and cavity insulation (with a vapor diffusion retarder) is placed between joists on the rim joist interior. Unlike Crawl Space 3, the vapor diffusion retarder placed on the floor of the crawl space continues up over the inside face and top of the foundation wall. In addition, faced batt insulation is laid on the perimeter of the crawl space floor. The above-grade wall shown here corresponds to Wall 4 in the previous section.

Key characteristics:
- *Rainwater is controlled by gutters and downspouts, impermeable soil cap over backfill, and grade sloping away from the building.*
- *Groundwater is controlled by a drain pipe at the footing.*
- *Capillary suction is controlled by a polyethylene sheet on the exterior wall, and a break over the footing.*
- *Air movement into the space is controlled by pressurizing the crawl space, limiting or sealing all penetrations, sealing the sill/ rim joist area, and placing a polyethylene sheet over the crawl space floor. All joints of the polyethylene ground cover are sealed and it extends over the foundation wall to form an air retarder.*
- *Vapor diffusion from the surrounding soil is controlled by the polyethylene on the wall exterior and the polyethylene ground cover.*
- *Vapor diffusion from the interior space is prevented from entering the construction assemblies by polyethylene covering the insulation in the wall cavity and in the rim joist area. Batt insulation on the floor has a vapor diffusion retarder backing.*
- *Insulation on the outside of the foundation wall and the rim joist raises the wall temperature and limits potential condensation.*
- *Drying toward the interior or exterior of the wall is limited. Therefore, framing and insulation materials should be dry or permitted to dry before enclosure.*

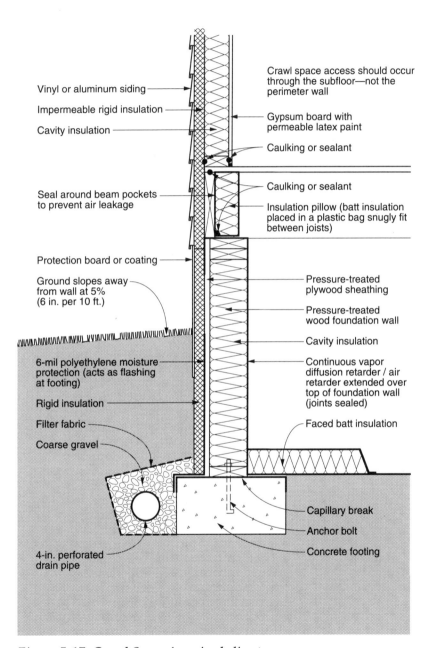

Figure 5-17: Crawl Space 4—mixed climate.

SUMMARY: FOUNDATION ASSEMBLIES IN MIXED CLIMATES

Rain and Groundwater

To control the entry of rainwater into the foundation, all buildings in this climate should utilize gutters and downspouts, along with careful site grading, which direct water away from the structure. Surface water penetration into the ground immediately adjacent to basements should be limited by a cap of impermeable backfill material.

The brick veneer construction shown in Basement 3 introduces an additional rain penetration concern. In this case, rainwater from the above-grade wall assembly controlled by the rain screen must be prevented from draining into the top of the perimeter concrete foundation wall. To do so, flashing is installed at the base of the brick veneer wall extending to the back of the rain screen cavity and up over the top of the concrete foundation wall. This flashing directs water to the exterior of the assembly.

A subgrade drainage system is necessary to control groundwater entry into basements and crawl spaces. The system shown for all assemblies in this climate consists of a drain pipe located at the perimeter of the concrete footings coupled with free-draining backfill material. An alternative approach utilizes a free-draining insulation board instead of the backfill. The drain pipe and the free-draining backfill material (or insulation board) act together to provide a drain screen.

The drain pipe is connected to a sump, storm sewer, or to daylight. Perforations in the perimeter drain pipe should be installed with the holes down to allow groundwater to rise up into the drain pipe and be carried away. Coarse gravel should surround the perimeter drain pipe and in turn be surrounded by a filter fabric. Filter fabric should be located both below and above the perimeter drain pipe, as drain pipe perforations face down and often clog from underneath. Drain tile should have at least 2 inches of gravel underneath, yet still be below the bottom surface of the basement floor slab.

Capillary Suction

Capillary moisture may move into a concrete or masonry foundation wall, a concrete floor slab, and the sill/rim joist area. Several methods are used to control moisture movement by capillarity into the foundation wall. The concrete foundation walls are protected by a dampproof coating on the exterior (Basements 1, 2, and 3; Crawl Spaces 1 and 2). The wood foundation walls are protected by a polyethylene sheet on the exterior (Basement 4; Crawl Spaces 3 and 4).

In all foundations shown here (except Crawl Space 2), a capillary break (dampproofing, low permeability paint, or elastomeric paint) is placed over the top of the concrete footing. It should be noted that dampproofing applied to footings presents a greater clean-up problem than the paint products. A granular pad beneath the footing also can serve as a capillary break. In Crawl Space 2, the break over the footing is not needed since there are capillary barriers on the other surfaces of the foundation wall.

Where the concrete foundation wall is in direct contact with the sill plate, capillary moisture can move into the sill/rim joist area. This moisture movement into the sill/rim joist assembly can be controlled by a capillary break at the top of the perimeter concrete foundation wall (Basements 1, 2, and 3; Crawl Spaces 1 and 2). In Basement 3, capillary moisture from the concrete foundation wall can migrate into the brick veneer. This is controlled by an impermeable flashing at the base of the brick veneer and the rain screen cavity.

In all four basements, capillary moisture movement into the floor slab is controlled by a granular capillary break under the slab. The break is a 4-inch- to 6-inch-thick layer of 3/4-inch gravel with fines removed.

Air Movement

In basement assemblies it is important to eliminate air flow between the surrounding soil and the basement space. This is also true for unvented crawl spaces. To control air-transported moisture infiltrating into the basement space, the basement or crawl space should be pressurized relative to the surrounding soil and air leakage openings should be limited (tight construction). Pipe penetrations and electrical conduits through concrete floor slabs and perimeter concrete walls, floor drains, and sump openings should be sealed or closed with tight covers.

In buildings with forced air systems, crawl spaces can be pressurized by a supply air register in the crawl space, with no corresponding return air register. With this approach the air distribution fan should run continuously. In enclosures without forced air systems, a separate fan for this purpose can be installed, taking air from the other conditioned spaces. The tighter the construction, the less air that has to be introduced to pressurize the crawl space.

Crawl spaces in this climate zone should not be pressurized at the expense of depressurizing the rest of the conditioned space during cooling periods. In other words, the entire building should be pressurized relative to the exterior, including the crawl space during cooling periods. Thus, air taken from the building to pressurize the crawl space needs to be replaced by outside air introduced in a controlled manner, typically to the air conditioning duct system. Pressurization will only occur when the forced air distribution fan is operating (when mechanical cooling or heating is occurring). This should be effective under most conditions.

Where perimeter concrete foundation walls are insulated on the interior, it is also important to prevent warm, interior, moisture-laden air from the basement space from coming in contact with cold, concrete surfaces during both heating and cooling periods.

Air leakage through a basement floor slab can be controlled by placing a polyethylene sheet beneath the slab and sealing it to the foundation wall assembly in various ways. Often it is sealed to the polyethylene or the gypsum board in wall assemblies with interior insulation (Basements 2 and 3). Similarly, in Basement 4 the polyethylene under the wooden floor is sealed to the wood foundation wall. In Basement 1, the concrete floor slab is sealed directly to the foundation wall with caulking.

In all crawl spaces, the polyethylene ground cover acts as an air retarder—it extends over the top of the footing and all joints are sealed. In some cases, the ground cover is sealed to the footing itself (Crawl Spaces 1 and 3). In others, it is taped to the foundation wall (Crawl Space 2), or even extends up to cover the wall (Crawl Space 4).

Air movement through the foundation wall assembly is typically controlled by a polyethylene sheet on the interior (Basements 2 and 3; Crawl Spaces 1, 2, and 4), or by sealing the gypsum board to the framing (Basement 4). This interior air barrier is particularly important in insulated wood foundation wall cavities to prevent warm, moisture-laden air from the basement from coming in contact with cold sheathing surfaces. In Basement 1 and Crawl Space 3, the air retarder occurs at the exterior of the foundation wall.

In almost all cases, the elements which form the sill/rim joist/floor assembly should

be sealed to control air movement in this area. There are many variations in rim joist construction practice. For example, the structural elements of the rim joist assembly are not sealed in Basement 2. Instead, the rim joist/floor assembly is wrapped by polyethylene and this polyethylene is sealed to both the foundation wall perimeter vapor diffusion retarder and the above-grade wall vapor diffusion retarder.

In Basement 3, the rim joist/floor assembly air leakage openings are controlled by installing blocks of rigid insulation between floor joists and sealing them to the top of the perimeter basement frame wall and the underside of the subfloor sheathing.

In several cases, a tight-fitting, insulation "pillow" is installed at the interior of the rim joist assembly between floor joists (Basement 1; Crawl Spaces 1, 2, and 4). The insulation pillow is formed by placing batt insulation in a plastic bag and snugly fitting the bag containing the insulation between the floor joists. Gaps at this location around the insulation pillow need to be minimized to control potential convective moisture transfer from the interior basement space to the interior surface of the rim joist.

In all basements and crawl spaces, exterior wall sheathing is extended down over the rim joist assembly to further reduce air leakage at this location. This exterior wall sheathing can be utilized as the principal air seal at this location if it is sealed directly to the exterior of the sill plate. This makes it possible to eliminate seals at the top and bottom of the rim joist.

Vapor Diffusion

Moisture movement by vapor diffusion can be controlled in several ways. When moisture moves from the surrounding soil into the concrete foundation wall, it is controlled by installing a vapor diffusion retarder on the exterior of the foundation wall. In several cases, the dampproof coating on the exterior of the foundation wall acts as a vapor diffusion retarder (Basements 1, 2, and 3; Crawl Spaces 1 and 2).

Similarly, in wood foundation assemblies (Basement 4; Crawl Spaces 3 and 4), a polyethylene vapor diffusion retarder on the exterior controls moisture entering from the surrounding soil. The impermeable sheathing on the exterior of the wood foundation walls also acts as a vapor diffusion retarder.

For all basements, vapor diffusion through the floor slab assembly from the surrounding soil can be controlled with a polyethylene vapor diffusion retarder under the slab (or wooden floor). In crawl spaces, moisture movement by vapor diffusion from the soil is controlled by a continuous polyethylene vapor diffusion retarder used as a ground cover.

Where there is interior insulation, moisture from the basement or crawl space is typically prevented from diffusing into the perimeter foundation wall framing by installing insulation with a vapor diffusion retarder backing or a polyethylene vapor diffusion retarder on the interior of the framing (Basements 2 and 3; Crawl Spaces 2, 3, and 4). Another approach, shown in Basement 4, utilizes a low permeability paint for this purpose.

In Basement 2, construction moisture contained in the perimeter concrete foundation wall is prevented from diffusing into the perimeter foundation frame wall cavity by applying dampproofing, low permeability paint, or elastomeric paint on the interior of the perimeter foundation wall. Alternatively, the wall can be allowed to dry prior to enclosure. Where interior dampproofing is used, consideration should be given to potential odors and other indoor environment concerns.

There are a number of approaches to controlling moisture diffusing from the interior basement or crawl space into the perimeter rim joist assembly during the heating season. In several cases, vapor diffusion is controlled by the plastic bag facing on the batt insulation (Basements 1; Crawl Spaces 1, 2, and 4). Other approaches utilize impermeable rigid insulation for this purpose (Basement 3), or rely on the vapor diffusion retarder backing on the batt insulation (Basement 2, Crawl Space 3).

In all foundation assemblies (except Basement 3), moisture accumulation at the rim joist assembly from vapor diffusion is reduced by installing insulating sheathing at the exterior of the rim joist. This elevates the temperature of the first condensing surface at this location (the interior surface of the rim joist).

Drying of Foundation Assemblies

Because the concrete foundation wall is exposed in Basement 1 and Crawl Space 1, the assembly can dry to the interior. In all other cases, however, drying toward either the interior or exterior is limited by an impermeable coating on the exterior of the wall and an interior vapor diffusion retarder. Should these wall assemblies become wet during service or be built wet due to wet framing materials or wet-applied cavity insulations (wet spray

cellulose or blown fiberglass), they may not dry. Accordingly, dry framing materials (wood at a moisture content of 19 percent by weight or lower) and dry-applied insulations are recommended. Alternatively, wall assemblies must be allowed to dry prior to enclosure.

For basements with limited drying (Basements 2, 3, and 4), interior basement moisture levels should be limited to 35 percent relative humidity at 70 degrees Fahrenheit during heating periods. This is needed to further control air-transported moisture and vapor diffusion with this wall assembly, since only limited drying of the assembly occurs.

Interior Finishes

Either vapor permeable or vapor impermeable interior surface finishes may be used in conjunction with any foundation wall assembly except for Basement 4 where an impermeable paint must be used to act as a vapor diffusion retarder.

Concrete floor slabs contain significant quantities of moisture when initially placed. Covering this surface with an impermeable surface finish or floor covering may lead to deterioration of these surfaces if the construction moisture is not allowed to dry. Initial drying of the construction moisture contained in concrete may also lead to elevated interior moisture levels during the first few months of occupancy.

Installing carpets on cold, damp, concrete floor slabs can cause serious allergenic reactions in sensitive individuals and other health-related consequences. It is not recommended that carpets be installed on concrete slabs unless the carpets can be kept dry and warm; that is, carpet relative humidities should be kept below 70 percent (Godish 1989). In practice this is typically not possible unless floor slab assemblies are insulated and basement areas are conditioned.

Details

In several cases (Basements 1 and 4; Crawl Spaces 1, 3, and 4), rigid insulation is installed on the exterior of the perimeter concrete foundation wall to reduce heating and cooling loads and is protected above grade on its exterior from mechanical damage. Appropriate below grade flashings or other protection may be necessary, since this rigid insulation can act as a conduit for insects to enter the enclosure.

In Basements 2 and 3, the perimeter foundation frame wall is held away from the concrete in order to enhance the durability of the wood members. This is accomplished by using a 2 x 4 top plate with 2 x 3 studs and a 2 x 3 bottom plate. The cavity insulation, however, fills the entire void and touches the interior face of the concrete foundation wall. Fiberglass batt insulation is recommended as the cavity insulation by virtue of its draining characteristics and nonhygroscopic nature.

The granular drainage pad located under basement floors can be integrated into a subslab ventilation system to control radon migration by adding a vent pipe connected to the surface and an exhaust fan. In all construction, it is good practice to install a passive vent pipe connecting this subslab gravel layer to the exterior through the roof. An exhaust fan can be added later if necessary.

In Basement 4, the rigid insulation under the basement floor framing requires a compressive strength of 25 psi to control settling. Regarding all the wood foundation assemblies, publications of the National Forest Products Association should be consulted including *Permanent Wood Foundation System: Design, Fabrication and Installation Manual* (NFPA 1987).

In unvented conditioned crawl spaces it is convenient to install ductwork, plumbing, and other mechanical components, since concerns about the effects of duct leakage and freezing pipes are minimized.

Roof Construction in Mixed Climates

In this section four roof assemblies are shown that can be used successfully in mixed climates. There are two assemblies with wood roof trusses and vented attics, and two examples of cathedral ceilings. One of the cathedral ceiling assemblies is ventilated and the other one is unvented. The basic characteristics of the roof assemblies are summarized in Table 5-3.

First, each roof assembly is illustrated and briefly described. Text adjacent to each drawing indicates how the assembly is designed to handle each of the critical moisture problems in this climate: (1) ventilation, (2) air movement, and (3) vapor diffusion. In addition, comments related to special concerns such as ice damming are summarized for each assembly. Following the drawings is a summary discussion of key moisture control strategies for roof assemblies in this climate.

Insulation levels in roof assemblies, except where specifically noted to control moisture accumulation on condensing surfaces, are left to the judgement of the reader.

Table 5-3: Characteristics of roof assemblies for mixed climates.

	ROOF TYPE	VENTILATION	CEILING INSULATION	OTHER FEATURES	DRYING
ROOF 1	Wood truss with flat ceiling	Vented attic	Cavity insulation	Polyethylene vapor diffusion retarder (Interior)	To the exterior
ROOF 2	Wood truss with flat ceiling	Vented attic	Cavity insulation	No vapor diffusion retarder in ceiling	To the exterior and the interior
ROOF 3	Cathedral ceiling	Vented	Cavity insulation	Polyethylene vapor diffusion retarder (Interior)	To the exterior
ROOF 4	Cathedral ceiling	Unvented	Cavity insulation with rigid insulation on the exterior	Rigid insulation acts as vapor diffusion retarder (Exterior)	To the interior

Prevent wind washing purpose of wind baffle

Roof 1—Mixed Climate: This conventional wood truss roof system is insulated above the flat ceiling. The attic space is ventilated. A polyethylene vapor diffusion retarder is placed above the ceiling gypsum board on the interior side of the insulation. The wood frame wall with brick veneer shown here corresponds to Wall 3 in a previous section of this chapter.

Key characteristics:
- *The attic is ventilated permitting drying to the exterior.*
- *The polyethylene sheet placed beneath the gypsum board acts as an air retarder to control air movement, and acts as a vapor diffusion retarder.*
- *Air movement is further controlled by limiting and sealing all penetrations between the conditioned space and the attic.*
- *The conditioned space should be depressurized relative to the attic during the heating season, and pressurized during cooling periods.*
- *The wind baffle prevents wind-washing of the perimeter insulation.*
- *A membrane over the roof sheathing protects against moisture damage from ice damming.*

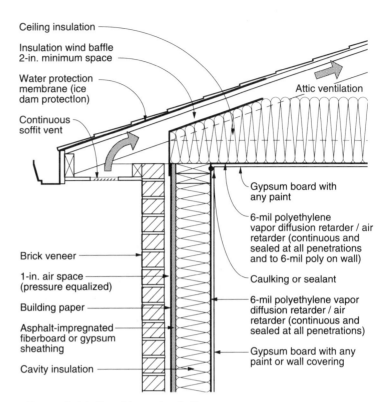

Ceiling insulation

Insulation wind baffle 2-in. minimum space

Water protection membrane (ice dam protection)

Continuous soffit vent

Attic ventilation

Brick veneer

1-in. air space (pressure equalized)

Building paper

Asphalt-impregnated fiberboard or gypsum sheathing

Cavity insulation

Gypsum board with any paint

6-mil polyethylene vapor diffusion retarder / air retarder (continuous and sealed at all penetrations and to 6-mil poly on wall)

Caulking or sealant

6-mil polyethylene vapor diffusion retarder / air retarder (continuous and sealed at all penetrations)

Gypsum board with any paint or wall covering

Figure 5-18: Roof 1—mixed climate.

Roof 2—Mixed Climate: Similar to Roof 1, this conventional wood truss roof system is insulated above the flat ceiling, and the attic space is ventilated. Unlike Roof 1, there is no polyethylene vapor diffusion retarder on the interior side of the ceiling insulation. The gypsum board ceiling is sealed to the wood frame construction in order to act as an air retarder. The wall assembly shown here corresponds to Wall 4 in a previous section of this chapter.

Key characteristics:
- *The attic is ventilated permitting drying to the exterior.*
- *There is no vapor diffusion retarder—vapor is permitted to move through this assembly in both directions and thus drying occurs both toward the interior and the exterior. Interior surface finishes must be vapor permeable.*
- *Air movement is controlled by limiting and sealing all penetrations between the conditioned space and the attic.*
- *The conditioned space should be depressurized relative to the attic during the heating season, and pressurized during cooling periods.*
- *Interior relative humidity should not exceed 35 percent at 70 degrees F during heating periods.*
- *The wind baffle prevents wind-washing of the perimeter insulation.*
- *A membrane over the roof sheathing protects against moisture damage from ice damming.*

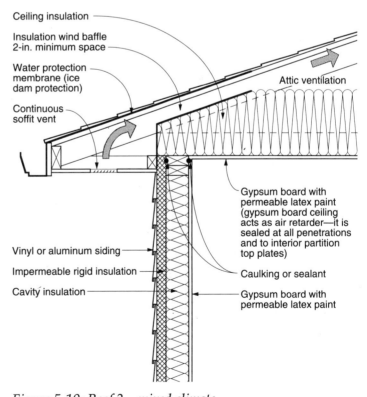

Ceiling insulation

Insulation wind baffle 2-in. minimum space

Water protection membrane (ice dam protection)

Continuous soffit vent

Attic ventilation

Vinyl or aluminum siding

Impermeable rigid insulation

Cavity insulation

Gypsum board with permeable latex paint (gypsum board ceiling acts as air retarder—it is sealed at all penetrations and to interior partition top plates)

Caulking or sealant

Gypsum board with permeable latex paint

Figure 5-19: Roof 2—mixed climate.

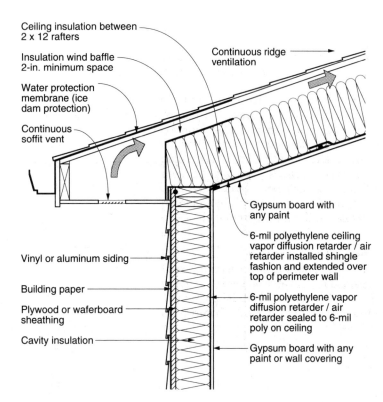

Ceiling insulation between
2 x 12 rafters

Insulation wind baffle
2-in. minimum space

Water protection
membrane (ice
dam protection)

Continuous
soffit vent

Continuous ridge
ventilation

Gypsum board with
any paint

6-mil polyethylene ceiling
vapor diffusion retarder / air
retarder installed shingle
fashion and extended over
top of perimeter wall

6-mil polyethylene vapor
diffusion retarder / air
retarder sealed to 6-mil
poly on ceiling

Gypsum board with any
paint or wall covering

Vinyl or aluminum siding

Building paper

Plywood or waferboard
sheathing

Cavity insulation

Figure 5-20: Roof 3—mixed climate.

Wood shake / shingle roof

Roofing paper

1 x 4 furring strips

R-15 rigid insulation
(insulation and sheathing
joints should be offset both
horizontally and vertically)

Rigid insulation
notched around rafters

Vinyl or aluminum siding

R-7 min. impermeable
rigid insulation

Cavity insulation

Roof sheathing

Roof joists with ceiling
insulation (R-28 maximum)

Gypsum board with
permeable latex paint

Caulking or sealant

Gypsum board with
permeable latex paint

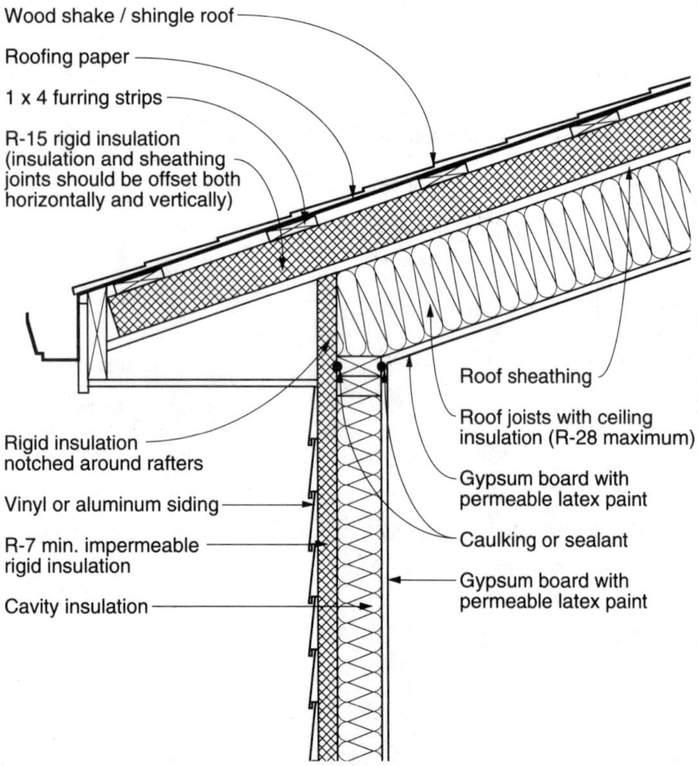

Figure 5-21: Roof 4—mixed climate.

Roof 3—Mixed Climate: In this roof assembly with a cathedral ceiling, cavity insulation is placed between 2 x 12 rafters. Ventilation is provided through a 2-inch air space above the insulation. A polyethylene vapor diffusion retarder is placed above the ceiling gypsum board on the interior side of the insulation. The wall shown here corresponds to Wall 1 in a previous section of this chapter.

Key characteristics:
* *Ventilation is provided by a 2-inch air space above the insulation with continuous soffit and ridge vents. This permits drying to the exterior.*
* *The polyethylene sheet placed beneath the gypsum board acts as an air retarder to control air movement, and acts as a vapor diffusion retarder.*
* *Air movement is further controlled by limiting and sealing all roof penetrations..*
* *The conditioned space should be depressurized relative to the attic during the heating season, and pressurized during cooling periods.*
* *The wind baffle prevents wind-washing of the perimeter insulation.*
* *A membrane over the roof sheathing protects against moisture damage from ice damming.*

Roof 4—Mixed Climate: This roof assembly illustrates a cathedral ceiling that is unvented. Cavity insulation is placed between 2 x 8 rafters, and above the roof sheathing is a layer of rigid insulation. Permeable latex paint on the gypsum board permits vapor to enter the roof cavity and then dry to the interior. This approach is dependent on limiting the cavity insulation to R-28, while installing at least R-15 rigid insulation. The wall shown here corresponds to Wall 4 in a previous section of this chapter.

Key characteristics:
* *Air movement is controlled by the rigid insulation installed with staggered joints, and sealing all roof penetrations.*
* *The conditioned space should be depressurized relative to the attic during the heating season, and pressurized during cooling periods.*
* *Impermeable rigid insulation acts as a vapor diffusion retarder during cooling periods.*
* *Insulation board raises the roof cavity temperature and limits potential condensation.*
* *A vapor permeable paint finish on the gypsum board permits drying toward the interior.*
* *Interior relative humidity should not exceed 35 percent at 70 degrees F during heating periods.*
* *The wind baffle (rigid insulation) prevents wind-washing of the perimeter insulation.*

Vaulted   1/150 Ventals
         Attic   1/300   per square foot

SUMMARY: ROOF ASSEMBLIES IN MIXED CLIMATES

Ventilation

Roofs 1, 2, and 3 are ventilated while Roof 4 is not. Where roof assemblies are ventilated in this climate, it is done to remove moisture from attic spaces and, to a limited extent, to reduce cooling loads by reducing solar heat gain. Where there is an open attic space (as in Roofs 1 and 2), a minimum of 1 square foot of vent area should be provided for every 300 square feet of insulated ceiling area. In addition, vents should be distributed between the soffit and ridge to prevent zones of dead or stagnant air and should not be blocked by roof assembly insulation or other obstructions.

If cathedral ceiling assemblies are ventilated (as is Roof 3), a minimum of 1 square foot of vent area should be provided for every 150 square feet of insulated ceiling area. Continuous soffit and ridge vents should be installed with a minimum 2-inch space between the top of the insulation and the underside of the roof sheathing.

It should be noted that during hot, humid periods, ventilation air into the attic will bring limited amounts of moisture into the roof assembly rather than remove it. However, during cooler periods this moisture is subsequently removed by ventilation.

In unvented cathedral ceiling assemblies (such as Roof 4), as in most wall assemblies, the emphasis is on the prevention of moisture movement into the assembly rather than the removal of moisture once it has entered the assembly by ventilation.

Air Movement

During the heating season, airborne moisture exfiltrates from the conditioned space into the attic or roof assembly cavities under typical conditions. To control this, the conditioned space should be depressurized relative to the attic or roof assembly cavities. During the cooling season, moisture infiltrates from the attic or roof assembly cavities into the enclosure. It is controlled by pressurizing the enclosure relative to the attic or roof assembly cavities. In all cases, penetrations through the ceiling where air leakage can occur should be limited as much as possible. The interior gypsum board ceiling and/or polyethylene is sealed to the roof framing and wall assembly to form a continuous air retarder.

In vented roof assemblies such as Roofs 1

and 2, it is important to eliminate air flow between conditioned spaces and the attic. The attic needs to be uncoupled from the conditioned space so that conditions within the building enclosure influence the attic to a minimum. This is best accomplished by not installing any forced air ductwork, furnaces, or air conditioners in attics. In addition, penetrations for plumbing, wiring, dropped ceilings, and kitchen cabinet bulkheads should be sealed.

In an unvented cathedral ceiling assembly such as Roof 4, the exfiltration of warm, moisture-laden air during the heating season is controlled by sealing the interior gypsum board to the roof joist framing, as well as by sealing the exterior rigid insulation to the roof sheathing. This air sealing can be with an adhesive, caulk, or some other sealant. Experience has shown that some exterior rigid insulations are thermally unstable, and may not be compatible with sealing techniques which provide little allowance for movement. The joints in the layers of rigid insulation should be staggered horizontally and vertically to form an effective air retarder. In addition, the joints in the roof sheathing should be staggered over the joints in the rigid insulation to enhance air tightness.

Vapor Diffusion

During heating periods, vapor diffusion from the interior may carry moisture into the attic or roof assembly, where it accumulates. During the cooling season, moisture diffuses from the attic into the enclosure. In Roofs 1 and 3, moisture movement by diffusion in either direction is controlled by a continuous ceiling vapor diffusion retarder. The polyethylene sheet is sealed to the perimeter wall vapor diffusion retarder in both cases. In Roof 3, the continuous ceiling vapor diffusion retarder is installed shingle fashion and extended over the top of the exterior perimeter wall to allow for drainage of any condensed moisture on the top surface and to provide secondary protection for roof rainwater leakage.

In Roof 4, the impermeable rigid insulation acts as a vapor diffusion retarder for exterior moisture during cooling periods. There is no vapor diffusion retarder on the interior, however. Consequently, during heating periods, vapor diffusion from the interior may transmit moisture into the cathedral ceiling assembly cavities, where it accumulates. Within an unvented cathedral ceiling assembly like Roof 4, vapor diffusion can be controlled by elevating the temperature of the first condensing surface—the cavity side of the roof sheathing. In this case, rigid insulation of sufficient thermal resistance is installed to limit periods of potential condensation to acceptable levels. An acceptable period would be sufficiently brief so that wood does not begin to decay or interior surface water stain marks or mold or mildew do not appear. This period is determined by the temperature of the first condensing surface and the interior moisture level. The temperature of the first condensing surface is determined by the ratio of the amount of thermal insulation installed to the exterior of the condensing surface compared with the amount of thermal insulation installed to the interior of the condensing surface. For Roof 4, the thermal resistance of the rigid insulation should be R-15 or greater, and the thermal resistance of cavity insulation should be R-28 or less.

In Roof 2, there is no ceiling vapor diffusion retarder. Consequently, moisture movement by vapor diffusion through the roof assembly in either direction is not controlled. Omitting the ceiling vapor diffusion retarder in this climate provides acceptable assembly performance as long as permeable paint is used on the interior. For this assembly to perform as intended, impermeable interior ceiling surface finishes should be avoided. For Roof 2, interior moisture levels should be limited to below 35 percent relative humidity at 70 degrees Fahrenheit.

Drying of Roof Assemblies

Roofs 1, 2, and 3 permit drying to the exterior since they are vented. Roof 3 also permits drying to the interior since there is no vapor diffusion retarder. In Roof 4, drying occurs only toward the interior. If Roof 4 is used, interior moisture levels should be limited to 35 percent relative humidity at 70 degrees Fahrenheit during heating periods. This is needed to further control airborne moisture and vapor diffusion with this cathedral ceiling assembly, since only limited drying of the assembly may occur.

Interior Finishes

Either vapor permeable or vapor impermeable interior surface finishes may be used in conjunction with Roofs 1 and 3 since there is no drying to the interior and a polyethylene sheet serves as a vapor diffusion retarder. In Roofs 2 and 4, a vapor permeable interior surface finish is required to permit some drying to the interior. Where roof assemblies with permeable interior surface treatments have been performing satisfactorily and are subsequently covered with impermeable interior surface treatments, mold and mildew problems may appear at the gypsum board/surface treatment interface.

Rain Absorption/Capillary Suction

Roof 4 illustrates the use of wood shakes or shingles on wood furring strips. With this approach, the rain screen principle is utilized which requires a pressure-equalized cavity behind the wood shakes/shingles to perform satisfactorily. Wood shakes/shingles are installed over a roofing paper—the shakes/shingles are loose; the roofing paper is tight. A roofing paper woven into the shakes/shingles installed over the top of the furring strips also helps drain rainwater to the exterior. Appropriate installation of flashings is critical in rain screen wood shake/shingle assemblies.

The air space beneath the wood shakes/shingles controls rain absorption and capillarity effects. The air space also acts as a receptor for both capillary moisture and absorbed moisture driven inward by incident solar radiation. Wood shakes/shingles can also be dipped (painting or coating the front and back surfaces) to limit their capillary and vapor absorption of moisture.

Comments

In Roofs 1, 2, and 3, a wind baffle is installed at the perimeter of the attic or cathedral ceiling area where the insulated ceiling intersects the exterior wall. This prevents thermal short-circuiting of the insulation by wind (wind-washing). In Roof 4, extending the exterior rigid insulation up on the perimeter wall so that it intersects the underside of the rigid insulation installed on top of the roof joists will effectively control wind-washing.

In this climate, wind-washing during the heating season can cool the perimeter wall top plate and ceiling gypsum board surfaces, subsequently causing interior mold and mildew growth. During the cooling season, wind-washing by hot, humid air can induce moisture deposition on perimeter wall top plate and ceiling gypsum board surfaces cooled by air conditioning.

Where exterior ventilation air enters soffit assemblies, it experiences a pressure drop, as the soffit assembly acts as an expansion space.

This is due to the combination of a narrow soffit vent opening up to a relatively large volume soffit assembly and then being squeezed into a narrow space between the underside of the roof sheathing and the wind baffle. This pressure drop induces the ventilation air to deposit airborne rain droplets and snow in the soffit assembly rather than transport them farther into the roof assembly. Accordingly, it may be desirable to back-prime wood soffit materials. In Roof 1, the pressure-equalized air space behind the brick veneer wall is open to the soffit assembly to promote moisture removal from the air space by ventilation.

Ice damming for Roofs 1, 2, and 3 in this climate is controlled by installing a water protection membrane over the sheathing at the eave. In addition, sufficient thermal insulation (along with air tightening) should be provided at the intersection of the perimeter wall and ceiling to reduce heat loss, which can lead to snow melt. In addition, where the soffit assembly is vented, it flushes heat from the conditioned space away from the roof sheathing to maintain a cold deck.

Some unvented roof assemblies have led to an elevation of shingle/shake/sheathing temperatures and subsequently to premature degradation of shingles/shakes/sheathings and a reduced service life. Accordingly, light-colored shakes and shingles should be utilized. In addition, it may be desirable to install roofing papers to provide additional protection against rainwater entry should shakes and shingles deteriorate prematurely. Rigid insulation placed over the roof sheathing in Roof 4 should be fastened with 5- to 6-inch wood screws penetrating into the rafters.

CHAPTER 6

Moisture Control Practices for Cooling Climates

This chapter includes four major sections that address moisture control practices for cooling climates in the United States. First, an introductory section defines the climate, identifies key moisture problems found there, and discusses some general approaches to solving these problems. The last three sections of the chapter address wall, foundation, and roof assemblies. For each component, several construction assemblies designed to control moisture in this climate are shown. There are detailed construction drawings, a list of the key characteristics for each assembly, and a summary discussion of the control strategies for this climate.

Introduction

This climate zone is defined as a warm, humid climate with a significant number of cooling (air conditioning) hours. It generally follows the ASHRAE definition of a humid climate where one or both of the following conditions occur:

1. A 67°F (19.4°C) or higher wet bulb temperature for 3000 or more hours during the warmest six consecutive months of the year.

2. A 73°F (22.8°C) or higher wet bulb temperature for 1500 or more hours during the warmest six consecutive months of the year.

The recommendations in this section will perform satisfactorily in climates meeting these conditions. Fringe areas of the ASHRAE humid climate definition are also included based on local experience with moisture problems. The recommendations in this section will also perform satisfactorily in warm, dry climates although these climates are not noted in the accompanying map (Figure 6-1).

The climate zone specified is broad and general for simplicity. For a specific location, designers and builders should consider weather records, local experience, and the microclimate around a building. Incident solar radiation, nearby water and wetlands, vegetation, and undergrowth can all affect the microclimate.

For residential buildings in this climate, both wood frame and concrete masonry walls are common. The absence of ground frost penetration in this climate zone results in the use of crawl space and slab-on-grade foundation construction—basements are rare, if not completely nonexistent.

KEY MOISTURE CONCERNS

In warm, humid climates the principle moisture concerns are rain penetration, groundwater, moisture within building assemblies, and mold and mildew. High exterior levels of humidity encourage mold and mildew growth, as do cool interior surfaces due to the air conditioning of enclosures. These are discussed below along with some other problems related to mechanical systems and the use of combustion appliances.

Rain and Groundwater

Controlling rain penetration and groundwater is a common concern to builders in all climates. Rain that is permitted to penetrate the exterior cladding of a building can cause material deterioration as well as contribute to other moisture problems within the building assemblies. Another source of external water—air conditioning condensate drains—should be plumbed directly to the graywater system.

Moisture within Building Assemblies

During cooling periods, mechanical cooling coupled with dehumidification is widespread. Air movement and vapor diffusion thus carry moisture from the exterior to the interior cooled area, because the vapor pressure is higher outdoors than it is indoors. These vapor pressure differences during cooling periods in this climate can be more significant than those found during heating periods in colder climates. High inward flow of moisture during cooling periods can increase energy costs due to high cooling loads, as well

as increase building deterioration.

Cladding systems that can absorb significant amounts of moisture when exposed to rain, such as brick, masonry, wood, and stucco, should only be incorporated in wall assemblies designed and built to deal with the inward migration of moisture. Solar radiation warms exterior wall surfaces, and this warming creates temperature gradients from the exterior to the interior. Along with the air conditioning of interior surfaces, this can cause problems if not taken into account.

An example of this is the installation of gypsum board covered with vinyl wallpaper on the interior of a masonry block wall without provision for an appropriate vapor diffusion retarder and air barrier system. Without these, the gypsum wall board is not protected from exterior moisture or from construction moisture which may be trapped in the masonry units. Thus, wherever vinyl interior wall coverings are used in this climate zone, precautions must be taken to prevent gypsum wall board from absorbing moisture either from the exterior or from construction moisture.

Building assemblies constructed with wet lumber (greater than 19 percent moisture content by weight) or employing wet-applied insulation (wet spray cellulose or wet blown fiberglass) merit special attention. These

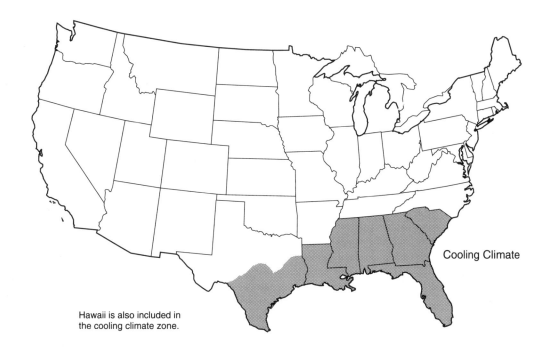

Hawaii is also included in the cooling climate zone.

Cooling Climate

Figure 6-1: Map of cooling climate zone in the United States.

assemblies must be designed and built so that they can dry to the exterior or interior, or the materials must be allowed to dry prior to enclosure.

High Interior Humidity Resulting in Mold, Mildew, and Condensation

Because of the high exterior humidity, elevated interior moisture levels can result from high air change due to infiltration/exfiltration, duct leakage, and excessive ventilation. This is contrary to heating climates, where the same mechanisms lead to low levels of interior moisture. Naturally, interior moisture levels increase as the amount of hot, humid exterior air brought into an enclosure increases. These elevated levels can lead to condensation and give rise to surface mold and mildew.

Mechanical System Concerns

During hot, humid cooling periods, leaky return ducts located in attics draw significant amounts of warm, moisture-laden air into the conditioned space from the attic, often creating moisture problems and increasing cooling loads. Leaky return ducts in vented crawl spaces draw significant amounts of soil gas, moisture, possibly pesticides, radon, and other pollutants into the conditioned spaces. This often creates moisture problems, increases cooling loads, and risks occupant health and safety.

Leaky supply ducts in attics or vented crawl spaces during cooling periods depressurize the conditioned space, leading to the infiltration of exterior warm air, often creating moisture problems and increasing cooling loads.

Combustion Appliances

Unvented combustion appliances such as gas stoves with standing pilot lights and room space heaters are significant sources of moisture as well as sources for other pollutants.

GENERAL STRATEGIES TO CONTROL MOISTURE PROBLEMS

For the potential moisture problems identified above for buildings in this climate, there are several control strategies. The control strategies generally fall into two groups: (1) those applying to the building envelope

assemblies, and (2) those related to the overall building and its mechanical systems. To be effective, all of these strategies must be applied as a complete system.

Building Envelope Strategies

Detailed presentations of building envelope strategies are found in the last three sections of the chapter for wall, foundation, and roof assemblies. Some of the key principles are:

- Control rain penetration in walls using rain screens, building papers, and appropriate placement of flashings.

- Direct water away from foundations using gutters and downspouts as well as careful site grading.

- Control groundwater with a subgrade drainage system.

- Control moisture movement by air leakage (the infiltration of exterior moisture-laden air) by limiting air leakage openings and installing air retarder systems in all assemblies.

- Place vapor diffusion retarders in walls, roofs, and foundations to control moisture movement by vapor diffusion from the exterior. In particular, place ground covers on all crawl space floors.

- If possible, permit wall assemblies to dry if they become wet. Wall design and construction in this climate typically locate vapor diffusion retarders and measures to control air leakage toward the exterior. Thus, it is convenient to allow walls to dry to the interior in the direction of typical vapor flow. Drying to the exterior is possible, but more difficult to facilitate and is usually intermittent.

- Ventilate roof assemblies to reduce cooling loads.

Whole Building System Strategies

The second group of strategies pertains to the overall design and operation of the building and its mechanical system in particular. These include:

- Minimize interior moisture sources by direct venting of clothes dryers, and providing kitchen and bath exhaust systems.

- To control air leakage, design the mechanical system to maintain above-grade spaces at a positive air pressure relative to the exterior. Unvented crawl spaces should also be maintained at a positive air pressure relative to the exterior in this climate. Pressurization of the above-grade conditioned space during cooling periods eliminates the infiltration of exterior moisture-laden air. Positive pressurization of unvented crawl spaces eliminates the infiltration of soil gas, radon, and other pollutants. This principle is shown in Figure 6-2 for three typical building configurations appropriate for this climate. All three buildings have vented attics while each illustrates a different foundation assembly: (1) a vented crawl space, (2) an unvented crawl space, and (3) a slab-on-grade.

- Limit controlled ventilation to minimum levels while maintaining indoor air quality. These levels are established by ASHRAE guidelines, the strength of pollutant sources within enclosures, and/or local authorities (ASHRAE 1989b). An effective controlled ventilation system must do the following: (1) exhaust stale air, (2) supply fresh outside air, (3) operate continuously when occupants are present, and (4) provide effective distribution. A schematic of such a system is shown in Figure 6-3 with notes describing its components, operation, and control. This type of system is essential with tight construction to control both health and moisture problems. The HVAC system, central exhaust, and fresh air supply must be balanced and commissioned in order to maintain the pressure relationships shown in Figure 6-2.

- It is preferable to install ductwork for forced air heating and cooling systems only within conditioned spaces. If possible, avoid attics or vented crawl spaces. Where ductwork is located in dropped ceilings adjacent to attics and exterior walls, it is important that air barrier continuity is maintained above the dropped ceiling or at the exterior wall.

- Seal all ductwork with mastic. Of particular concern are return systems utilizing floor joist and stud wall cavities to form return air ducts. Utilize multiple return registers (particularly located in bedrooms), and transfer grills between bedrooms and interior corridors to prevent pressurization of above-grade rooms.

- Utilize the dehumidification capabilities of the air conditioning system to control

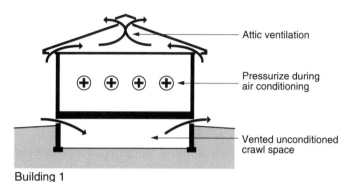

Building 1

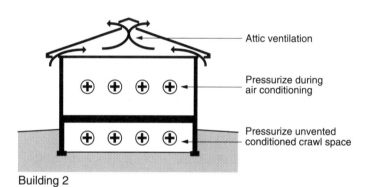

Building 2

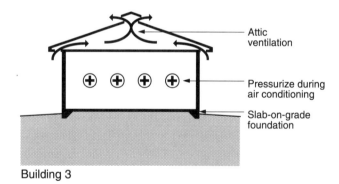

Building 3

Figure 6-2: Recommended air pressure distribution to reduce moisture problems in cooling climate buildings.

interior humidity. Since latent cooling loads on air conditioning systems can be higher than sensible cooling loads, proper sizing of air conditioning systems is important. Oversizing of air conditioning equipment can lead to high interior humidity problems since oversized equipment will not operate as often, and therefore will dehumidify less than properly sized equipment.

- Locate air conditioning supply air registers so that cold air is not blown directly across wall and ceiling surfaces, potentially chilling the surfaces below dew point temperatures. This could cause condensation or high surface relative humidities and potential mold and mildew growth.

- Insulate and protect air conditioning supply ductwork with an exterior vapor diffusion retarder to control condensation on cold duct surfaces.

- Insulate cold water piping if exposed to warm, humid air during the cooling season.

- Avoid unvented combustion appliances. Gas stoves and cook tops without standing pilot lights should be installed in conjunction with vented range hoods or some other vent provision.

- Use combustion appliances that are aerodynamically uncoupled (not influenced by enclosure air pressures or supply air availability) from the conditioned space. In other words, combustion devices that are sealed, power vented, induced draft, condensing, or pulse should be used. Devices with traditional draft hoods should be avoided.

- Provide fireplaces with their own air supply (correctly sized) from the exterior as well as tight-fitting glass doors. Wood stoves should also have their own supply of exterior air ducted directly to their firebox.

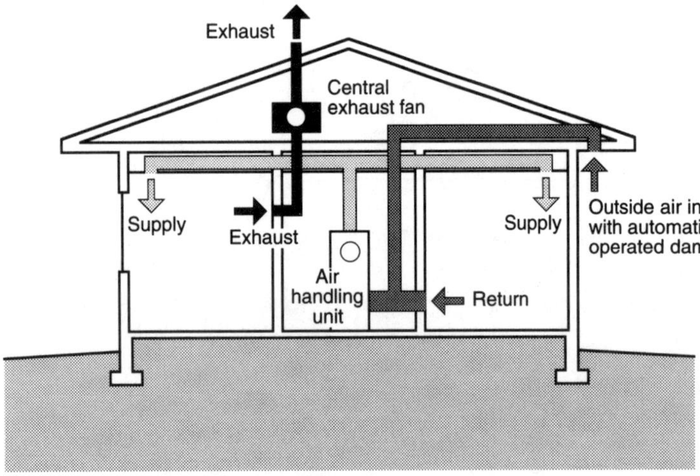

Figure 6-3: Controlled ventilation system for a house in a cooling climate.

Notes for Figure 6-3:
An effective controlled ventilation system in a heating climate should have the following characteristics:

- *Stale air is removed through a central exhaust system. Exhaust vents are located in the kitchen and bathrooms.*
- *The central exhaust system operates continuously – at least 15 minutes per hour whenever occupants are present.*
- *The outside air supply is connected to the return side of the air handling unit. An automatically operated damper covers the outside air intake.*
- *The forced air system provides effective distribution of fresh air throughout the house.*
- *The control system is designed so that the central exhaust system only operates when the outside air damper is open and the air handling unit is running.*
- *The overall system must be designed, balanced, and commissioned so that the pressure relationships recommended for cooling climate buildings are maintained (see Figure 6-2).*
- *To maintain the air pressure relationships for cooling climate buildings, the outside air damper should be open when the air handler is operating.*

Wall Construction in Cooling Climates

In this section eight wall assemblies are shown that can be used successfully in cooling climates. The first five examples are wood frame walls—three with siding, one with brick veneer, and one with stucco cladding. The last three wall assemblies are concrete masonry—one with brick veneer, and two with stucco cladding. Other differences between the wall assemblies include the type of sheathing as well as the use and location of a vapor diffusion retarder. The basic characteristics of the wall assemblies are summarized in Table 6-1.

First, each wall assembly is illustrated and briefly described. Text adjacent to each drawing indicates how the assembly is designed to handle each of the critical moisture problems in this climate: (1) rain penetration, (2) rain absorption, (3) air movement, and (4) vapor diffusion. In addition, comments concerning the ability of the wall to dry and other limitations of each wall assembly are included. Following the drawings is a summary discussion of key moisture control strategies for wall assemblies in this climate.

Insulation levels in wall assemblies, except where specifically noted to control moisture accumulation on condensing surfaces, are left to the judgement of the reader.

4 - Critical Moisture Problems

Table 6-1: Characteristics of wall assemblies for cooling climates.

	WALL TYPE	EXTERIOR COMPONENT	SHEATHING	OTHER FEATURES	DRYING
WALL 1	Wood frame	Plywood siding (Impermeable)	None	Plywood siding acts as vapor diffusion retarder (Exterior)	To the interior
WALL 2	Wood frame	Wood, vinyl, or aluminum siding	Rigid insulation (Impermeable)	Rigid insulation acts as vapor diffusion retarder (Exterior)	To the interior
WALL 3	Wood frame	Wood siding over air space	Plywood or waferboard (Impermeable)	Plywood sheathing acts as vapor diffusion retarder (Exterior)	To the interior
WALL 4	Wood frame	Brick veneer over cavity	Asphalt-impregnated fiberboard or gypsum (Permeable)	Polyethylene acts as vapor diffusion retarder (Exterior)	To the interior
WALL 5	Wood frame	Stucco cladding	Plywood, waferboard, or gypsum covered with polyethylene	Polyethylene acts as vapor diffusion retarder (Exterior)	To the interior
WALL 6	Concrete block with wood frame wall on interior	Brick veneer over cavity	None	Coating or membrane acts as vapor diffusion retarder (Exterior)	To the interior
WALL 7	Concrete block	Stucco cladding	Rigid insulation (Impermeable)	Rigid insulation acts as vapor diffusion retarder (Exterior)	To the interior
WALL 8	Concrete block	Stucco cladding	None	Rigid insulation acts as vapor diffusion retarder (Interior)	To the exterior

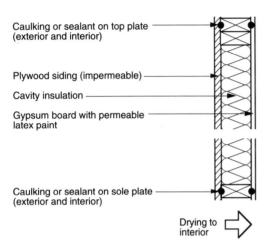

Caulking or sealant on top plate
(exterior and interior)

Plywood siding (impermeable)

Cavity insulation

Gypsum board with permeable
latex paint

Caulking or sealant on sole plate
(exterior and interior)

Drying to
interior

Figure 6-4: Wall 1—cooling climate.

Wall 1—Cooling Climate: Plywood siding with no sheathing material underneath is used in this wood frame wall assembly. The impermeable siding serves as a vapor diffusion retarder on the exterior. Permeable latex paint on gypsum board permits drying to the interior.

Key characteristics:
- *The barrier approach (sealing all openings in the plywood) controls rain penetration.*
- *Appropriate paints and stains control rain absorption and plywood capillarity effects. The insulated cavity acts as a receptor for moisture driven inward by solar radiation.*
- *To control air movement, the exterior plywood and the interior gypsum board are sealed to the framing to form air retarders.*
- *Plywood siding acts as a vapor diffusion retarder for vapor entering from the exterior during cooling periods.*
- *A vapor permeable paint finish on the gypsum board permits this wall to dry toward the interior. Vapor permeable interior surface finishes must be used.*

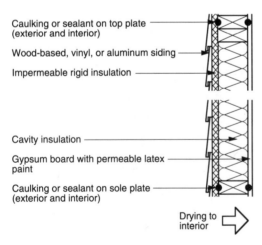

Caulking or sealant on top plate
(exterior and interior)

Wood-based, vinyl, or aluminum siding

Impermeable rigid insulation

Cavity insulation

Gypsum board with permeable latex
paint

Caulking or sealant on sole plate
(exterior and interior)

Drying to
interior

Figure 6-5: Wall 2—cooling climate.

Wall 2—Cooling Climate: Impermeable rigid insulation is used as the sheathing material in this wood frame wall assembly. Wood-based, vinyl, or aluminum siding is applied over the sheathing. The rigid insulation serves as a vapor diffusion retarder on the exterior. Similar to Wall 1, permeable latex paint on gypsum board permits drying to the interior.

Key characteristics:
- *The rain screen principle controls rain penetration when vinyl or aluminum siding is used. With wood siding, the barrier approach (sealing all openings) is used.*
- *No building paper is required to control rain absorption since rigid insulation is impermeable.*
- *To control air movement, the exterior sheathing and the interior gypsum board are sealed to the framing to form air retarders.*
- *Impermeable rigid insulation acts as a vapor diffusion retarder for vapor entering from the exterior during cooling periods.*
- *Insulating sheathing raises the wall cavity temperature and limits potential condensation.*
- *A vapor permeable paint finish on the gypsum board permits this wall to dry toward the interior. Vapor permeable interior surface finishes must be used.*
- *With wood-based siding, utilize dry materials, back-prime the siding, and nail according to manufacturers' recommended installation practices. Using spacers, wedges, or installing siding over furring should be considered.*

Wall 3—Cooling Climate: Plywood or waferboard is used as the sheathing material in this wood frame wall assembly. Wood-based siding is applied and an air space between the siding and the sheathing is a receptor for moisture. The impermeable sheathing serves as a vapor diffusion retarder on the exterior. Similar to the previous wall assemblies, permeable latex paint on gypsum board permits drying to the interior.

Key characteristics:
- The rain screen principle controls rain penetration.
- Building paper controls rain absorption into the sheathing.
- The air space beneath the wood siding acts as a receptor for capillary moisture and absorbed moisture driven inward by solar radiation.
- Back-prime the siding and utilize dry materials.
- To control air movement, the exterior sheathing and the gypsum board on the interior are sealed to the framing to form air retarders.
- Plywood sheathing acts as a vapor diffusion retarder for vapor entering from the exterior during cooling periods.
- A vapor permeable paint finish on the gypsum board permits this wall to dry toward the interior. Vapor permeable interior surface finishes must be used.

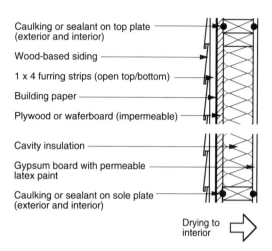

Caulking or sealant on top plate (exterior and interior)
Wood-based siding
1 x 4 furring strips (open top/bottom)
Building paper
Plywood or waferboard (impermeable)
Cavity insulation
Gypsum board with permeable latex paint
Caulking or sealant on sole plate (exterior and interior)

Drying to interior

Figure 6-6: Wall 3—cooling climate.

Wall 4—Cooling Climate: This wood frame wall is covered on the exterior by a brick veneer. An air space between the brick and the wood frame assembly is a receptor for moisture. The sheet membrane (typically adhered) over the sheathing serves as an air retarder and a vapor diffusion retarder on the exterior. Similar to the previous wall assemblies, permeable latex paint on gypsum board permits drying to the interior.

Key characteristics:
- The rain screen principle controls rain penetration.
- The air space behind the brick veneer acts as a receptor for capillary moisture and absorbed moisture driven inward by solar radiation.
- To control air movement, the gypsum board on the interior is sealed to the framing to form an interior air retarder.
- The polyethylene sheet placed over the sheathing acts as an exterior air retarder, and acts as a vapor diffusion retarder for vapor entering from the exterior during cooling periods.
- A vapor permeable paint finish on the gypsum board permits this wall to dry toward the interior. Vapor permeable interior surface finishes must be used.

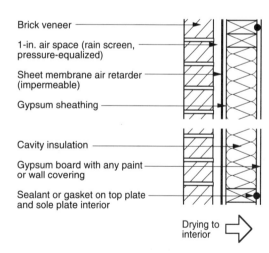

Brick veneer
1-in. air space (rain screen, pressure-equalized)
Sheet membrane air retarder (impermeable)
Gypsum sheathing
Cavity insulation
Gypsum board with any paint or wall covering
Sealant or gasket on top plate and sole plate interior

Drying to interior

Figure 6-7: Wall 4—cooling climate.

Pressure Equalization—seal the outside or use rain screen

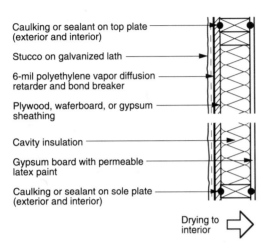

Caulking or sealant on top plate (exterior and interior)

Stucco on galvanized lath

6-mil polyethylene vapor diffusion retarder and bond breaker

Plywood, waferboard, or gypsum sheathing

Cavity insulation

Gypsum board with permeable latex paint

Caulking or sealant on sole plate (exterior and interior)

Drying to interior

Figure 6-8: Wall 5—cooling climate.

Wall 5—Cooling Climate: *Plywood, waferboard, or gypsum sheathing material is used in this wood frame wall assembly. Stucco over galvanized lath is applied over the sheathing. A polyethylene sheet placed between the sheathing and the stucco cladding serves as a vapor diffusion retarder on the exterior. Similar to the previous wall assemblies, permeable latex paint on gypsum board permits drying to the interior.*

Key characteristics:
- *Stucco cladding forms a barrier to control rain penetration.*
- *Rain absorption and capillary suction through the stucco are controlled by the polyethylene sheet.*
- *To control air movement, the exterior sheathing and the interior gypsum board are sealed to the framing to form air retarders.*
- *The polyethylene sheet placed over the sheathing acts as an exterior air retarder, and acts as a vapor diffusion retarder for vapor entering from the exterior during cooling periods.*
- *A vapor permeable paint finish on the gypsum board permits this wall to dry toward the interior. Vapor permeable interior surface finishes must be used.*

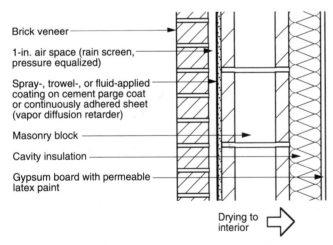

Brick veneer

1-in. air space (rain screen, pressure equalized)

Spray-, trowel-, or fluid-applied coating on cement parge coat or continuously adhered sheet (vapor diffusion retarder)

Masonry block

Cavity insulation

Gypsum board with permeable latex paint

Drying to interior

Figure 6-9: Wall 6—cooling climate.

Wall 6—Cooling Climate: *This concrete block wall assembly with brick veneer includes an interior wood frame wall filled with cavity insulation. There is a cement parge coat on the outside face of the concrete block wall. An air space between the brick and the block walls is a receptor for moisture. A coating or sheet membrane applied to the exterior face of the cement parge coat on the block wall serves as a vapor diffusion retarder. Similar to the previous wall assemblies, permeable latex paint on gypsum board permits drying to the interior.*

Key characteristics:
- *The rain screen principle controls rain penetration.*
- *The air space behind the brick veneer acts as a receptor for capillary moisture and absorbed moisture driven inward by solar radiation.*
- *To control air movement, the coating or sheet membrane placed over the cement parge coat acts as an exterior air retarder.*
- *The coating or sheet membrane placed over the cement parge coat acts as a vapor diffusion retarder for vapor entering from the exterior during cooling periods.*
- *A vapor permeable paint finish on the gypsum board permits this wall to dry toward the interior. Vapor permeable interior surface finishes must be used.*

Wall 7—Cooling Climate: This concrete block wall assembly utilizes rigid insulation placed on the exterior covered with stucco applied over galvanized lath. The impermeable rigid insulation along with a coating or membrane over the concrete blocks creates an air retarder and vapor diffusion retarder on the exterior. On the interior of the block wall, gypsum board with permeable latex paint permits drying toward the interior.

Key characteristics:
- *Stucco cladding forms a barrier to control rain penetration.*
- *Rain absorption and capillary suction through the stucco are controlled by the impermeable rigid insulation.*
- *To control air movement, the impermeable rigid insulation and the coating or sheet membrane placed over the masonry blocks form an exterior air retarder.*
- *The coating or sheet membrane placed over the masonry blocks acts as a vapor diffusion retarder for vapor entering from the exterior during cooling periods.*
- *A vapor permeable paint finish on the gypsum board permits this wall to dry toward the interior. Vapor permeable interior surface finishes must be used.*

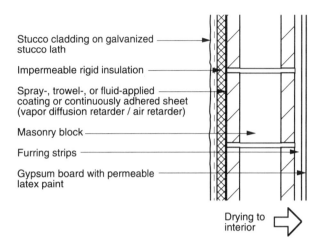

Stucco cladding on galvanized stucco lath

Impermeable rigid insulation

Spray-, trowel-, or fluid-applied coating or continuously adhered sheet (vapor diffusion retarder / air retarder)

Masonry block

Furring strips

Gypsum board with permeable latex paint

Drying to interior

Figure 6-10: Wall 7—cooling climate.

Wall 8—Cooling Climate: Similar to Wall 7, this concrete block wall assembly utilizes stucco on the exterior. In this case, the stucco is applied directly to the exterior face of the block wall. Rigid insulation is placed on the interior of the concrete block, and then covered with gypsum board. The impermeable rigid insulation serves as a vapor diffusion retarder on the interior. This permits intermittent drying toward the exterior.

Key characteristics:
- *Stucco cladding forms a barrier to control rain penetration.*
- *Rain absorption and capillary suction through the stucco are not controlled by an impermeable material. Instead, moisture may enter and then is permitted to dry toward the exterior.*
- *To control air movement, the impermeable rigid insulation on the interior is sealed at all joints and to the masonry wall.*
- *The impermeable rigid insulation on the interior acts as a vapor diffusion retarder for moisture from both the interior and the exterior.*
- *Vapor permeable or impermeable interior surface finishes may be used.*

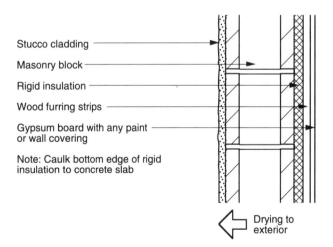

Stucco cladding

Masonry block

Rigid insulation

Wood furring strips

Gypsum board with any paint or wall covering

Note: Caulk bottom edge of rigid insulation to concrete slab

Drying to exterior

Figure 6-11: Wall 8—cooling climate.

SUMMARY: WALL ASSEMBLIES IN COOLING CLIMATES

Rain Penetration

There are two basic approaches to controlling rain penetration through walls: the rain screen, and the barrier approach. The rain screen principle requires a pressure-equalized cavity behind the cladding. In Wall 2, for example, vinyl or aluminum siding is installed over a tight sheathing. The cavities created behind vinyl or aluminum siding serve this purpose and they should not be filled with insulation material. For pressure to be equalized in these cavities, the exterior sheathing must be significantly tighter than the cladding. It should be installed vertically, with all joints falling on framing members, with the option of utilizing a sealant or adhesive at sheathing joints and edges. Alternatively, a tightly installed building paper (lapped or taped joints) may be utilized to equalize pressure.

Wall 3 illustrates another application of the rain screen concept. In this example, wood-based siding is installed on furring strips to create an air space open at the top and bottom of the wall. This space may be screened to prevent insect entry.

In Walls 4 and 6, the rain screen is created using a brick veneer over a minimum 1-inch air space. This air space must be clear of mortar droppings and should be open at the top of the brick veneer wall as well as vented at its base. Such brick veneer walls should be vented at their base by leaving open every other vertical mortar joint in the first course of brick.

These vertical open joints serve two functions, first to allow inward air movement to equalize pressure and second to provide a weep or drainage function. As in all rain screen systems, the sheathing must be significantly tighter than the cladding for pressure to be equalized in the cavity. This is accomplished by both tightening the inner surface of the cavity and making the brick veneer deliberately leaky. Venting the air space at the top and bottom make the brick veneer sufficiently leaky. In Wall 4, the sheet membrane over the sheathing provides an airtight inner surface, while the cement parge coat over the masonry wall serves the same purpose in Wall 6. Flashings at the base of brick veneer walls are also critical so that cavity moisture can be directed to the exterior through the weep holes under the influence of gravity. These base flashings must extend to the back of the rain screen cavity and be placed behind the sheathing or building paper.

Appropriate installation of flashings over window and door openings is critical in all rain screen assemblies, ideally tucking in behind exterior sheathings or building papers. In drain screen assemblies, flashings over window and door openings are also critical to direct rainwater to the exterior of the assembly.

A barrier approach, or face-sealing, controls rain penetration in several wall assemblies shown for this climate. In Wall 1, the exterior plywood siding serves as the rain penetration barrier. Since this approach requires the elimination of all exterior openings, the plywood must be sealed at all penetrations and openings—particularly around windows and exterior doors. Similarly, in Wall 1, wood-based siding may be used instead of vinyl or aluminum, but all exterior holes in the building paper and sheathing then must be eliminated to control rain penetration. Whenever the barrier approach is used, appropriate installation of flashings over window and door openings is critical.

The barrier approach (or face-sealing) is also applied in Walls 5, 7, and 8 where an exterior stucco cladding is installed. In order to eliminate all exterior openings, the stucco cladding needs to be continuous and sealed at all penetrations such as at window and door openings.

Uncontrolled cracking of the exterior stucco cladding can lead to significant rain penetration, so control joints are often utilized. The effectiveness of stucco control joints is often dependent on a bond breaker placed between the stucco cladding and any sheathing material. Where a bond breaker is not utilized, control joints need to be spaced closer together. Control joint detailing is important since they often provide entry points for rainwater. Thus, selection of appropriate sealants and/or flashings for use at these locations is critical. Effective bond breakers include sheet polyethylene, impermeable rigid insulation, as well as both absorptive and nonabsorptive building papers.

Rain Absorption/Capillary Suction

In the eight wall assemblies shown here, there are two basic concepts to control moisture from rain absorption and capillary suction: (1) impermeable materials or coatings are used to keep moisture out of the wall assembly, and (2) a space or permeable material acts as a receptor for this moisture, providing a path for it to leave the wall assembly.

In Wall 1, rain absorption by the exterior plywood siding and plywood siding capillarity effects are controlled by appropriate exterior surface treatments such as paints and stains, which seal capillary pores in the exterior plywood siding. The insulated cavity also acts as a receptor for absorbed siding moisture driven inward by incident solar radiation.

Rain absorption by vinyl or aluminum siding (as shown in Wall 2) and siding capillarity effects are not a concern as a result of the inherent material properties of the vinyl and aluminum. Where wood-based siding may be utilized (in Walls 2 and 3, for example), back-priming (painting or coating the back surfaces) is recommended to limit capillary and vapor absorption by the siding. Installing the wood siding on furring strips (as in Wall 3), or using spacers or wedges to create openings between siding pieces is also recommended. It is important to use dry materials and nail according to the manufacturers' recommended installation practices.

In Wall 3, building paper protects the exterior sheathing material from capillarity effects and rain absorption. A vapor permeable, nonabsorptive building paper should be used. In Walls 4 and 5, sheet membranes control capillarity effects and rain absorption by the exterior sheathing material. In Wall 2, where the sheathing material is impermeable rigid insulation, building paper is not required to prevent water absorption by the sheathing.

In Walls 5 and 7, rain absorption by the stucco cladding and stucco capillarity effects are controlled by the impermeable rigid insulation (a capillary break) installed behind the stucco. Wall 8 has no bond breaker—instead it relies on the formulation and material properties of the stucco cladding itself (which are important whether or not a bond breaker is present). Traditional stuccos, which have provided the best service life, have been composed of three layers, where each successive layer to the exterior has been weaker and more permeable than the layer under it. In other words, the base coat is the thickest and has the lowest water to cement ratio, and therefore is the most impermeable. The second coat is thinner and weaker (more permeable) than the base coat, and the finish coat is the thinnest, weakest and most permeable of the three.

The result of this three-layer stucco application is that the farther that water penetrates into the wall, the more resistance it meets. A further advantage is that once water has penetrated the stucco it is always easier for it to migrate toward the exterior than to penetrate any farther to the interior. Thus, any paint finishes or hydrophobic sealants installed over the outermost surface of a stucco cladding should be more permeable than the outermost surface of the stucco cladding. This is typically very difficult to achieve in practice. Consequently, stains or colorants added to stuccos during application are often more successful than paint films applied to the stucco at a later time. This concern is significantly reduced, however, in cooling climates where the principle direction of moisture migration (or drying) is inwards.

Rain absorption by the stucco cladding and stucco capillarity effects can also be controlled by exterior paint films and hydrophobic coatings. However, caution and judgement need to be exercised in the application of this control strategy. Although these coatings reduce rain absorption and capillarity, they also often retard the drying of the wall assembly to the exterior if it gets wet through other mechanisms such as interior moisture or failure at control joints.

The second concept of creating a receptor for moisture from rain absorption and capillarity is demonstrated in three cases. In Walls 4 and 6, an air space behind the brick veneer controls rain absorption and brick veneer capillarity effects. The air space also acts as a receptor for both capillary moisture and absorbed moisture driven inward by incident solar radiation. The air space behind the wood siding in Wall 3 performs a similar function. In some cases, a building paper may be installed to limit rain absorption by the sheathing material. In such cases a vapor permeable, nonabsorptive building paper should be used.

Air Movement

In this climate, the infiltration of warm, humid air transports moisture into the building from the exterior. To control this moisture, an air seal (air retarder) is installed at either the interior or exterior of the wall. In wood frame walls, this air sealing can be accomplished with adhesive, caulk, or some other sealant. To ensure effectiveness, it is desirable to create both an interior and exterior air retarder when possible.

In all of the wood frame walls (Walls 1 through 5), the gypsum board is sealed to the wall framing and acts as the interior air retarder. An exterior air retarder is also shown in these walls. This has the added advantage of equalizing the pressure behind the exterior cladding to create the rain screen. In most cases, the exterior air barrier is formed by sealing the sheathing material to the framing. For Wall 4, however, an exterior air seal at the asphalt-impregnated fiberboard is not shown. It has proven difficult in practice to seal this type of sheathing. Consequently, in wall assemblies with asphalt-impregnated fiberboard sheathing, the plane of airtightness is often located to the interior of the wall assembly. In this case, however, a sheet membrane over the sheathing serves as an exterior air retarder.

Each of the concrete masonry walls utilizes three techniques to minimize the transport of airborne moisture from the exterior: (1) an air retarder is installed at the interior or exterior of the assembly, (2) the upper course of masonry blocks is filled with mortar, and (3) the ceiling gypsum board (or vapor diffusion retarder) is sealed to this masonry block wall. In Wall 6, a cement parge coat is applied to the outside of the masonry block wall. It is covered with a spray-, trowel-, or fluid-applied vapor diffusion retarder and sealed to the ceiling gypsum board or to the ceiling sheet membrane, which should be extended over the top of the masonry wall (see roof assemblies). The upper course of blocks of all masonry perimeter walls should be filled with mortar in order to reduce the migration of hot, humid exterior air down the masonry cavities from the attic space.

In Walls 7 and 8, the exterior stucco cladding contributes to an airtight assembly. In addition, the rigid insulation on the exterior (Wall 7) or the interior (Wall 8) can be sealed to the masonry wall to further tighten the construction. For the rigid insulation to be effective as an air retarder it must be installed continuously, taped, and sealed to the ceiling vapor diffusion retarder.

Vapor Diffusion

Similar to air-transported moisture in this climate, vapor diffusion enters a wall assembly from the exterior during the cooling season. During cooling periods, vapor diffusion from the exterior can be controlled by two methods. Almost all the wall assemblies shown for this climate (Walls 1 through 7) utilize a vapor diffusion retarder on the exterior of the assembly. In Wall 1, the plywood siding is impermeable and acts as an effective vapor diffusion retarder. The plywood sheathing in Wall 3 performs a similar function. In Wall 2, an impermeable rigid insulation is installed as the exterior wall sheathing and acts as the exterior

vapor diffusion retarder. To control vapor diffusion in Walls 4, 5, 6, and 7, a sheet membrane or coating is located toward the exterior side of each assembly.

An alternative approach to controlling vapor diffusion from the exterior is shown in Wall 8. The impermeable rigid insulation serves as a vapor diffusion retarder at the interior of the wall assembly. Although installing a vapor diffusion retarder at this location does not prevent moisture from entering the wall, the vapor diffusion retarder effectively protects the interior gypsum board and any interior finishes from moisture damage.

This interior vapor diffusion retarder can get wet on the cavity side during the day as a result of exterior absorbed moisture driven inward by incident solar radiation and the air conditioned interior. This moisture then typically migrates outward in the evening when the temperature gradient reverses. *2 conditions*

Drying of Wall Assemblies

In almost all wall assemblies recommended for this climate (except Wall 8), a vapor permeable paint finish on the interior gypsum wall board promotes wall drying toward the interior. Drying will occur due to (1) an inward temperature and vapor pressure gradient present as a result of air conditioning the enclosure during the cooling season, and (2) ambient climatic conditions during the spring and fall.

Faced cavity insulations in these walls can retard drying to the interior if the facing is installed toward the interior. Faced cavity insulations can be installed where drying to the interior is not required, or alternatively, the cavity insulation can be installed with the facing material toward the outside of the cavity.

Wall 8 represents the only case in this climate where the wall assembly is designed to dry to the exterior. Installing only vapor permeable surface finishes on the stucco cladding promotes intermittent wall drying toward the exterior. Should the wall assembly become wet during service or be built wet through the use of wet masonry blocks, it can dry intermittently to the exterior during cool weather or during cool dry evenings.

In instances where the rigid insulation is installed discontinuously, or has been punctured (at electrical wall outlets), hot, humid exterior air has been shown to infiltrate down the masonry cavities and through the openings.

This causes mold and mildew on the interior gypsum wall board. This failure mechanism can be dramatically enhanced if several other conditions are present: (1) the masonry wall is saturated from rain penetration or construction moisture; (2) the enclosure is air conditioned, possibly under a slight negative air pressure due to poorly designed or installed HVAC systems; and (3) incident solar radiation drives moisture inward. To reduce the migration of air down the masonry cavities, the upper course of blocks should be filled with mortar.

Interior Finishes

In Walls 1 through 7, a vapor permeable interior surface finish is required to permit drying to the interior. Where wall assemblies with permeable interior surface treatments have been performing satisfactorily and are subsequently covered with impermeable interior surface treatments, mold and mildew problems may appear at the gypsum board/ surface treatment interface. In Wall 8, either vapor permeable or vapor impermeable interior surface finishes may be used since there is no drying to the interior and impermeable rigid insulation serves as a vapor diffusion retarder on the interior.

Foundation Construction in Cooling Climates

In this section seven foundation assemblies are shown that can be used successfully in cooling climates. There are four crawl space assemblies and three slab-on-grade foundations. All four of the crawl spaces are concrete or masonry construction—two are vented, and two are unvented. Two of the slab assemblies include concrete or masonry foundation walls, while the third illustrates a grade beam foundation. A key difference between the foundation assemblies is the type and placement of insulation. The basic characteristics of the foundation assemblies are summarized in Table 6-2.

First, each foundation assembly is illustrated and briefly described. Text adjacent to each drawing indicates how the assembly is designed to handle each of the critical moisture problems in this climate: (1) rain and groundwater, (2) capillary suction, (3) air movement, and (4) vapor diffusion. In addition, comments concerning the ability of the wall to dry and other limitations of each foundation assembly are summarized. Following the drawings is a summary discussion of key moisture control strategies for foundation assemblies in this climate.

Insulation levels in foundation assemblies, except where specifically noted to control moisture accumulation on condensing surfaces, are left to the judgement of the reader. Guidance regarding optimum insulation levels for foundation assemblies can be found in the *Builder's Foundation Handbook* (Carmody et al. 1991).

Table 6-2: Characteristics of foundation assemblies for cooling climates.

	FOUNDATION TYPE	FOUNDATION INSULATION	OTHER FEATURES	DRYING
CRAWL SPACE 1	Concrete masonry (Vented)	Rigid insulation beneath floor joists	Polyethylene vapor diffusion retarder on floor	Limited drying of floor assembly—ventilation dries crawl space
CRAWL SPACE 2	Concrete (Vented)	Faced batt insulation between floor joists	Polyethylene vapor diffusion retarder on floor	Limited drying of floor assembly—ventilation dries crawl space
CRAWL SPACE 3	Concrete masonry (Unvented)	Rigid insulation vertically on wall (Exterior)	Polyethylene vapor diffusion retarder on floor and interior wall	Limited
CRAWL SPACE 4	Concrete (Unvented)	Rigid insulation vertically on wall (Interior)	Polyethylene vapor diffusion retarder on floor and interior wall	To the exterior
SLAB 1	Concrete masonry wall supporting wood frame	Rigid insulation vertically on wall (Exterior)	Polyethylene vapor diffusion retarder beneath slab	Limited
SLAB 2	Concrete wall supporting block with brick veneer	Rigid insulation horizontally beneath slab perimeter and in wall/floor joint	Polyethylene vapor diffusion retarder beneath slab	Limited
SLAB 3	Grade beam supporting concrete block	Rigid insulation covers exterior vertical face of grade beam	Polyethylene vapor diffusion retarder beneath slab and grade beam	Limited

Crawl Space 1—Cooling Climate: This is a vented crawl space with insulation placed in the ceiling. In this case, the foundation wall is concrete masonry, and impermeable rigid insulation board is attached to the underside of the floor joists. Cavity insulation is placed between joists on the rim joist interior. Rigid insulation sheathing also covers the exterior of the rim joist. A continuous vapor diffusion retarder is placed on the floor of the crawl space. Except for the air space beneath the wood siding, the above-grade wall shown here is similar to Wall 2 in the previous section.

Key characteristics:
- *Rainwater is controlled by gutters and downspouts, as well as grade sloping away from the building.*
- *Groundwater is controlled by a drain pipe at the footing.*
- *Ventilation through open vents in the crawl space walls removes moisture from the crawl space interior.*
- *Capillary suction is controlled by a break on top of the foundation wall.*
- *Air movement is controlled by pressurizing the above-grade conditioned space, limiting or sealing all penetrations between the crawl space and the conditioned space, and sealing the sill/rim joist area. The joints of the rigid insulation placed beneath the floor joists are sealed to form an air retarder.*
- *Vapor diffusion from the soil into the crawl space is controlled by the polyethylene ground cover.*
- *Vapor diffusion from the crawl space is prevented from entering the construction assemblies and the above-grade space by the rigid insulation placed beneath the floor joists.*
- *Drying toward the interior or exterior of the floor joist assembly is limited. The crawl space itself can dry since it is vented.*

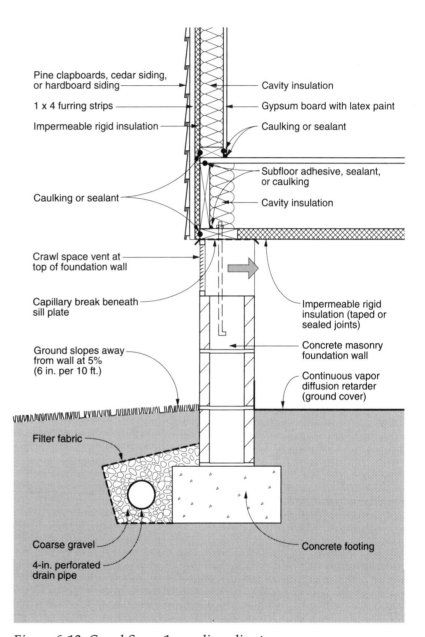

Pine clapboards, cedar siding, or hardboard siding

1 x 4 furring strips

Impermeable rigid insulation

Caulking or sealant

Crawl space vent at top of foundation wall

Capillary break beneath sill plate

Ground slopes away from wall at 5% (6 in. per 10 ft.)

Filter fabric

Coarse gravel

4-in. perforated drain pipe

Cavity insulation

Gypsum board with latex paint

Caulking or sealant

Subfloor adhesive, sealant, or caulking

Cavity insulation

Impermeable rigid insulation (taped or sealed joints)

Concrete masonry foundation wall

Continuous vapor diffusion retarder (ground cover)

Concrete footing

Figure 6-12: Crawl Space 1—cooling climate.

Crawl Space 2—Cooling Climate: This vented crawl space utilizes a concrete foundation wall. Faced batt insulation (with the faced side down) is placed between the floor joists above the crawl space. This batt insulation partially covers the rim joist on the interior. A continuous vapor diffusion retarder is placed on the floor of the crawl space. Except for the type of siding used, the above-grade wall shown here is similar to Wall 3 in the previous section.

Key characteristics:
- Rainwater is controlled by gutters and downspouts, as well as grade sloping away from the building.
- Groundwater is controlled by a drain pipe at the footing.
- Ventilation through open vents in the crawl space walls removes moisture from the crawl space interior.
- Capillary suction is controlled by a break on top of the foundation wall.
- Air movement is controlled by pressurizing the above-grade conditioned space, limiting or sealing all penetrations between the crawl space and the conditioned space, and sealing the sill/rim joist area. If sealed properly, the subfloor forms an air retarder.
- Vapor diffusion from the soil into the crawl space is controlled by the polyethylene ground cover.
- Vapor diffusion from the crawl space is prevented from entering the above-grade space by the impermeable subfloor material. A vapor diffusion retarder backing protects the batt insulation between the joists from crawl space moisture.
- Drying toward the interior or exterior of the floor joist assembly is limited. The crawl space itself can dry since it is vented.

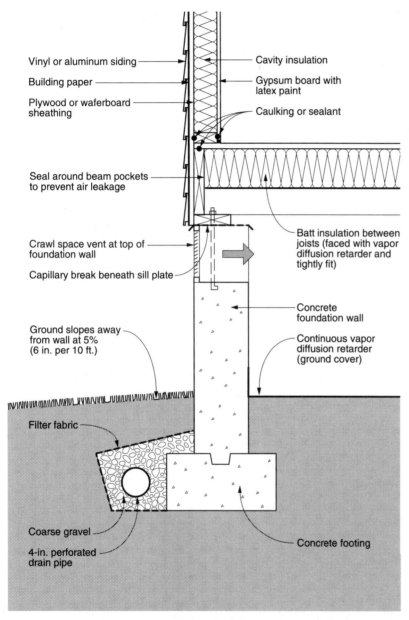

Vinyl or aluminum siding

Building paper

Plywood or waferboard sheathing

Cavity insulation

Gypsum board with latex paint

Caulking or sealant

Seal around beam pockets to prevent air leakage

Crawl space vent at top of foundation wall

Capillary break beneath sill plate

Batt insulation between joists (faced with vapor diffusion retarder and tightly fit)

Ground slopes away from wall at 5% (6 in. per 10 ft.)

Concrete foundation wall

Continuous vapor diffusion retarder (ground cover)

Filter fabric

Coarse gravel

4-in. perforated drain pipe

Concrete footing

Figure 6-13: Crawl Space 2—cooling climate.

Insulation in contact
convective heat loss

Crawl Space 3—Cooling Climate: Unlike the previous two foundation assemblies, this crawl space is unvented. The concrete masonry foundation wall is covered with rigid insulation board on the exterior. Rigid insulation covers the exterior of the rim joist, and cavity insulation (with a vapor diffusion retarder) is placed between joists on the rim joist interior. A continuous vapor diffusion retarder is placed on the floor of the crawl space and extends up the interior face and over the top of the foundation wall. The above-grade wall shown here corresponds to Wall 2 in the previous section.

Key characteristics:
- *Rainwater is controlled by gutters and downspouts, impermeable soil cap over backfill, and grade sloping away from the building.*
- *Groundwater is controlled by a drain pipe at the footing.*
- *Capillary suction is controlled by a break on top of the foundation wall.*
- *Air movement into the space is controlled by pressurizing the crawl space, limiting or sealing all penetrations, sealing the sill/ rim joist area, and placing a polyethylene sheet over the crawl space floor. All joints of the polyethylene ground cover are sealed and it is taped to the polyethylene on the wall to form an air retarder. The polyethylene extends over the top of the wall.*
- *Vapor diffusion from the soil is controlled by the polyethylene ground cover.*
- *Vapor diffusion from the interior space is prevented from entering the construction assemblies by polyethylene covering the insulation in the rim joist area.*
- *Drying toward the interior or exterior of the foundation wall is limited.*

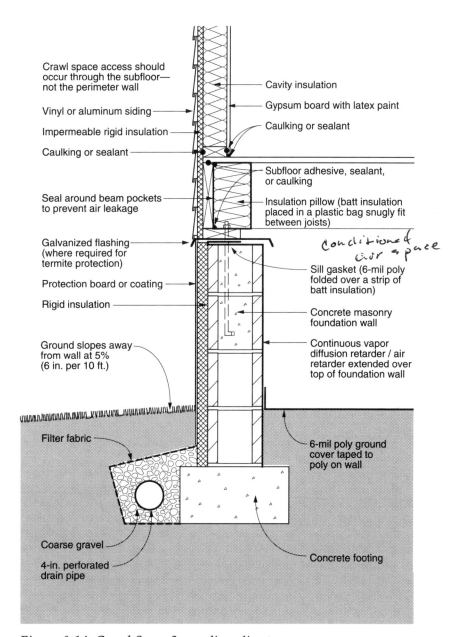

Figure 6-14: Crawl Space 3—cooling climate.

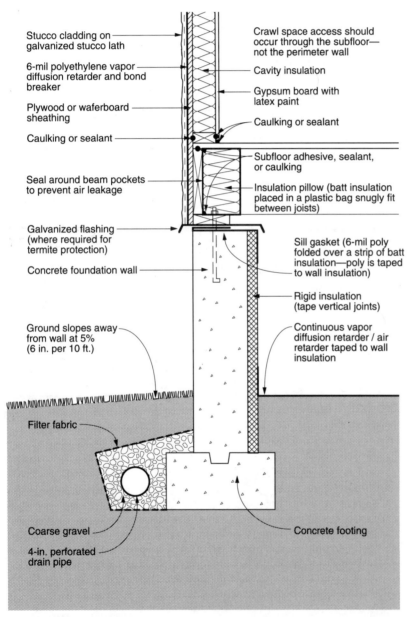

Stucco cladding on galvanized stucco lath

6-mil polyethylene vapor diffusion retarder and bond breaker

Plywood or waferboard sheathing

Caulking or sealant

Seal around beam pockets to prevent air leakage

Galvanized flashing (where required for termite protection)

Concrete foundation wall

Ground slopes away from wall at 5% (6 in. per 10 ft.)

Filter fabric

Coarse gravel

4-in. perforated drain pipe

Crawl space access should occur through the subfloor—not the perimeter wall

Cavity insulation

Gypsum board with latex paint

Caulking or sealant

Subfloor adhesive, sealant, or caulking

Insulation pillow (batt insulation placed in a plastic bag snugly fit between joists)

Sill gasket (6-mil poly folded over a strip of batt insulation—poly is taped to wall insulation)

Rigid insulation (tape vertical joints)

Continuous vapor diffusion retarder / air retarder taped to wall insulation

Concrete footing

Figure 6-15: Crawl Space 4—cooling climate.

Crawl Space 4—Cooling Climate: Similar to Crawl Space 3, this crawl space is also unvented. In this case, however, the foundation wall is concrete and the rigid insulation board is placed on the interior rather than the exterior. Cavity insulation (with a vapor diffusion retarder) is placed between joists on the rim joist interior. A continuous vapor diffusion retarder is placed on the floor of the crawl space, extends up the interior face of the insulation board, and over the top of the foundation wall. The above-grade wall shown here corresponds to Wall 5 in the previous section.

Key characteristics:
- Rainwater is controlled by gutters and downspouts, impermeable soil cap over backfill, and grade sloping away from the building.
- Groundwater is controlled by a drain pipe at the footing.
- Capillary suction is controlled by a break on top of the foundation wall.
- Air movement into the space is controlled by pressurizing the crawl space, limiting or sealing all penetrations, sealing the sill/rim joist area, and placing a polyethylene sheet over the crawl space floor. All joints of the polyethylene ground cover are sealed and it is taped to the rigid insulation on the wall to form an air retarder. The polyethylene sill gasket on top of the wall is also taped to the rigid insulation.
- Vapor diffusion from the soil is controlled by the polyethylene ground cover.
- Vapor diffusion from the interior space is prevented from entering the construction assemblies by polyethylene covering the insulation in the rim joist area.
- The exposed concrete wall can dry toward the exterior.

Slab 1—Cooling Climate: This slab-on-grade foundation assembly illustrates the use of a concrete masonry foundation wall. Rigid insulation covers the exterior vertical face of the wall. A polyethylene vapor diffusion retarder is placed beneath the floor slab and continues through the wall/slab joint and over the top of the foundation wall. The above-grade wood frame wall corresponds to Wall 2 in the previous section.

Key characteristics:
• *Rainwater is controlled by gutters and downspouts, and grade sloping away from the building.*
• *Air movement into the space from the ground is controlled by a polyethylene sheet placed beneath the floor slab.*
• *Vapor diffusion from the surrounding soil is also controlled by the polyethylene sheet placed beneath the floor slab.*
• *Avoid ductwork beneath the slab and minimize other slab penetrations to control air movement and vapor diffusion.*
• *Capillary suction is controlled by a layer of gravel under the slab, and the polyethylene sheet which extends over the top of the foundation wall.*

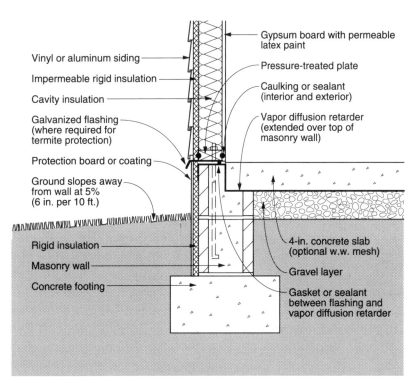

Gypsum board with permeable latex paint
Pressure-treated plate
Caulking or sealant (interior and exterior)
Vapor diffusion retarder (extended over top of masonry wall)
Vinyl or aluminum siding
Impermeable rigid insulation
Cavity insulation
Galvanized flashing (where required for termite protection)
Protection board or coating
Ground slopes away from wall at 5% (6 in. per 10 ft.)
Rigid insulation
Masonry wall
Concrete footing
4-in. concrete slab (optional w.w. mesh)
Gravel layer
Gasket or sealant between flashing and vapor diffusion retarder

Figure 6-16: Slab 1—cooling climate.

Slab 2—Cooling Climate: This slab-on-grade foundation assembly illustrates the use of a concrete foundation wall supporting a concrete block above-grade wall assembly with brick veneer. Rigid insulation is laid horizontally beneath the perimeter of the concrete floor slab and in the wall/slab joint. A polyethylene vapor diffusion retarder is placed beneath the floor slab and continues through the wall/slab joint and over the top of the foundation wall. The above-grade concrete block wall corresponds to Wall 6 in the previous section.

Key characteristics:
• *Rainwater is controlled by gutters and downspouts, and grade sloping away from the building.*
• *Air movement into the space from the ground is controlled by a polyethylene sheet placed beneath the floor slab.*
• *Vapor diffusion from the surrounding soil is also controlled by the polyethylene sheet placed beneath the floor slab.*
• *Avoid ductwork beneath the slab and minimize other slab penetrations to control air movement and vapor diffusion.*
• *Capillary suction is controlled by a layer of gravel under the slab, and the polyethylene sheet which extends over the top of the foundation wall.*

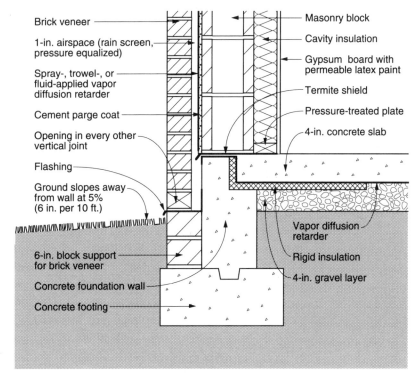

Brick veneer
1-in. airspace (rain screen, pressure equalized)
Spray-, trowel-, or fluid-applied vapor diffusion retarder
Cement parge coat
Opening in every other vertical joint
Flashing
Ground slopes away from wall at 5% (6 in. per 10 ft.)
6-in. block support for brick veneer
Concrete foundation wall
Concrete footing
Masonry block
Cavity insulation
Gypsum board with permeable latex paint
Termite shield
Pressure-treated plate
4-in. concrete slab
Vapor diffusion retarder
Rigid insulation
4-in. gravel layer

Figure 6-17: Slab 2—cooling climate.

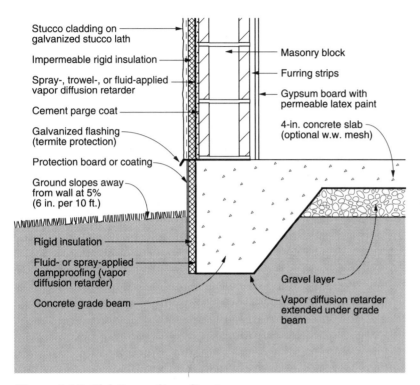

Stucco cladding on galvanized stucco lath

Impermeable rigid insulation

Spray-, trowel-, or fluid-applied vapor diffusion retarder

Cement parge coat

Galvanized flashing (termite protection)

Protection board or coating

Ground slopes away from wall at 5% (6 in. per 10 ft.)

Rigid insulation

Fluid- or spray-applied dampproofing (vapor diffusion retarder)

Concrete grade beam

Masonry block

Furring strips

Gypsum board with permeable latex paint

4-in. concrete slab (optional w.w. mesh)

Gravel layer

Vapor diffusion retarder extended under grade beam

Figure 6-18: Slab 3—cooling climate.

Slab 3—Cooling Climate: This slab-on-grade foundation assembly illustrates the use of a shallow grade beam supporting an above-grade concrete block wall. Rigid insulation covers the vertical face of the grade beam. A polyethylene vapor diffusion retarder is placed beneath the floor slab and extends under the grade beam. A dampproof coating covers the exterior face of the grade beam. The above-grade concrete block wall with stucco cladding corresponds to Wall 7 in the previous section.

Key characteristics:
- *Rainwater is controlled by gutters and downspouts, and grade sloping away from the building.*
- *Air movement into the space from the ground is controlled by a polyethylene sheet placed beneath the floor slab and grade beam.*
- *Vapor diffusion from the surrounding soil is also controlled by the polyethylene sheet placed beneath the floor slab and grade beam.*
- *Avoid ductwork beneath the slab and minimize other slab penetrations to control air movement and vapor diffusion.*
- *Capillary suction is controlled by a dampproof coating on the exterior face of the grade beam, the polyethylene sheet beneath the grade beam, and a layer of gravel under the slab.*

SUMMARY: FOUNDATION ASSEMBLIES IN COOLING CLIMATES

Rain and Groundwater

To control the entry of rainwater into the foundation, all buildings in this climate should utilize gutters and downspouts, along with careful site grading, which direct water away from the structure. A subgrade drainage system may be required to control groundwater entry into crawl spaces. Whether or not subsurface drainage is necessary depends on the groundwater level. The system shown for all four crawl spaces in this climate consists of a drain pipe located at the perimeter of the concrete footings. The drain pipe is connected to a sump, storm sewer, or to daylight. Perforations in the perimeter drain pipe should be installed with the holes down to allow groundwater to rise up into the drain pipe and be carried away. Coarse gravel should surround the perimeter drain pipe and in turn be sur-

rounded by a filter fabric. Filter fabric should be located both below and above the perimeter drain pipe, as drain pipe perforations face down and often clog from underneath. Drain tile should have at least 2 inches of gravel underneath.

Ventilation

In order to remove moisture from crawl spaces, Crawl Spaces 1 and 2 are ventilated by openings in the crawl space walls. The vent openings should be based on the 1/1500 ratio (at a minimum), where 1 square foot of vent area is provided for every 1500 square feet of subfloor area. In addition, vents should be distributed over the crawl space perimeter to prevent zones of dead stagnant air and should not be blocked by shrubs, plants, or other obstructions.

It should be noted that during hot, humid periods, ventilation air will often bring moisture into the crawl space rather than remove it. However, during cooler periods this moisture is subsequently removed by ventilation. Under severe ambient hot/humid conditions, moisture accumulation in the crawl space from ventilation air can exceed moisture removal on a seasonal basis. When this is combined with a heavily air conditioned enclosure, it is necessary to protect the floor system from this moisture. Crawl Space 1 illustrates how rigid impermeable insulation can be installed on the underside of the floor system for this purpose.

Capillary Suction

Capillary moisture may move into a concrete or masonry foundation wall or a concrete floor slab. Where the concrete foundation wall is in direct contact with the sill plate, capillary moisture can move into the sill/rim joist area. This moisture movement into the sill/rim joist assembly can be controlled by a capillary break at the top of the concrete foundation wall. In most of the crawl spaces and slabs shown here, a polyethylene vapor diffusion retarder extends over the top of the foundation wall. In addition, a metal flashing is shown which can both serve as a capillary break as well as provide termite protection where necessary. In Slab 2, capillary moisture from the concrete foundation wall can migrate into the brick veneer. This is controlled by an impermeable flashing at the base of the brick veneer and the rain screen cavity.

In all three slabs, capillary moisture movement into the floor slab is controlled by a granular capillary break under the slab. The break consists of a 4-inch- to 6-inch-thick layer of 3/4-inch gravel with fines removed. Where slab construction is utilized with a perimeter concrete grade beam (Slab 3), the slab vapor diffusion retarder is extended under the concrete grade beam to act as a capillary break at this location. Furthermore, dampproofing is installed on the exterior of the perimeter of the grade beam also to act as a capillary break. This dampproofing, if it is fluid or spray applied, must be chemically compatible with any rigid insulation installed over it.

Air Movement

In vented crawl space assemblies (1 and 2), it is important to eliminate air flow between the crawl space and the conditioned space. The crawl space needs to be uncoupled from the conditioned space so that conditions within the crawl space influence the building enclosure to a minimum. This is best accomplished by not installing any forced air ductwork, furnaces, or

air conditioners in the crawl space. Experience has shown that it is difficult to seal such units or ductwork sufficiently to prevent leakage. In addition, penetrations for plumbing, wiring, bathtubs, etc., must be sealed, making the crawl space subfloor assembly airtight.

Where vented crawl spaces experience extremely humid conditions during heavy air conditioning, the installation of impermeable rigid insulation on the underside of the floor joists protects the entire floor system from moisture brought into the crawl space by ventilation air (Crawl Space 1). This rigid insulation acts as both a vapor diffusion retarder and air retarder system. Consequently, it needs to be installed airtight and should completely enclose any supporting beam structures.

Airborne moisture infiltrating from the crawl space into the conditioned space is minimized by pressurizing the conditioned space relative to the exterior, and by limiting air leakage openings (tight construction). Unvented crawl spaces (3 and 4) can be pressurized as well by a supply air register in the crawl space, with no corresponding return air register. With this approach the air distribution fan should run continuously. In enclosures without forced air systems, a separate fan for this purpose can be installed, taking air from the other conditioned spaces. The tighter the construction, the less air that has to be introduced to pressurize the crawl space.

Unvented crawl spaces in this climate zone should not be pressurized at the expense of depressurizing the rest of the conditioned space during cooling periods. In other words, the entire building should be pressurized relative to the exterior, including the crawl space during cooling periods. Thus, air taken from the building to pressurize the crawl space needs to be replaced by outside air introduced in a controlled manner, typically to the air conditioning duct system. Pressurization will only occur when the forced air distribution fan is operating (when mechanical cooling or heating is occurring). This should be effective under most conditions.

Air movement through the foundation wall assembly in an unvented crawl space is typically controlled by a polyethylene sheet (Crawl Space 3) or impermeable rigid insulation (Crawl Space 4) on the interior of the wall. A polyethylene ground cover acts as an air retarder on the floor. To form a continuous air retarder system in these crawl spaces, the floor membrane is taped to the polyethylene sheet or rigid insulation on the foundation wall.

In all cases, the elements which form the sill/rim joist/floor assembly in crawl spaces should be sealed to control air movement in this area. In Crawl Spaces 3 and 4, a tight-fitting, insulation "pillow" is installed at the interior of the rim joist assembly between floor joists. The insulation pillow is formed by placing batt insulation in a plastic bag and snugly fitting the bag containing the insulation between the floor joists. Gaps at this location around the insulation pillow need to be minimized to control potential convective moisture transfer.

In all crawl spaces, exterior wall sheathing is extended down over the rim joist assembly to further reduce air leakage at this location. This exterior wall sheathing can be utilized as the principal air seal at this location if it is sealed directly to the exterior of the sill plate. This makes it possible to eliminate seals at the top and bottom of the rim joist.

In slab assemblies it is important to eliminate the moisture flow from the exterior into the enclosure by air flow and vapor diffusion. To do this, a polyethylene sheet is installed under the slab and construction is tight. Ductwork should be avoided in slabs. Groundwater, soil gas, and moisture from surrounding soil can seep into ducts and become significant sources of moisture to the conditioned space.

Vapor Diffusion

Vapor diffusion through the slab-on-grade assemblies from the surrounding soil can be controlled with a polyethylene vapor diffusion retarder under the slab. In crawl spaces, moisture movement by vapor diffusion from the soil is controlled by a continuous polyethylene vapor diffusion retarder used as a ground cover.

Vented crawl spaces must be designed to prevent moisture movement by diffusion from the crawl space into the conditioned space. In Crawl Space 1, this moisture movement is retarded by the impermeability of the rigid insulation installed on the underside of the floor joists.

The impermeability of the subfloor sheathing in Crawl Space 2 retards moisture movement by diffusion from the crawl space into the conditioned space. However, the impermeability characteristics of the subfloor sheathing can create moisture accumulation on the bottom surface of the subfloor. Vapor diffusion retarder faced insulation (faced-side down) is recommended to prevent moisture accumula-tion in the insulation. In less humid climates, unfaced insulation can be installed to promote drying should such moisture accumulate at the underside of the subfloor. Local experience can determine the correct choice.

In unvented crawl spaces, moisture from the crawl space must be prevented from diffusing into the insulation on the foundation wall interior. This can be accomplished by installing insulation with a vapor diffusion retarder backing, a polyethylene vapor diffu-sion retarder, or impermeable rigid insulation on the interior (Crawl Spaces 3 and 4).

There are a number of approaches to controlling moisture diffusing from the interior crawl space into the perimeter rim joist assem-bly during the heating season. In Crawl Spaces 3 and 4, vapor diffusion is controlled by the plastic bag facing on the batt insulation. Other approaches utilize impermeable rigid insula-tion for this purpose (Crawl Space 1), or rely on the vapor diffusion retarder backing on the batt insulation (Crawl Space 2).

Drying of Foundation Assemblies

The purpose of the open ventilation in Crawl Spaces 1 and 2 is essentially to dry the spaces by dilution with outside air. The floor assembly over the vented crawl space forms the boundary between the warmer, moist crawl space air and the cooler air conditioned air in the above-grade space. Similar to other construction assemblies, this floor can be designed to dry toward the crawl space or be enclosed by vapor retarding materials to limit drying. In the two vented crawl spaces (1 and 2) shown here, drying is limited.

In unvented crawl spaces, the wall assem-bly may be designed to dry to the exterior, the interior, or be enclosed on both sides so that drying is limited. Because the concrete founda-tion wall is exposed in Crawl Space 4, it can dry to the exterior. In Crawl Space 3, however, drying toward either the interior or exterior is limited by impermeable rigid insulation on the exterior of the wall and an interior vapor diffusion retarder.

Interior Finishes

Concrete floor slabs contain significant quantities of moisture when initially placed. Covering this surface with an impermeable surface finish or floor covering may lead to deterioration of these surfaces if the construc-tion moisture is not allowed to dry. Initial drying of the construction moisture contained in concrete may also lead to elevated interior moisture levels during the first few months of occupancy.

Installing carpets on cold, damp, concrete floor slabs can cause serious allergenic reactions in sensitive individuals and other health-related consequences. It is not recommended that carpets be installed on concrete slabs unless the carpets can be kept dry and warm; that is, carpet relative humidities should be kept below 70 percent (Godish 1989). In practice this is typically not possible unless floor slab assemblies are insulated and basement areas are conditioned.

Details

In several cases (Crawl Space 3, Slabs 1 and 3), rigid insulation is installed on the exterior of the perimeter concrete foundation wall to reduce cooling loads and is protected above grade on its exterior from mechanical damage. Appropriate below-grade flashings or other protection may be necessary, since this rigid insulation can act as a conduit for insects to enter the enclosure.

As a result of fire code flame spread requirements, rigid insulation installed on the interior of unvented, conditioned crawl space foundation walls (Crawl Space 4) may need to be protected on its interior surface by gypsum wall board or some other treatment. Local authorities may need to be consulted.

In some assemblies it may not be practical or possible to extend the vapor diffusion retarder over the top of the perimeter masonry wall foundation assembly. In such cases, the cavities in the masonry blocks should be filled with mortar to create an air seal with a strip of sheet polyethylene installed under the wall framing to act as a capillary break.

The granular drainage pad located under concrete slab floors can be integrated into a subslab ventilation system to control radon migration by adding a vent pipe connected to the surface and an exhaust fan. In all construction, it is good practice to install a passive vent pipe connecting this subslab gravel layer to the exterior through the roof. An exhaust fan can be added later if necessary.

In unvented conditioned crawl spaces it is convenient to install ductwork, plumbing, and other mechanical components, since concerns about the effects of duct leakage and freezing pipes are minimized.

Roof Construction in Cooling Climates

In this section four roof assemblies are shown that can be used successfully in cooling climates. All four assemblies utilize wood roof trusses and vented attics. They illustrate ways of connecting to different wall assemblies, as well as different approaches to vapor diffusion retarders and insulation. The basic characteristics of the roof assemblies are summarized in Table 6-3.

First, each roof assembly is illustrated and briefly described. Text adjacent to each drawing indicates how the assembly is designed to handle each of the critical moisture problems in this climate: (1) ventilation, (2) air movement, and (3) vapor diffusion. In addition, comments related to special concerns are summarized for each assembly. Following the drawings is a summary discussion of key moisture control strategies for roof assemblies in this climate.

Insulation levels in roof assemblies, except where specifically noted to control moisture accumulation on condensing surfaces, are left to the judgement of the reader.

Table 6-3: Characteristics of roof assemblies for cooling climates.

	ROOF TYPE	VENTILATION	CEILING INSULATION	OTHER FEATURES	DRYING
ROOF 1	Wood truss with flat ceiling	Vented attic	Cavity insulation	No vapor diffusion retarder	To the exterior and the interior
ROOF 2	Wood truss with flat ceiling	Vented attic	Cavity insulation with rigid insulation beneath trusses	Rigid insulation acts as vapor diffusion retarder (Interior)	To the exterior
ROOF 3	Wood truss with flat ceiling	Vented attic	Cavity insulation	No vapor diffusion retarder	To the exterior and the interior
ROOF 4	Wood truss with flat ceiling	Vented attic	Cavity insulation	No vapor diffusion retarder	To the exterior and the interior

limited drying potential w/ poly on inside & out

Roof 1—Cooling Climate: This conventional wood truss roof system is insulated above the flat ceiling and the attic space is ventilated. There is no polyethylene vapor diffusion retarder in this assembly. The gypsum board ceiling with permeable latex paint permits drying of the roof assembly toward the interior.

Key characteristics:
- The attic is ventilated promoting drying to the exterior.
- There is no vapor diffusion retarder—vapor is permitted to move through this assembly in both directions and thus drying occurs both toward the interior and the exterior. Interior surface finishes must be vapor permeable.
- Air movement is controlled by limiting and sealing all penetrations between the conditioned space and the attic. The gypsum board ceiling is sealed to the wood frame construction in order to act as an air retarder.
- The conditioned space should be pressurized relative to the attic during cooling periods.
- The wind baffle prevents wind-washing of the perimeter insulation.

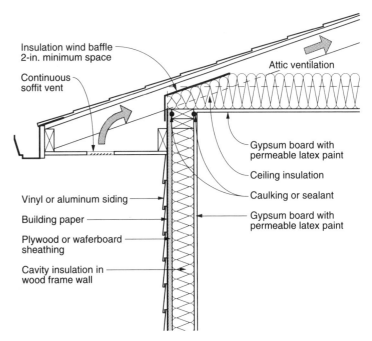

Figure 6-19: Roof 1—cooling climate.

Roof 2—Cooling Climate: Similar to Roof 1, this conventional wood truss roof system is insulated above the flat ceiling and the attic space is ventilated. In this case, however, rigid insulation is attached to the underside of the trusses with cavity insulation above. The impermeable rigid insulation serves as a vapor diffusion retarder on the interior side of the cavity insulation in the ceiling.

Key characteristics:
- The attic is ventilated promoting drying to the exterior.
- The impermeable rigid insulation placed beneath the gypsum board acts as an air retarder to control air movement, and acts as a vapor diffusion retarder.
- Air movement is further controlled by limiting and sealing all penetrations between the conditioned space and the attic.
- The conditioned space should be pressurized relative to the attic during cooling periods.
- The wind baffle prevents wind-washing of the perimeter insulation.
- Any type of interior finish material may be used on the ceiling of this assembly.

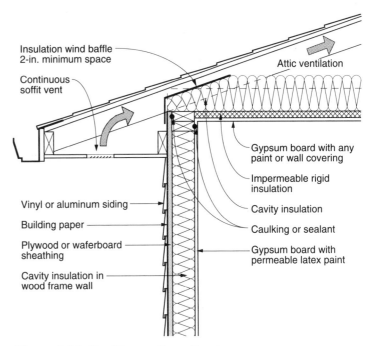

Figure 6-20: Roof 2—cooling climate.

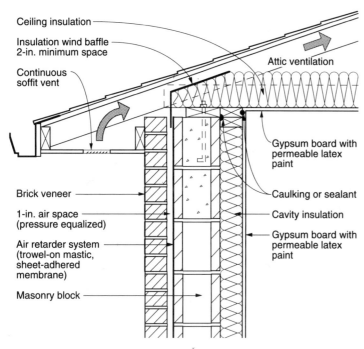

Ceiling insulation

Insulation wind baffle
2-in. minimum space

Continuous
soffit vent

Attic ventilation

Gypsum board with
permeable latex
paint

Brick veneer

1-in. air space
(pressure equalized)

Caulking or sealant

Cavity insulation

Air retarder system
(trowel-on mastic,
sheet-adhered
membrane)

Gypsum board with
permeable latex
paint

Masonry block

Figure 6-21: Roof 3—cooling climate.

Roof 3—Cooling Climate: This conventional wood truss roof system, insulated above the flat ceiling, is similar to Roof 1. The attic space is ventilated, and there is no vapor diffusion retarder. This case illustrates how this roof assembly is attached to a masonry wall assembly with brick veneer. The wall shown here corresponds to Wall 6 in a previous section of this chapter.

Key characteristics:

• The attic is ventilated promoting drying to the exterior.
• There is no vapor diffusion retarder—vapor is permitted to move through this assembly in both directions and thus drying occurs both toward the interior and the exterior. Interior surface finishes must be vapor permeable.
• Air movement is controlled by limiting and sealing all penetrations between the conditioned space and the attic. The gypsum board ceiling is sealed to the wood frame construction in order to act as an air retarder.
• The conditioned space should be pressurized relative to the attic during cooling periods.
• The wind baffle prevents wind-washing of the perimeter insulation.

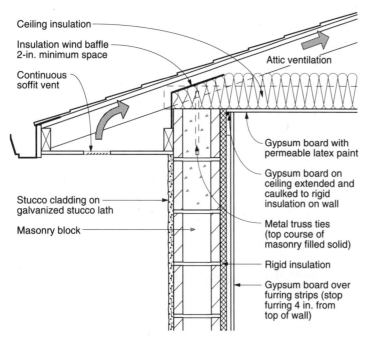

Ceiling insulation

Insulation wind baffle
2-in. minimum space

Continuous
soffit vent

Attic ventilation

Gypsum board with
permeable latex paint

Gypsum board on
ceiling extended and
caulked to rigid
insulation on wall

Stucco cladding on
galvanized stucco lath

Metal truss ties
(top course of
masonry filled solid)

Masonry block

Rigid insulation

Gypsum board over
furring strips (stop
furring 4 in. from
top of wall)

Figure 6-22: Roof 4—cooling climate.

Roof 4—Cooling Climate: Similar to the previous roof assemblies, this conventional wood truss roof system is insulated above the flat ceiling. The attic space is ventilated, and there is no vapor diffusion retarder. This case illustrates how this roof assembly is attached to a masonry wall assembly with stucco. The wall shown here corresponds to Wall 8 in a previous section of this chapter.

Key characteristics:

• The attic is ventilated promoting drying to the exterior.
• There is no vapor diffusion retarder—vapor is permitted to move through this assembly in both directions and thus drying occurs both toward the interior and the exterior. Interior surface finishes must be vapor permeable.
• Air movement is controlled by limiting and sealing all penetrations between the conditioned space and the attic. The gypsum board ceiling is sealed to the wood frame construction in order to act as an air retarder. It is also sealed to the rigid insulation which forms the air retarder in the wall assembly.
• The conditioned space should be pressurized relative to the attic during cooling periods.
• The wind baffle prevents wind-washing of the perimeter insulation.

SUMMARY: ROOF ASSEMBLIES IN COOLING CLIMATES

Ventilation

All four roof assemblies shown for this climate are ventilated in order to reduce cooling loads by reducing solar heat gain. For open attic spaces such as these, a minimum of 1 square foot of vent area should be provided for every 300 square feet of insulated ceiling area. In addition, vents should be distributed between the soffit and ridge to prevent zones of dead or stagnant air and should not be blocked by roof assembly insulation or other obstructions.

It should be noted that during hot, humid periods, ventilation air into the attic will bring moisture into the roof assembly rather than remove it. However, during cooler periods this moisture is subsequently removed by ventilation. Under severe conditions, such as those experienced by some gulf coast regions, moisture accumulation in the attic from ventilation air will exceed moisture removal by the same ventilation air on a daily, monthly, or seasonal basis. When this is combined with a heavily air conditioned enclosure, using rigid insulation on the interior to reduce condensation should be considered (see Roof 2).

Air Movement

In this climate moisture infiltrates from the attic or roof assembly cavities into the enclosure. This can be reduced by pressurizing the enclosure relative to the attic space. In addition, penetrations through the ceiling where air leakage can occur should be limited as much as possible. In Roofs 1, 3, and 4, the interior gypsum board ceiling is sealed to the roof framing and wall assembly to form a continuous air retarder. The rigid insulation beneath the trusses forms the air retarder in Roof 2. To ensure airtightness in this assembly (Roof 2), the ceiling gypsum board is extended to the edge of the rigid insulation on the wall and sealed. The furring strips on the masonry perimeter wall installed for the attachment of the interior gypsum wall board are cut short. The ceiling gypsum board is installed first, and the perimeter wall gypsum wall board subsequently conceals the bead of sealant.

In vented roof assemblies, it is important to eliminate air flow between conditioned spaces and the attic. The attic needs to be uncoupled from the conditioned space so that conditions within the building enclosure influence the attic

to a minimum. This is best accomplished by not installing any forced air ductwork, furnaces, or air conditioners in attics. Experience has shown that it is difficult to seal such units or ductwork sufficiently to prevent leakage. In addition, penetrations for plumbing, wiring, dropped ceilings, and kitchen cabinet bulkheads should be sealed.

It should be noted that in concrete masonry walls, hot, humid air can infiltrate from the attic/soffit area down through the masonry cavities and into other cavities within the wall assembly. This may cause mold and mildew on the interior gypsum wall board. To reduce this air migration down the masonry cavities, the upper course of blocks should be filled with mortar as shown in Roofs 3 and 4.

Vapor Diffusion

During the cooling periods in this climate, moisture diffuses from the attic into the enclosure. In Roof 2, moisture movement by diffusion in either direction is controlled by a continuous ceiling vapor diffusion retarder—impermeable rigid insulation installed beneath the ceiling framing. This impermeable rigid insulation, which is sealed to the perimeter wall vapor diffusion retarder, also protects the ceiling gypsum board from moisture accumulation which can lead to mold and mildew growth or water staining. It therefore allows impermeable wall/ceiling coverings, paints, and textured treatments to be installed.

In severe hot, humid conditions, the installation of the rigid, impermeable insulation at the underside of the ceiling framing has two effects. First, it raises the temperature of the upper surface of the impermeable rigid insulation above the dew point temperature, thus making condensation unlikely, even if the enclosure is heavily air conditioned. Second, because it is a vapor diffusion retarder, it prevents vapor from reaching the upper surface of the ceiling gypsum board, which is normally the first condensing surface.

In Roofs 1, 3, and 4 there is no ceiling vapor diffusion retarder. Consequently, moisture movement by vapor diffusion through the roof assembly in either direction is not controlled. Omitting the ceiling vapor diffusion retarder in this climate provides acceptable assembly performance as long as permeable paint is used on the interior. For this assembly to perform as intended, impermeable interior ceiling surface finishes should be avoided.

Drying of Roof Assemblies

All four roofs permit drying to the exterior since they are vented. Roofs 1, 3, and 4 also permit drying to the interior since there is no vapor diffusion retarder.

Interior Finishes

Either vapor permeable or vapor impermeable interior surface finishes may be used in conjunction with Roof 2 since there is no drying to the interior and rigid insulation serves as a vapor diffusion retarder. In the remaining roofs (1, 3, and 4), a vapor permeable interior surface finish is required to permit drying to the interior. Where roof assemblies with permeable interior surface treatments have been performing satisfactorily and are subsequently covered with impermeable interior surface treatments, mold and mildew problems may appear at the gypsum board/surface treatment interface.

Comments

In severe hot, humid conditions, the temperature of the ceiling gypsum board may be below the dew point temperature of the ambient air if the enclosure is heavily air conditioned. This may result in condensation, mold, and mildew growth on the ceiling gypsum board. Under such extreme conditions, using rigid insulation on the interior to reduce condensation should be considered (see Roof 2).

In all roof assemblies shown for this climate, a wind baffle is installed at the perimeter of the attic where the insulated ceiling intersects the exterior wall. This prevents thermal short-circuiting of the insulation by wind (wind-washing). Wind-washing by hot, humid air can induce significant amounts of moisture deposition on perimeter wall top plate and ceiling gypsum board surfaces cooled by air conditioning.

Where exterior ventilation air enters soffit assemblies, it experiences a pressure drop, as the soffit assembly acts as an expansion space. This is due to the combination of a narrow soffit vent opening up to a relatively large volume soffit assembly and then being squeezed into a narrow space between the underside of the roof sheathing and the wind baffle. This pressure drop induces the ventilation air to deposit airborne rain droplets in the soffit assembly rather than transport them farther into the roof assembly. Accordingly, it may be desirable to back-prime wood soffit materials. In Roof 3, the pressure-equalized air space behind the brick veneer wall is open to the soffit assembly to promote moisture removal from the air space by ventilation.

CHAPTER 7

Case Studies of Moisture Problems and Solutions

This chapter consists of six case studies of moisture problems and solutions. The principles and practices described in the first six chapters of this handbook are applied to problems in actual buildings. Building types include single-family housing, row house complexes, and a school. Five of the buildings are located in predominantly heating climates, while one is in a cooling climate.

Each case study presents the problem, a description of the building, the investigation procedures and results, a statement of the pertinent principles of moisture movement, the underlying causes, and a list of recommended solutions. The basic characteristics of the six case studies are shown in Table 7-1.

Table 7-1: Summary of moisture problem case studies.

	LOCATION	CLIMATE	BUILDING	PROBLEM
CASE STUDY 1	Fort Lauderdale, Florida	Cooling	Single family house	Mold behind vinyl wall covering
CASE STUDY 2	Trenton, New Jersey	Heating	School	Odor and indoor environment complaints
CASE STUDY 3	Cleveland, Ohio	Heating	Single family house	Roof condensation
CASE STUDY 4	Sturbridge, Massachusetts	Heating	Single family house	Roof decay
CASE STUDY 5	Chicago, Illinois	Heating	Row houses	Peeling paint on wood trim
CASE STUDY 6	Hoffman Estates, Illinois	Heating	Row houses	Hardboard panel problems

Case Study 1:
Mold Behind Wall Coverings

Building: Single family detached house.

Location: Fort Lauderdale, Florida.

Climate Zone: Predominantly cooling.

Problem

A homeowner became rather agitated when pink spots began to bleed through the dining room vinyl wall covering on an interior wall. When a corner of the wall covering was pulled away from the wall, both the wall gypsum board and the back of the wall covering were covered with mold.

Description

The home was a single story building over a concrete slab foundation. The exterior walls were concrete masonry block. The exterior cladding was painted stucco. Interior framing was a combination of metal studs and metal furring. Roof construction was wood sheathing installed over wood trusses. Interior cladding was predominantly painted gypsum board. In one room, the dining room, an interior partition wall was highlighted with a vinyl wall covering.

The space conditioning system was a forced air high efficiency heat pump. The air handler was located in the attic, as were all the supply and return ductwork. Exhaust fans were installed in bathrooms, and a recirculating range hood was installed in the kitchen. A fireplace was in the living room with tight-fitting glass doors and exterior combustion air ducted directly to the firebox.

Investigation

The principle means of investigation were visual examinations, temperature and interior relative humidity measurements, and smoke pencil and air pressure differential testing using a digital micromanometer.

Discussions with the homeowner revealed that in addition to the complaint regarding the discoloration of the wall covering it was also very difficult to establish draft in the fireplace.

The home was visited during hot, humid weather during August. Exterior temperature was measured at approximately 85 degrees Fahrenheit, and exterior relative humidity was measured at 80 percent. Interior temperatures were taken at several locations in various rooms in the house in conjunction with relative humidity measurements. Interior temperatures ranged from 73 degrees to 76 degrees Fahrenheit. Interior relative humidities were measured and ranged from a low measurement of 60 percent to a high of 65 percent.

In the dining room, where the pink spots were most prevalent, it was noticed that a supply air diffuser was blowing air conditioned air against the wall. Although pink spots were distributed across the entire wall, they were most concentrated where this cold air came in contact with the surface of the wall covering.

A smoke pencil indicated that air was being drawn out of the interior partition wall at an electrical outlet location when the air handler switched on, suggesting that the dining room operated at a negative air pressure with respect to the exterior. Smoke pencil readings also indicated that air was being drawn out of exterior walls at electrical outlets.

This was confirmed when the digital micromanometer was used to measure interior dining room, exterior wall cavity, and dining room demising wall interstitial (wall cavity) air pressures relative to the exterior. When the air handler was operating the dining room would drop to 4 Pascal negative relative to the exterior and the demising wall interstitial air pressure would drop to 3 Pascal negative relative to the exterior. Exterior wall cavities would also drop to 3 Pascal negative relative to the exterior. When the air handler was not operating, the dining room and the dining room exterior and interior wall cavities would come to a neutral air pressure with respect to the exterior.

The air handler was found to depressurize both the interior conditioned space and the interstitial cavities of interior demising walls as well as exterior walls.

Air pressure measurements were repeated under various conditions of interior doors being opened and closed. Greatest depressurization of both the dining room area and wall cavities occurred when the bedroom doors were closed. The single greatest drop in pressure occurred with the opening and closing of the master bedroom door. However, even with all interior doors open, the building still operated under a negative air pressure relative to the exterior when the air handler was on.

The wall covering in the dining room was completely pulled off the wall. Mold growth was rampant on both the back side of the wall covering and the newly exposed face of the gypsum board.

Mold growth was not visible on any other wall. However, a noticeable musty odor was detected coming out of several exterior wall electrical outlets when the investigator was close to the electrical outlets when the air handler was operating.

Principle

Mold and other biologicals will grow on a surface if mold spores are present, if nutrients are available, temperatures are between 50 degrees and 100 degrees, and the relative humidity adjacent to the surface is above 70 percent. Of these conditions, relative humidity near surfaces is the most practical to control. Spores are almost always present in outdoor and indoor air. Almost all of the commonly used construction materials can support mold growth, therefore control of available nutrients is not feasible, and human comfort constraints limit the use of temperature control.

Where relative humidities near surfaces are maintained below 70 percent, mold and other biological growth can be controlled. Since relative humidities are dependent on both temperature and the amount of moisture in the air, mold control is dependent on controlling both the temperature and the amount of moisture near surfaces.

The colder the surface, the higher the relative humidity at that surface. When the relative humidity at a surface reaches 100 percent, condensation occurs. The temperature at which the air/vapor mix reaches 100 percent relative humidity is called the *dew point* temperature. The dew point temperature of 85 degree Fahrenheit air at a relative humidity of 80 percent is 78 degrees Fahrenheit. In other words, if exterior air at a temperature of 85 degrees and 80 percent relative humidity contacts a cooled surface at a temperature below 78 degrees Fahrenheit, condensation will occur.

The operation of air handlers depressurizes the building enclosure and thereby draws hot, humid exterior air into the building from the attic and through exterior walls into interior demising walls. Once inside the demising walls, this hot, humid exterior air is cooled below its dew point temperature, leading to condensation. The installation of impermeable wall coverings (vinyl wall paper) prevents the moisture from drying into the interior conditioned space where it would be removed by the air conditioning system. Mold growth appears

at the interface of the wall covering and the gypsum board since moisture accumulates at this location. The secretions from the biological growth react with the plastics and adhesives in the wall covering, leading to pink spots bleeding through the wall covering.

Causes

In cooling climates, interior mold growth occurs because interior surfaces are typically cold (due to air conditioning) and subsequently contacted by air containing high moisture levels. When exterior hot air is cooled, its relative humidity increases. If the exterior hot air is also humid, cooling this air will typically raise its relative humidity above the point at which mold growth can occur (70 percent).

Where air conditioned cold air is supplied to a room, and this air is blown against interior surfaces due to poor diffuser design, location, or performance, it can create cold spots on the interior gypsum board surfaces. Although this cold air is typically dehumidified before it is supplied to the conditioned space, it can create a mold problem on room surfaces as a result of high levels of airborne moisture already existing within the room. This typically raises relative humidity near the surface and creates a corresponding mold problem.

If exterior humid air comes in contact with the interstitial cavity side of cooled interior gypsum board, mold and other biological growth can occur. Cooling this exterior hot, humid air will typically raise its relative humidity above 70 percent. When nutrients are present mold and other growth occurs. This is exacerbated with the use of impermeable wall coverings such as vinyl wallpaper, which can trap moisture between the interior finish and the gypsum board. When these interior finishes are coupled with cold spots and exterior moisture, mold and other growth can occur.

Air handlers create air pressure differences in buildings in two ways, by duct leakage and by unbalanced air flows. If ductwork is installed in such a manner that it leaks, the air leakage can change air pressure. For example, if leaky supply ductwork is installed in an attic, air is extracted out of the building, depressurizing the conditioned space (Figure 7-1). If leaky return ductwork is installed in an attic, air is supplied to the building from the attic, pressurizing the conditioned space (Figure 7-2). In buildings where both supply and return leaks occur, one mechanism typically dominates. In this example, supply leaks appear to be

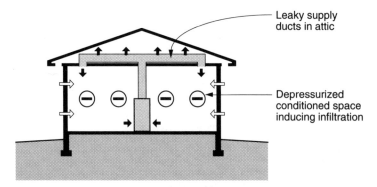

Figure 7-1: Leaky supply ducts in attic spaces cause depressurization of the conditioned space.

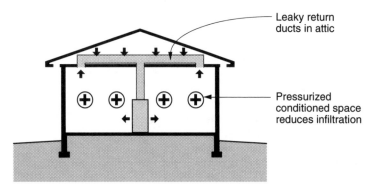

Figure 7-2: Leaky return ducts in attic spaces cause pressurization of the conditioned space.

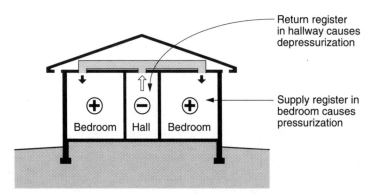

Figure 7-3: When bedroom doors are closed, bedrooms with supply registers become pressurized, while corridors with return registers become depressurized.

dominating, as the building enclosure operates at negative air pressure with respect to the exterior when the air handler is operating.

When the amounts of supply and return air are the same, no air pressure differential occurs. If more air is supplied to a room than is returned, the room will become pressurized. In the house investigated, only a single return register for the entire enclosure was installed. This return register was located in the main hallway of the house. However, each bedroom had a supply register. When bedroom doors are closed, it is difficult for air to pass from the bedrooms to the main body of the house where the return is located. Hence, the bedrooms become pressurized and the main body of the house becomes depressurized (Figure 7-3). The effect is greatest with a master bedroom suite, since it gets significantly more supply air than the other bedrooms.

Undercutting of doors has traditionally been the accepted method of returning air from bedrooms to centrally located return registers. However, in newer, recently constructed buildings, the circulating airflows in high efficiency space conditioning equipment can be substantial and undercuts are no longer able to function as an adequate return path.

In the house investigated, the effects of bedroom door closure and supply leakage were both present. Supply duct leakage was evidenced by the building enclosure's shift to negative air pressure when all interior doors were open and the air handler was operating. The effect of bedroom door closure was demonstrated by the changing air pressures when interior doors were opened and closed.

The measured negative pressures created by door closure, duct leakage, and operation of the air handler were also responsible for the difficulties reported in establishing fireplace draft. When the house enclosure was depressurized by the air handler, the fireplace chimney was unable to establish draft or maintain it.

The nature of the construction of the interior and exterior walls allowed air to travel along exterior walls in the air spaces created by metal furring and into the interstitial spaces of interior demising walls when negative air pressures occurred from the operation of the air handler (Figure 7-4).

Moisture also moves from the warm side of building assemblies to the cold side by vapor diffusion. In cooling climates vapor diffusion helps dry walls to the interior. Vapor retarders should be installed on the exterior of walls to help prevent them from getting wet from the exterior, and should be avoided on the interior

Chapter 7—Case Studies of Moisture Problems and Solutions

of walls to allow drying toward the interior. An interior wall covering in a cooling climate acts as a vapor retarder and prevents drying to the interior and is thus in effect a vapor retarder located on the wrong side of the wall. Wall coverings in cooling climates should be avoided.

Solutions

One of the most practical solutions in controlling mold and other biological growth in cooling climates is the prevention of hot, humid exterior air, or other forms of moisture transport, from contacting the interior cold (air conditioned) gypsum board surfaces. This can be accomplished by preventing the conditioned space from operating at a negative air pressure to the exterior. In addition, the installation of interior vapor diffusion retarders should be avoided.

Interior moisture levels within the conditioned space should also be limited to 60 percent relative humidity at 78 degrees Fahrenheit by dehumidification through proper sizing and operation of the air conditioning system. The following steps are recommended:

1. Seal all supply and return leaks in ductwork using mastic.

2. Provide transfer grills to facilitate air flow from bedrooms to main return (Figure 7-5). Pressure balance house (check air pressure relationships, avoid negative air pressure).

3. Remove all wall coverings and damaged gypsum board. Replace with new gypsum board. Do not install any wall coverings. Paint interior surfaces with latex paint only.

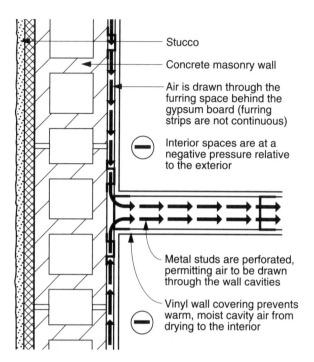

Figure 7-4: Moist outside air is drawn into the cavity within the interior partition wall that is covered with vinyl. This is caused by negative pressures within wall cavities and conditioned spaces created by an air handling system with leaky return ducts.

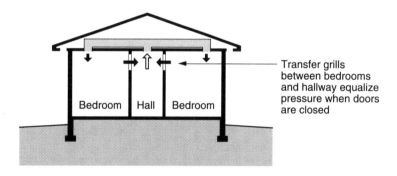

Figure 7-5: Transfer grills placed between bedrooms and corridors permit supply air to flow toward return ducts without creating pressure differences.

Case Study 2: Odor and Indoor Environment Complaints

Building: Single story masonry school.

Location: Trenton, New Jersey.

Climate Zone: Predominantly heating.

Problem

Teachers and students in a school were concerned about intermittent odors detected in several classrooms. A teacher in one of the classrooms in the affected area was complaining of headaches, fatigue, and flue-like symptoms. Discussions with the teacher indicated that similar complaints were also common among the students.

Description

The single story masonry school building is constructed over a crawl space foundation. The facility consists of several wings constructed at different periods over the past 60 years. Each wing has a separate foundation system, although communication between the various crawl space foundations was present. The crawl space in the affected area of the facility consists of a perimeter cast concrete foundation wall on concrete strip footings. The floor deck consists of precast concrete planks supported on precast concrete beams resting on the perimeter foundation walls and interior cast concrete bearing walls. The crawl space floor surfaces were uncovered earth. Crawl space ventilation consisted of numerous 8- by 12-inch vents, distributed in an approximate ratio of 1 to 1500 between vent area and floor area.

Investigation

The principle means of investigation were a visual examination, tests for air pressure differences, intrusive disassembly, fan depressurization testing, review of drawings, and discussions with school district staff.

Upon entering the classroom which the affected teacher and students occupied, visible deterioration of plaster and baseboard surfaces were observed along interior and exterior walls. The deterioration was most intense at the baseboard level, and decreased in intensity with height. Paint had peeled from the plaster at many locations. Water markings were observed on the plaster surfaces. The plaster was soft to the touch and disintegrated when probed. When the plastic covering over the wood baseboard trim was removed, noticeable musty odors were encountered. The wood was soft and punky, and significant decay was observed. When the wood baseboard was pulled away from the wall, the intensity of the musty odors increased significantly.

Visual observations revealed a joint between the concrete floor slab and the masonry perimeter wall. Other joints were observed in the concrete floor slab at the interior concrete foundation walls. Smoke

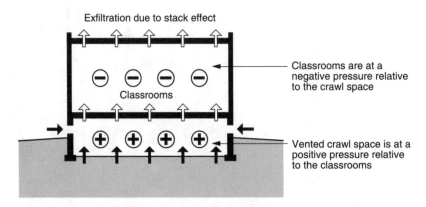

Figure 7-6: The crawl space in this school operates at a positive pressure with respect to the classrooms.

pencil testing indicated substantial air flow between the crawl space and the classroom through these exposed joints. Readings taken with a digital micromanometer indicated that the crawl space was operating at a 4 Pascal positive air pressure with respect to the classroom (Figure 7-6).

Removal of deteriorated plaster verified wall construction. Specifically, interior plaster was installed over wood furring strips, creating an air spaces (or channels) between the plaster and the masonry wall. Removal of ceiling tiles indicated that the plaster finish extended just above the dropped ceiling level and that the air spaces (or channels) between the plaster and the masonry wall were open at the top and connected to the air space above the dropped ceiling. This wall geometry created chimneys which extended from the crawl space to the air space above the dropped ceiling.

Photographs and discussion with school district staff indicated that no ground cover was present in the crawl space. According to staff, the top surface of the soil appeared dry. In addition, many of the steam lines in the crawl space were reported to be uninsulated due to ongoing asbestos mitigation work. Crawl space temperatures in excess of 100 degrees Fahrenheit were typical according to staff.

Fan depressurization testing of the crawl space under the affected classroom area was conducted. Crawl space vents were sealed. The access opening connecting the affected crawl space and the adjacent crawl space was also sealed. The depressurization equipment was installed in the main external access opening to the crawl space under the affected classroom area. Air pressure differentials between the affected classroom and the crawl space were monitored. Testing determined that extracting approximately 650 cfm of air from the crawl space by exhaust fan would depressurize the crawl space 4 Pascals with respect to the classroom area. This was shown to reverse air flow between the crawl space and the classroom—when the exhaust fan was operating, air moved from the classroom into the crawl space instead of the opposite flow which occurs under normal conditions.

Principle

Complaints from the teacher and students were due to musty odors resulting from the deterioration of wood trim and other building materials. These odors and deterioration were due to excessive moisture migrating from the crawl space under the classrooms into the interstitial spaces of interior and exterior walls as a result of the air pressure relationship between these spaces and the crawl space.

Causes

For an odor or indoor air quality problem to occur, four factors are necessary: (1) a receptor (people), (2) a pollutant, (3) a pathway, and (4) a driving force (air pressure difference or concentration gradient).

It is obvious that people must be present in order for a problem to be detected, or for a problem to exist. Although removing people is an effective short-term solution, this strategy is not appropriate for the long-term.

A pollutant is also necessary. In this case the primary pollutant is moisture, and this moisture pollutant leads to the creation of the secondary pollutants, mold and other biological agents. Eliminating the pollutant (source control) is a very effective approach to controlling indoor air quality problems.

A pathway connecting the pollutant and receptor is also necessary. If pollutants and receptors are isolated from each other by perfect barriers, then problems can also be eliminated. In this case the pathway connecting the moisture pollutant and the receptor are the openings connecting the crawl space and the channels between the plaster surfaces and the masonry walls.

Finally, a driving force is required to push the pollutant through the pathway to the people (receptor). In this case the driving force is an air pressure difference between the crawl space and the classrooms. This air pressure difference is created by a combination of the stack effect (heated air rising due to buoyancy effects) and the exhaust operation of the classroom ventilators.

Moisture (the primary pollutant) in the soil in the crawl space is evaporated due to the elevated temperatures in the crawl space. Warm, moisture-saturated air migrates through openings in the floor slab into the air space created by the plaster and wood furring (the pathway). The air is pulled into the air space by its temperature and the building's stack effect combined with the operation of the classroom ventilators (the driving force). The moisture-saturated air cools once it is in the furring space, leading to condensation and saturation of the building materials at this location (Figure 7-7). This saturation degrades building materials and creates odors and other biological agents (the secondary pollutants).

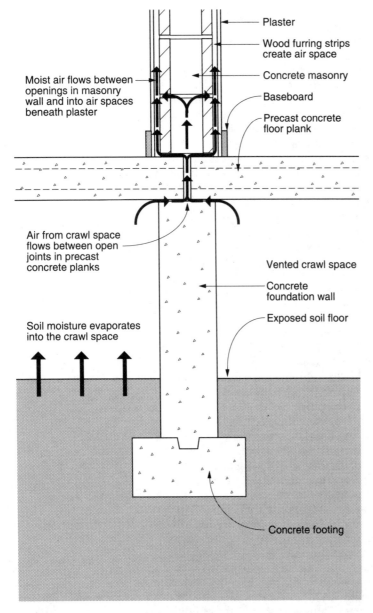

Plaster

Wood furring strips
create air space

Moist air flows between
openings in masonry
wall and into air spaces
beneath plaster

Concrete masonry

Baseboard

Precast concrete
floor plank

Air from crawl space
flows between open
joints in precast
concrete planks

Vented crawl space

Concrete
foundation wall

Exposed soil floor

Soil moisture evaporates
into the crawl space

Concrete footing

Figure 7-7: This wall section illustrates moisture movement from the crawl space floor into the wall cavities adjacent to the conditioned spaces above grade.

These secondary pollutants enter the classroom and come in contact with the teacher and students.

The dry crawl space soil surface observed is hypothesized to be dry due to the rapid rate of moisture evaporation (vapor diffusion) from the upper surface of the crawl space soil into the crawl space enclosure due to the heat from the uninsulated steam lines. Where it was possible to probe several inches beneath the crawl space floor surface, the ground material became damp to the touch, supporting this hypothesis.

Ventilation as a moisture removal mechanism was evident by the presence of crawl space vents and because the ambient (exterior) vapor pressure was lower than the crawl space enclosure vapor pressures. However, the rate of moisture removal by ventilation was judged to be extremely low due to the small number of vents, their location, and small cross-sectional areas.

Moisture levels within enclosures are determined by a combination of moisture source strength (rate of moisture generation or entry) and air change or ventilation (rate of moisture removal). If the rate of moisture generation or entry is higher than the rate of moisture removal, then high enclosure moisture levels can occur. The crawl space airborne moisture levels were high. It is our belief that these crawl space airborne moisture levels were high because the rate of moisture generation or entry in the crawl spaces is high compared with the rate of moisture removal by ventilation. This is consistent with our observations of low moisture removal (poor ventilation) and the lack of an effective ground cover.

Solutions

All four factors active in air quality and odor problems (receptor, pollutant, pathway and pressure) should be controlled in this case.

In the short term, the receptor should be removed. Students and teachers should not be allowed access to the affected classroom until the rehabilitation measures have been implemented.

Source control for the primary and secondary pollutants should be undertaken. The secondary pollutants should be removed by stripping the damaged portions of the interior plaster surfaces and removing all wood baseboard trim. The carpets should be lifted and examined for deterioration and cleaned with a HEPA vacuum.

The primary pollutant, airborne moisture

from the crawl space, should be controlled at the source. Crawl space enclosure moisture levels can be reduced only two ways, by limiting moisture source strength (moisture entry) or by dilution (moisture removal by ventilation or dehumidification). A desired result would be where the rate of moisture entry is lower than the rate of moisture removal. To achieve this desired result, it is practical to control the source strength (moisture entry by the bulk, capillary, air transport, and vapor diffusion transport mechanisms) and not rely on dilution (moisture removal by ventilation).

A temporary polyethylene ground cover should be installed immediately. A permanent stabilized, reinforced polyethylene ground cover should be installed after mechanical system work is completed in the crawl space. As part of this work, all steam lines should be insulated.

The pathway for the primary pollutant (moisture) should be sealed by installation of foam sealants after damaged and deteriorated materials have been removed at baseboard locations.

Finally, the driving force for pollutant transfer—specifically, the air pressure relationship between the crawl space and the classrooms—should be altered by the installation and operation of an exhaust fan (Figure 7-8). This exhaust fan should run continuously. To control air pressure, the crawl space vent openings should be closed. Specific recommendations follow:

1. Do not use the affected classroom until the principal remedial measures have been implemented.

2. Install a continuously operating 1000 cfm exhaust fan in the crawl space below the affected portion of the school. Seal all the crawl space exhaust vents and any major penetrations in the demising crawl space wall between the crawl space under the affected classroom and the crawl space under the remainder of the facility.

3. Check with a digital micromanometer the depressurization of the crawl space with the exhaust fan operating. Depressurization should be in the 4 to 8 Pascal range with respect to the classrooms.

4. Install a temporary 6-mil crawl space ground cover in both the affected and unaffected portions of the facility.

5. Remove the damaged baseboard, plaster, lath, and furring strips in the affected classroom and other classrooms with visible damage. Seal exposed floor slab penetrations with Class 1 expanding foam sealant. Replace with gypsum board and replacement trim.

6. Lift edges of carpet and visibly examine for mold and/or decay as well as odor. If mold, decay, or odor is detected, replace and discard the carpet. Otherwise, use a HEPA vacuum to clean carpet prior to re-use of classrooms.

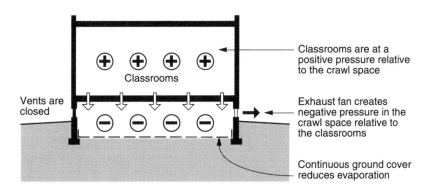

Figure 7-8: Closing the crawl space vents and using an exhaust fan depressurizes the crawl space relative to the classrooms.

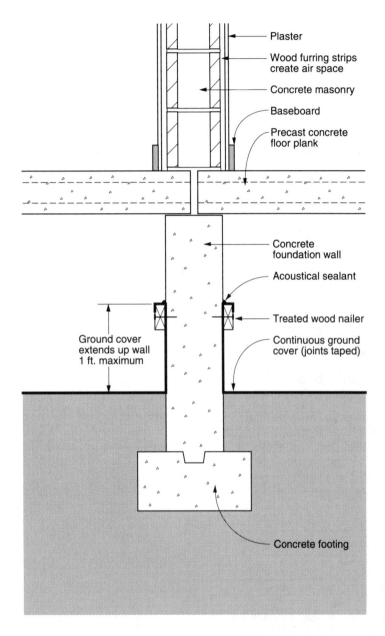

Plaster

Wood furring strips create air space

Concrete masonry

Baseboard

Precast concrete floor plank

Concrete foundation wall

Acoustical sealant

Ground cover extends up wall 1 ft. maximum

Treated wood nailer

Continuous ground cover (joints taped)

Concrete footing

Figure 7-9: This wall section illustrates proper installation of the polyethylene ground cover.

The above actions should be taken immediately. Upon completion of these actions, the classroom can resume normal occupancy. The following additional measures should also be implemented as soon as practical.

7. Install a permanent ground cover using cross-laminated stabilized polyethylene, taped seams, and a positive attachment to perimeter and demising walls. This ground cover should be installed after asbestos abatement has been concluded. This work should be implemented as shown in Figure 7-9:

   • Place ground cover on crawl space floor surfaces, insuring adequate material can extend up perimeter and interior concrete foundation walls approximately 12 inches. Ground cover material should be stabilized, reinforced sheet polyethylene.

   • Tape seams in ground cover with tape.

   • Fasten treated wood nailer (2 x 3 or 2 x 4) to concrete at 24-inch centers with either explosive actuated fasteners or drilled/plug mechanical fasteners.

   • Caulk/seal ground cover to perimeter concrete foundation wall with acoustical sealant.

8. Insulate all heating pipes.

9. Open the crawl space vents and switch off the crawl space exhaust fan.

Case Study 3: Roof Condensation

Building: Single family detached house.

Location: Cleveland, Ohio.

Climate Zone: Predominantly heating.

Problem

A homeowner registered complaints of water dripping from ceiling light and electrical fixtures, staining of interior gypsum board finishes, water stains on exterior walls at facia vent locations, and mold on the underside of the roof sheathing.

Description

The recently constructed residence was approximately 5,000 square feet in living area. The house contained five full baths and a water closet, each with an exterior ducted exhaust fan. An additional exhaust fan was located in the kitchen. Three induced-draft, gas-fired, forced air heating systems serviced the conditioned space. Two induced-draft, gas-fired water heaters supplied domestic hot water. A fireplace with integral glass doors and dedicated exterior combustion air was located in the living room. A laundry room was located on the main floor and contained an exterior ducted clothes dryer.

The roof of the residence was constructed of 2 x 10 wood rafters installed at 16 inches on center. A plywood deck was attached to the upper surface of the rafters and was covered with a shingled roof (Figure 7-10). Faced batt insulation was installed between the rafters. The underside of the roof rafters was covered with 1/2-inch gypsum board prime-coated and sprayed with a textured finish. Roof ventilation was attempted through intermittent screened holes drilled through facia boards coupled with continuous ridge ventilation at peaks. Where cathedral roofs terminated at the midheight of walls, no upper elevation vent openings were provided.

The exterior walls were constructed from 2 x 6 wood studs at 16 inches on center sheathed with 1/2-inch fir plywood. The wall cavities were filled with faced batt insulation and covered on the interior with 1/2-inch painted gypsum board. Expanded polystyrene (1 inch thick) was mechanically fastened to the plywood sheathing with screws and plastic washers and covered with stucco and a silicone-based acrylic sealer.

The foundation system was masonry block

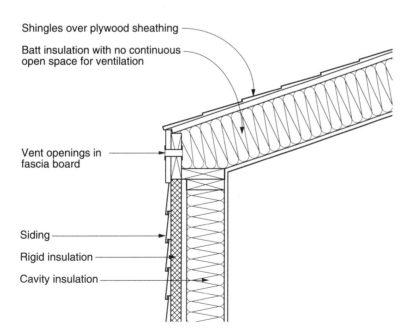

Figure 7-10: Existing roof construction. Vents openings are provided in the fascia board but there is no continuous air space in the roof cavities above the insulation. Moist interior air reaches the underside of the plywood sheathing and condenses.

on strip footings. A subgrade drainage system was located to the inside of the footings under a cast concrete basement floor slab. The basement was finished to the interior with an insulated wood frame wall which terminated at interior ceiling level. A dropped ceiling covered the basement ceilings.

Investigation

A visual examination, field testing, review of drawings and specifications, and discussions with the owner were the principle means of investigation.

Visual observations indicated numerous water stains at interior sloped ceiling surfaces and at facia locations on the exterior stucco.

Photographs taken by the owner during previous investigations revealed mold and mildew on the underside of the plywood roof sheathing. The photographs also indicated the lack of a continuous air space between the underside of the roof sheathing and the top of the roof cavity insulation. Cardboard and EPS baffles appeared to be intermittently installed.

Air pressure differential measurements taken with a digital micromanometer indicated that the upper portion of the building was operating under a positive air pressure with respect to the exterior and with respect to the interstitial cathedral ceiling spaces.

Testing with portable fan pressurization equipment indicated that approximately 1,000 cubic feet per minute of air exhausted from the interior was required to alter the positive pressure condition at the upper portions of the building. While under this exhaust flow, all combustion appliances were examined to determine positive exhaust flow of flue gases. Some leakage was observed at the furnace/flue connection of two of the three furnaces. No leakage/spillage was observed at the remaining combustion appliances.

Readings taken with a digital hygrometer indicated relative humidities in the range of 50 percent at 70 degrees Fahrenheit. Exterior temperatures were approximately 35 degrees Fahrenheit.

An infrared scan conducted while the building was depressurized 20 Pascals (at grade) by calibrated fan pressurization/depressurization equipment revealed various air leakage pathways between the interstitial spaces of the cathedral ceiling assemblies and the conditioned space. The air leakage pathways appeared typical of construction of this type (custom built) and age (recent construction).

In the basement area, smoke pencil investigation indicated substantial air flow out of the perimeter masonry blocks into the dropped ceiling area above the basement conditioned space. A mirror placed in the flow path fogged instantly.

Principle

The water stains on interior sloped ceiling surfaces occur as a result of condensation of air-transported moisture (from the interior) on the underside of the roof sheathing dripping through ceiling openings and staining visible surfaces. The condensation was due to the availability of a cool surface coupled with interior moisture. The mold on the underside of the roof plywood occurred as a result of a high surface relative humidity at the underside of the roof plywood due to the condensed air-transported moisture accumulating at this surface. The moisture source was soil gas infiltration through the perimeter masonry block foundation walls.

Causes

Moisture can only enter a building three ways: (1) from the exterior by rain leakage, groundwater, capillarity, air transport, and vapor diffusion; (2) be generated within the enclosure by occupants or occupant activity; or (3) be built into the structure initially.

Readings indicated that a major (or several major) interior moisture sources were present. Internally generated moisture from occupant loading and activities was not sufficient to account for the high moisture levels in an enclosure of such a large volume. Examination of the foundation system indicated high moisture levels in the masonry cores and substantial air flow up the cores and into the basement conditioned space above the dropped ceiling. This moisture source can easily account for the measured interior moisture levels. External entry of moisture by rain leakage, capillarity, air transport, and vapor diffusion can be discounted by virtue of the nature of the wall structure. Construction moisture can be discounted due to the pattern of damage.

Where interior moisture contacts cool or cold surfaces, surface condensation can occur. The condensing surface in the building was the underside of the roof decking. Moisture can only access the underside of the roof decking from the interior by two transport mechanisms: air transport and/or vapor diffusion.

Vapor diffusion can be discounted due to the presence of a vapor diffusion retarder on the batt insulation (the facing on the insulation). Since vapor diffusion is a function of surface area, and since the facing of the batt insulation covers more than 95 percent of the surface area of the underside of the roof assembly, the vapor diffusion retarder can be judged to be 95 percent effective in controlling moisture transport by vapor diffusion.

The process of elimination leaves air transport as the mechanism responsible for moisture access to the underside of the roof decking. Air transport requires three components: (1) moisture in the air, (2) an opening, and (3) a driving force (air pressure difference).

All three were present in this building. The presence of interior moisture has already been noted. The openings consisted of the typical gaps or openings found in wood frame construction such as between the gypsum board and wall framing, electrical outlet openings, recessed ceiling fixtures, split level framing details, and dropped ceilings. These gaps connected the interior conditioned space to the interstitial space bounded by the underside of the roof plywood and the ceiling gypsum board. The driving force (air pressure difference) was provided by the natural buoyancy of heated air (stack effect). Warm moisture-laden air was seen to be passing through the openings into the ceiling interstitial space, thereby accessing the underside of the roof plywood. Although the facing on the batt insulation can be effective in controlling moisture transport by vapor diffusion, it has been shown historically to be completely ineffective in controlling air-transported moisture.

Since moisture can access the underside of the roof plywood by air transport, when the temperature of the underside of the roof plywood drops below the dew point temperature of the air/vapor mixture of the conditioned space, condensation occurs at this location. Since no thermal insulation exists above the roof plywood, the temperature of the roof plywood can be approximated by the local ambient temperature. An examination of weather records and an estimate of interior moisture levels suggest that dew point temperatures occur regularly at the underside of the roof plywood during the heating season in Cleveland, Ohio.

When sufficient condensation occurs at the underside of the roof plywood, the condensed water drips through the gaps in the batt insulation under the influence of gravity, passes through openings in the ceiling gypsum board, and stains the surfaces below. This same process also accounts for the stain marks at facia openings on the exterior stucco.

Since condensed water can access the underside of the roof plywood, this leads to high relative humidities at the underside of the roof plywood. This then leads to mold at this location and decay and structural failure over time.

Had a continuous air space above the cathedral ceiling insulation been present to allow for roof ventilation to remove interior moisture from the interstitial spaces, the observed problems would not have occurred.

Solutions

Condensation at a surface can be controlled by reducing the amount of moisture accessing the surface, elevating the temperature of the surface, or by removing the moisture once it gets to the surface.

Since air-transported moisture is believed to be the method of moisture transport to the surface, and since air transport of moisture requires moisture in the air, openings, and an air pressure difference, the following strategies for control are possible:

1. Remove moisture by ventilation.

2. Control moisture in the interior air.

3. Control openings.

4. Control air pressure differences.

5. Control condensing surface temperatures.

Removal of moisture from roof and attic spaces by ventilation has been the traditional method of control of surface condensation at the underside of roof sheathing. For ventilation to be effective, a clear path for ventilation air flow needs to be present (an air space above the insulation and below the roof sheathing). The following requirements would be necessary to provide for sufficient removal of moisture by ventilation to eliminate the observed problems: (1) a continuous air space between the underside of the roof plywood and the top of the cavity insulation, and (2) continuous ridge and soffit ventilation.

Although these recommendations can be successful in controlling the observed ceiling moisture problems, they will not be able to be implemented unless the existing roof plywood is removed, or unless the existing ceiling gypsum board is removed. Removing the existing roof sheathing and/or removing the interior ceiling gypsum board would be a major undertaking (cost and coordination) and seriously inconvenience the owner. Accordingly, this approach is not recommended.

Interior moisture levels can be reduced only two ways, by limiting source strength (interior generation or entry) or by dilution (air change or ventilation). It is not practical to control the source strength from occupant activities. However, it is practical and necessary to control the moisture entering the building through the foundation masonry blocks. It is cost-effective to increase the air change rate or ventilation (dilution) to reduce moisture levels to limit (not eliminate) condensation. Consequently, control of the moisture in the foundation system and control of the moisture in the interior air is recommended in this building as a partial rehabilitation measure. This can be accomplished by the installation of two controlled ventilation systems. The first system extracts air from the foundation masonry block cavities and from under the perimeter of the basement floor slab. The second system extracts air based on the interior relative humidity within the conditioned space and contains a provision for make-up air from the exterior.

Control of openings can take several forms. It can be accomplished by the installation of an air retarder system on the underside of the batt insulation. This requires a great deal of workmanship to be implemented effectively. It would necessitate the removal of either the existing ceiling gypsum board or the existing roof plywood and the installation of a continuous air retarder system. This is not practical given the constraints. However, an interstitial air retarder system installed in the cavities bounded by the existing roof plywood, the ceiling gypsum board, and the 2 x 10 rafters is recommended. Dense pack cellulose installed in these cavities can provide sufficient flow resistance to limit condensation from air leakage. This would need to be coupled with the air sealing of accessible openings, specifically the recessed lights and electrical outlet boxes.

Control of air pressure differences is not practical due to the large volume of air within the conditioned space required to be continuously extracted (1,000 cfm plus). However, temporary extraction to provide immediate

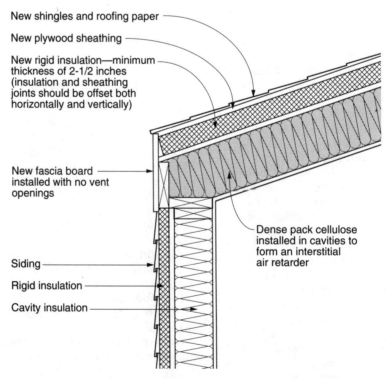

New shingles and roofing paper

New plywood sheathing

New rigid insulation—minimum thickness of 2-1/2 inches (insulation and sheathing joints should be offset both horizontally and vertically)

New fascia board installed with no vent openings

Siding

Rigid insulation

Cavity insulation

Dense pack cellulose installed in cavities to form an interstitial air retarder

Figure 7-11: Proposed retrofit roof construction. Vents openings in the fascia board are closed, dense pack cellulose is installed in the roof cavities to form an air retarder, and rigid insulation raises the temperature of the first condensing surface above the dew point.

relief via depressurization is recommended until permanent remediation measures are implemented. Depressurization of the building will raise the neutral pressure plane above the ceiling line and induce infiltration through all building envelope openings.

Control of the temperature of the condensing surface is possible by removing the existing roof shingles and installing rigid insulation, plywood, and shingles above the existing roof plywood.

Of the possible approaches, the installation of the controlled ventilation systems, the installation of an interstitial air retarder system (dense pack cellulose), and the elevation of the temperature of the condensing surface by installing insulation over the existing roof plywood are all recommended (Figure 7-11). Specific recommendations follow:

1. Install a temporary exhaust fan extracting 1,000 cfm to eliminate the exfiltration of warm, interior, moisture-laden air into the interstitial spaces of the cathedral ceiling assemblies by raising the neutral pressure plane above the ceiling. During the operation of this temporary exhaust fan the fireplace should not be used and plumbing traps should be continuously refilled with water. Seal the connections between the chimney flue pipes and the furnaces with high temperature sealant to prevent leakage. Do not use existing humidifiers. Once the other remedial measures have been implemented (specifically the installation of the interstitial air retarder), remove this exhaust fan. The exhaust fan is only a temporary measure utilized to prevent additional deterioration of the existing roof assembly. Care should be taken not to achieve excessive depressurization with this temporary exhaust fan. Excessive depressurization could lead to serious air quality problems should continuous backdrafting of combustion appliances and sewer gas migration occur.

2. Blow dense pack cellulose (an interstitial air retarder system) into the cathedral ceiling spaces over the existing batt insulation. Recessed lights should be IC-rated fixtures and retrofitted with airtight liners. Should the recessed lights not be IC rated, they will have to be replaced due to the risk of fire. Seal existing ceiling fixtures. Then use infra-red scans to verify installation of the dense pack cellulose interstitial air retarder system. As part of this work the existing facia boards will need to be removed and replaced without vents (depth of facia boards will have to be increased to accommodate rigid insulation installed over existing roof plywood). Remove but do not replace the existing ridge vents. During the installation of the interstitial air retarder system (dense pack cellulose), care will have to be taken to prevent blowing the drywall off the rafters. Although this cannot be guaranteed, the risk can be reduced with an experienced installer. Considering the other alternatives, the risk is worth accepting.

3. Install rigid insulation, plywood and shingles over the existing roof plywood. This insulation and membrane system should have a minimum of 2.5 inches of rigid roof insulation. Screw this new plywood sheathing into the existing rafters through the new rigid insulation. Offset rigid insulation and new plywood joints from existing plywood sheathing joints. Install bituthane at eaves, around skylights, and at valleys. Install roofing paper throughout. Raise skylights to accommodate the thickness of the rigid insulation and new plywood. Rigid metal flashing should be regletted into intersecting walls as necessary.

4. Install a primary controlled ventilation system to limit the interior relative humidities to below 35 percent at 72 degrees Fahrenheit. An exhaust only ventilation system is recommended. The capacity of this system should be approximately 150 cfm. Install a make-up air duct that supplies exterior air directly to the return side of the principle air handler.

5. Install a second controlled ventilation system to extract air from the perimeter masonry foundation block cavities and from the perimeter subgrade drainage system located to the interior of the foundation footings. This system will provide radon abatement as well reverse the flow of the soil gas moisture source for the building. A standard radon abatement depressurization fan system should be used.

Case Study 4:
Roof Decay

Building: Two-story detached house.

Location: Sturbridge, Massachusetts.

Climate Zone: Predominantly heating.

Problem

During the late spring after the first winter of occupancy, a homeowner indicated concern over the staining of ceiling gypsum board at a cathedral ceiling over the main living room. In the winter during sunny weather, water would occasionally drip from several ceiling light fixtures.

Description

The recently constructed home was of wood frame construction, two stories in height, with a concrete basement foundation. Space conditioning was through the use of a high efficiency induced-draft gas furnace.

The roof was constructed of wood rafters with cavities insulated with backed fibrous insulation. A plywood deck attached to the upper surface of the rafters was covered with a shingled roof. The underside of the roof rafters were covered with 1/2-inch painted gypsum board. Roof ventilation was provided through a combination of continuous soffit and ridge ventilation according to the 1 to 300 ratio.

Investigation

The principle means of investigation were visual examinations, temperature measurements, relative humidity measurements, along with smoke pencil testing.

The home was visited in early April. The exterior temperature was approximately 45 degrees Fahrenheit. Visual observations revealed numerous openings and penetrations in the interior gypsum board finish at electrical service openings. The cathedral ceiling area contained approximately 20 recessed lights.

Smoke pencil investigation indicated air from the house exfiltrating into ceiling cavities around recessed electrical light fixtures. Interior temperatures were measured to be approximately 72 degrees Fahrenheit, and interior relative humidities ranged from 40 to 45 percent.

Access openings cut through the gypsum board at several locations revealed mold and water stains on the underside of the plywood roof sheathing. The observations indicated that a continuous air space between the underside of the roof sheathing and the top of the roof cavity insulation was present.

Principle

Water stains on interior sloped ceiling surfaces typically occur in heating climates as a result of the condensation from air transported moisture (from the interior) on the underside of the roof sheathing dripping through ceiling openings. The condensation is due to the availability of a cool surface coupled with interior moisture (Figure 7-12).

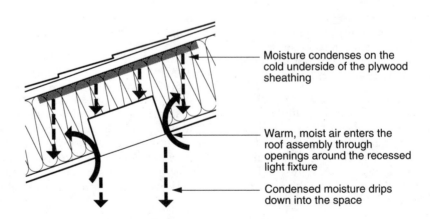

Moisture condenses on the cold underside of the plywood sheathing

Warm, moist air enters the roof assembly through openings around the recessed light fixture

Condensed moisture drips down into the space

Figure 7-12: Warm, moist air from the interior enters the roof cavities and condenses when it reaches the cold underside of the plywood sheathing.

Mold and decay on the underside of roof plywood occurs as a result of a high surface relative humidity at the underside of the roof plywood due to the accumulation of condensed air-transported moisture.

Roof ventilation will control moisture accumulation in a roof assembly if the rate of removal of moisture exceeds the rate of moisture entry.

Causes

Where interior moisture contacts cool or cold surfaces, surface condensation can occur. The condensing surface in this case is believed to be the underside of the roof decking. Moisture can only access the underside of the roof decking from the interior by two transport mechanisms: air transport and/or vapor diffusion.

Vapor diffusion can be discounted due to the presence of a vapor diffusion retarder (the interior paint surface and the backing on the batt insulation). Since vapor diffusion is a function of surface area, and since the interior paint surface and the batt insulation facing cover more than 95 percent of the surface area of the underside of the roof assembly, the vapor diffusion retarder can be judged to be 95 percent effective in controlling moisture transport by vapor diffusion.

The process of elimination leaves air transport as the mechanism responsible for moisture access to the underside of the roof decking. Air transport requires three components: (1) moisture in the air, (2) an opening, and (3) a driving force (air pressure difference).

All three are present in this building. The presence of interior moisture was confirmed from measurements and the likely source is respiration from typical occupancy. The openings consist of the electrical outlet openings at the recessed ceiling fixtures. These gaps connect the interior conditioned space to the interstitial space bounded by the underside of the roof plywood and the ceiling gypsum board. The driving force (air pressure difference) is provided by the natural buoyancy of heated air (stack effect). The smoke pencil testing demonstrated that warm moisture-laden air passed through the openings at the electrical fixtures into the ceiling interstitial space, thereby accessing the underside of the roof plywood.

Since moisture can access the underside of the roof plywood by air transport, when the temperature of the underside of the roof plywood drops below the dew point tempera-

ture of the air/vapor mixture of the conditioned space, condensation will occur at this location. Since no thermal insulation exists above the roof plywood, the temperature of the roof plywood can be approximated by the local ambient temperature. An examination of weather records and an estimate of interior moisture levels suggest that dew point temperatures occur regularly at the underside of the roof plywood during the heating season in Sturbridge, Massachusetts.

When sufficient condensation occurs at the underside of the roof plywood, the condensed water can drip through the gaps in the cavity insulation under the influence of gravity, pass through openings in the ceiling gypsum board, and stain the surfaces below.

During cold weather, the condensed water can freeze and remain in the roof assembly for extended periods of time. During sunny conditions, solar radiation can warm the roof plywood, leading to melting of the frost and subsequent water leakage.

Since condensed water can access the underside of the roof plywood, this leads to high relative humidities at the underside of the roof plywood. This then leads to mold and decay at this location, and structural failure over time.

Had airtight recessed ceiling fixtures been installed, the continuous air space above the ceiling insulation coupled with the continuous ridge and soffit ventilation would have removed sufficient moisture from the interstitial ceiling spaces to prevent the observed problems.

Solutions

Condensation at a surface can be controlled by reducing the amount of moisture accessing the surface, elevating the temperature of the surface, or by removing the moisture once it gets to the surface.

Removal of moisture from roof and attic spaces by ventilation has been the traditional method of control of surface condensation at the underside of roof sheathing. For ventilation to be effective, the rate of moisture removal has to be greater than the rate of moisture entry. The existing roof assembly contained substantial ventilation openings, yet moisture problems still occurred. The rate of moisture entry was exceeding the rate of moisture removal. It is not practical to increase the rate of moisture removal beyond what is already present, therefore, the rate of moisture entry from air transport must be reduced.

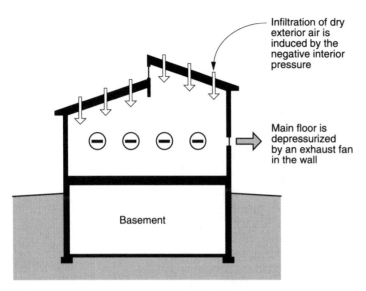

Infiltration of dry exterior air is induced by the negative interior pressure

Main floor is depressurized by an exhaust fan in the wall

Basement

Figure 7-13: Condensation is controlled by an exhaust fan that depressurizes the building envelope, thus inducing infiltration of dry exterior air.

Air-transported moisture requires moisture in the air, openings, and an air pressure difference. The following strategies for control are therefore possible:

1. Control moisture in the interior air.

2. Control openings.

3. Control air pressure differences.

Control of moisture in the interior air is effective, but has limits with respect to occupant comfort. It is unlikely that sufficient moisture can be removed from the interior air in this particular case to eliminate the condensation in the roof assembly.

Control of air pressure differences is possible. An air leakage test with fan depressurization equipment (a calibrated blower) will be able to establish air flows necessary to induce infiltration across the structure (Figure 7-13). Should these measured air flows be sufficiently low, depressurization control may be cost-effective.

The air leakage openings have been identified as the recessed light fixtures. Retrofit kits are readily available commercially which are designed to eliminate air leakage at recessed light fixtures.

Of the two options available—air pressure control and air leakage opening control—eliminating the air leakage openings appears to be the most cost-effective approach. Accordingly, the following recommendation results:

• Seal all recessed light fixtures (Figure 7-14).

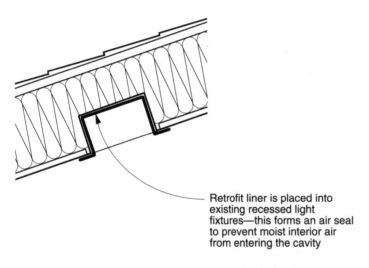

Retrofit liner is placed into existing recessed light fixtures—this forms an air seal to prevent moist interior air from entering the cavity

Figure 7-14: A retrofit liner seals existing recessed light fixtures and prevents the movement of moist air into the roof cavities.

Case Study 5: Peeling Paint on Wood Trim

Building: Two story row houses.

Location: Chicago, Illinois.

Climate Zone: Predominantly heating.

Problem

Peeling paint began to occur at exterior wood trim locations of three-year-old buildings. The peeling paint was located on vertical trim pieces located at exterior corners and horizontal trim pieces over windows and between floors. The incidence of peeling paint was more pronounced at locations with direct exposure to the sun, specifically the south and southwest elevations. Peeling paint on trim on north facing elevations was also evident, but to a much lesser extent. Horizontal hardboard lap siding was unaffected.

Description

The row houses, located in several subdivisions, were wood frame buildings over cast concrete basement foundations. Exterior cladding was hardboard lap siding over foil-covered pressed paper noninsulating impermeable sheathing. The trim was kiln-dried eastern white pine.

Investigation

The principle means of investigation were visual inspections, along with intrusive disassembly (trim was removed and examined).

Visual examinations confirmed the distribution of peeling paint, specifically on the south and southwest exposures. Vertical trim around windows appeared to be more affected than horizontal pieces. Similarly, vertical trim at exterior building corners appeared to be more effected than the horizontal trim which provided aesthetic separation between floors. Vertical trim surrounding door openings (including garage doors) appeared to be the worst of all.

When trim was removed, it was evident that only the exposed surfaces were primed and painted. Water stain marks were observed along the back surfaces of many trim boards. Particularly disconcerting was evidence of decay at vertical trim butt ends.

Principle

Capillary suction can draw water into porous materials (blotting paper, wood, concrete). The smaller the pores in a material, the greater the capillary suction. Wood and concrete are typically coated in order to provide a capillary break. Paint and caulking are used to fill capillary pores in wood, while dampproofing is used in concrete. Capillary suction can also act when two materials tightly overlap each other (the spacing between the materials becomes a capillary). A common example of this is the overlap of horizontal wood lap siding. The cut end grain of wood lumber and trim is particularly susceptible to capillary suction due to the oriented nature of wood fibers.

Causes

There are three possible sources of moisture responsible for the peeling paint and decay problems affecting the trim: (1) interior moisture from air leakage and vapor diffusion, (2) construction moisture, and (3) exterior moisture from rain leakage and capillarity.

Interior moisture can be eliminated as a source by the presence of impermeable sheathing isolating the trim from interior moisture. Construction moisture can be eliminated since kiln-dried lumber was used for the trim. Exterior moisture is the only remaining possibility. The pattern of damage (the decay of trim board ends and water stains on the back surfaces of the trim) is consistent with rainwater/capillary effects. Rainwater is drawn behind trim boards by capillary suction (Figure 7-15), leading to water stains on the back surfaces of the trim. Rainwater is also drawn into the unprotected end grain of vertical trim boards, leading to decay. Once water accesses the unprotected surfaces (not painted, primed, or otherwise sealed/coated) of the wood trim, it is absorbed.

When wood absorbs moisture it expands, stressing any coating which may be adhered to it. When wood is subsequently dried by exposure to solar radiation it contracts, relieving the stress on any coating. Repeated expansion and contraction leads to repeated stretching and shrinking of adhered coatings (paints) and subsequent failure of coating adhesion (peeling paint). Wood trim experiences more cycles on elevations exposed to solar radiation. Accordingly, south-facing trim peels more readily than north-facing trim.

Solutions

From the field observations, the following recommendations result:

1. Continue using kiln-dried wood for all wood trim. Wood trim should also continue to be eastern white pine (or equivalent), as eastern white pine exhibits better paint holding characteristics than most other woods. Western red cedar, cypress, and redwood also have excellent paint holding characteristics principally due to their densities and dimensional stability when exposed to moisture.

2. Prime-coat all wood trim on all six surfaces. Special consideration should be made to coat/seal ends of trim boards. Trim material should come to the job site pre-primed. When trim material is cut to size on the site, the cut ends and/or cut edges should be immediately sealed with primer (or caulking smeared over the end grain filling all pores).

3. Prime-coat with either a premium latex or oil-based primer. Top coating should occur within two weeks of trim exposure to solar radiation, and should consist of two coats of acrylic latex paint. A superior system would utilize the application of a paintable water repellant preservative prior to the prime coating of all six surfaces. Unpainted prime-coated trim material exposed to solar radiation for an extended period should be reprimed prior to top coating.

4. Alter trim details to minimize rain entry, promote drainage of rainwater, and minimize capillarity effects.

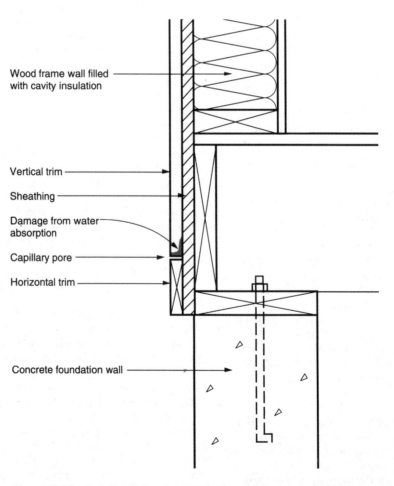

Wood frame wall filled with cavity insulation

Vertical trim

Sheathing

Damage from water absorption

Capillary pore

Horizontal trim

Concrete foundation wall

Figure 7-15: Existing trim detail. Rainwater is drawn behind trim boards by capillary suction leading to stains and decay.

The ideal coating system for wood and wood-based materials is a system which is hydrophobic (sheds water), vapor permeable, resistant to ultraviolet light, and has good adhesion and cohesion properties. Acrylic latex top coats coupled with premium latex primers are preferred when they are applied over stable substrates (dry, dimensionally stable and able to hold paint) as they are more vapor permeable than other paint finishes while providing similar hydrophobic, ultraviolet resistance, adhesion and cohesion properties to other paint systems. Oil-based prime coats coupled with latex top coats do not provide as permeable a system as a latex prime coat based system. However, oil-based prime coats provide superior adhesion for difficult substrates. Accordingly, oil-based prime coats should be utilized over hardboard claddings. As advances in latex paint technology occur, latex-based prime coats should outperform oil-based prime coats even on difficult substrates.

Stains are not as hydrophobic or resistant to ultraviolet light as paints but are more vapor permeable. As stains break down more rapidly due to ultraviolet light than do paints, recoating more frequently with stains will be likely. Solid body stains are thin paints and should not be used. Wood trim should be dry when coated. Latex paint systems should not be applied at temperatures below 50 degrees Fahrenheit.

Figure 7-16 illustrates the use of flashing and sealants to protect the cut ends of trim material as well as provide drainage from joints at the exterior corners of buildings. Trim around window and door openings should use flashing and sealant in a similar manner. Ideally the top edges of all horizontal trim should be covered with flashing for protection and drainage. If flashing cannot be used, the top edge should be sloped and a bead of caulking placed where the trim meets the wall.

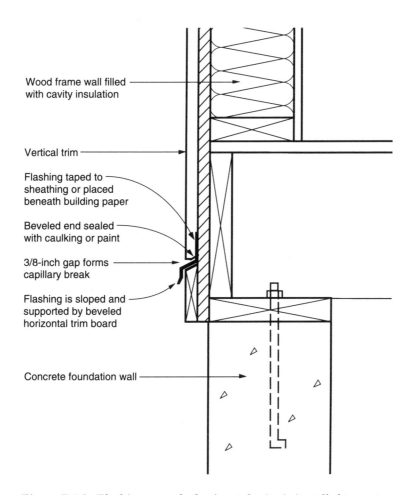

Wood frame wall filled with cavity insulation

Vertical trim

Flashing taped to sheathing or placed beneath building paper

Beveled end sealed with caulking or paint

3/8-inch gap forms capillary break

Flashing is sloped and supported by beveled horizontal trim board

Concrete foundation wall

Figure 7-16: Flashing over the horizontal trim is installed to protect the wood and provide drainage beneath the vertical trim board.

Case Study 6:
Hardboard Panel Problems

Building: Townhouse complex.

Location: Hoffman Estates, Illinois.

Climate Zone: Predominantly heating.

Problem

Complaints of paint discoloration on hardboard siding panels began to occur after a three- to four-year period at several townhouse projects. The discoloration of the hardboard panels was accompanied by peeling paint on wood trim as well as some trim and panel edge decay.

Description

The buildings were two-story single family wood frame row houses constructed over concrete basement foundations. Exterior cladding was a stucco-like hardboard panel siding with wood trim installed in a "Tudor" style.

The space conditioning systems were forced air gas furnaces with atmospherically vented chimneys and draft hoods located in the basements. Gas water heaters were similarly vented.

Wall framing was 2 x 4 at 16 inches on center with faced batt insulation installed within the cavities. Painted gypsum board was installed on the interior of the frame walls. Foil-covered, pressed paper noninsulating impermeable sheathing was installed on the exterior of the frame walls. Trim and hardboard siding panels were installed over the exterior sheathing.

Investigation

The principle means of investigation were visual inspections, along with intrusive disassembly (hardboard panels, trim and exterior sheathing were removed and examined).

As part of the investigation, the projects were subject to a complete "walk through" visual inspection. During this visual inspection several buildings were selected for detailed investigation. Five siding panels were subsequently removed from a gable end wall identified as having maximum wind, rain, and solar exposure. Three of these cladding panels were removed adjacent to the insulated envelope, and two cladding panels were removed adjacent to the unconditioned attic space. Associated trim boards were also removed, as well as exterior sheathing and cavity insulation.

Panels were removed at end wall locations to evaluate the effect of conditioned and unconditioned spaces behind the panels. In contrast to the lower wall panels, the panels removed at the attic level would not be affected by conditions within the conditioned spaces.

The walk through visual inspection revealed that the majority of the panels were deteriorating at their base where they intersected the Z flashing. This deterioration consisted of edge swelling, paint discoloration, and some paint peeling. The hardboard material at the panel bottom edge felt soft and *punky* when probed.

Paint discoloration was observed throughout the project. Where it was observed, it was concentrated principally over the bottom quarter of the panel surfaces. However, numerous panels also had surface discoloration over the center portions of the panels. This panel center discoloration manifested itself as large blotches approximately centered between vertical framing studs. There was no discernible difference in discoloration between panels located at the attic level and those located below the attic level.

The removed panels were observed to be nailed/fastened rigidly to the framing members. The bottom edges of the backside of the removed panels were stained and water marked. The water stain marks extended upwards approximately 1.5 inches from the lower bottom edge of the panels.

Vertical trim boards which were removed were observed to be at the early stage of deterioration at their bottom edges where they were in contact with the Z flashing. Horizontal trim boards at many locations were observed to be *cupping*.

No staining or water marks were observed on the foil-faced sheathing. Sheathing sheet edges were overlapped and tight. Sheathing sheet joints occurred directly over framing elements.

The batt fiberglass cavity insulation was observed to be dry. No dustmarking was observed anywhere over batt insulation surfaces or within the batt insulation. Particular attention was focused on possible dustmarking at electrical outlets, but none was found.

The cavity framing was observed to be dry

and in a pristine state. Bottom plates showed no evidence of water stains or condensation. Gypsum board surfaces were unmarked.

The observed wall construction and cladding geometry is presented in Figure 7-17. It is important to note the following:

1. The sheathing was vapor impermeable.

2. The observed gap between the bottom edge of the panels/vertical trim and the Z flashing was less than 3/8 inch.

3. The hardboard panels were not factory or site sealed/coated/painted at their edges and back surfaces particularly where edges overlap the Z flashing and/or each other

4. The Z flashing was horizontal and not sloped.

5. The ends of the vertical trim, or back surfaces of both vertical and horizontal trim were not sealed/coated/painted.

Principle

Capillary suction can draw water into porous materials (blotting paper, wood, concrete). The smaller the pores in a material, the greater the capillary suction. Wood and concrete are typically coated to provide a capillary break. Paint and caulking are used to fill capillary pores in wood, while dampproofing is used for concrete. Capillary suction can also act when two materials tightly overlap each other and the spacing between them becomes a capillary. A common example of this is the overlap of horizontal wood lap siding. The cut end grain of wood lumber and trim is particularly susceptible to capillary suction due to the oriented nature of wood fibers.

Causes

There are three possible sources of moisture responsible for the damage to the exterior cladding/trim (peeling paint, water stains, swelling hardboard panel edges, deterioration along hardboard panel lower edges, trim board cupping and warping). These are: (1) interior moisture from air leakage and vapor diffusion, (2) construction moisture, and (3) exterior moisture from rain leakage and capillarity.

Interior moisture can be eliminated as the moisture source for three reasons. First, there was no difference in the pattern of damage between locations at attic level and locations below attic level. Second, the foil-covered exterior sheathing is impermeable and installed in a tight manner, thereby isolating the panels and trim from interior moisture. Finally, it is unlikely that any interior moisture was present as the cavities were observed to be completely dry with no evidence of prior moisture accumulation.

Construction moisture can be eliminated due to the period of time required for the

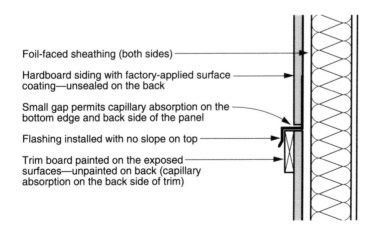

Foil-faced sheathing (both sides)

Hardboard siding with factory-applied surface coating—unsealed on the back

Small gap permits capillary absorption on the bottom edge and back side of the panel

Flashing installed with no slope on top

Trim board painted on the exposed surfaces—unpainted on back (capillary absorption on the back side of trim)

Figure 7-17: Existing trim and hardboard panel detail. Flashing is not sloped and there is a small gap beneath the panel. Rainwater is drawn behind trim and panel boards by capillary suction leading to stains and decay.

complaints to surface. In addition, the panels come from the manufacturer in a dry state and it is very unlikely that the panels were allowed to get wet prior to installation. Exterior moisture is the only remaining possibility.

Direct rain entry is not likely due to the geometry of the cladding/trim installation. Air leakage and vapor diffusion from the exterior are unlikely because the exterior cladding/trim surface temperatures are typically very close to the ambient exterior temperature. (Exceptions occur when incident solar radiation significantly raises surface temperatures, making condensation extremely unlikely.) The only remaining moisture transport mechanism is capillarity. Furthermore, the observed pattern of damage (staining and water marks along panel bottom edge back surfaces) is consistent with capillary suction.

The observed geometry and material properties of the cladding/trim/flashing interface are very susceptible to capillarity. Capillarity at this interface can occur two ways:

1. Through the unsealed bottom edge of the hardboard panels.

2. Through the back surfaces of the hardboard panels where they are in contact with the vertical portion of the horizontal Z flashing.

When it rains, a film of water is deposited on the surface of the panel. As the water flows downwards under the influence of gravity it forms into a droplet at the bottom edge of the panel and flows around it (Figure 7-17). With water present at the intersection of the vertical portion of the horizontal Z flashing and the bottom edge of the back of the panel, capillary suction will draw the water upwards into the tiny crack between the two materials. Water can now be absorbed into the material both along the bottom unsealed edge as well as through the back of the panel at the bottom edge. When this occurs, the panel edge also can swell, leading to more water absorption. Over time, surface finishes can become discolored and ultimately the bottom panel edge can deteriorate. The observed water stain marks at the back, bottom edges of the removed panels and the associated edge swelling are consistent with this mechanism. The geometry of the installation and the material properties of the hardboard which allow water absorption through unsealed surfaces lead to the observed damage.

This same mechanism is believed to be responsible for the observed deterioration at the bottom end of the vertical trim boards where they come in contact with the horizontal Z flashing.

Manufacturers' recommended installation practice is presented in Figure 7-18. Note the site-applied caulking at the bottom edge of the panel. This caulking seals both the bottom untreated edge of the panel as well as the capillary pore between the vertical portion of the horizontal Z flashing and the back surface

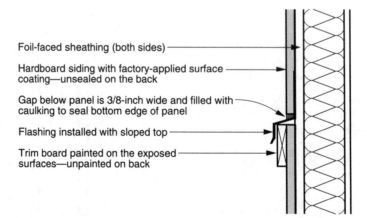

Foil-faced sheathing (both sides)

Hardboard siding with factory-applied surface coating—unsealed on the back

Gap below panel is 3/8-inch wide and filled with caulking to seal bottom edge of panel

Flashing installed with sloped top

Trim board painted on the exposed surfaces—unpainted on back

Figure 7-18: Manufacturers' recommended detail for hardboard panel and trim installation. The flashing is sloped and the gap beneath the panel is filled with caulking.

of the bottom of the panel. This caulking must be installed with a high degree of workmanship so that the bottom edge and capillary gap are completely sealed. The recommended 3/8-inch gap is to facilitate panel expansion due to changing moisture content and to allow the caulking to seal the bottom of the panel, not to act as a capillary break. Over time this caulking will fail, leading to problems similar to the ones observed. Regular, frequent maintenance of this caulked joint would be essential for satisfactory performance.

A detail which is not as dependent on workmanship and maintenance is presented in Figure 7-19. In this detail, the bottom edges and back of the panel are sealed with paint prior to installation and the horizontal gap is opened up to facilitate drainage and drying.

The surface discoloration observed at the bottom edges and at panel centers as blotches is also believed to be related to the moisture entry via capillarity at the horizontal joints. Once moisture accesses the back of the panels, it will migrate outwards when the exterior temperature and vapor pressure are lower than the temperature and vapor pressure at the back of the panel. This occurs in evenings and during cool weather. The outward migration of moisture toward the exterior finish also transports char residue and colorants within the hardboard to the exterior. If the surface finish is not sufficiently opaque, these materials will become visible. When the temperature reverses and the moisture is driven inwards

again (typically due to incident solar radiation), the discolorants are left behind, and the moisture is pushed out the back of the panel.

Panel center discoloration or blotches occur centered between studs. It is hypothesized that this is due to the air space between the sheathing and panels at this location. The sheathing and panels are not perfect planes, and therefore not in continuous contact with each other. Contact only occurs at studs due to the nailing pattern. As such, air pockets/air spaces can occur between the studs. The air spaces get larger as the panel expands due to changing moisture content. The moisture content of the panel changes due to ambient relative humidity, and due to the local relative humidity at the back of the panel. Expansion of the panel leads to buckling, as the panel is restrained at the stud line by nailing. The resultant air spaces facilitate the accumulation of moisture at these locations due to convection and the subsequent migration of moisture outwards.

The outward/inward cycling of moisture through the panels pumps the stains to the surface. The panels are not affected structurally because this repeated wetting is followed by repeated drying almost on a daily cycle. Limiting the absorption of moisture through the back surface (*back-priming*) or coating the exterior with an opaque surface finish would likely resolve this issue.

Trim board cupping is believed to be due to the absorption of moisture by the wood trim due to both exposure to ambient relative

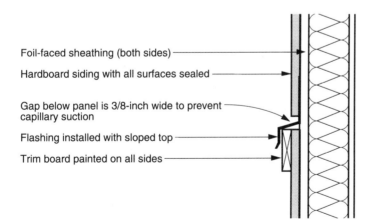

Foil-faced sheathing (both sides)

Hardboard siding with all surfaces sealed

Gap below panel is 3/8-inch wide to prevent capillary suction

Flashing installed with sloped top

Trim board painted on all sides

Figure 7-19: Alternative recommended panel and trim detail. Panels must be painted on the bottom edges and back, and a full 3/8-inch gap must be left beneath the panel to prevent capillary suction. This detail does not depend on caulking (with excellent workmanship) to be successful.

humidity and absorption through back surfaces due to capillarity. Once moisture is present in the wood, the moisture tends to migrate between the front and back surfaces of the wood under the action of solar radiation and other temperature gradients. The sun tends to push the moisture to the back of the trim board, leaving the front dry and the back wet. The back expands, while the front contracts, leading to cupping. The repeated expansion/contraction of the wood due to changing moisture content within the wood, stresses the paint film, and peeling/blistering occurs.

Cupping, blistering, and peeling can be reduced by utilizing narrower trim boards, back-priming the trim to reduce water absorption, and by increasing the restraint of the trim against movement (more nails).

Solutions

From the field observations, the following recommendations result:

1. Remove and replace panels that have deteriorated bottom edges with deterioration and swelling extending upwards beyond 1.5 inches. Install replacement panels as per Figure 7-19. All replacement panels should have all surfaces and edges painted, including the rear surface, with an alkyd primer prior to installation. Any cutting and trimming of replacement panels should occur only along panel upper edges.

2. For all panels that have not been replaced, cut away the bottom 1.5 inches (including vertical trim boards) and bend/slope horizontal flashing downwards. Seal the newly cut/exposed bottom edges of panels and vertical trim boards by painting with an alkyd primer and latex finish coat.

3. Remove and back-prime all horizontal trim boards, or paint/seal over all surfaces. Replace deteriorated trim board. All horizontal trim should be reinstalled/ replaced so that horizontal flashings are able to slope downwards as shown in Figure 7-19.

4. Prime-coat all wood trim on all six surfaces. Special consideration should be made to coat/seal ends of trim boards. If possible, trim material should come to the job site pre-primed. When trim material is cut to size on the site, the cut ends should be immediately sealed with primer (or caulking smeared over the end grain to fill all pores).

5. Clean and repaint all panels with an alkyd prime coat and latex finish coat. Wood trim should be dry when coated. Latex paint systems should not be applied at temperatures below 50 degrees Fahrenheit.

(Note: It is not necessary to install caulking at the bottom edge of the panels if bottom edges have been sealed by an alkyd prime coat and a latex finish coat of paint. Furthermore, it is not necessary to replace panels which have stains or blotches visible on exposed surfaces as long as panel bottom edges have not decayed or swollen. After the edge geometry has been modified, stained panels can be painted.)

References and Bibliography

AHMA (American Hotel and Motel Association), 1991. *Mold and Mildew in Hotel and Motel Guest Rooms in Hot, Humid Climates*, AHMA, Washington, D.C.

Angell, W.J., 1988. *Home Moisture Sources*, (CD-FO-3396), Minnesota Extension Service, University of Minnesota, St. Paul, Minnesota.

Arg, N., A.L. Sescius, and J. Timusk, 1988. *The Control of Wind Cooling of Wood Frame Building Enclosures*, Energy Efficient Building Association Conference, Portland, Oregon.

ASHRAE (American Society of Heating, Refrigerating and Air Conditioning Engineers, Inc.), 1989a. *ASHRAE Handbook: 1989 Fundamentals*, Atlanta, Georgia.

ASHRAE (American Society of Heating, Refrigerating and Air Conditioning Engineers, Inc.), 1989b. *Ventilation for Acceptable Indoor Air Quality*, ASHRAE Standard 62-1989, Atlanta, Georgia.

Baker, M.C., 1980. *Roofs: Design, Application and Maintenance*, Multi-Science Publications, Ltd., Montreal, Canada.

Blasnik, M., 1990. *Attic Insulation Performance, Air Leakage and Ventilation*, ACEEE 1990 Summer Study, Vol. 9, Pacific Grove, California.

Burge, H.A., 1985. "Indoor Sources for Airborne Microbes," *Indoor Air and Human Health*, edited by R.B. Gaminage and S.V. Kaye, Lewis Publishers, Chelsea, Michigan.

Canada Mortgage and Housing Corporation, 1987. *Moisture Problems*, Canada Mortgage and Housing Corporation, Ottawa, Canada.

Carmody, J., J. Christian, and K. Labs, 1991. *Builder's Foundation Handbook*, Oak Ridge National Laboratory, ORNL/CON-295.

Cleary, P., 1984. *Humidity in Attics - Sources and Control Methods*, Lawrence Berkeley Laboratory, California, January.

EPA (Environmental Protection Agency), 1991. *Building Air Quality—A Guide for Building Owners and Facility Managers*, DHHS (NIOSH) publication No 91-114, December.

Fitzgerald, J., G. Nelson, and L. Shen, 1990. "Sidewall Insulation and Air Leakage Control," *Home Energy Magazine*, Berkeley, California, January.

Forgues, Y.E., 1986. *The Ventilation of Insulated Roofs*, Building Practice Notes NO57, (NRCC/DBR).

Garden, G.K., 1983. *Rain Penetration and its Control*, Canadian Building Digest 40, DBR/NRCC, April.

Godish, T., 1989. *Indoor Air Pollution Control*, Lewis Publishers, Chelsea, Michigan.

Handegord, G.O., 1985. "Prediction of the Moisture Performance of Walls," *ASHRAE Transactions*, Vol. 91.

Handegord, G.O., 1991. Personal communication.

Handegord, G. O. and Giroux, G., 1984. *An Attic Condensation Ventilation Model*, Division of Building Research/National Research Council of Canada.

Hutcheon, N. and G.O. Handegord, 1983. *Building Science for a Cold Climate*, Construction Technology Centre Atlantic, Inc., January.

Iowa Department of Natural Resources, 1987. *A Builder's Guide to Iowa's Idea Homes*, Des Moines, Iowa.

Joy, F.A., 1951. *Basic Concepts of Water Vapor Migration and Their Application to Frame Walls*, Pennsylvania State College Engineering Experiment Station, Technical Paper NO89.

Latta, J.K., 1973. *Walls, Windows, and Roofs for the Canadian Climate*, Division of Building Research/National Research Council of Canada, October (NRCC 13487).

Lischkoff, J.K. and J.W. Lstiburek, 1987. *The Airtight House*, University of Iowa Research Foundation, Ames, Iowa, October.

Lischkoff, J. and J. Timusk, 1984. "Moisture and Thermal Aspects of Insulating Sheathing," paper presented at Second CSCE Conference on Building Science and Technology, London.

Lstiburek, J.W., 1989. "Insulation Induced Paint and Siding Failures," paper presented at CIB W40 Conference, Victoria, Canada, September.

Lstiburek, J.W., 1991. *Contractor's Field Guide*, Building Science Corporation, Chestnut Hill, Massachusetts, April.

Lux, M.E., and Brown,W.C., 1986. "Air Leakage Control," proceedings of Building Science Insight '86, Institute for Research in Construction/National Research Council of Canada, (NRCC 29943).

Marshall, Macklin, and Monaghan, 1983. *Moisture Induced Problems in NHA Housing*, Canada Mortgage and Housing Corporation, Ottawa.

Merrill, J.L., 1986. *Moisture Problems in the Home*, University of Wisconsin - Extension, Madison, Wisconsin.

NAHB (National Association of Home Builders), 1988. *Frost-Protected Shallow Foundations: Design Details Developed by the Norwegian Building Research Institute*, NAHB Research Center, Upper Marlboro, Maryland, January.

NCAT (National Center for Appropriate Technology), 1983. *Moisture and Home Energy Conservation: How to Detect, Solve and Avoid Related Problems*, DOE/CE/15095-4.

NFPA (National Forest Products Association), 1987. *Permanent Wood Foundation System: Design, Fabrication and Installation Manual*, Washington, D.C.

Oatman, L. and C.A. Lane, 1988. *Mold and Mildew in the Home*, (CD-FO-3397), Minnesota Extension Service, University of Minnesota, St. Paul, Minnesota.

Peterson, R.A. and L.T. Hendricks, 1988. *A Systems Approach to Cold Climate Housing*, (CD-FO-3566), Minnesota Extension Service, St. Paul, Minnesota.

Quirouette, R., 1985. *The Difference Between a Vapor Barrier and an Air Barrier*, Building Practice Note 54, Division of Building Research/National Research Council of Canada.

Quirouette, R., M. Rousseau, J. Rousseau, 1984. *Humidity, Condensation and Ventilation in Houses*, Division of Building Research/National Research Council of Canada, Ottawa.

Rose, W., 1991. "More Data on Shingle Overheating with Unvented Roofs," *Energy Design Update*, March.

Spengler, J.D., H. Burge, and H.J. Su, 1991. *Biological Agents and the Home Environment*, Workshop Proceedings, Bugs, Mold & Rot, BTECC, Washington, D.C, May 20-21.

Samuelson, I. and R. Samuelson, 1990. *Conditions for Growth of Mold on Wood Products*, Swedish Testing Institute, Boras, Sweden.

Tamura, G.T., G.H. Kuester, and G.O. Handegord, 1974. "Condensation Problems in Flat Wood Frame Roofs," paper presented at second International CIB/RILEM Symposium on Moisture Problems in Buildings (NRCC 14589), Rotterdam.

Timusk, J., 1981a. *Design of the Building Envelope*, M.W. Huggins Symposium on Structural Engineering, University of Toronto, September.

Timusk, J., 1981b. *External Insulation of Basement Walls*, Housing and Urban Development Association of Canada Task Force on Basements, Ottawa.

Timusk, J., 1983. *Insulation Retrofit of Residential Basements*, Ontario Ministry of Municipal Affairs and Housing, ISBN 0-7743-1052-1, October.

Tooley, J. and N. Moyer, 1991. "Pressure Differential: Measurement of the New Decade," paper presented at Energy Efficient Building Association Conference, Indianapolis, Indiana, March.

Torp, A. and T. Graee, 1964. *The Effect of Air Currents in Moisture Migration and Condensation in Wood Frame Structures*, Norwegian Building Research Institute, Reprint DBR/NRCC.

White, J.H., 1991. "Moisture, Mould, Ventilation and Energy," paper presented at ENERhouse 91 Conference, Halifax, Canada, March.

White, J., 1984. *Ventilation for Humidity Control*, Canada Mortgage and Housing Corporation, Ottawa, Canada.

Wilson, A.G., 1965. *Condensation in Insulated Masonry Walls in Summer*, CIB/RILEM Symposium on Moisture Problems in Building (NRC 9130), Helsinki.

Wilson, A.G., and G.T. Tamura, 1968. *Stack Effect and Building Design*, Canadian Building Digest 107 (DBR/NRCC), November.

Index

See also specific building assemblies in ch. 4–6.

Floor insulation   102, 107-08, 137, 139, 141-45, 173-74

Floor slabs   110-12, 142-44, 174-75

Footings, concrete   26-27, 110, 142

Forced-air heating systems   40-42, 92, 121, 123, 142, 155

Foundation assemblies   100-12, 133-145, 166-75. *See also* Concrete foundations; Concrete masonry foundations; Wood frame foundations.

Foundation insulation. *See* Insulation, foundation

Foundations, types of
basements   41, 100-12, 133-37, 142-45
crawl spaces   123, 133, 138-45, 154, 156, 166-70, 172-75
slabs   109-12, 166, 171-75

Free-draining materials   18-19, 109, 142

Furring strips   23, 28, 30, 130, 162-63

G

Grade beam   109-112, 166, 172-75

Gravel pad   27, 44, 110, 112, 142, 145, 172-73, 175

Gravity   21

Groundwater   16-20, 88-90, 109-110, 120, 142, 153, 172. *See also* specific building assemblies in ch. 4–6.

Gutters   17, 90, 109, 122, 142, 154, 172

Gypsum board   57, 72, 75, 79, 130-32, 180-85. *See also* specific building assemblies in ch. 4–6.

H

Health, occupant   3-4, 90, 112, 121, 154, 175, 186

Heating climate
case studies   186-206
defined   88-89
foundation assemblies   100-12
moisture concerns and strategies   55-61, 88-92
roof assemblies   76-87, 113-18
wall assemblies   47-61, 93-99
whole building systems   91-92

High-heel trusses   10

House-wraps   25, 37-39

Humidity ratio   1

HVAC system   92, 123, 155

Hydrostatic pressure   16-19

I

Ice damming   87, 89, 114-15, 118, 146-48, 151. *See also* Roof assemblies

Inlet/outlet openings   52, 57, 71-72, 78-79

Insect pathways   112, 144, 162, 173

Insulation, foundation   110-12, 133-45, 166-75

Insulation, horizontal in soil   109, 112

Insulation, rigid
in cooling climates   162-65, 172-75, 179-80
in heating climates   94-99, 111-12
in mixed climates   129-32, 142-45

Insulation pillow   111, 143, 174

Insulation/sheathing interface   48-52

Interior finishes
in cooling climates   63-64, 153, 164-65, 174-75, 179-80
in heating climates   55-57, 61, 99, 112
in mixed climates   132, 144, 150

Interstitial condensation   57, 72

J

Joints, control   20, 129

Joints, vertical open   97, 129, 162

K

Kerfs   21, 26

Kitchens   31-32, 90, 122, 154, 156

L

Leaks, preventing roof   76

Lights, recessed   39, 195, 198

Liquid flow   15-26. *See also* Groundwater; Rain penetration/absorption.

M

Masonry foundations, concrete
in cooling climates   166-67, 169, 174-75
in heating climates   104-05, 109-12,
in mixed climates   136, 139, 142-45

Masonry walls, concrete   27, 70, 160-65

Mechanical system concerns   40-42, 66, 72, 90-92, 121-23, 154-56

Mixed climate
defined   119-20
foundation assemblies in   133-45
moisture concerns and strategies   119-24
roof assemblies in   78, 83, 146-51
wall assemblies in   125-32
whole building systems   122-23